THE GOUGEON BROTHERS
ON BOAT CONSTRUCTION

THE GOUGEON BROTHERS ON BOAT CONSTRUCTION

WOOD & WEST SYSTEM* MATERIALS

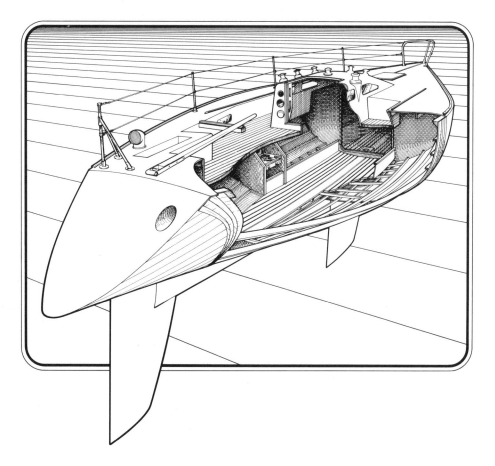

NEW REVISED
(FOURTH)
EDITION

*TRADEMARK OF GOUGEON BROTHERS, INC., U.S.A.

COVER — IOR ½-ton racer, based on Gary Mull's design for HOT FLASH (now BOOMERANG). Cover design and artwork by Michael Barker.

Copyright © 1985, 1982, 1979 **Gougeon Bros. Inc., P.O. Box X908, Bay City, Michigan 48707 U.S.A.** New, Revised (Fourth) Edition. World Rights Reserved. Library of Congress Catalog Card Number: 79-84319. ISBN: 0-87812-166-8. Printed by The McKay Press, Inc., Midland, MI

Contents

Color Photographs

Every year we receive photographs of boats built with WEST SYSTEM epoxy. In the section between pages 142 and 143, we print a representative sample of them. A few projects and shops remain unidentified. We apologize to their owners for our oversight.

1. Trimaran, modified Norman Cross design.
2. Inverted trimaran interior, Jay Kantola design, built by California Custom Coatings (Bob Perkins photo).
3. ROGUE WAVE, Dick Newick design, built by Gougeon Brothers, Inc.
4. Plywood power boat, Freeport, Bahamas (A. Edwards photo).
5. Large cruising catamaran.
6. BAY BEA, Britt Chance design, built by Palmer Johnson.
7. GOLDEN DAZY, Ron Holland design, built by Gougeon Brothers, Inc.
8. ROGUE WAVE, Dick Newick design, built by Gougeon Brothers, Inc.
9. LOVE, proa designed by Russell Brown, built by Lewis McGregor.
10. Trimaran, Jay Kantola design, built by California Custom Coatings.
11. Modified John L. Hacker design 21 foot speed boat, built by Jim Forrest, Ace Speed Boat Co.
12. Catamaran, built by Yigal Havkin.
13. HOT FLASH interior, Gary Mull design, built by Gougeon Brothers, Inc.
14. Catamaran, fairing set-up.
15. Trimaran launching, Dick Newick design, built by Damian McLaughlin.
16. ROGUE WAVE, main hull, Dick Newick design, built by Gougeon Brothers, Inc.
17. Varnished catamaran hull, Cecil Ross, builder.
18. Overland transportation of catamaran hull, Cecil Ross, builder.
19-36. WHITEHAWK, 92 foot luxury racing ketch, various stages of construction and launching, Bruce King design, built by Lee's Boat Shop.
37. Herschel Payne built 20 foot stripper canoe.
38. PRIME COMPUTERS, 18 foot racing skiff.
39. Strip planked sailing trimaran canoe.
40. OLLIE, self-righting test, Gougeon Brothers, Inc.
41. PERFECT DAZY, 30 foot catboat, wood composite wing spar built by Gougeon Brothers, Inc. (J. R. Watson photo).
42. SLINGSHOT, Georg Thomas design, built by Gougeon Brothers, Inc. (Dave Powlison photo).
43-44. OLLIE, 35 foot trimaran, designed and built by Gougeon Brothers, Inc.
45. SHARK, McAlpine Downey design, built by John Rogers.
46-47. Dashboard and hull, replica, modified John L. Hacker design, built by Morin Mahogany Marine (J. R. Watson photo).
48. ADAGIO, designed and built by Gougeon Brothers, Inc.
49. Pram, Frank ("Red") Davis/GBI design, built by Paul Butler.
50. STREAKER, 7-litre hydroplane designed and built by John Staudacher (R. Koch photo).
51-52. Boiler, steam launch, built by California Custom Coatings (J. R. Watson photos).
53. 21 foot speed boat, modified John L. Hacker design, built by Jim Forrest, Ace Speed Boat Co.
54. Plywood composite dory.
55. Strip planked fishing boat.
56. MILLENIUM FACTOR, land yacht, built by Harken Vanguard Inc.
57. ROGUE WAVE, Dick Newick design, built by Gougeon Brothers, Inc., wood composite wing spar by Gougeon Brothers, Inc.
58. Traditional rowing boat.
59. Solo canoe, built by Mentha Wooden Boat Co.
60. ATOM, modified Jim Brown design, built by J. R. Watson.
61. Wood/epoxy composite offshore cruising ketch.
62. SPLINTER, designed and built by Gougeon Brothers, Inc.
63. Stripper canoe, designed and built by Ted Moores (J. R. Watson photo).
64. DN ice boats (Pam Thomas photo).
65. Sea kayak, built by Richard Hardy.
66. ANNA J. LUGIANTONIO, designed by Halsey Herreshoff, wing spar by Gougeon Brothers, Inc. (Benjamin Mendlowitz photo).

Acknowledgements

From its beginnings, this book has been a team effort. Back in 1978 and 1979, Meade Gougeon took primary responsibility for its writing and sequestered himself in the bedroom of a mobile home. Rob Monroe, working in the living room, drew the original illustrations and provided technical advice. Jan Gougeon, trailer owner and night resident, provided enormous quantities of expertise and information.

Several outsiders were brought in to supplement the workforce. Kay Harley, an English professor and avid sailor, edited the text. Lily Jarmin and Loren Mohn took care of the details of printing. Barbara Livingston proofread and double-checked for accuracy.

The team has expanded for this edition of *The Gougeon Brothers on Boat Construction,* but we continue to rely on several original members. Although Meade relinquished writing duties and Rob moved on to manage the GBI engineering department, they offer advice when asked, as they often are. The tasks of compiling material and describing techniques were assigned to the WEST SYSTEM technical and marketing staff. Jan, J.R. Watson and Randy Koch patiently read over multiple drafts of each chapter. Mike Barker revised illustrations, drew new ones and assembled the color insertion with photos organized by Pat Gougeon. Jim Derck answered his share of questions. The entire effort has been accomplished in about a year, under the gentle but persistent prodding of B. Livingston. Her original job of editor evolved to that of primary writer: with the help and guidance of the entire Gougeon team, she wrote most of the new revised text.

We all wish in turn to acknowledge the great help provided by the office, manufacturing and engineering departments of Gougeon Brothers, Inc. Kay Harley was unable to participate in this edition, but her family was ably represented by Catherine Fahlgren, who assisted on chapters on WEST SYSTEM materials and safety. Bruce Peasley and Dave Rogers proofread the revised text and Joe Mayville and Jeff Smithwick again made dealing with Pendell Printing one of the easier aspects of publishing a book.

The Gougeon Brothers on Boat Construction remains very much the project of families. We therefore also thank wives, husbands and children not otherwise involved or already acknowledged. Many of our ideas have come from our customers, and to them we are very grateful.

October 1985

Bay City, Michigan

Chapter 1

Introduction

In 1979, the year we published the first edition of *The Gougeon Brothers on Boat Construction,* we were three brothers who had been building boats since we were kids. We ran a shop, and had turned out DN iceboats, Olympic medal-winning Tornado class catamarans, several well-known trimarans and some very fast monohull racers. Jan had served an apprenticeship with Superior Sailboats in Port McNicol, Ontario. Joel, who had served as an Air Force pilot for five years, had graduated from General Motors Institute with a B.S. in Mechanical Engineering. Meade had a degree in business administration and had worked for a number of years for a large corporation.

In 1985, Gougeon Brothers, Inc. is a high-tech manufacturer of engineered wooden laminates. We now have a laboratory and a materials testing facility. With the support of the U.S. Department of Energy and the National Aeronautics and Space Administration, we have designed the most successful wind generator blades in use in the United States and have performed the first conclusive testing of the long-term fatigue behavior of wood.

In addition to establishing a data base for wood/epoxy composites, we have pushed production methods to new extremes of scale. Although it is a bit dangerous to claim the "largest ever," we believe that our finger joint demonstration process unit, which measured approximately 14 feet deep, 17 feet wide and 8 feet high, with about 60 individual 12 inch long joints, was the largest ever successfully bonded. In April of 1985, we set the record for our biggest, fastest lay-up. In a little over two hours, a team laminated a 66 foot long half of a wind turbine blade for the Advanced Energy Systems Division of the Westinghouse Corporation. The section, which tapered from a maximum thickness of 6.3 inches to .5 inch, weighed a little over 2,000 pounds. Our shop has produced up to 100 smaller blades per week.

Jan now manages the WEST SYSTEM* division of the company and has won the DN World Championship three times. Last year, our boat shop completed OLLIE, a 35-foot trimaran he designed. Joel, no longer as active in the company as he once was, devotes much of his time to community affairs and prod-

uct research. Meade races his 16 year old trimaran ADAGIO and operates the production division of GBI. He has guided the development of wind turbine blades and is currently focusing on new applications of our materials technology.

Over the past six years, as our work has developed from a craft to a post-industrial technology, we have learned a great deal, and have acquired technical expertise we didn't have when we first wrote our book. In the Introduction to the first edition of *The Gougeon Brothers on Boat Construction,* we apologetically mentioned that our methods were immature and that some were considered experimental because they had not yet stood the test of time. This edition reflects the results of that testing. Few of our experiments failed, and those which did have been corrected. We've attempted to clarify all our instructions, and have double and triple-checked them for accuracy.

We had two goals in writing a book. We wanted to make boatbuilding so simple and straightforward that anyone with a few tools, some wood and some WEST SYSTEM epoxy could turn out a good, safe boat. At the same time, we wanted to give experienced builders a base of information from which to produce increasingly sophisticated hulls and other structures. We think that we succeeded in meeting these objectives.

Many wood/epoxy composite boats, from prams to sloops, have been built by beginners and professionals since 1979. Notable among them are WHITEHAWK, the 105 feet L.O.A. wood/epoxy ketch built by O. Lie-Nielson in Maine, and RED HERRING, one of Eric Goetz's many projects. MOXIE, a 50-foot trimaran designed by Dick Newick for the late Phil Weld and built by Walter Greene, won the 1980 OSTAR. These boats demonstrate the levels of sophistication which professionals have developed in working with WEST SYSTEM materials.

We continue to believe in our basic approach to boat construction. Boatbuilding must overlap with engineering because improper boat construction can have serious consequences. We assume that the builder of a 10 to 60 foot long boat will make many engineering decisions. To complicate matters, even the best engineers have not been totally successful in predicting the loads to which a given hull will be subjected. Because of this, tradition plays a large part in the development of marine engineering: the wise builder considers what has worked in the past as a basis for what will work in the future.

There have now been enough boats built with new methods to provide a sound foundation of knowledge, but wood/resin composite construction has not matured to the point where hard and fast scantling rules can be made to apply to every situation. To help fill this void, we have provided technical data which we hope will be of help. These include updated scantlings from successful boats built with wood and WEST SYSTEM materials and the results of testing performed in our lab and elsewhere.

We think of wood and WEST SYSTEM epoxy-based resins as primary engineering materials. With these two basic ingredients, it is possible to make a composite material which has significant advantages for boatbuilding.

Wood has traditionally been viewed as a dimensional material. To build a boat, you took boards and planks and shaped, fit and assembled them with fasteners. We approach wood from another direction: it is a fiber which can be bonded with epoxy into the profiles and forms needed for boatbuilding. To us, wood is a bit like fiberglass, in that we use it as a reinforcing material. But unlike fiberglass, which has little structural value until it is incorporated in resin, wood fiber is an excellent structural material on its own. We have found that it functions even better as a boatbuilding material when it is used in a composite with an appropriate epoxy.

This composite has many practical benefits. Wood/epoxy laminates have clear structural advantages. With them, it is possible to build very advanced structures, such as wind turbine blades and trimarans, with very high strength-to-weight ratios. Our materials produce boats which are strong, stiff and resistant to fatigue — boats are now built at weights which were only dreamed of a decade or two ago. Composite wooden sailboats have been highly successful in nearly every kind of racing, and at least part of this is due to the superiority of the materials used in their construction. At a time when materials failure is a major problem in radically-designed non-wood racing boats, wood composites offer the safety and flexibility of very high strength over years.

The moisture content of wood/epoxy composites is stable, so many of the maintenance problems traditionally associated with wooden boats, such as joint cracks and surface checking, are minimized or entirely eliminated. Because the base beneath it is stable, paint is less likely to peel. Joints bonded with resin can be made as strong as wood itself.

We differ from many boat builders in one major respect: we have looked to the design and construction of wooden aircraft, especially from the World War II period, for inspiration. Wooden airplanes developed from wooden boats, and were innovative because they depended on bonded joints and load-transferring gussets rather than fasteners. We have completed the circle, bringing aircraft technology to boats. As a result, certain of our components, such as bulkheads, are often more similar to those found on aircraft than to those on traditional boats. One of the most valuable and informative trips we have taken since the publication of our first book was to examine the Spruce Goose, Howard Hughes' famous airship.

This book specifically recommends the use of WEST SYSTEM resins in all manufacturing. While this may appear to be self-serving, the fact is that our instructions would be of little value if the bonding and sealing materials which are central to our method of boatbuilding were not discussed in detail. Our techniques depend on the predictable physical properties of epoxy and fillers.

Years of using these products have given us an intimate knowledge of their properties and the ways in which they interact with wood. WEST SYSTEM materials have two characteristics which are crucial to success. The first is their physical capabilities and the ability to stand up to the effects of the environment. The second characteristic is the versatility of the materials, how they can be used in many different building situations and under varying environmental conditions. It takes time to establish both of these features. Over the years, improvements in our products and in their application have been key factors in developing composite construction techniques. No doubt, in years to come, there will be continued development in these areas.

The New, Revised Edition of The Gougeon Brothers on Boat Construction is loosely divided into the same basic sections as its predecessor. We begin with what we think are important matters for consideration before you buy or build a boat. The second group of chapters is devoted to WEST SYSTEM materials and core techniques used in almost all boats — bonding and laminating, scarfing, coating and finishing — as well as to safety procedures. Next, we discuss lofting and setting up, steps which are usually necessary before laminating a hull. Finally, we have chapters on various methods of hull laminating, on non-laminated hulls and on what were once radical techniques for fold-up hulls, hardware bonding and interior construction. Our scope is limited to building the basic boat. We do not discuss wiring, plumbing, engine installation or rigging, but there are excellent texts on these subjects available.

We believe that it is extremely important for any builder planning to use wood and resin composite construction to develop an understanding of these materials and a feel for working with them. We strongly recommend that you perform simple tests as you proceed.

If you know your materials, your solutions to problems will be better and you will gradually evolve the technique which works best for you. In revising this book, we have recognized that there are many ways to do some jobs. We urge you to be creative and develop your skills. After you have become familiar with our techniques, you may wish to develop your own.

Our shop has concentrated on building sailboats up to 60 feet long. As a result of providing technical assistance to other builders, and because we watch the use of our products with keen interest, we have received a great deal of information about other applications of our methods and materials. We hope to share this, as well as our personal experience, with you.

We wish you good luck on your projects. Should you need technical assistance on the use of WEST SYSTEM products, please write or give us a call. We are always interested in hearing about the work of our customers and hope that you will share new ideas and better solutions with us so that we can pass them along.

Chapter 2

Before You Build

There are many reasons to build your own boat. You may enjoy the process and regard boatbuilding as a source of challenge and pride. The boat you want may not be available in the marketplace. You may feel that you cannot find the quality of workmanship you are looking for unless you build your own. If you are like many people, you want to build your own boat to save money.

To enjoy any of these advantages and savings, you must plan carefully and have realistic expectations of what your project will entail. Builders who start their boats with no firm idea of the time, money and difficulty involved are often forced to abandon their work. You do not want to be one of them.

Chapter 3 presents guidelines for estimating how much you will spend on materials and hardware and for calculating the time it will take you to finish your project. It assumes not only that you have decided to build, but also that you have a specific design in mind. In this chapter, we will discuss factors which we think you should consider before committing yourself to a boatbuilding venture. If you have never built a boat before, this may help you to decide if you have the resources to finish one.

Our goal is not to discourage would-be boatbuilders. In fact, we hope that you will enjoy the process so much that you will do it again and again. We've built everything from plywood dinghies to our most recent STRESFORM* 35-foot trimaran, so we know how exciting it is to get started on a new boat. It will be easier to maintain enthusiasm throughout your boatbuilding project if you give it some serious thought before you build.

Should You Build Your Own Boat?

Before devoting significant resources to a project, fully consider the arguments for and against building your own boat. You will save some money. More importantly, you will end up with exactly the boat, with exactly the detail and workmanship, that you want. But in order to achieve this, you will have to make a significant investment of time, energy and patience.

Labor costs represent about 50% of the price of some mass-produced boats and a considerably higher percentage of the cost of one-off hulls. If you build your boat yourself, you will not pay for someone else's work. Unless you quit your job in order to take up boat construction, you will save money on labor.

By building your own boat you will eliminate sales costs. A boat priced at $10,000 in the showroom was probably built for $8,000. The extra $2,000 goes for shipping from the factory to the dealer, the dealer's overhead and profit and the salesman's commission. You will not have to pay these markups.

While you will have to pay sales taxes on materials and hardware, you can pare down your tax bill by building for yourself. You will not owe sales tax on a price inflated by commissions and overhead, and you will not pay indirect taxes on labor.

If you plan to borrow money to finance a boat, you may save a bit by building it yourself. You will pay less interest because you will need less capital. If you can delay ordering materials until you need them, you may be able to pay for some as you go along and your loan period may be shorter.

Over time, an owner-built boat will generally cost less to service. Because you built the boat, your troubleshooting will be more effective. A boat is a collection of components. Since you constructed or purchased and installed each of these yourself, you will be able to recognize malfunctions at an early stage. Since you bought the original hardware and instruments, you will know where to go for replacements and repairs. By the end of your project, you should be capable of almost any major hull repair.

Finally, should you ever sell a boat you have built, you will be able to convert some of your investment into cash. If you did your job quickly and well, you may even recoup a minimal wage for your labor. Surveyors judge boats on their merits. The prices they set are determined, within certain limits, as much by the condition and quality of workmanship as by who did the building. A home-built boat will probably never be worth as much as one built at a famous yard, but if your standards of craftsmanship are high and materials are good, you should be able to sell your boat for a reasonable amount.

* TRADEMARK OF GOUGEON BROTHERS, INC., U.S.A.

Figure 1—ROGUE WAVE ocean-racing trimaran designed by Dick Newick for the late Phil Weld. Stock plans are available from the designer. (Experimental wing spar design by Gougeon Brothers, Inc.)

The economics of mass production also affect boat detail. Interior construction requires time and skill. Manufacturers interested in maintaining competitive prices tend to offer minimal accommodations with few personalized conveniences. A home-built boat has a better chance of having exactly the drawers, lockers and color scheme you want.

Although reputable manufacturers do not compromise the safety of their boats, the boat you build may be safer than one you buy. Your intimacy with your boat's design will give you a head start in knowing its safe performance limits. Further, a wood and WEST SYSTEM* Brand epoxy hull will probably be stronger for its weight than an equivalent glass-reinforced plastic hull.

You will enjoy these advantages only if you have the basic skills needed to build a boat. Wood epoxy composite construction techniques may be somewhat easier than traditional boatbuilding methods, but woodworking experience is necessary. Lofting is tricky and will call on geometry you probably haven't used since high school. Read through the Lofting chapter in this book to be sure that you are up to the task. You can take a shortcut and buy plans that do not require lofting, but your boat's curves may not end up as smooth as you want them.

To build a boat, you must be willing to give up a great deal of time, including the hours you usually spend sailing. Your weekends and evenings will be taken up by the jobs of planning, purchasing and building, so your family must support your goal. If your spouse and children join you in your project, you will share the learning, frustration, pride and satisfaction that are part of every boatbuilding endeavor. Family cooperation may even result in the boat being built more quickly.

Boatbuilding requires patience and perseverance. The joys can be great, but so can the tedium and frustration. No one likes to sand, but it must be done if your boat is to be finished properly. You must be prepared to devote long hours to hard and repetitive work.

If you plan to build your own boat, you must be willing to accept the risk that accompanies any large personal commitment. At some point in the future, due to factors beyond your control, you may be forced to abandon your project. This may cause some financial hardship: it is extremely difficult to sell a half-finished hull. Worse, though, are the psychological results of giving up something on which you have lavished time and effort.

If you have never built a boat before, try a small project first. Practice on a dinghy will give you experi-

After imagining all that you will save by building yourself, you must come back to earth. It is very easy to bank imaginary money and draw from it, especially if you have not set straightforward financial limits. Know what you can spend. Do not make the mistake of figuring that small changes in your original plans will only cost a little, and that because you are saving so much by building you can well afford them. A number of tiny modifications can add up to financial overextension, which may put your boat in jeopardy.

If you build your own, you may get more boat for your money. You will certainly have more freedom to choose the design, however radical or traditional, you want. Because manufacturers must rely on large sales volumes, their designs are usually tailored to appeal to as many buyers as possible. If you cannot afford to have a one-off hull built, and your ideas of the perfect hull shape are out of the ordinary, you may have no alternative except building for yourself.

ence with the materials and methods described in this book. Mistakes on a small boat take less time to correct than mistakes on a large one, and the exercise will help you decide if you have the skill, time and dedication required for a larger enterprise.

Choosing The Right Boat

Once you have decided to build your own boat, choose the specific design carefully. Ask yourself some questions. How will you use your boat? What can you afford? Failure to carefully consider these factors can lead to the selection of a boat which will not meet your needs.

With whom will you be sailing? Will you be taking day or weekend cruises or do you plan longer trips? Take a long-range view and balance it against the length of time you will own your boat. Young families tend to increase in size, but if your children are older, you may soon need less space. While every boat has an absolute load limit, this is not the number of people who will actually be comfortable on board. As a rule, more passengers can be taken for short outings, fewer for overnights and fewer still on weekend cruises.

Boats with long-term, live-aboard accommodations with large fuel and water tanks are expensive to build and maintain. Before investing in them, think about where you will be cruising and how the boat should be fitted out. Live-aboard amenities for shorter periods necessitate more frequent port calls, but are much less costly.

Where will you be operating your boat? Look over a chart of your cruising area and take prevailing water and wind conditions into account. These should have significant impact on your choice of design. If you will be in shallow waters, think twice about a boat with deep draft. Some boats perform better in light air than others. You will need fewer instruments and a simpler boat if you sail in sheltered waters within visual range of navigational aids than if you go to open areas. Your interior will vary according to whether you plan trips to places where provisions are readily available.

Will you race your boat? If so, investigate racing in your area. Many different rating rules are used to fairly equate different types of sailing craft. These usually favor certain designs, so if you want a competitive edge, check local rules carefully.

Do you plan to put your boat on a trailer? Trailering is often a lot of work and sometimes a matter of waiting in line at launch ramps, but it cuts expenses and expands cruising range. Consider transporting your boat overland as you pick your design, remembering that long, heavy boats are particularly difficult to haul and launch.

How much can you afford to spend each year on the costs of owning and operating your boat? Items such as dockage, launch and haul-out are hard to predict because they vary from region to region. Maintenance, insurance, repair and equipment replacement expenses will depend on the workmanship, quality of accessories and general condition of the boat. The combined costs of owning a boat annually amount to from 3% to 5% of the vessel's showroom cost, plus engine fuel. If you budget for 5% plus fuel, you will be able to build up a reserve for major repairs.

Boat Plans

Once you have clear ideas of the kind of boat you want and how much money you have available, begin looking at specific designs. We recommend that you seek out reputable naval architects and boat designers. These professionals understand the various loads that will be placed on a vessel and know how to make sure that the boat will withstand them. You can save some money by designing your boat yourself, but we advise against this. Designers' fees are small compared to the total cost of a boat. Doing without an experienced designer is a gamble in which a lot of money is bet against very little.

Figure 2—OLLIE, 35-foot STRESFORM trimaran designed and built by Gougeon Brothers, Inc.

Shop for plans with as much diligence as you would shop for any other boatbuilding material. Designers should be willing to offer advice. Talk with them or write to them about the boats you are considering and inquire about performance. Ask about the prices and details of plans. If you plan to build with WEST SYSTEM materials, inform your designer and make sure that the construction details provided are applicable. If you want a class racing boat, check to see if the class association sells detailed plans.

You have a choice of four different kinds of drawings. Custom plans, which run about 10% of total construction cost, are specifically drawn for one client's exclusive use. Semi-custom plans are based on one of a designer's stock hulls, but are modified for a single client. They sell for about 4% of total construction cost. Stock plans cost ½% to 2% of total construction and have no guarantee of exclusivity. Study plans are insufficiently detailed for building, but do provide enough information for the browsing shopper. Designers either lend these to potential customers or charge a very minimal fee.

Even within these different types, plans vary greatly in the amount of detail they provide. Some describe and illustrate every aspect of construction, include full-scale templates for fabricating parts, and suggest specific woods and hardware. Others assume that you already know a good deal about boatbuilding techniques and offer little more than a set of hull lines and a table of offsets. Quality and price are not necessarily determined by the amount of detail a set of drawings contains.

Blueprint-type illustrations showing the size and position of every component are rarely included in plans. Instead, your designer will probably either provide you with a set of scantlings or refer you to Lloyd's, Nevin's or Herreshoff's scantling rules for wooden yachts. These prescribed dimensions are critical to the safe and efficient operation of your boat. Your designer has determined them by balancing specific loads against overall hull weight, and so they are not readily interchangeable between boats. If you have any questions about scantlings, or if you are considering altering them in any way, ask for professional advice.

Overbuilding is one of the most common errors in boatbuilding. Erring on the side of safety by using overly heavy scantlings can be quite wasteful. If you use 1¼ inch decking where 1 1/16 inch would be more appropriate, you will pay for more wood than you really need and end up with a boat which is heavier than it should be. Added load will stress the rigging of sailboats and increase fuel consumption of powerboats. If a hull is heavier than its designer intended, it

Figure 3—Popular and competitively raced worldwide, the DN class iceboat is a good project for beginners.

will ride in the water below the waterline and its performance will suffer.

Just as different boats have different scantlings, the different boatbuilding methods in this book may require different scantlings systems. There is no easy way to directly translate, for example, the scantlings for a laminated hull to hard chine construction. If you are inclined to switch from the method specified in your plans, consult your designer. While we are always willing to offer broad technical advice, we are unable to provide scantlings for specific applications.

Modifying Plans for WEST SYSTEM Materials

We are often asked if our construction methods can be used to build traditional boats. They can, but you must make some changes.

Most available plans for traditional small craft were drawn many years before the development of modern resins. They rely on traditional building techniques: a typical design might indicate carvel planking over closely-spaced ribs, a large rabbeted keel and stem, and copper nails or bronze screws. This sort of construction is not compatible with our methods and, unfortunately, any attempt to blend old and new will probably result in an unsuccessful hybrid.

The solution is to maintain all of the traditional lines, but to alter the scantlings so that one of the building methods described in this book may be used. We recommend that this, like any other changes in scantlings, be done under the supervision of an experienced designer. Every boat must be considered individually because, again, no conversion tables exist.

Good plans for modern hull designs are readily available, but their construction often calls for building materials such as fiberglass, steel and ferrocement. When designers choose these materials, it's frequently because they have little knowledge of or preference for wood. It follows, then, that they may not be able to help you very much if you want to convert their plans to wood and WEST SYSTEM epoxy. We suggest that you continue your search for a design if you find yourself contemplating major changes in materials.

Many excellent boat designers are familiar with our construction methods and offer plans for wood epoxy hulls. We will be happy to refer you to the professionals who might be best able to advise you about the particular boat you wish to build.

Chapter 3

Estimating Material and Labor

Realistic projections of material costs and labor requirements greatly increase the odds that you will finish your boat. If you are lucky, your designer has included an estimate in the plans. If not, take the time to make one yourself before you get started. While you can get some idea of what a boat will cost by finding a similar mass-produced model and dividing its price in half or by two thirds, we recommend more reliable methods.

As you look over your plans, prepare a rough estimate based on the price per pound of the materials your boat will require. If this figure seems affordable and you've decided on your design, move on to a more detailed estimate. Calculate your hull costs according to its surface area, and add up the prices of hardware and miscellaneous items. Make realistic guesses about the amount of time you'll spend on each step of construction. Consider all of these expenses before committing yourself to the project.

Revise your estimate when you loft the boat. As you lay out your lines, build the boat in your head to double-check the accuracy of your numbers.

Rough Estimates

We divide the beginning estimate into two parts: bare hull costs and hardware costs. From these, you'll

get a rough indication of how much you'll spend to finish your boat, not including labor.

To figure the rough estimate, you need a list of the materials used in your hull and deck and a firm idea of your boat's weight. This information should be included in your plans. If it isn't, ask your designer.

To determine hull costs, work out the proportion of each building element to the entire weight of the hull. If, for example, you're thinking about a design with a bare hull weight of 5,000 pounds, you might find that the materials required are 1,000 pounds each of Douglas fir, Western red cedar and mixed WEST SYSTEM* Brand epoxy, and 2,000 pounds of ¼ inch okoume plywood. Next, work out the per-pound price of each of these materials. Some, such as WEST SYSTEM resin, are sold by the pound and will be easy to figure, but others will require some calculation. Lumber is sold by volume and its price is listed in board feet. To compute its cost per pound, multiply board foot price by 12 to establish cubic foot price. Divide this by the weight of the wood per cubic foot.

In the case of the 5,000 pound hull, you might work out the following table. To spare yourself expensive surprises, add a 20% waste factor to the total.

While this breakdown may not be absolutely accurate, a small error is unlikely to cause any great change in the final per-pound cost. The price of a basic hull structure will vary a great deal according to the materials used to build it. For most boats, in 1985 prices, hull

Figure 1—Sample bare hull rough estimate.

SAMPLE BARE HULL ROUGH ESTIMATE

MATERIAL	PRICE/BOARD FOOT OR SHEET			PRICE/CUBIC FOOT	WEIGHT/CUBIC FOOT		PRICE/POUND		POUNDS NEEDED		PRICE MATERIALS
DOUGLAS FIR	$ 1.75	×	12 =	$ 21.00	÷	36 LBS.	=	$ .58	×	1000 LBS.	=	$ 583.00
WESTERN RED CEDAR	$ 2.50	×	12 =	$ 30.00	÷	24 LBS.	=	$ 1.25	×	1000 LBS.		$ 1,250.00
¼ INCH OKOUME PLYWOOD, (4X8 SHEET)	$ 48.00/SHT.				÷	20 LBS/SHT.	=	$ 2.40	×	2000 LBS.	=	$ 4,800.00
WEST SYSTEM EPOXY								$ 2.35	×	1000 LBS.	=	$ 2,350.00

SUB TOTAL MATERIALS	$ 8,983.00
+ 20% WASTE	$ 1,797.00
TOTAL, BARE HULL MATERIALS	$ 10,780.00

and deck construction will run between $2.00 and $3.00 per pound, although it may be more if you plan to use sophisticated materials or exotic woods.

The second part of the rough estimate, hardware costs, includes rigging, sails, engine, keel, interior fixtures and deck items and cannot be figured on a weight basis. For a very general idea of these expenses, multiply your bare hull costs by three. Hardware costs for a performance racing boat might be as high as four times the bare hull estimate, while simpler or smaller projects will have hardware costs only double those of basic materials.

Adding together bare hull and hardware estimates for the 5,000 pound design, total material costs would be

Bare hull	$10,780
Hardware	32,340
TOTAL ROUGH ESTIMATE	$43,120

Detailed Estimates — Hull Costs

The beginning estimate is far from accurate, especially for larger boats. To refine it, draw up a detailed list of boatbuilding materials. Everything from keel to cabin to spar should be included. Think through the stages of construction, from buying the plans to commissioning the vessel, to be sure that your list is complete.

The detailed estimate is broken into three parts: hull costs, hardware costs and labor. The first of these consists primarily of wood and epoxy, while hardware costs, as in the rough estimate, include manufactured items such as engine and winches. You will find labor requirements by far the most troublesome to predict.

To determine hull costs, consult your plans and write down all the basic materials you'll need. Designers often specify lumber dimensions and quantities on their drawings, listing, for example, 24 4 x 8 foot sheets of plywood, 420 board feet of Douglas fir and 690 board feet of Western red cedar. If no such information appears on your plans, scale off measurements yourself.

Once you have a list of hull materials, break it down into five categories:

(1) Hull skin, cabin, cockpit, deck, centerboard and rudder;

(2) Hull framework, including stringers, frames, sheer clamp, stem, bulkheads, floors and centerboard case;

(3) Interior items, from bunks and cabinets to shelves and partitions;

(4) WEST SYSTEM epoxy for stabilization, adhesive and surface coatings, pigments and fillers;

(5) Miscellaneous materials, such as paint, molds, cloth, cores, staples, fasteners and sandpaper.

Hull skin material costs are based on the exact surface area of the hull and deck. If this is not given in your plans or is not available from the designer, derive it from your drawings. Lay a string along the curves of your body plan to measure the girth of each station. Add these measurements for the total girth and divide this number by the number of stations measured. To find the hull area, multiply this figure by the length of your hull.

Before making the detailed estimate, it's necessary to know what building method — strip plank, mold, stringer-frame, hard chine or whatever — you will be using. If you are laminating your hull, you will need to know how many layers of wood you will apply. For the purpose of a sample estimate, we will assume that a hull with 300 square feet of surface area will be built with four layers of ⅛ inch cedar veneer.

Hull framework costing is a bit trickier. To arrive at any sort of accurate estimate, you must look over your list item by item. Be prepared to find that your local lumberyard does not carry exactly what you need. Use your best judgment in deciding what base stock sizes are most suitable to your applications. Try to work out the most economical uses of materials, especially plywood, but allow generous margins for waste. Some areas are particularly difficult, so pay extra attention to them.

Few lumber dealers will be able to sell you a perfect 2½ inch x 1½ inch board, 25 feet long, for a sheer

Figure 2—Sample detailed veneer estimate.

DETAILED VENEER ESTIMATE

MATERIAL	HULL SURFACE AREA	PRICE/SQUARE FOOT	PRICE/LAYER	No. LAYERS	PRICE MATERIALS
⅛ INCH SLICED CEDAR VENEER	300 SQUARE FEET ×	$ .44	= $ 132.00 ×	4	= $528.00
			SUB TOTAL VENEER		$ 528.00
			+ 20% WASTE		$ 105.60
			TOTAL VENEER COST		$ 633.60

Figure 3—Estimating WEST SYSTEM epoxy.

The following chart shows approximate coverage rates per pound of mixed WEST SYSTEM epoxy by type of application.

Application	Square feet covered per pound of epoxy	Waste rate
Initial coating	35	20%
Secondary and build-up coats	35	20%
Interlaminate adhesive coat (per glue line)	13	20%
Glass coat (10 oz.)	15	10%

clamp. You may choose, therefore, to buy two 1 inch x 6 inch boards, each 25 feet long, and laminate it from them. This will require more lumber than you really need and result in some waste. If you can't find any 25 foot boards and decide to scarf up shorter ones, order at least an extra few feet of wood for the joint.

You may plan to use many layers of wood to laminate the stem. The layers must be sawn from stock of adequate size, but before actually bending them to your curves, you won't know the best thickness of each layer. As a result, you won't really know how much stock to buy. Take an educated guess, remembering that a saw blade removes about ⅛ inch of wood with each cut. If you will be using ⅛ inch layers, you'll have a 50% waste factor. If you can bend ¼ inch laminating stock, waste will be noticeably reduced.

Before lofting them, it's very hard to know how many frames can be cut from a sheet of plywood. Given the price of plywood, you don't want to buy too much more than you will need. To work around this difficulty, use your imagination — and scraps of paper if necessary — to come up with the most efficient use of material. Order a little extra to be on the safe side.

Because of the unusually high waste rate in their construction, the costs of interior items are sometimes difficult to predict. Lumber requirements are usually not very critical, since you probably will have plenty of short ends and scrap for cleats and framework. Wood trim sizes and quantities are often indicated in plans. Plywood, however, can pose some problems.

Look over your plans to identify which interior components will be built with one or more sheets of plywood. If, say, you plan six 30 inch x 6 foot bunks, and use a sheet for each, you'll have six leftover pieces which are not particularly useful for anything else. Think of areas where they might fit, and consider scarfing them into a larger piece. Ask yourself if any rounded partitions, bulkheads, shelves or bunks can be cut out of rectangular stock. When you've finished this process, count up the number of full sheets you'll need.

All wood surfaces on your boat should be coated with WEST SYSTEM epoxy. Plan to apply at least two coatings — one stabilization and one surface — to interiors, and several more to exterior surfaces. Epoxy will be used as an adhesive between layers of laminated hulls and in joints and fillets. See Chapters 9 through 12 for detailed discussion of application techniques.

To estimate costs for WEST SYSTEM resin and hardener, use your study of the hull framework and interior to figure out total interior surface area. Remember to include frames, stringers, bulkheads and cabinets. Make educated guesses about the quantity of epoxy you will need for joints. Refer to the hull surface area to estimate your requirements for exterior and laminating applications.

WEST SYSTEM epoxy application rates vary according to the kind of job and work habits. For the purposes of your estimate, plan on coating an average of 35 square feet with one mixed pound of resin and hardener. Rates for interlaminate coats on hulls can be harder to predict because they depend a great deal on the quality of the fit and on the quantities of filler and clamping pressure used. A good figure to use for hand lay-ups, with clamps rather than vacuum pressure, is 12.8 square feet per pound per glue line. If you have many small jobs, or if you will be working at cool temperatures, coverage rates may be lower. On the other hand, careful fitting of joints and good planning will improve your application rate. Always add a 20% waste allowance to your total estimate.

When you have established interior area, divide this figure by 35 to find how many pounds of epoxy you'll need for each coating. Multiply this number by two, to account for stabilization and surface applications, and add a reasonable amount to cover your interior joints and fillets.

Before estimating the hull's exterior epoxy requirements, count the stabilization, adhesive and finish coats you will apply. When you have a firm idea of the number of exterior coats, divide your entire hull surface area by 35 and multiply by the number of coatings to determine pounds of mixed epoxy needed. A laminated hull requires at least one adhesive coating between each layer of plywood or veneer in addition to its minimum three exterior coatings. To find out how many pounds you will need for these applications, divide the surface area by 13 and multiply by number of interlaminate glue lines.

Add interior and exterior estimates and a waste factor for a total epoxy estimate. Look over your plans and consider your construction technique to determine required quantities of WEST SYSTEM additives and fillers. Chapter 7 provides guidelines for estimating each of these materials.

There are two things to consider as you price out WEST SYSTEM epoxy. First, you have only estimated the number of pounds of *mixed* resin and hardener you will use. Be sure to include resin and hardener totals so that you won't make the very common mistake of over-ordering. Second, consider ordering epoxy more than once, especially if you are working on a big boat, depending on your storage facilities, your financial situation and your experience. We recommend that you buy in volume to take advantage of price breaks, but you may want to order a little less than you think you'll need rather than the full quantity. This way, when it comes time to reorder, you are much more experienced and better able to correctly estimate what's required to finish the project.

To complete the hull estimate, think through your boatbuilding project. Add up the cost of plywood for lofting and molds and the cost of staples and screws for molds and hull laminations. If you plan to use glass cloth or graphite fibers on your hull, rudder or centerboard, price out the quantities you'll need. Work out the cost of paint or varnish. Estimate and include the prices of core materials. Don't forget disposable tools and equipment such as sandpaper, rollers and brushes.

Add the five portions of the bare hull estimate, making sure to include a waste allowance in all areas. Raw materials can represent as little as 10% of the cost of a finished boat, so it makes sense to overestimate, particularly in questionable situations. If you order a little more plywood or lumber than you anticipate needing, you may be able to avoid the expense and frustration of running short late in the project.

Detailed Estimates — Hardware Costs

The second major part of the detailed estimate, hardware costs, begins with an item-by-item inventory of your boat's hardware, rig, instruments and engine. These will vary greatly from vessel to vessel, but their costs will generally amount to a very high percentage of total costs.

Because hardware is so expensive, we recommend that you collect catalogs and price lists from several manufacturers and distributors. Shop around for the best deal you can find. Most marine products wholesalers extend 10% to 50% discounts to professional boatbuilders and dealers. Some will sell to individual builders at these prices if they see the prospect of a reasonable amount of business. Although you probably won't be able to get everything you need from a single source, you might consider sending your hardware inventory to several distributors and wholesalers and asking for quotations on it.

A good set of boat plans will list all of the hardware items needed. Some designers specify manufacturers, parts and numbers, and save their builders a great deal of time during estimating. If there are no hardware specifications on your drawings, develop an inventory yourself. This may not be easy. Many different types and qualities of hardware are sold, and it may be difficult to choose among them. Apparent bargains may turn out to be unsuited to your use. Research persistently and thoroughly and look through publications which objectively evaluate specific equipment. Ask for professional advice, especially on high-price items like winches, engines and rigging. Your final list should include a description of each piece you need, its manufacturer and model number.

Organizing hardware into groups will help you keep track of them. If the groupings are similar to catalog categories, you can save time in locating individual pieces. The comments about hardware which follow are broken into the divisions we've used over the years.

Interior hardware includes everything below the deck, and for large boats can be a major part of overall hardware cost. Your living area may require sinks, stove, icebox or refrigerator, toilet, portholes, vents and latches. The electrical system includes wiring, switches, fuse panels and accessories for lights, instruments, engine and appliances. You may need tanks for fuel and water and holding tanks, as well as plumbing. Last on the interior hardware list are the engine and its muffler, shaft, strut and stuffing box. The engine itself may be the single most costly item on your boat.

Most decisions on interior hardware are based on personal taste and the uses to which the boat will be put. High performance racing yachts and family cruisers have very different requirements. You may wish to build some items yourself. If so, see instructions for iceboxes, portholes, vents and tanks in later chapters of this book.

Engine type and size may be specified by your designer. If no engine is recommended in your plans, you must decide on one yourself. A good rule of thumb for determining engine size is to allow 1 horsepower for every 500 pounds of total boat displacement.

We suggest that you consider the choice between diesel and gasoline engines very carefully. Although more expensive initially, diesels are usually cheaper to operate in the long run because of their fuel economy and lower maintenance costs. Diesel fuel is much safer than gasoline. Since more boats are lost to fire than to any other single hazard, we think this is a good argument for using diesel.

Cost should be a secondary factor in engine selection. More important over time is the availability of parts and experienced repair personnel. Cruising boats in particular may break down in out-of-the-way places. You can avoid some very significant potential problems by choosing an engine which can be easily fixed.

Deck hardware requirements can be divided into three parts. Sail-handling hardware includes blocks, tracks, winches and cleats. Life lines, cleats, chocks and ground tackle are practical necessities. Structural hardware can include items such as chain plates and steering systems.

Because hardware needs vary so widely, we cannot offer firm advice to guide your choices. We do recommend, however, that you read over the principles of hardware installation discussed in Chapter 26, which may affect your selection of fasteners and metals, before you estimate your deck hardware costs.

Rig, a third grouping of hardware costs, contains mast and boom, with tang, sheaves and blocks, rigging, including stays, halyards, turnbuckles and all electrical items wired through the mast, sails and sheet lines. Contact your designer before making any alterations in the rig specified in your plans.

You have three options when it comes to masts and booms. You may decide to follow the instructions in later chapters of this book and build your own, or you can purchase parts and assemble a rig yourself. Finally, several companies now sell high-quality, inexpensive assembled masts and booms. You may want to ask one of them for an estimate on your designer's specifications. Boat builders often have trouble finding specified extrusions. Ask for professional advice if you find yourself in this position.

The fourth group of hardware is *instruments*. If you will need only a compass, depth sounder, log and radio, your list will be short. It may, however, be much longer. We think it's best to buy all your instruments from one manufacturer. The advantages of having a single source are twofold: you may pay less for a package deal, and you will have to remember only one name if any instrument stops functioning. Instrument repair is beyond the capability of most of us, so consider availability of parts and service when you make your estimate.

Keels, the final hardware category, are made of iron or lead. They are usually poured by specialized foundries into molds made from patterns you provide. Find foundry addresses in advertisements in marine publications, and request a few estimates. In order to avoid the big job of fairing up a keel, specify the tolerance and finish you want. The foundry's quote, a per-pound price, will include mold costs. Lead keels are more common than iron because they require simpler molds.

When you have worked out all five groups of the hardware inventory, add them for a total hardware estimate. Add this to the bare hull estimate to determine your potential total cash outlay.

Detailed Estimates — Labor

There are so many variables involved in estimating labor hours for boatbuilding projects that it is almost impossible to give good general advice. Some spouses of experienced builders insist that there's really only one rule — every stage will take two or three times as long as they thought it would — but we believe that it is possible to set a completion date for a boat and to meet it.

As we see it, four factors determine the amount of time it takes to build a boat: the size and type of the boat, the construction method used, the skill of the builder and the quality of shop and tools. If you can control any of these elements, you can significantly reduce your labor investment.

Builder's skill is by far the most important of these factors. We have seen inexperienced boatbuilders turn out excellent work right from the beginning of their projects, but they took much longer than experienced people to do equivalent jobs. We have also seen nonprofessionals perform as quickly and as well as professionals. Builder efficiency is closely related to tools and facilities; although you can sometimes compensate for inexperience by having the right tool for the job, it's also true that you'll never work effectively if you're poorly set up in the first place. See Chapter 4 for a discussion of tools and boat shops.

Experience has taught us that time requirements also vary with hull area, especially if scantlings systems remain constant. As boats get bigger, scantlings usually grow heavier and labor increases. A 40-foot boat can take half again as long to build as a 30-footer. Construction method, too, clearly affects labor hours: a one-off hull built with the mold method requires a relatively labor-intensive mold but less hull construction time than other techniques might. Second and third boats built on the same mold or with another method will require much less labor.

To develop your labor hour estimate, figure the time it will take you to finish a square foot each of hull, deck and interior, and multiple these figures by your actual areas. Do not forget to estimate labor for lofting and setting up a mold. Then add estimates for installing miscellaneous but necessary appendages like rudder, engine and hardware. Finally, include the time it will take you to commission the boat.

We find that on average, with a professional crew, custom one-off hulls and decks for boats up to 30 feet require approximately 2 hours per square foot. This climbs to 3 hours per foot when boats are 40 feet long. The same hulls built with the mold method need an extra hour per foot for mold building, but 30 minutes less for hull construction. Time requirements for decks may be slightly less than for hulls, but this depends on the complexity of cockpit and cabin.

Because interiors can be spartan or luxurious, the hours they take to complete can vary widely. We usually estimate interior labor as a function of hull area and figure that, depending on how elaborate it is, an interior will take 1½ to 2½ hours per square foot of hull. A more accurate method is to add up the hours you think it will take to construct each interior fixture. This is tricky, though, because even the most experienced builders find it hard to predict the time it will take to build complex features such as galleys, lockers and bunks.

Some jobs demand such significant blocks of time that they must be separately scheduled and estimated. Installation of deck hardware, including life lines, pulpits, winches, sail tracks and cleats, on sophisticated racers can take an hour per square foot of deck surface. There are no guidelines for establishing the time it will take to install keels, rudders and electronic gear. Because these features differ so much from boat to boat, we advise that you look at each closely and make the best guesses you can.

The process of installing an engine and its tanks, plumbing, electrical connections and through-hull fittings is notoriously time-consuming. Allow well in excess of 100 hours, according to its complexity, for this part of your project.

Commissioning is the business of taking the boat out of the shop, putting it in the water and making it work. It is almost inevitable that something will not be as it should be and that you will have to correct minor flaws and problems. This can use up a sizable chunk of time, so follow the example of professional builders and budget extra for it in your estimate.

After tallying various time requirements, you may wish to add something similar to a materials waste factor. When we estimate labor for a job, we include a factor of 20% to account for the time workers spend discussing their work. This is by no means wasted, unproductive time, but it does represent a lot of minutes that aren't devoted to actual boatbuilding. If you work alone, you might use the extra time to worry over difficult details or work around the problems of handling big pieces by yourself.

Set a completion date for your boat and establish intermediate goals for finishing each phase of the project. Maintain a log of your hours as you go, to keep track of the actual time you're spending and to indicate progress. Adjust your timetable if necessary by comparing weekly and monthly totals to your estimate. This may help improve your efficiency, keep the project on target and keep up your morale.

Estimating material costs and labor is not easy, nor is it scientific. It's unlikely that anyone has ever predicted boat costs to the dollar. Consider a materials estimate that turns out to be within 10% of actual costs excellent and a labor estimate within 20% of actual time superior.

With an estimate, even if it's off by 30%, you have a sound framework for planning, building and financing. Without an estimate, you may have to rely on wild guesses and blind luck. As you buy your materials and finish your boat, keep track of receipts and actual hours and compare these with your projections. This is an interesting exercise for those so inclined, and the records will come in handy for your next boatbuilding project.

Tools and the Boat Shop

You could, if you wanted to, build a boat in a closet, using no tool but a crooked knife. On the other hand, you might, in preparation for a major boatbuilding project, choose to build a solid new workshop and stock it with thousands of dollars of boatbuilding tools. We suggest that you settle somewhere between these extremes.

There are no strict rules about tools and boat shops. We think that in most cases it's best to wait to buy tools until you know you need them, and that in all cases, boats should be built in some sort of shelter. In this chapter we will present guidelines for tool inventories and shops to help you to decide what you need to build your boat.

Good power tools and working space save time and increase efficiency. Professional woodworkers, always mindful that labor is by far the most expensive of their materials, find that labor-saving electric and air-powered tools quickly pay for themselves. The cost of maintaining a well-lighted, heated shop with ample space for work and materials is justified by higher productivity and less frustration.

If you are an amateur, you will probably have to live with a compromise. Expensive power tools and an ideal workshop will save you time, but since you are not paying for your labor, they may not save you money. At the same time, you don't want to skimp so much on overhead that your project becomes a miserable exercise in muddling through with dull tools or tripping around cluttered floor space. Boatbuilding is much more fun when you have good, sharp tools and a well-ordered shop.

Your financial situation and personal tastes will ultimately determine your best balance of tools, shop, time and money. Within certain limits, boats can as easily be built in the living room as in a specially-built shop, so the flexibility and income of your household may determine your work space. If you plan to continue building boats, or if you are the kind of person who takes special pride in tools, it may be worthwhile to invest in some major equipment. If, on the other hand, your funds are limited or your interest uncertain, you will be able to finish your boat with a minimal tool inventory.

* TRADEMARK OF GOUGEON BROTHERS, INC., U.S.A.

Tools

The boatbuilding methods we use with wood and WEST SYSTEM* Brand epoxy require fewer tools than traditional techniques. We rarely need hard-to-find tools like adzes and slicks. In fact, one of the great advantages of wood-epoxy composite structures is that they can be built with a small number of readily available hand and power tools.

Over the years, our shop has developed an inventory of hand and power tools, and, like most builders, we probably have more tools than we really need. Some of them, particularly some hand tools, are indispensable. Others have been chosen because we are professionals and it is important that we cut down on labor. From the discussion of tools and their uses which follows, you should be able to decide what you will need for your project.

Bear several things in mind as you assess your tool requirements. Most pieces of equipment are sold in various qualities for professionals and hobbyists. Heavy-duty power tools are substantially more expensive than home shop models, but break down less frequently and last longer. Hand tools, too, come in different grades. The best way to find out what tools and what grade equipment you need is to get into your job. Check tool company catalogs for the best prices and invest your dollars wisely.

As professional builders, we can amortize large power tool expenditures over many projects. Tool reliability is a major consideration in our selection process because downtime due to malfunctions can be expensive. We are therefore willing to pay a premium for equipment that will hold up through a lot of abuse.

Most amateurs have different criteria for choosing their inventories. You will put less wear and tear on your power equipment if you only use it to build one boat a year. If your electric drill breaks down, you can probably move on to another job until it's fixed. Given the relative costs of different tool grades, the possibility of slight inconvenience doesn't really justify your buying top quality industrial tools. Less expensive models will serve you well.

Hand tools are a slightly different matter. We suggest that you do as we do, and buy the best chisels and planes that you can find at your local hardware store.

Figure 1—Minimal tool inventory: (1) combination square; (2) 24 inch level; (3) scissors; (4) sliding bevel or bevel square; (5) standard drill bits; (6) spade drill bits; (7) electric drill motor; (8) block plane; (9) compass; (10) 25 foot tape measure; (11) chalk line; (12) hammer; (13) screwdrivers; (14) rasp; (15) utility knife; (16) keyhole saw; (17) chisel; (18) staple removing tool; (19) staple gun.

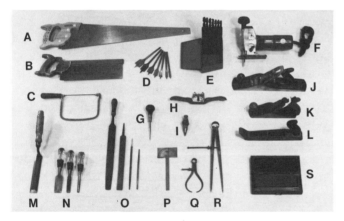

Figure 2—Broader tool inventory: (A) crosscut saw; (B) back saw; (C) coping saw; (D) large set spade bits; (E) large set drill bits; (F) electric saber saw; (G) awl; (H) spokeshave; (I) plumb bob; (J) jack plane; (K) bench or smoothing plane; (L) Surform™ tool; (M) offset chisel; (N) chisel assortment; (O) file and rasp assortment; (P) protractor; (Q) calipers; (R) dividers; (S) whetstone.

Keep your tools sharp, and let yourself enjoy handling them. Cured epoxy is harder than the wood for which good edge tools were intended, so you may occasionally want to protect your investment by using a few lower-quality, disposable pieces. Purchase good clamps because they will save you a great deal of frustration.

A small boatbuilding project can go smoothly with a small inventory of hand tools and some basic safety equipment. Figure 1 shows a minimal, economical col-

* TRADEMARK OF GOUGEON BROTHERS, INC., U.S.A.

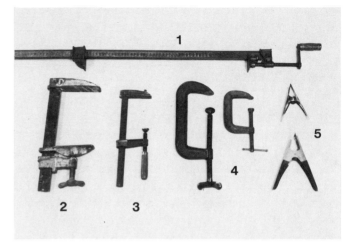

Figure 3—Clamps: (1) sliding bar clamp; (2) heavy-duty, large pad clamp; (3) quick action clamp; (4) C-clamps; (5) spring clamps.

lection of tools. It would be impractical to do without these even on an 8-foot pram. Figure 2 illustrates a broader inventory which will get you through a project more comfortably. You might consider beginning with the tools in Figure 1, and buying more as you need them. Most of the pictured tools are well-known and available at hardware stores.

Construction with WEST SYSTEM epoxy requires a few specialized tools, some of which can be purchased and others made in the shop. Syringes, rollers, squeegees, pans and cups are available in most hardware stores or through us. Instructions for making other useful gadgets are provided throughout this book.

Three or four well-chosen hand held power tools will make your work easier and cut down on the need for major equipment. A saber saw is a little less accurate than a band saw, but it can do most of the same work and more. A good ¼ or ⅜ inch electric drill with bits and accessories is useful for many jobs. If you plan to scarf a great deal of plywood, ½ inch thick or less, a 7¼ inch electric circular saw with a SCARFFER* attachment will ease your task considerably. A circular saw can also be set up with guides and used as a table saw. An orbital polisher with a selection of foam pads will speed up finishing. If you buy these tools for a project and later find that your interest in woodworking has vanished, you can usually sell them to regain a portion of their price.

The first major piece of equipment to think about buying is a table saw. This versatile tool is used primarily to saw lumber to exact specifications, but it's also handy for beveling and tapering. A good table saw can masquerade as a jointer and put a straight edge on a warped board, and, with the addition of a sliding miter gauge, it can serve as a cut-off saw. With dado blades and other heads, a table saw also can act as a shaper.

At some point, now or in the future, you may think about purchasing other power tools. The following inventory of our shop equipment may help you in deciding whether or not to supplement your basic inventory.

Gougeon Brothers Power Tool Inventory

In listing the equipment we use in our shop, we hope to give you an idea of the possibilities available to the modern boatbuilder. We are in no way suggesting that amateur builders should try to duplicate this inventory.

Our list is arranged in categories according to use, so tools do not appear in order of importance. Tool choice is a personal matter: as we talked this list over, we realized that we didn't always agree about individual items. We do not claim that these are the best on the market and our purpose is not to endorse particular manufacturers or products. Because they change so quickly, model numbers are not included.

These tools have served best in reducing labor in a professional boat shop. Many of them are industrial quality and therefore may require additional electrical wiring for safe use. Some are air-powered and so require an air compressor. Should you decide to buy air-powered tools, ask for advice about their operation. Almost all of these tools may be somewhat powerful for a home shop, and all are expensive. Note that we use a number of auto body shop tools.

Saws

Bosch electronic saber saw: The saber saw is one of the essential boatbuilding tools. This particular

Figure 4—Makita finishing sander.

Figure 5—Skil electric plane used here to trim a wing mast during construction.

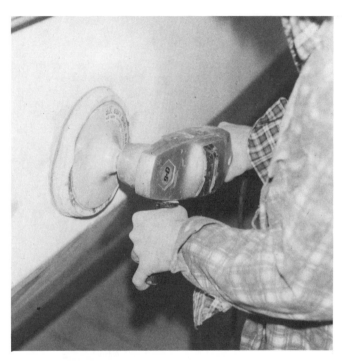

Figure 6—Black & Decker polisher is used with foam disc pad for sanding.

model offers much more than most and is also about three times as expensive. It features adjustable orbital blade action and a variable and very accurate speed control which enable you to set it to best cut a variety of materials. It has a cutting oil attachment for use with stainless steel and other hard-to-cut metals, and it is extremely accurate in cutting wood. This saber saw is particularly helpful in natural finishing because it has a guard which keeps the blade from chipping plywood.

Milwaukee and Skil® 7¼ inch hand held electric circular saws: Use a circular saw to cut lumber or plywood that is too unwieldy or too large to handle on a table or radial arm saw and to notch frames and beams. We have several and keep one permanently set up with the SCARFFER attachment to cut 8 to 1

Figure 7—Black & Decker polisher, with foam disc pad shown. We bond a piece of 1/16 inch birch plywood on the face of the disc. This plywood is still flexible enough to follow major contours, and is effective for sanding and fairing surfaces with varying densities, such as WEST SYSTEM resins and various fillers.

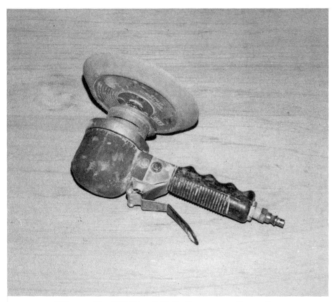

Figure 8—DAQ orbital air-powered sander.

scarfs on plywood up to ½ inch thick.

Rockwell 4½ inch circular electric panel saw: This tool is wonderful for cutting thin plywood and veneer, but it's not a necessity.

Rockwell 10 inch tilting arbor table saw: Rockwell makes the best — and most expensive — saw of this type. Less costly brands may be more practical for most individuals. Look for a solidly-constructed unit that has a well-positioned arbor with good bearings. An easily adjusted rip fence is a necessity. We also have a 14 inch Rockwell table saw which can handle very large stock, but it is not needed very often.

Rockwell 14 inch wood cutting band saw: After the table saw, the band saw is the most important stationary power tool in any boat shop. It is the most accurate saw for cutting curves and bevels. We often use an older Crescent 36 inch band saw and a 14 inch metal cutting band saw.

Rockwell 14 inch radial arm cut-off saw: This is not a particularly important tool in our shop, but we use it with a special jig to cut perfect splices on stringers. It produces very good miter cuts.

Electric Planes, Polishers and Sanders

Black & Decker ® 7 inch electric orbital polisher: We use this polisher with high-density foam disc pads to work on large areas such as hulls and decks, and with two kinds of low-density pads on interiors and strip construction. Stick with a 2,000 r.p.m. polisher because faster models will scorch finished epoxy. We think this tool is an important labor saver.

Chicago Pneumatic Co. air-powered file sander or body file: This tool, more commonly found in body shops, is used for fairing. We have modified it by replacing the standard 14 x 2 inch pad with a 22 x 4½ inch wood pad, which is perfect for 9 x 11 inch sheets of sandpaper split in half lengthwise and held in place with feathering disc adhesive. With the long pad, the file sander does a good job of rough fairing hulls and decks. Final fairing is still done by hand.

DAQ air-powered orbital circular sander: Another auto shop tool, this sander is light in weight, which

Figure 9—Chicago Pneumatic air-powered file with the standard 2 inch x 14 inch pad.

makes it very handy on irregular surfaces and in tight areas such as the interiors of hulls. We use it mainly as a finish sander with 180 grit and finer sandpaper, although it does a good job of rough sanding with coarse grit paper.

Rockwell block plane: This electric plane is very good for speeding up the removal of stock on curved surfaces and for changing the bevels on frames, bulkheads and deck beams.

Rockwell heavy-duty orbital sander: This is the best orbital sander we have found to date, both because of its efficiency and because it is easily maintained. We use it with 80 grit and finer sandpapers on wood and well-cured resin.

Rockwell 48 inch belt and 12 inch disc sander/finisher: We use this stationary tool constantly to mill wood and metal to close tolerances.

Makita finishing sander: Small and lightweight, this sander is wonderful for getting into corners. You can easily hold it with one hand. Its pad is approximately 4 inches square.

Skil electric plane: This tool is excellent for planing large surface areas, such as keels and shear clamps, where a lot of stock is to be removed. A long 18 inch bed provides excellent fairing ability and saves labor.

Skil 4 inch electric belt sander: This sander spends most of its time on the shelf in our shop, but comes in handy for sanding scarfs and other surfaces which must be flat. To use this properly, you must have a great deal of skill.

Staplers, Tackers, and Nailers

Staples are cheaper than other fasteners and they require less labor. There are many large companies besides Duo-Fast® in the stapling equipment field, Bostitch™, Senco™ and Swingline® among them, and all make excellent products. The major consideration in choosing one over another is the availability of non-rusting alloy staples in the size you need. Some manufacturers provide alloy staples for some staple gun sizes, but not for others. This is something to think about before making a purchase.

Duo-Fast air-powered staple gun: This staple gun shoots broad back wire staples from ¼ to 9/16 inch long. We use it mainly for clamping pressure when laminating veneers and plywood up to ¼ inch thick.

Duo-Fast air-powered nailer: This countersinks strong wire nails up to 2 inches long. We use it primarily in assembling jigs and fixtures.

Duo-Fast air-powered tacker: This shoots narrow back, fine wire staples up to ⅝ inch long. It leaves very small holes to be plugged or filled and is often used for

Figure 10—Duo-Fast staplers and tackers. Clockwise from upper left: air-powered staple gun; heavy duty tacker; hand-powered stapler; light duty tacker.

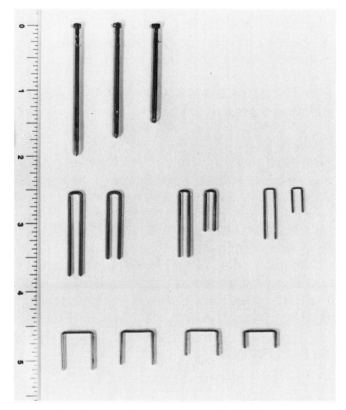

Figure 11—Fasteners. Top row: wire nails. Middle row: narrow crown staples. Bottom row: wide crown staples.

assembling in fine cabinet work.

Duo-Fast electric tacker: Electric version of air-powered staple gun.

Duo-Fast heavy duty tacker: This shoots narrow crown 19 gauge staples up to 1 inch long. Consider using it with bronze or Monel™ staples for installing stringers and for assembling centerboard cases and other larger structural elements.

Routers

Milwaukee 1½ horsepower router: Because it is well-powered, this router is good for heavy jobs where a lot of material must be removed. We regularly use it for notching and shaping, too.

Skil ⅞ horsepower router: This is best for light shaping. Plywood and veneer edge trimming is easy if you use its fly-cutting knives with ball bearing guide.

Miscellaneous tools

Dayton heat guns: We have a number of heat guns, and use them to speed up epoxy cures, especially in cold weather. We recommend the 750°F models. Heat guns can cause fires, so be careful with them.

Rockwell drill press: We use ours often for accurate drilling of both wood and metal.

Rockwell light-duty wood shaper: This is for large shaping jobs, such as rounding edges on stringers.

Rockwell 13 inch thickness planer: A planer is a necessity if you buy rough lumber which must be surfaced. The alternative is to have millwork done by a local cabinet shop or lumberyard. Our planer is also used to smooth up rough saw cuts as it is quicker than sanding.

Rockwell tool grinder: Sharp tools are essential to efficient production, so a well-balanced grinder with good stones is essential to any shop. Dull tools are no fun.

Rockwell-Delta 6 inch jointer: This does a good job of smoothing saw marks on planks.

WEST SYSTEM resin metering dispensers: A metered dispensing system is a big help on any sizable project. Our dispensers mix precise ratios, save time and reduce waste.

The Boat Shop

Boatbuilders have demonstrated great resourcefulness and ingenuity in the selection of appropriate shelter for their activities. We have seen barns and living rooms converted, with varying degrees of success, into permanent and temporary shops. Your working space will be determined by how much you can afford to spend, by the size of your project and by whether your shop will be permanent or temporary.

Don't try to build a boat without a shelter. Wooden hulls and components suffer when exposed to rain, snow and sunlight. Tools left out in the open may rust or disappear, and the alternative, hauling them in and

out, is time-consuming. Your boatbuilding time will be restricted by the weather if you work outside, and you will be forced to quit at nightfall, even if it's only 6:00 P.M. While WEST SYSTEM resins can withstand most weather conditions, their efficacy will be reduced by improper storage and by use in very cold conditions or on wet wood.

Plan your boat shop carefully. It should provide you, your hull and your tools with adequate protection from the elements. Your shop should have room enough for your boat, tools and lumber, and some extra space for working and maneuvering. It must be warm and well-lighted if you are to do your best work, and it must be safe. Your shop must be operated within the boundaries of acceptable behavior as established by your neighborhood. As you plan it, think about ways to expand your work space should you ever decide to build a larger vessel.

Whether you buy, rent or build your shop, make sure that you will have enough floor space. In order to work comfortably, you will need an area that is at least twice as large as your hull. Multihull builders, who usually construct hulls one at a time, will require twice the area of their largest hulls. This general rule will allow minimal room for tools, workbench, layout, small parts manufacture and lumber storage. If you have a large collection of power tools, your needs may be a little different.

In some cases it is convenient to split total work area into different buildings. In colder climates, a good arrangement might be to use a large shed for actual hull construction and a smaller shop — basement, utility room or garage — for other functions. With some planning, little jobs can be reserved for months when the larger shop is difficult to heat. Because they would otherwise require extraordinarily large workshops,

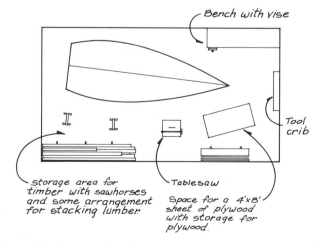

Figure 12—Layout of typical home shop or shelter for building 25 foot to 30 foot boat.

multihulls are built hull by hull indoors and assembled outside.

An efficient floor plan will pay dividends in productivity. Allow plenty of room around each power tool. You will need from 15 to 20 feet of clear area on each end and 5 feet on each side of a table saw or planer in order to run stock through it. Portions of this space may be shared with a band saw, since it's unlikely that you'll operate these machines simultaneously. Figure 12 illustrates a typical and effective shop layout. Don't forget to plan for walking room at either end of your hull.

Because a poorly organized shop can be hazardous as well as irritating, pay some attention to safety factors as you think over your building. Reduce potential fire hazards by finding metal cabinets in which to store solvents and paints. Make sure that no combustibles will be stored near your heater. Incorporate good housekeeping procedures and venting devices into your floor plan to reduce dust and fume inhalation. If young children may visit you as you work, redouble your precautions. Buy a lock for your boat shop to prevent vandalism and to keep curious visitors out of danger.

Shop electrical installations require special care. Plan on a minimum of 30 amps of power — more if you have an extensive lighting system. Use heavy-duty wiring and extension cords. All of your tools, cords and wiring should be double-grounded, especially if you will be working on a damp earth floor. If you will be using power tools on a dock or near water, protect circuits with ground fault interrupters.

Boatbuilders often wonder about the best way to heat their shops and about the effects of cold on WEST SYSTEM epoxy. Any type of fuel can be used as long as it presents no fire hazard. It is important that your heating system be well-vented, for your personal safety and because carbon dioxide emissions, especially from kerosene heaters, can adversely affect resin cures. See Chapter 7 for futher information if you will be working with WEST SYSTEM materials in cold weather.

Before getting down to work on your boat shop, stop to consider the people around you. At some point in your project, you will undoubtedly want to work into the night. Will the noise of your power tools disturb neighbors? If you have decided on an addition to your garage, will your neighbors approve? If you plan to carry out portions of your project in your home, have you figured out some way to control dust?

A Temporary Shelter — One Option

If you are unable to rent or buy a boat shop, or if you cannot afford to build a permanent structure to accommodate your project, you may decide to build a temporary shelter. This might be freestanding or it might butt up against a pre-existing building. Garages and sheds can be enlarged simply and quickly with temporary extensions. Your choices will depend on the land and buildings you have to work with and on the size of your boat.

Many different techniques have been used to build satisfactory temporary shelters, but one stands out. We suggest that you consider using heavy standard or reinforced polyethylene sheeting on wood frames. This construction system requires limited quantities of labor and materials and can be used in warm or cold regions. Conventional buildings certainly offer better insulation from the weather, but polyethylene shops are inexpensive and adequate for boatbuilding purposes.

Before erecting a temporary shelter, talk with your neighbors and check local zoning ordinances. Polyethylene buildings and additions are not beautiful, they will not enhance your neighborhood, and they can lead to hard feelings. If you explain your project to the people next door and ask their blessings before you begin, they will probably be very understanding. Zoning officials can offer less latitude. Some towns permit free-standing temporary structures while others allow only temporary additions to pre-existing buildings.

To determine your shelter's minimum size, double the area of your boat. A 30-foot boat, 10 feet wide, has a total area of about 300 square feet and will require 600 square feet of construction space. A 36 x 17 feet shop, with a total area of 612 square feet, would be adequate and would permit 3 feet of work room at each end of the hull. Less area would be insufficient, while more would make things go a bit easier. Weigh the convenience of extra elbow room against the costs of building and heating additional space.

Figure 13—Garage extension. (Art Briggs)

When you know your ideal shop size, look around to see if you can extend any outbuildings to suitable dimensions. If you don't mind evicting your car, it's far easier to enlarge a high-ceilinged garage than it is to build an entirely new structure. If you are able to use pre-existing rigid walls, you will save time and have a stronger shelter. An extension to a heated structure will pick up some radiant heat and can share an electrical system. Figure 13 illustrates a single-car garage enlarged successfully with polyethylene and wood to build a 24-foot trimaran. Timber dimensions and framework will of course vary with the size of your addition.

If you plan to construct an independent building, or if your addition is so large as to require substantial support, we recommend using arches to form a basic structural skeleton. The ends of your building can butt up against a house or garage or be covered with plastic or plywood, but provisions should be made for opening them in warm weather. Figures 14, 16, 17 and 18 show an arched shelter in which a 37-foot trimaran was built.

It is not possible for us to provide a detailed materials list for polyethylene shops because each is different. Most will require arches every 4 feet along their lengths, but this may vary. The basic instructions which follow provide an outline for building. The dimensions and quantities of lumber you need will depend on the size of your structure and on the degree of curvature you choose to build into its roofline.

Begin by building arches, half-section by half-section. Each of these pieces consists of two boards separated by regularly-spaced 2 inch blocks. Construct half-sections by bending one board around a simple form. Use WEST SYSTEM epoxy and nails to attach blocks at 18 inch intervals, and then form a sandwich

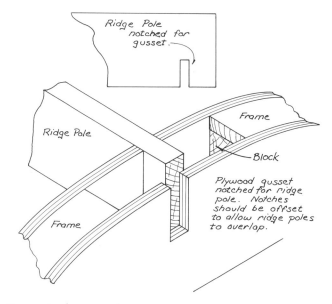

Figure 15—Detail of ridge pole arrangement for temporary shelter.

Figure 16—Framework for shelter completed. Diagonal bracing and stringers in place.

by bonding the second board to your assembly. Remove this from the form when the adhesive has cured, and continue until you have made as many half-arches as your shop will need.

When you have completed the half-sections of the arches, join them at the roof peak with plywood gussets. Use two gussets per arch, one on either side of the joint, and bond with WEST SYSTEM epoxy and nails or staples. Notch the gussets to receive a ridgepole. Sand outside surfaces smooth so that polyethylene will not snag when it is installed.

To erect your frame, drive heavy stakes — 4 or 5 foot long 2 x 4's work well — every 4 feet along the sides of the area to be enclosed. Make sure that the angle of your stakes matches the angle of your arches. Then raise the arches and clamp them to the stakes.

Figure 14—Assembling arches for temporary shelter.

Figure 17—Plastic covering stretched over framework.

Fair up your roofline, adjusting arches where necessary. Drill and bolt through two points on each joint/arch overlap so that the stake becomes a rigid extension of the arch. The arches will be freestanding and will not require temporary bracing.

Ridgepoles are easy to install if you put them up in 4 foot sections corresponding to stake and arch spacing. Make these segments out of ¾ inch stock and notch them to lock into the gussets as shown in Figure 15. As you align each arch, drop the next ridgepole section into its notched position to maintain a straight roofline.

When your skeleton is erect, set up diagonal bracing for longitudinal support. One way to do this is to build the framework for end walls at a sloping angle, as in Figure 17. You may need additional interior bracing or stringers.

Polyethylene sheeting can be purchased at hardware and building supply stores. Both black and translucent sheets are usually available in 6 mil thicknesses.

Figure 18—Shelter completed. Plywood walls were used at both ends to give structure extra rigidity.

Black polyethylene will absorb heat from the sun, so if you have a choice and live in a cold climate you may prefer it. While its color does tend to retard the damage caused by ultraviolet light, black plastic will not last significantly longer than clear polyethylene. You can repair rips and tears in your sheathing with duct tape, but you should plan on replacing it every year.

If your shelter will be subjected to strong winds or if you are willing to spend more to avoid annual re-sheathing consider using reinforced rather than standard polyethylene. This material is three-layered, with nylon webbing sandwiched between two layers of plastic, and therefore costs more and lasts longer.

Whichever type of sheeting you use, apply the entire arched roof covering in one piece. If you cannot buy a single sheet large enough for your shop, use duct tape to put one together. Spread smaller pieces out on a flat surface, allowing about a foot of overlap at each joint. Apply equal tension to the sheets as you tape them together and put on the tape itself with the greatest possible pressure. Remember to turn your plastic over to tape both sides.

If you are particularly concerned about conserving heat, consider covering your framework with the heavy cardboard used for appliance shipping crates before you apply plastic sheeting. When you work on the interior of your shop, you can fill in your "walls" with fire-resistant insulating material before sheathing them with additional cardboard.

After you have pulled the plastic over your framework, fasten it along the end arches, nailing through a thin batten to distribute the load evenly. To fasten it at ground level, place a board over the polyethylene and drive nails through to the arches. Move inside your shelter, place more battens over your sheeting and nail through them to the board.

Floors for polyethylene sheds are expensive and time-consuming to make. You can probably make do with a plastic-covered dirt floor if you plan drainage carefully. Dig a trench around the perimeter of your structure and lay polyethylene sheeting over the entire floor area out into the trench. For a more solid floor surface, cover the plastic with fiberboard.

If you intend to heat your workshop, we suggest that you install inside walls to form dead air spaces. You can do this with an inner polyethylene liner, but heavy cardboard is a better insulating material and can add some rigidity to your structure. If you staple and tape cardboard neatly in place, your shop may begin to look, at least on the inside, like a real building. Further heat savings are possible if your building is tall enough to allow you to nail joists across your arches for a dropped ceiling. You will find that heated air rises to the ceiling and investment in a fan will help push it back down.

Install your heating and electrical systems and your temporary shelter is ready for a boat. Vent your heater in an approved manner, using a large flashing if you must run a stovepipe through an end wall. Avoid coal and wood stoves, because their sparks may damage your plastic sheathing, and remember that open flames can ignite some solvents and all woods.

Chapter 5

Wood as a Structural Material

Wood has many advantages as a boatbuilding material. It's probably easier, less expensive and more satisfying to build a boat from it than from any other material. Wood is relatively easy to cut and shape and almost everyone has some experience with it. It's satisfying to work with because it's beautiful. It is readily available and it costs less than steel, aluminum or fiberglass. Although lumber prices have increased in the past decade, wood is still comparatively inexpensive in terms of both its own cost and the cost of tools to work it. Most importantly, however, wood has physical characteristics which make it ideal for boatbuilding. Its strength, stiffness, light weight and resistance to fatigue give wood advantages over other materials.

While wood has many advantages as a structural material, it also has some well-known disadvantages, most of which are caused by the passage of water in and out of its cells. Wood can rot. It shrinks and swells with changes in moisture and temperature and it loses some of its strength and stiffness when its moisture content is high. In the past, difficulties arose in constructing boats with wood because of changes in the condition of the wood caused by changes in moisture content. As its moisture level increased, the wood changed in dimension and lost some of its strength and stiffness. The design of boats built of wood had to make allowances for this instability.

To a very great extent, the use of WEST SYSTEM* Brand epoxy overcomes the problems previously associated with wood construction. All joints in boats built with the methods described in this book are bonded with, and all surfaces encapsulated in, resin. In this way, every piece of wood, inside and out, is covered with a barrier coating of WEST SYSTEM epoxy through which no significant amount of water or air can pass. As a result, the moisture content of the wood is stabilized.

This stabilization means that the wood will shrink and swell very little. The moisture level at which the stabilization occurs and at which the wood remains ensures a continuation of design strength and stiffness. Encapsulation in WEST SYSTEM resin also prevents dry rot not only by stabilizing moisture content, but also by restricting oxygen supply to the wood surface.

Since World War II, there has been tremendous research and development in the field of epoxy and other thermosetting plastics. Little experimentation, however, has been done on wood. We are among the few to work specifically to develop a wood/epoxy composite material, and the only group to test it exhaustively, especially in high-cycle fatigue. Our efforts clearly show that a wood/WEST SYSTEM epoxy composite is one of the best structural materials currently available for building boats when strength and stiffness-to-weight are primary considerations. Because of the superiority of the composite in fatigue, wood/epoxy hulls are less liable to failure over time and after hard use than hulls built of other materials. We will explain why this is so in this chapter and discuss WEST SYSTEM resin in greater detail in Chapter 7. See Appendix A for additional data on wood's mechanical properties.

Engineering for Wooden Boats

Boats present unique engineering problems. They require an outer skin which may or may not be load-bearing but which must withstand and deflect tons of water. Boats must also survive the kind of high point loadings that occur during launching, and hauling out and if objects are struck at sea. Even small vessels have tremendous amounts of vulnerable hull and deck surface which must be properly supported to retain their streamlined shapes. Large sailing rigs may cause torsion and bending in hulls which have inadequate shear bracing. Finally, boats must survive these loads continuously over many years. The overall task in addressing these problems is the successful integration of proper design, construction methods and material choices.

Boats demand a material which is strong and lightweight. It must also be stiff, as demonstrated by ability to resist deformation under load. Within certain limits, the lighter and stiffer a boat is, the better its potential for performance and durability. The less a hull weighs, the faster it will move under a given amount of power. The stiffer a boat, the better it holds its true shape and resists "softening" or weakening through flex and fatigue. Boatbuilding materials must retain their strength and stiffness over time and after use, and the

26

boat's structural components and construction method must be designed to fully exploit the materials' capabilities.

These principles may be best understood by thinking of a boat hull as a box beam enclosed by hull planking, deck planking and keel. This total outer skin, plus the stringers and other longitudinal members, provides support fore and aft. Frames and bulkheads, at right angles to these, form a strengthening lattice athwartships and provide torsional rigidity. If this lattice is loose and weak and its skin flexible from poor design, bad construction or inappropriate choice of materials, the entire beam may lose its shape. In boats, problems of inadequate support most commonly show up as hogging, sagging, leaking and slow performance.

Adequate structural strength is required of any material used in boats. Usually, enough material is used to provide an adequate safety margin against material fatigue and unseen loads, and beyond this basic requirement, ultimate strength is less critical. Stiffness, however, continues to be important and maximum stiffness is very desirable. All materials must deflect — either stretch or compress — under load, but usually any deformation in a boat hull is undesirable. While both strength and stiffness can generally be increased by using more material in the form of a thicker hull skin, this will increase hull weight. A basic problem with boats is that skin weight alone becomes the major factor in overall boat weight.

In the quest for more speed, reducing weight is of major importance. Materials have been pushed to their limits for many years. Recently, strong competition and the desires of clients have caused many designers and builders to go further, and to sometimes test margins of safety. The results of this — boats which never finish races because of materials failure — point to the importance of fatigue resistance in any boatbuilding material. When a material loses most of its strength after a single high loading, it may quickly fail, no matter how strong it was originally.

Fatigue is an *accumulation* of damage caused by repeated loading of a structure. When boats, wind turbine blades and masts are subjected to a continuing series of loads, the fatigue behavior of the material of which they are made is more important than its ultimate one-time strength. If a boatbuilding material loses most of its strength after a few thousand hours of service, it may fail. Failure in fatigue is probably one of the leading causes of breakdowns in racing boats.

Materials differ widely in their resistance to fatigue. Some are very strong for a limited number of loads, but lose a high percentage of this strength as the loads are repeated. Others, particularly wood, begin with

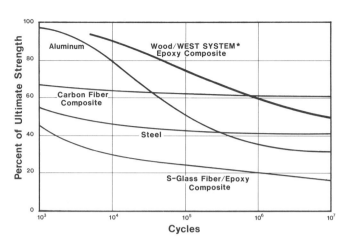

Figure 1—Tensile fatigue comparison. Fatigue strength of various structural materials as percentage of static strength.

slightly lower one-time load strengths, but retain most of their capabilities even after millions of cycles of tension and compression. One-time, load-to-failure figures may not, therefore, be very representative of how a material behaves under long-term cyclic fatigue stress.

Figure 1 illustrates the cyclic tension fatigue behavior of some popular boatbuilding materials. The left side of

Figure 2—Gougeon MTS test machine with dogbone sample.

this chart displays the load capability of each material expressed as a percentage, with 100% representing the ultimate one-time strength of each. All of these materials lose strength as a given load is repeated at steadily increasing numbers of cycles. The plotted fatigue curves show the relative percentages of strength which remain after any given range of loads and cycles to failure.

Millions of cycles of stress are difficult to imagine, but they can be translated into operating hours. Boats at sea have been carefully instrumented where cyclic load increases associated with waves were measured once every 3 seconds. At this rate, after about 833 hours, the equivalent of about four years of seasonal weekend sailing, a hull would experience about a million cycles. The material used in a wooden boat would at this time still have about 60% of its ultimate strength, while aluminum would retain 40% and fiberglass composite 20% of their respective ultimate capabilities. Given the anticipated life of a hull and the fact that human lives depend on its strength over time, these figures deserve serious consideration.

Some boat designers set their priorities and trade off between stiffness, one-time strength, weight and resistance to fatigue. We use wood, so we don't have to compromise. It is the material of choice when the primary goal is to gain maximum stiffness and excellent strength and at least weight, and it will retain these qualities for many years of hard sailing.

Wood Strength

In *The New Science of Strong Materials*, J. E. Gordon suggests that a simple way to understand the strength of wood is to think of a bundle of drinking straws which have been glued together. These represent tubular cellulose fibers bonded with lignin, and clearly illustrate what happens to a piece of wood under load.

When equal tension and compression loads are applied to opposing faces of this bundle, effects differ. The bundle is *anisotropic:* longitudinal strength, with the grain of the straws, is much greater than horizontal or crossgrain strength. When too much compression is applied to any face, the straws buckle and then crush. The bundle is generally stronger in tension than in compression, but in spite of all this pushing and pulling the straws are very hard to actually break.

Strength is a measurement of the amount of force needed to break something. In wood, strength values vary significantly according to the orientation and type of load. Mechanical properties are about 20 times higher in the direction of grain than across it, either

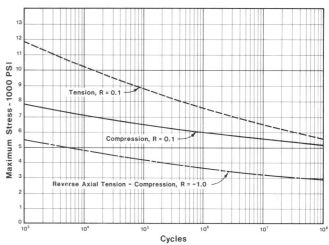

Figure 3—Laminate fatigue properties. Maximum stress adjusted to 12% wood moisture content vs. total cycles for BG-1 Douglas fir/epoxy laminate with 12:1 slope scarf joints, 3 inch stagger, 31.8 cubic inch test volume parallel to grain load direction, room temperature.

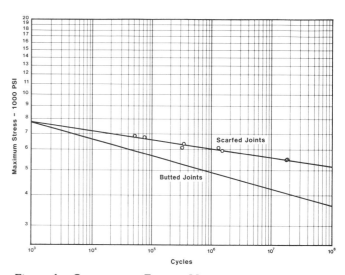

Figure 4—Compression Fatigue. Maximum stress vs. total cycles for Douglas fir/epoxy laminate with 12:1 slope scarf *and* butt joints with three inch stagger. 31.8 cubic inch test volume, parallel to grain directions, room temperature, 12% wood moisture content.

parallel to or at right angles to growth rings. Tensile strength of most woods is quite high and compressive strength somewhat lower. When it is overloaded, wood will buckle and crush, with cells deforming up to 20% before initial failure. It will then gradually yield before finally breaking.

The strength of any particular piece of wood is greatly dependent on its quality, moisture content and density. Grain irregularities, knots and other defects may cause local weakness. Variation in moisture content may increase or reduce the ultimate strength of an entire board. Figure 10 illustrates how changes in levels of moisture affect wood's ultimate mechanical

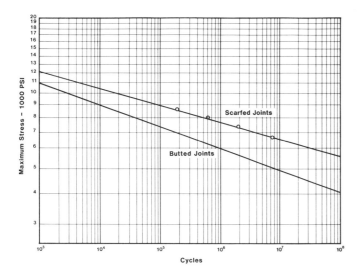

Figure 5—Tension Fatigue. Maximum stress vs. total cycles for Douglas fir/epoxy laminate with 12:1 slope scarf *and* butt joints with three inch stagger. 31.8 cubic inch test volume, parallel to grain directions, room temperature, 12% wood moisture content.

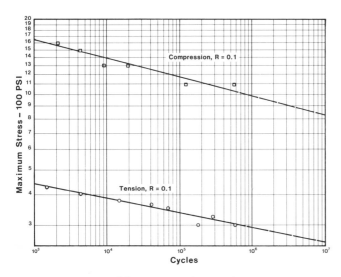

Figure 6—Tangential fatigue, wood/epoxy laminate.

properties, especially in compression. Wood density varies from species to species. See Appendix A for a listing of the static ultimate mechanical properties of selected boatbuilding woods.

Wood has unusually good resistance to fatigue. Although its one-time load capability may not be as high as that of other materials, a significantly high percentage of it is available for long-term fatigue life. This is not surprising when we consider that nature spent millions of years evolving trees in a competitive environment. But while this capability was empirically proven for years — anyone who watches a tall old tree survive repeated winds knows that wood is strong over time — little specific design data was available to support

engineering efforts for repetitively loaded wooden structures.

In 1978, with the sponsorship of NASA, we began a program to determine the fatigue characteristics of wood in laminate form. Earlier fatigue testing, performed in 1943, showed that Sitka spruce exhibits excellent fatigue behavior, but failed to provide enough specific information for us to develop design allowables for our wind turbine blades. Our tests, which are described more fully in Appendix B, have centered on ultrasonically graded Douglas fir veneers laminated with WEST SYSTEM epoxy, with and without synthetic fiber augmentation. The discussion of our results which follows is limited to wood/epoxy composites; details about other laminates made with wood and glass aramid and graphite fiber reinforcement are provided in Appendix B. No similar comprehensive data exist for solid timber, but values are usually lower.

Figure 3 shows the resulting fatigue curves in tension, compression and reverse axial tension to compression. Wood is considerably stronger in tension than in compression at low load cycles. At ten million cycles, however, their capabilities are very similar and the two fatigue curves move closer together.

We have designed blades for wind turbines up to 400 feet in diameter and built blades which are 65.5 feet long. Veneers are only 8 feet long and must be joined in some fashion in order to build larger rotors. For this reason, all of our test samples have included either staggered butt or scarf joints — built in manufacturing defects. In one group of tests, we used a 12 to 1 slope scarf joint between mating veneers and in a second series we induced the much more serious flaw of three butted joints. While the difference between the scarfed and butted specimens, logarithmically plotted in Figures 4 and 5, was significant, it was much less than we anticipated. In any other material this type of induced defect would likely cause a much more significant reduction in fatigue capability.

These were tests for longitudinal mechanical properties, measuring fatigue when loads were applied parallel to the grain of the wood. Just as important are *secondary properties* or *crossgrain material capability*. Trees have very simple load paths, with most loads longitudinal to wood grain direction, but boats and other complex structures do not. In these, loads will vary from fiber direction, so some understanding of a material's ability to carry loads radially and tangentially is needed for safe design.

All unidirectional composites exhibit substantially less strength across their fibers than parallel to them. Wood laminates are generally about five times stronger in tension parallel to the fiber direction than tangentially to the fiber direction. Dense high strength fiber bundles such as glass or carbon have a much worse problem in this regard: their crossfiber strength may only be a very small fraction of longitudinal capability. It is our view that a majority of composite material failures in the marine field are in these secondary properties, and it is also in these areas where limited or no fatigue data exists.

Shear and crossgrain properties with wood are difficult to test. Figure 6 shows data that we have developed with Douglas fir laminate in across-the-grain tension and compression. More thorough testing in this area is scheduled and its results will be published when completed.

Wood Stiffness

Stiffness may be quantified by measuring deflection under a given cyclic load. It describes how floppy, flexible, rigid or stiff a material or structure is. Since repeated deflection can cause cumulative damage, resistance to deflection is often important to the integrity of rigid structures. In boats, adequate hull stiffness prevents the excessive working which may result from repeated high point loadings. Wood has excellent stiffness potential and, as indicated in Figure 7, it is relatively light in weight.

To illustrate wood stiffness, we conducted a simple bending test and compared it to other materials used in boat construction. For this experiment, we made up samples of the following:
(1) unidirectional glass fiber with polyester resin (50% fiber volume)
(2) aluminum (5054-H34 commercial grade)
(3) Kevlar™ aramid fiber with epoxy resin (50% fiber)
(4) graphite fiber with epoxy resin (50% fiber)
(5) White ash
(6) Sitka spruce
(7) Western red cedar.
Each sample was 24 inches long x ½ inch wide. Thickness was determined by the density of each material so that all samples weighed exactly 25 grams. In theory, the samples represent small sections of a hull skin taken from boats of the equal size and weight manufactured with each of these materials.

To test our samples, we clamped them to a bench and used them as cantilever beams, with weights hung from their free ends. Figure 8 lists the amount of deflection measured under uniform weight in all samples, and it also lists the price per pound of each material. Wood and graphite fiber/epoxy composite clearly resisted deflection better than the others. When cost is

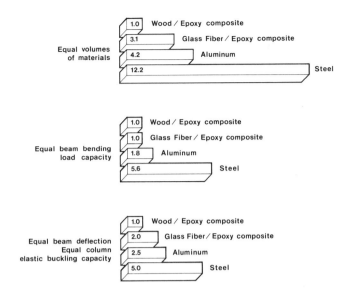

Figure 7—Relative weights of flat panels built with various structural materials. Wood/epoxy composite built with ultrasonically-graded Douglas fir and WEST SYSTEM resin.

factored in, wood is the winner of the stiffness test. Graphite fiber composite is almost twenty times as expensive as Sitka spruce.

The beam test compares equal weights of materials, but not equal volumes. A section of ⅛ inch thick aluminum would resist deflection far better than a piece of wood with the same dimensions, but it would also weigh about seven times as much. Two hulls, one made of ⅛ inch aluminum and the other of ⅞ inch wood, would weigh about the same, but the wooden hull would be significantly stiffer.

When weight is a major consideration, as it is in boat hulls, there are advantages to choosing low rather than high density materials to generate stiffness. On a weight per square foot basis, a thicker, lighter, material has a natural advantage over a thinner, heavier one. In

Figure 8—Stiffness comparison of cantilever beams with 7 engineering materials[1]

Material[2]	Deflection in inches with 200 gram weight	Deflection in inches with 500 gram weight	Specific gravity	Pounds per cubic foot	Cost per pound in dollars[3]
Glass fiber/ polyester (50% fiber volume)	10	Failed	1.52	104	2.58
Aluminum (5054-H34 sheet)	9½	Failed	2.7	170	2.50
Kevlar™/epoxy (50% fiber)	6¼	11½	1.18	81	10.45
Graphite fiber/epoxy (50% fiber volume)	1-11/16	4	1.54	105	24.40
White ash (select)	1-11/16	4	.64	42	.77
Sitka spruce (select)	13/16	1-13/16	.38	26	1.48
Western red cedar (select)	11/16	1-10/16	.31	21	1.63

[1] Test conducted by Gougeon Brothers, August 1976.
[2] All samples weigh 25 grams and measure 24 inches x ½ inch.
[3] Prices as of September 1985.

a beam, longitudinal stresses are better carried as far as possible from the neutral axis, provided that the loads do not exceed material strength. A wooden beam may be thicker than a steel one for the same weight and may also offer some thermal and acoustic insulation. It is only in areas where space is limited and strength requirements are high that strong, high density materials become preferable. Masts, booms and centerboards may require more strength in smaller dimensions than unreinforced wood can offer.

Our test does not reflect the fact that both the strength and stiffness of glass reinforced composites may be manipulated with the use of core materials. The technique of bonding skins of fiberglass over wood is enormously successful for small boats, most notably stripper canoes, but as we will discuss more fully in Chapter 20, it can present significant practical problems in other applications.

Considerations About Wood

To understand wood as a structural material, it's necessary to know a little about its growth. While certain of its properties, most notably resistance to repeated buffeting of wind and water, stem from its functions in supporting and feeding the tree, some of wood's problems also result from its original role in life.

As a tree grows, cellulose molecules are organized into strands, and these are become parts of the cell walls of wood fiber. Cellulose, lignin and hemicellulose give wood its physical properties. New wood is laid around a core of older wood and pith and reflects the growing seasons in which it was made. *Earlywood* cells, produced in the spring, may have thinner walls and larger cavities than *latewood* cells. The transition between the two is visually apparent in annual growth rings, which vary in size by tree species and by the general conditions in which the tree grew. In areas like the tropics, where trees grow year round, distinct rings do not appear. By contrast, trees which grow in northern climates, where seasonal changes are extreme, have distinct rings of early and late woods.

Two kinds of wood develop in the tree trunk. Sapwood or xylem, recently formed, stores food and transports sap. When a tree has grown so large that its innermost sapwood is no longer close to the cambium, its cells undergo chemical and physical change to become heartwood. Material deposited in heartwood cells may make it darker than sapwood in color, and usually increase its durability.

The terms *hardwood* and *softwood* describe neither strength nor toughness. Softwood trees bear cones and, often, needle-like leaves. Hardwoods may be evergreen or deciduous; it is their broad leaves which distinguish them from softwoods. Both types of trees have *fibers* or *tracheids,* long, pointed cells which serve as their basic support. In hardwoods, sap flows through a system of vessels. Softwoods rely on thinwalled tracheids laid down early in the year for controlling sap and on thicker-walled, later tracheids for support. Sap is carried horizontally from pith to bark in hardwoods and softwoods by cellular structures called *rays.*

The majority of fibers in any standing tree are aligned vertically. When the log is cut up into boards, the length of the board is always parallel — or nearly so — to the fibers, or *with the grain* of the wood. Straightness of grain varies from species to species, but grain is usually straighter in heartwood and in sapwood than in pith, where the fibers are burled. Rays are twined through the fibers perpendicularly and are aligned more or less along the radius. Looking at the end of a log, the wood rays may appear like spokes of a wheel.

Some species — Sitka spruce is probably the most extreme example — have abundant wood rays and therefore do not split easily along the grain. They are said to have a great deal of *grain strength.* Other species, such as redwood and Western red cedar have few rays and therefore split easily.

The rate at which a tree grows varies according to its species and within the species, depending on soil conditions and the weather at the spot where it is growing. We have seen Sitka spruce with as few as eight growth rings per radial inch, indicating that the tree from which it came grew in diameter at the rate of ¼ inch per year, and we have also seen wood with as many as 30 growth rings per inch, indicating that the tree from which it came had increased its diameter at the rate of only 1/15 inch per season. Slow-growing trees, which have a higher number of growth rings per inch, have a higher percentage of late wood than faster-growing trees. For this reason, lumber from slow-growing trees is usually heavier and stronger.

Wood Into Lumber

Harvested wood is processed in many ways, for paper, chemicals and lumber. Boat builders are concerned with the techniques used to manufacture planks and plywood veneers. In each of these, two distinctly different methods are used, and in each case one is preferable for wood used in boat construction.

Boards may be cut from the log in two ways. In *plain* or *slab sawn lumber,* all cuts are parallel and annual rings are at angles of 0° to 45° with the wide side of a board. *Quarter* or *radial sawn boards,* on the other hand, are cut with growth rings at angles of 45° to 90° to their wide sides, and so are approximately parallel to the tree's rays. Although these distinctions may be a bit confused by the terminology of the marketplace — plainsawn softwoods may be called *flat* or *slash grained* and quartersawn softwoods may be advertised as *edge* or *vertical grained* — they are significant.

Plywood is made of layers or plies of thin veneer glued together so that the grain of each layer is at right angles to the grain of the plies on either side of it. The veneers themselves may be either *peeled* or *sliced* from the log. In the rotary-cutting or peeling operation, knives "unwind" a continuous length of wood until perhaps six inches of the original log remain. Sliced veneers, less common, are made by first sawing the log into quarters or eighths, and then slicing it into thin strips with a straight knife.

Wood and Moisture

Freshly-cut wood, however sawn, has two major problems. Heartwood, sapwood, earlywood and latewood, all of which may have slightly different densities and properties, may appear in the same plank. High moisture content, distributed unevenly between heartwood and sapwood, compounds what might not otherwise be a significant difficulty and creates its own set of troubles for the boat builder. Wood derives its strength from cellulose, lignin and hemicellulose, and some of its greatest weaknesses from its other major component, water.

The moisture content of trees and wood is expressed as a percentage of the weight of the wood after it has been dried in an oven. In a living tree, where water and water vapor occupy cell cavities and are held in cell walls, moisture content can range from 30% to 200%. In softwoods especially, heartwood and sapwood of the same tree usually contain different levels of water. In Western red cedar, an extreme example, sapwood holds almost five times as much water as heartwood. While sapwood is generally "wetter" than heartwood, in some trees, such as birch, oak and tupelo, the opposite is the case.

When a tree is cut, its wood is "green." Moisture remains in cell cavities and walls. As water and sap are dispelled, the wood reaches its *fiber saturation point:* cell walls are still saturated but cell cavities have dried out. At this time, moisture content is between 25% and 30% of dry weight. Wood is dimensionally stable above its saturation point but not below it.

Wood continues to lose water until it reaches an *equilibrium moisture content* at which it neither gains

Figure 9—Shrinkage and distortion for wood of various cross sections as affected by direction of annual rings. Tangential shrinkage is about twice as great as radial. (From *Wood Handbook: Wood as an Engineering Material,* U.S. Department of Agriculture Handbook, No. 72, p. 3-10.)

nor loses water. Cell walls dry out, stiffen and shrink until their moisture content is in balance with the temperature and relative humidity of their environment. Wood continuously seeks this equilibrium as long as it is exposed to fluctuations in the atmosphere. Every day, as temperatures and humidity change, unprotected wood absorbs and releases water vapor to maintain equilibrium moisture content. Constant contraction and expansion cycles over time lead to fiber deterioration.

Heartwood and sapwood begin with different moisture contents and therefore reach fiber saturation and equilibrium points at different times. As lumber shrinks during cure, its cells tend to pull at each other and become taut. This has the desired effect of stiffening the board, but if heartwood dries up and stiffens long before sapwood in the same plank does, the inconsistent drying rates may set up excessive internal stressing which results in warping, checking, cracks and grain rise. Wood shrinks less radially than it does tangentially and this may lead to further distortion. For all practical purposes, shrinking occurs only across the width and thickness of a board: a green board which is 10 feet x 8½ inches x 1 inch will still be 10 feet long when cured, but it will be only about 8 inches wide and 15/16 inches thick. There is generally less difference in tangential and radial rates in the tropical species without growth rings than in species with well-defined growth rings, where the difference is substantial.

One obvious solution to the problems caused by moisture is to cut boards so that they contain either heartwood or sapwood, but not both. Quartersawn boards, which have sapwood only at their edges and are cut radially rather than tangentially, will shrink, swell and cup far less than slabsawn lumber. Quarter-sawn boards are more dimensionally stable and they also tend to be a little stronger and easier to shape and mill. In slabsawn lumber, hard latewood and soft ear-lywood appear in wide bands on major surfaces and cause difficulty in sanding, planing and finishing. Rotary-peeled veneers are cut with no regard what-soever to patterns of heartwood, sapwood and growth rings and therefore have considerable potential for internal stressing. Sliced veneers, by contrast, are cut perpendicular to growth rings and are more stable.

Another, sometimes more practical way to reduce internal stressing in wood is to cut it up into thin boards for drying. The reduction in volume while the wood is still above fiber saturation relieves the lines through which excessive tension could develop during cure. We usually resaw stock over 1 inch thick, and laminate keels and sheer clamps which require thicker stock. This is usually much easier than trying to find a single piece of wood good enough for the job, and even if we were able to find such a piece, a lamination would probably serve better.

Moisture and Physical Properties

If wood is taken at its fiber saturation point and al-lowed to dry to 5% moisture content, its crushing strength and bending strength may easily be doubled and in some woods tripled. The reason for this is the actual strengthening and stiffening of cell walls as they dry out. Not all strength properties are changed in such a dramatic way. Figure 10 gives a tentative average for several species of wood of the change of various physi-cal properties per 1% decrease in moisture content. By multiplying the values in the table, you can see that reducing the moisture content of wood results in sub-stantial increase in its physical properties.

These data are averages for several species of wood and therefore are not suitable for engineering work. We present them only to illustrate the fact that up to a point, dry wood makes a stronger boat. The percent-age increases in strength are the average for the entire range, from 25% to 0%. The first test, for instance, shows that in fiber stress at proportional limit in static bending the increase in value is 5% for every percent-age point moisture content is reduced below 25%. One hundred percent is the reference value for 25% moisture content; 225% becomes the value at 0%. It is incorrect, however, to conclude that the value is a straight line function of moisture content and that it would be 105% at 24%, 110% at 23% and so on. It's most likely that in most species of wood the percentage increase in the value is higher as the moisture content

Figure 10 — Physical Properties
Average increase in value affected by lowering the moisture content 1% from fiber saturation point [1,2]

Static Bending	Increase
Fiber stress at proportional limit	5%
Modulus of rupture, or crossbreaking strength	4%
Modulus of elasticity or stiffness	2%
Work to proportional limit	8%
Work to maximum load or shock-resisting ability . .	½%

Impact Bending	
Fiber stress at proportional limit	3%
Work to proportional limit	4%

Compression Parallel to Grain	
Fiber stress at proportional limit	5%
Maximum crushing strength	6%

Compression Perpendicular to Grain	
Fiber stress at proportional limit	5½%
Hardness, end grain	4%
Hardness, side grain	2½%
Shearing strength parallel to grain	3%
Tension perpendicular to grain	1½%

[1] Approximately 24% in most woods.
[2] References: "Strength and Related Properties of Woods," Forest Products Laboratory, Forest Service, U.S. Department of Agricul-ture Technical Bulletin No. 479.
Wood Handbook: Wood as an Engineering Material, Forest Prod-ucts Laboratory, U.S. Department of Agriculture Handbook, No. 72.

is first lowered from 25%, then lower as it aproaches 0%.

While the effects of moisture on maximum load-to-failure static properties are substantial, for most marine applications the designer should not be overly con-cerned. Most marine structures are subjected to stress levels well below maximum static one-time load-to-failure conditions and the effect of moisture on lower load levels in long-term fatigue is a more pertinent issue. Recent scattered and preliminary Gougeon-developed fatigue data indicate that the detrimental effects of higher moisture content may diminish or even disappear at 10 million cycles and beyond. These early indications require further substantiation before the extent of the phenomenon will be accurately known.

Wood/Epoxy Composites

Wood is strong, lightweight, stiff and resistant to fatigue. Some of its shortcomings as a material for en-gineering result from inherent defects such as knots and grain irregularity, but most are related to moisture. By using wood as a reinforcing fiber which may be bonded into many shapes and forms with epoxy resin, we are able to make the most of its structural advantages and overcome its limitations.

The primary goal of incorporating wood in a composite with resin is to provide its fibers with maximum practical protection against moisture. When it is able to resist violent seasonable fluctuations in moisture and its moisture level is stabilized at lower levels, wood maintains good physical properties and dimensional stability.

Wood/epoxy composites may also, when properly engineered, provide a means of homogenizing the defects and variations of lumber and of increasing its strength in compression. Chances of failure of structural boat members may be greatly reduced by using beams laminated of a number of pieces of thinner wood instead of a single board, particularly when grain alignment within a laminate is manipulated to best receive predicted loads.

We seal all wood surfaces, those which come into contact with water as well as those which come into contact with air, with WEST SYSTEM epoxy and use it as a bonding adhesive in all joints and laminates. When applied in correct quantities, the resin forms a thin continuous film which serves as a moisture barrier on exterior surfaces, in joints and between layers of veneer.

While this barrier is not perfect, it is far more realistic than wrapping a boat in plastic. Moisture passage into wood is limited to such an extent that any change in moisture content within the wood itself is minimal. If dry wood encapsulated in our resin is put in a high humidity chamber and left for months, the wood's moisture content will eventually rise. The rate of moisture change in wood/epoxy composites is so slow under normal circumstances, however, that wood remains at virtually constant levels in exact equilibrium with average annual humidity. In most areas, this equilibrium is between 8% and 12% moisture content.

A minimum of two unsanded coats of WEST SYSTEM resin on all surfaces will form an adequate moisture barrier. More coatings are desirable, especially if the boat will be subjected to extremes between dry and moist environments. Coating effectiveness reaches a point of diminishing returns, four or five coats, where improved moisture resistance does not balance the weight of the extra resin. Any more than five coats of resin may contribute to abrasion resistance but will add little to the moisture barrier.

Large amounts of resin are used in coating and bonding boats. Although ratios vary, depending primarily on hull size, it's not uncommon to find that 25% of the weight of the basic hull structure is resin. About 20% is more typical. Wood performance domi-

nates, but because so much of a boat is epoxy, the physical properties of the resin have a large effect on the physical properties of the composite. For this reason, it's important that the epoxy resin portion of the composite contribute more than weight.

There is a large range of physical properties which can be developed within present epoxy resin technology. Very flexible resins, with good resistance to a single impact, can be formulated, but they otherwise might contribute little to a hull's overall structure in their ability to pay for their own weight in added stiffness and strength. Flexible resins also have high strain rates which can limit long-term fatigue performance at higher load levels.

WEST SYSTEM epoxy is specifically formulated to develop maximum physical properties while retaining just enough toughness and flexibility to live with the sight deformations which inevitably occur in any boat. The most significant driving force in developing our WEST SYSTEM epoxy formulation has been long-term fatigue resistance. Wood is one of the most fatigue resistant materials on earth. Any bonding adhesive used to make joints or laminates must be of equally high capability or the wood's long-term performance will be compromised. We have conducted a great deal of fatigue testing on WEST SYSTEM epoxy and have achieved performance at 10 million cycles, which is approximately 40% of ultimate in torsional shear. (See Appendix B.)

Determining Moisture Content

When using wood in composite with WEST SYSTEM resins, it's important to use only wood which has a moisture content of 12% or less. Eight to 12% moisture content is ideal. Boats can be built with wood with moisture levels up to 18%, but in long-term equilibrium they may lose some moisture which could affect structural integrity because of internal stressing.

As we explained earlier, the moisture content of wood varies according to the relative humidity and temperature of the atmosphere which surrounds it. For every combination of temperature and humidity there is a moisture level which wood will seek, absorbing and dispelling moisture until it reaches this equilibrium. We keep our shop at 65°F, with relative humidity averaging around 50%. In these conditions, the moisture level equilibrium is 8%, and most of the wood we work with has a moisture content near that percentage.

Atmospheric conditions vary according to geography and type of shelter. In most situations, the prevailing conditions will be such that the equilibrium percentage is below 12%. Figure 11 shows the equilib-

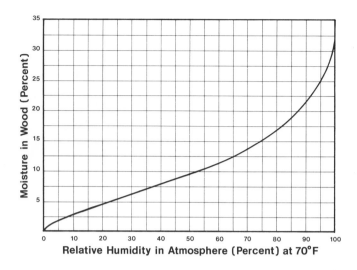

Figure 11—Equilibrium moisture content as a function of relative humidity.

rium percentages of moisture content of wood as a function of relative humidity. The graph is good for that temperature only. As Figure 12 illustrates, relative humidity throughout the United States is such that the 8% to 12% moisture range is accessible.

The speed with which a piece of wood reaches equilibrium depends on the span between existing moisture content and the percentage at equilibrium and on the ratio between exposed surface area and volume. Wood tends to reach equilibrium faster when the difference between equilibrium percentage as deduced from atmospheric data and moisture content is greater. Extremely wet wood expels moisture rapidly in an oven and very dry wood absorbs moisture quickly in a steam bath. Thin veneer, which has a very large surface area and relatively little volume, dries to brittleness or steams until it is very pliable within hours. Whole logs, which have huge volumes and little surface area, can take years to reach equilibrium.

If you have any doubts about the moisture content of lumber, test it. Tests are necessary on newly-acquired lumber or lumber which has been stored under questionable conditions. We use an electronic tester, but these machines are expensive and their cost isn't justified for limited use. Some local building inspectors and lumber yards have moisture meters and will test specimens brought to them. Failing more accurate instrumentation, you can perform moisture tests in your kitchen.

To do this, weigh wood samples on a gram or postage scale before and after placing them in a 225°F oven. It's impossible to predict how quickly a sample will lose all of its moisture because this depends on variables such as sample size and original moisture

content. Continue baking and checking every half hour until no further weight reduction takes place and moisture level is therefore reduced to 0%.

Apply the following formula to your results:

$$\frac{100(W_1 - W_2)}{W_2} = P$$

W_1 is the weight before drying, W_2 is the weight after drying and P is the percentage moisture content of the specimen before drying.

Dry Rot (and Other Vermin)

While some of the effects of moisture in wood may be eliminated by careful selection of quartersawn and sliced boards or veneer and by careful control of moisture levels, others cannot. When its moisture level is at or near fiber saturation point, seasoned wood becomes susceptible to fungus damage, often called dry rot or brown rot. This causes millions of dollars of damage each year to wooden structures of all kinds; more wooden ships may have been lost to it than to all of the storms and naval battles of history.

Neither very dry nor totally submerged wood is likely to decay — in fact, wood sealed for 3,000 years in Egyptian tombs at a constant temperature and humidity level has lost none of its physical properties — but wood used in boats is usually damp and therefore, if oxygen is present and temperatures warm, subject to the types of fungi which cause rot by feeding on the cellulose in cured lumber. When this happens, the wood becomes browner and it may crack, shrink and collapse. Attempts to eradicate the fungi have usually revolved around poisoning their food supply. Most of the commercial wood preservatives which use this approach have only limited success on boats because marine moisture levels are so high that the poisons are quickly diluted.

We suggest a different solution to dry rot. In order to survive long enough to cause decay, brown rot fungi need food and oxygen. In warm weather, the fungi make rapid progress, but in temperatures above 90°F and below 50°F they are much slower. Despite its name, dry rot will not occur in dry wood or in wood moistened only by humid air. Neither is it a problem when wood is so saturated with water that air cannot penetrate to fungi in its interior.

It's impossible to keep wood boats dry. When cured wood is encapsulated in WEST SYSTEM epoxy, however, its moisture level cannot reach fiber saturation point and it therefore is no longer susceptible to fungi. Coatings of resin provide additional insurance against rot by restricting oxygen supply.

Figure 12 — RELATIVE HUMIDITY
in Selected U.S. Cities

STATE	STATION	Length of record (yr.)	Jan. 7:00 a.m.	Jan. 1:00 p.m.	Mar. 7:00 a.m.	Mar. 1:00 p.m.	May 7:00 a.m.	May 1:00 p.m.	July 7:00 a.m.	July 1:00 p.m.	Sept. 7:00 a.m.	Sept. 1:00 p.m.	Nov. 7:00 a.m.	Nov. 1:00 p.m.	Annual 7:00 a.m.	Annual 1:00 p.m.
Ala.	Mobile	17	81	62	83	56	86	54	89	61	88	61	85	56	85	57
Alaska	Juneau	36	79	76	79	69	74	62	81	70	87	77	85	81	81	73
Ariz.	Phoenix	19	45	32	33	23	18	13	28	20	31	23	37	28	32	22
Ark.	Little Rock	19	80	62	78	56	86	57	87	58	89	59	82	57	83	57
Calif.	Los Angeles	20	56	60	62	65	66	66	69	68	66	67	57	63	62	65
	Sacramento	19	85	70	68	52	50	36	47	28	50	31	75	59	63	46
	San Francisco	20	79	67	70	63	64	60	66	60	65	59	73	64	69	62
Colo.	Denver	19	45	48	42	40	39	37	35	35	38	34	45	50	40	40
Conn.	Hartford	20	72	57	72	53	73	47	79	51	87	56	80	57	77	53
Del.	Wilmington	32	75	60	74	53	76	53	80	54	85	56	80	56	78	55
D.C.	Washington	19	68	54	68	49	72	51	76	53	80	56	74	53	73	52
Fla.	Jacksonville	43	87	57	85	49	84	50	88	58	91	62	89	55	87	55
	Miami	15	84	60	82	56	82	61	85	64	89	68	85	61	84	62
Ga.	Atlanta	19	78	60	78	51	83	55	90	63	90	61	82	54	83	57
Hawaii	Honolulu	10	80	63	73	58	67	55	66	51	66	52	74	59	71	56
Idaho	Boise	40	73	70	55	44	45	34	33	21	39	30	65	60	52	44
Ill.	Chicago	21	76	68	79	62	76	54	81	57	84	57	80	64	79	60
	Peoria	20	77	68	81	64	81	57	85	58	88	58	83	66	82	61
Ind.	Indianapolis	20	81	70	80	63	82	57	87	60	91	59	85	67	84	62
Iowa	Des Moines	18	76	68	78	63	78	55	81	57	84	59	79	64	80	61
Kans.	Wichita	26	79	63	76	54	83	55	78	49	82	55	79	57	79	55
Ky.	Louisville	19	77	65	76	59	83	56	86	59	89	60	79	61	81	59
La.	New Orleans	31	85	67	85	61	89	60	91	66	89	66	86	61	88	63
Maine	Portland	39	77	62	75	59	75	58	80	60	86	61	84	63	80	60
Md.	Baltimore	26	71	58	71	51	77	53	82	53	85	56	77	55	77	54
Mass.	Boston	15	68	58	68	57	71	58	73	56	79	61	75	61	72	58
Mich.	Detroit	45	78	69	77	60	71	51	74	51	82	55	79	64	77	58
	Sault Ste. Marie	38	82	76	83	68	80	56	89	62	92	67	87	76	85	67
Minn.	Duluth	18	74	68	77	63	76	54	83	58	86	63	80	69	80	63
	Minneapolis-St. Paul	20	72	66	76	63	76	52	81	54	86	60	80	66	79	60
Miss.	Jackson	16	87	66	88	57	92	56	93	60	94	61	91	58	91	59
Mo.	Kansas City	7	74	65	78	62	83	59	82	56	86	60	78	62	80	60
	St. Louis	19	83	66	82	59	83	56	86	57	91	59	85	63	84	60
Mont.	Great Falls	18	63	62	53	48	46	40	38	29	45	36	55	54	50	45
Nebr.	Omaha	15	76	65	76	57	79	55	83	56	87	61	80	62	80	59
Nev.	Reno	16	68	50	47	33	33	25	28	19	34	21	56	41	44	31
N.H.	Concord	14	74	60	78	56	79	48	86	52	91	57	85	61	82	55
N.J.	Atlantic City	15	75	58	76	55	79	57	84	58	86	59	82	57	80	57
N. Mex.	Albuquerque	19	50	39	32	23	24	17	35	27	40	31	42	35	37	28
N.Y.	Albany	14	79	64	74	54	76	52	80	54	88	59	81	63	79	57
	Buffalo	19	80	74	80	67	76	56	79	55	83	60	82	70	80	63
	New York	58	68	60	67	55	71	53	75	55	79	57	73	59	72	56
N.C.	Charlotte	19	78	56	80	51	84	54	88	59	90	58	84	53	83	54
	Raleigh	15	79	55	80	49	87	56	90	59	93	60	85	51	85	54
N. Dak.	Bismark	20	72	66	78	62	79	49	83	47	82	49	79	62	79	56
Ohio	Cincinnati	17	79	68	77	60	80	54	85	57	88	59	80	63	81	60
	Cleveland	19	77	70	78	65	77	58	82	58	84	61	79	66	79	63
	Columbus	20	76	68	73	58	79	55	84	56	88	59	81	64	80	59
Okla.	Oklahoma City	14	79	61	75	52	83	58	81	50	84	56	78	54	80	54
Oreg.	Portland	39	82	76	72	60	66	53	61	45	67	49	82	74	72	60
Pa.	Philadelphia	20	73	59	71	53	75	53	79	55	83	57	77	56	76	55
	Pittsburgh	19	76	66	74	58	76	51	82	53	86	57	79	63	78	57
R.I.	Providence	16	72	58	70	54	72	52	77	57	82	57	78	59	75	55
S.C.	Columbia	13	82	55	83	48	87	51	89	56	93	58	88	49	87	52
S. Dak.	Sioux Falls	16	74	67	80	63	80	53	81	52	85	57	82	64	80	59
Tenn.	Memphis	40	78	63	76	56	82	55	85	57	86	56	79	55	81	57
	Nashville	14	80	65	78	54	87	56	91	59	92	61	81	59	85	58
Tex.	Dallas-Fort Worth	16	80	61	80	57	88	61	81	50	87	59	81	56	82	57
	El Paso	19	44	34	28	20	22	15	39	29	44	34	38	32	35	27
	Houston	10	88	66	89	60	94	60	94	59	95	65	91	60	92	60
Utah	Salt Lake City	20	70	68	52	45	37	31	26	20	34	27	57	58	46	42
Vt.	Burlington	14	70	64	73	59	75	51	80	54	87	64	79	69	78	60
VA.	Norfolk	31	75	59	74	54	78	57	82	60	84	62	79	56	78	58
	Richmond	45	81	57	78	49	79	51	85	57	90	57	85	50	83	53
Wash.	Seattle-Tacoma	20	78	74	74	62	67	54	65	48	74	59	80	74	73	62
	Spokane	20	82	77	67	54	52	40	39	25	50	34	81	74	62	51
W. Va.	Charleston	32	77	63	74	53	82	50	90	61	91	56	80	56	82	56
Wis.	Milwaukee	19	75	68	79	66	79	61	82	61	87	63	81	67	81	65
Wyo.	Cheyenne	20	45	48	44	45	39	41	34	37	35	36	42	47	40	42
P.R.	San Juan	24	80	64	77	60	77	65	78	66	79	67	81	66	79	64

Please note: These figures, given in percentages, represent the average for the period of record through 1979. Eastern Standard Times are indicated.

From *1984 American Express Appointment Book*. (American Express Co.: NY, NY, 1983), p. 209.

Encapsulation in WEST SYSTEM epoxy also seems to provide wood with some protection against two other common predators. Testing has shown that exterior coatings of WEST SYSTEM resin will restrict termite damage. Although no scientific investigations have conclusively proven the phenomenon, shipworms and other wood-boring mollusks seem to be unwilling to pass through lines of WEST SYSTEM resin. They may typically attack the bottom of a laminated rudder or centerboard and go no farther than its first glueline.

Chapter 6

Buying Wood

Boat builders use a very small percentage of the lumber sold in the United States, so few local dealers sell very much of the quality and type needed for boat construction. It may be difficult to find materials for your project, but keep a few things in mind as you shop.

Lumber, plywood and veneer are by far the cheapest materials in a boat. Buy the highest quality wood available. When the waste which results from knots and grain run out in lower quality boards is factored in, the best becomes a bargain. You will put an enormous amount of time into a boat, and it makes sense to guarantee the longevity of your investment by using top grade materials.

Also remember that the moisture content of the wood at the time you use it may determine the success or failure of a project. As we noted in Chapter 5, wood is strong, stiff and dimensionally stable when its moisture levels are relatively low. Careful selection and storage, with a keen eye to maintaining moisture level equilibrium in the range between 8% and 12%, will minimize the chances of moisture-related problems and maximize the effectiveness of WEST SYSTEM* Brand epoxy.

In later chapters we discuss the specifics of the wood needed for various methods of hull and interior construction. The general information presented here is useful whether you plan to build a traditionally-planked boat, a laminated hull, a strip composite canoe or a hard chine or compounded plywood vessel.

Ordering Lumber

Be prepared for some difficulty in buying boat lumber. Your local dealer may sell clear Douglas fir, Honduras mahogany and white ash, but his doing so reflects commercial demand in other fields — the construction, pattern making and mill work industries respectively — rather than an attempt to meet a demand for boat construction materials. The rare dealer will stock Sitka spruce and cedar. We always hope that the resurgence of wooden boat building will increase availability and permit better distribution of quality boat lumber.

If you can't find wood locally, you may have to order it from a mail order specialty house. Freight rates

on unimproved lumber are quite low, so shipping costs over long distances are fairly reasonable. Since they serve large markets and specialize in specific types and qualities of wood, the mail order houses are able to offer quality materials at moderate prices. There are, however, problems with ordering by mail: you must often buy wood sight unseen, with the reputation of the company as your only assurance of quality, and you may have to schedule around the lag time between ordering and receiving your lumber.

It's sometimes possible to acquire wood in other ways. If you live where timber is harvested, you may be able to purchase top quality boards directly from a small sawmill. This lumber is usually green and rough sawn, but its price is accordingly low. Other potential sources are wholesale houses which provide special woods to a regional industrial market. These firms like to deal with large volume trade, but they often accept smaller orders at a slight premium.

Choose the kind of wood you will use in your boat before you order. You may need more than one species. Check plans for specifications or select particular woods for their physical properties. You will probably discover that relatively few of the better boatbuilding varieties are available at one time, and if you can't find what you want, you may be forced to make substitutions. In most applications several different species will work equally well, so if you can't find your first choice, another with similar physical properties and density might stand in its place. See Appendix A for the mechanical properties of selected boatbuilding woods. Price may also be a factor in your selection.

If at all possible, buy lumber which has been dried to approximately 12% moisture content. Green wood is heavier than dry wood and therefore costs more to ship. If your lumber has not been seasoned, give it time to reach equilibrium or dry it in a kiln. Although wood may be damaged by very high temperatures, we've never had any problems with the kiln-dried lumber we've received. Before using any wood, follow the procedure described in Chapter 5 to check its moisture level.

The amount of time it takes to air dry wood depends on the moisture content of the wood, its ratio of exposed surface area to volume, its density — softwoods tend to dry more quickly than hardwoods — and the temperature and humidity of the atmosphere in which it is seasoned. There is no magic formula for predicting how long you will have to wait before you can use a board. Green ⅛ inch cedar veneer might reach 8% to 12% moisture content in weeks, while 2 inch white ash will take much longer to cure.

When ordering lumber, specify dimensions in thickness, width and length. In the United States, thickness, the most important of these measurements, is often given in quarter inch fractions, although it is also sometimes listed in inches. In the *quarter* system, 1 inch thick stock may, for example, be referred to as 4/4, 1½ inch as 6/4, 2 inch stock as 8/4 and so on. Width is always measured in inches and length in feet. A board foot of lumber measures 12 inches x 12 inches x 1 inch.

We prefer to buy thinner, rather than thicker, stock because it dries faster and can be used sooner. We do purchase thick lumber, however, when there is a price advantage or when it is the least wasteful way to develop the size we need. To expedite drying and reduce stressing, we usually resaw lumber which is more than 1 inch thick.

As you work out a lumber list, calculate the board sizes which will result in the least waste. Unless we are buying boards in specific sizes, we try to get the widest and longest stock we can without paying a premium. As a rule, lumber over 20 feet long or over 8 or 10 inches wide is more expensive and prices are usually high enough to warrant scarfing shorter pieces for length and laminating thinner pieces for width.

Thickness and width dimensions stated in inches measure the stock before surfacing or finishing: a 1 inch board is 1 inch thick rough and ¾ inch thick finished. Wood measured by the quarter, on the other hand, is identified by its finished measurement. A 4/4 board was 5/4, or 1¼ inches, thick before planing and is 1 inch thick at the time of sale.

Boat lumber is usually available either rough sawn or finished. Rough sawn boards are generally simply called *rough*. If a board is marked *S2S*, two of its major surfaces have been planed. The marking *S4S* means that all four sides of a plank have been put through a planer. We often purchase rough lumber because with careful surfacing we can use more wood from the board than typically survives commercial planing. Boat lumber prices are often quoted for rough sawn, with an extra charge for surfacing.

Quality — What To Look For

There is no formal grading system for boat lumber. Standard markings and descriptions refer to surface, dimensions and sawing techniques, but not to quality.

While it is assumed that only clear, properly sawn lumber is acceptable for boat building, high quality wood commands high prices, creating some incentive for unscrupulous dealers to substitute lower grades. The best defense against this is to inspect wood piece-by-piece before buying it and to accept only high quality lumber. If you order by mail, be sure to deal with a company which has a reputation for honest business practices. We have ordered from many firms and have rarely found wood quality misrepresented.

Some top quality wood is *quarter sawn* and sold as *vertical grain* lumber, labelled *VG*. Quarter sawn wood is far superior to slab sawn wood because it has greater dimensional stability, it is less liable to internal stressing and it is easier to machine. Vertical grain stock is easy to inspect: the edge grain can be "read" to determine overall quality. In a true vertical grain board, growth rings run perpendicular to the flat surfaces. Lower quality quarter sawn planks may have rings which run as much as 45° off the vertical.

You can saw your own vertical grain planks from thicker stock. Use a table saw to cut 2 inch or 3 inch stock down to 2 inch x 2 inch boards. Turn the squared planks and saw the faces which show the most consistent vertical grain in the dimensions you need. Stringers and other boat parts which are less than 2 inches thick can often be cut from 2 inch slab sawn stock so that they will have vertical grain. For more information on preparing planking for stripper canoes, see Chapter 20.

In many boards, general grain direction is not exactly parallel to board surfaces. With *grain run out,* grain may typically run more or less parallel to the board and then, marking the spot of a branch in the standing tree, curve radically toward one end. Grain run out is not a serious problem until the angle of difference between the board and its grain exceeds 4°. Boards with severe grain run out should be used for less structurally-demanding parts.

Knots are obvious major flaws. More difficult to deal with, however, are the radical grain changes within a board caused by the proximity of a knot in the tree. The grain of wood which grew within 2 inches of a knot can vary 20° to 30° from the general run of the grain and this can lead to extreme weakening. Look at all four sides to be sure that you have not missed other grain distortions.

Avoid planks which have combinations of heartwood and sapwood. These two types of wood dry at different rates and can set up internal stresses in a board. You can usually see this situation in distinct color changes, since heartwood is generally slightly darker than sapwood.

Pith, the wood from the very center of the tree, tends to have burled grain which is difficult to work, so avoid it as well. Some species, such as Douglas fir, are more likely than others to develop pitch pockets. Pockets which are large enough to cause significant weakening are usually plainly visible.

Even with careful selection, some of the planks you buy will be better than others. When the wood is delivered, inspect it again and separate it into two or three groups by quality. We usually identify deck and hull stringers and other components with high structural requirements and save the best stock for them. Use lower quality lumber for items like joining cleats, where grain is not particularly important. Every boat has many areas which require short pieces, so saw around flaws and use the cut-up lumber for them. Careful planning and efficient use of available lumber are necessary, but it's possible to safely use lesser quality wood without making structural compromises.

If it is not yet perfectly dry, stack the wood in a dry place after sorting it. Place thin sticks between each layer of boards so that they will cure without sagging and to permit good air circulation around each piece.

Veneer and Plywood

Sophisticated manufacturing techniques are used to make both veneer and plywood. It's helpful to know a little about these processes before buying either materials.

Veneers are thin sheets of wood which can be made with various species of wood and in a range of thicknesses. They are cut from logs in two different ways: by slicing and, more frequently, by rotary cutting or peeling. With the latter technique, the log is held on lathe-like spindles and rotated while a knife peels off a continuous ribbon of wood. Slice cut veneers are made by quartering a log and then slicing it repeatedly with a straight knife as shown in Figure 1. In both processes the log is thoroughly soaked before cutting. Plywood is made of dried veneers, bonded in *plies* or layers with the grain of each layer at right angles to the grain of the layers on either side of it. At least three plies of veneer are used in a sheet of plywood.

Buying Veneer

Slice cut veneers are preferable to rotary cut veneers for several reasons. Peeled veneers are very unstable: their tangential cut results in maximum expansion and contraction. Sliced veneers are more expensive, but they are more like vertical grain, quarter sawn lumber and are very stable and unlikely to warp. They have an additional advantage in that they are available in

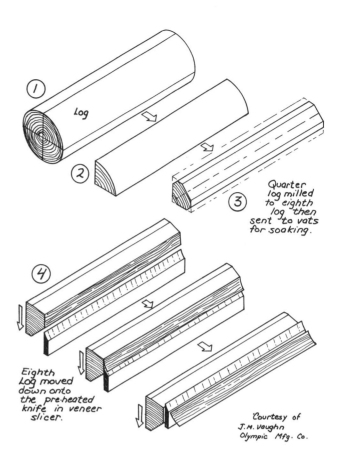

Figure 1—Manufacturing sequence in veneer slicing.

longer pieces. In general laminating, where limited clamping pressure is used, sliced veneers are easier to hold in place and require fewer staples.

Few lumber yards sell sliced veneers. In fact, so far as we know, you will have to order veneers from the companies which cut them. This sole source situation works well for those who can use fairly large quantities of veneer because manufacturers' prices are usually low. Sliced veneers are commonly sold by the square foot — in 1985, 1,000 square feet of ⅛ inch cedar veneer cost $450 — and are shipped in flitches, bundles 1 foot to 18 inches wide. Each flitch contains from 500 to 1,000 square feet of veneer. Smaller quantities, as might be needed for a dinghy, can be more expensive to buy and ship.

Sliced veneers up to 17 feet long are usually available, but 12 foot pieces are adequate for most laminating. Pieces less than 12 feet long can be used less wastefully in smaller boats. Widths are random in all lengths, but generally range between 6 and 12 inches. As we explain in later chapters, we advise against cutting veneers to standard widths until after you have experimented with bending them around a hull's most severe curves.

The thickness of sliced veneers is limited by the technology used to produce them. The maximum thickness which can be cut without damage to the wood is ⅛ inch. Thinner veneers are rarely needed, since ⅛ inch pieces bend easily over most curves.

If you want to, you can buy veneers and laminate plywood yourself. This takes extra time, but it guarantees absolute control over both the wood and the adhesive in the laminate. In home-made plywood, veneers may be oriented in the best directions for specific applications and sheets can be made to exact length and thickness desired. If you have cheap veneer and labor and an organized approach, it may be less expensive to make panels than to buy them.

Buying Plywood

Plywood panels are easy to work with and their use in boatbuilding is discussed throughout this book. Plywood is an excellent material for manufacturing flat boat components and it can also be helpful for making parts with limited curvature. Commercial plywood is used for compounded and hard chine construction, as well as in other applications. It does, however, have a few disadvantages.

Both domestic and imported plywood panels are sold in the United States. Imported plywood is more expensive than the domestic variety, but we prefer it in many situations. Most domestic plywood contains peeled Douglas fir, inside if not on either or both surfaces. While this wood can be strong and tough, the combination of early wood and late wood which results from the peeling process makes it somewhat unstable. Different expansion and contraction rates in interior Douglas fir plies can set up stresses in an entire panel. Peeled fir is also so hard to finish that the best approach is often to sheathe it in fiberglass cloth.

Marine grade plywood imported from the Netherlands, United Kingdom, West Germany and Israel, by contrast, is usually made of medium density tropical woods. Okoume (Gaboon), utile (sipo), Lauan (Philippine mahogany), meranti and mecore are generally more desirable for boatbuilding than Douglas fir because they do not have distinct growth rings and the problems associated with them. All of these species easily take natural finishes and they all have low expansion/contraction rates.

Plywood is almost always sold in 4 foot x 8 foot sheets, in various thickness and with different numbers of plies. Larger sheets are available, but usually at considerably higher prices. When we need big plywood panels, we scarf regular sheets to size. For instructions on scarfing plywood, see Chapter 10. Quarter inch plywood may be constructed with three layers of veneer or with five plies. The 5-ply is more difficult to make and therefore more expensive, but it is also more evenly balanced, with greater stiffness and strength in both directions. The thickness of imported marine plywood may be listed in millimeters. A 6mm panel is roughly equivalent to a ¼ inch panel, while 9 mm is slightly thinner than ⅜ inch.

When you buy plywood, consider the quality and species of internal veneers and the suitability of the adhesive used in the laminate. Voids within the plywood may cause failure and the glues used in marine applications must be waterproof. A strict grading system, outlined in Figure 2, describes the quality of surface veneers in domestic plywood, but other markings are used to identify adhesives and to grade interior plies.

For plywood panels manufactured in the United States, veneers are graded like lumber into various quality groupings and the trade standards generally adhered to are those of the American Plywood Association. There are six veneer grades:

Grade N: Smooth surface "natural finish" veneer; select, all heartwood or all sapwood; free of open defects; not more than six repairs — of wood only — per 4 × 8 foot panel, made parallel to grain and well-matched for grain and color.

Grade A: Smooth, paintable; not more than 18 neatly-made repairs of the boat, sled or router type, and parallel to grain; may be used for natural finish in less demanding applications.

Grade B: Solid surface; shims, circular repair plugs and tight knots to 1 inch across grain permitted; some minor splits permitted.

Grade C: Tight knots to 1½ inches; knot holes to 1 inch across grain and some to 1½ inches if total width of knots and knot holes is within specified limits; both synthetic and wood repairs permitted; discoloration and sanding defects not affecting strength permitted; limited splits allowed.

Grade C Plugged: Improved C veneer with splits limited to ⅛ inch in width, and knot holes and borer holes limited to ¼ inch × ½ inch; some broken grain; synthetic repairs permitted.

Grade D: Knots and knot holes to 2½ inches width across grain and up to 3 inches within specified limits; limited splits permitted.

Figure 2—Veneer grades.

A typical piece of domestic plywood suitable for use in boats is stamped *MARINE AA EXT*. *MARINE* indicates that interior veneers are of B quality or better. *AA* means that both faces are grade A, just as NA would tell you that one surface is suitable for natural finishing and the other is of A quality. AC describes a panel which has one A quality face and one C quality face. The interior veneers of panels which are not labelled MARINE may be better than C quality, but there is no guarantee that they are.

EXT panels are made with waterproof adhesive as, indeed, are most pieces of plywood manufactured today. If you are uncertain about the glue used in a laminate, domestic or imported, or if it is not marked, boil a sample in water for 30 minutes, dry it in an oven for an hour, and then repeat the process. If the piece survives without delaminating, its adhesive is probably good enough for marine construction.

Grading and marking systems differ from country to country, so ask questions when you purchase imported plywood. Most panels brought into the United States fall into the American Plywood Association's MARINE grade, and some are of higher quality. Waterproof adhesive is usually used in imported plywood, but you should boil a sample as described above if you have any doubts.

Chapter 7

WEST SYSTEM Products

In the 1960's, when we began building boats professionally, we had a few ideas about what we wanted from our materials. We needed practical, low-cost and versatile methods. We knew how to work with wood, but as boat owners we also knew about the problems of maintaining wooden boats. We wanted to build fast, lightweight boats which were tough and strong enough to survive the high loads of hard racing. We had limited time and money, so our materials and methods couldn't be fussy or expensive.

After some experimenting, we found what we were looking for. Post-World War II technological advances had led to the development of epoxide resins. We began using epoxy and wood together, building composite structures with methods which had been used to construct wooden airplanes. Realizing that a boat's ability to stand up to a single impact was not as important as its long-term resistance to the daily assaults of wind and water, we modified epoxy formulations until we found the best balance between flexibility and high strength. In a few years we had worked out a safe and effective way to build boats. Our materials were inexpensive and our methods balanced the benefits of using wood against its shortcomings. We polished our techniques to reduce labor and, at the same time, to establish safe handling procedures for the new resin system.

Because we worked with the epoxy resin every day, we became concerned very early about the potential short and long term health hazards of the new materials. We were very cautious in choosing ingredients for our product. Just as we aimed for a balance between flexibility and high strength, we looked for a formulation which was as effective but as low in toxicity as possible. This is not to say that our products are without some health risk — all epoxy resin systems are potentially toxic — but WEST SYSTEM* Brand epoxy can be used safely if reasonable precautions are taken.

We began to market WEST SYSTEM resin and associated products in 1972. Since then, we've continued to improve our methods and materials and we've learned a great deal more about them. WEST

SYSTEM epoxy seemed strong. We now know, after intensive test programs, that its physical properties, and particularly its ability to withstand repeated loads, are extremely high. Our hunch that our boatbuilding techniques could be applied to volume production of high-quality airfoils has been confirmed. Gougeon Brothers, Inc. is recognized as a leading manufacturer of composite structures. After five years of work with NASA on the development of laminated wind turbine blades, we have proved that our wood/epoxy composite is a competitive modern material.

Product diversification has been our way to make sure that we can continue to build and sail boats. If our lab generates data for wind turbine blades, we look at boatbuilding applications. If we make modifications in formulations or techniques, we test to see where they can be used in boats. WEST SYSTEM epoxy resin has been intensively studied, particularly for cyclic fatigue resistance, in several laboratories and it has been proven in the field on ocean-racing boats. Our most recently designed boats reflect years of engineering and production with wood and epoxy.

Our line of products grew as the use of WEST SYSTEM materials increased. We still blend resin and hardeners with additives to make a strong, moisture and fatigue resistant epoxy resin. Ongoing research has led to the development of a new and greatly improved high density filler, and the epoxy formulation has been fine tuned so that it is easier to work with in difficult conditions. We now distribute epoxy, fillers, additives, fibers and associated tools world-wide.

WEST SYSTEM Materials

WEST SYSTEM resin and hardeners are the base components of a two-part epoxy developed specifically for use in wooden boatbuilding. Our epoxy and additives are formulated to provide maximum physical properties and, at the same time, to be as easy to use as possible. WEST SYSTEM products are designed to be versatile so that boat builders can mix epoxy and fillers on site in the specific formulations needed for various jobs.

Cured WEST SYSTEM epoxy is a hard, solid plastic with superior mechanical properties. It is a specific adhesive formulation which can also create an effective moisture barrier. When small amounts of filler are added to mixed resin and hardener, WEST SYSTEM epoxy becomes a very strong, gap-filling adhesive. Joints bonded with it are often stronger than the wood fibers which surround them. Other combinations of WEST SYSTEM epoxy and fillers produce mixtures which can be used in fairing and filleting. WEST SYSTEM epoxy resin has been relied on for many years as a medium for transferring loads from wood fiber to metals. It will serve as an efficient interface for distributing high point loading over greater surface area than would otherwise be possible. WEST SYSTEM products will bond fiberglass, Kevlar™ aramid, graphite and other synthetic fibers in structural and reinforcing applications. To our knowledge, they are the only epoxy resins to have been tested in high cycle (10 million cycles) fatigue.

The success of any epoxy/wood composite depends in part on the resin's ability to shield the wood beneath it from moisture. While WEST SYSTEM epoxy does not form a complete moisture barrier, as little as two coatings of it will impede the passage of moisture vapor to such an extent that the moisture content of the encapsulated wood is relatively stable. When its constant fluctuations of moisture content are under control, wood has predictable mechanical properties and dimensional stability. When moisture content is low and oxygen restricted, dry rot fungi cannot survive.

A WEST SYSTEM epoxy moisture barrier creates a stable base for paint and varnish. Wood surfaces protected with coatings of WEST SYSTEM epoxy cannot become saturated with water. Paint therefore adheres better, with less cracking and lifting, than it does to untreated wood. Boats built with wood and epoxy require less maintenance than traditional wooden boats and they will not blister as polyester boats do. So many boat owners have used WEST SYSTEM epoxy to repair and prevent gelcoat blisters on polyester hulls that we now distribute a Gelcoat Blister Repair Kit.

Boats built with epoxy and wood are relatively inexpensive. Wood itself is among the cheapest of boatbuilding materials, but high labor and maintenance costs have made the price of traditional wooden boats non-competitive. Wood/epoxy construction methods require less labor and equipment than earlier planking systems. Epoxy will bond at room temperatures with little clamping pressure, so few specialized tools and molds are needed. As a result, overhead can be drastically reduced and parts manufacture is flexible.

Our body of knowledge about wood/epoxy composites grows with each day of testing. Current product data is published in WEST SYSTEM Technical Manuals and in our newsletter, *The Boatbuilder*. Our technical staff is always available to answer questions and to help solve application problems.

Fatigue Behavior of WEST SYSTEM Epoxy

For many years we have used WEST SYSTEM epoxy as a medium to transfer loads from low density wood to high density metals. Our techniques for bonding large and small fasteners, hardware and keels are fully explained in Chapter 26. In most cases, all load is transferred through resin which has been thickened with fillers. This idea has been very successful and is now widely used in the marine industry.

In the process of developing wind turbine blades, we quickly found that the resin interface between load take-off studs and wood fiber was the critical element in blade performance. Blade failure usually initiates failure of the entire wind machine. To predict blade load capability and performance life, we needed to learn more about the long-term fatigue behavior of WEST SYSTEM epoxy. Very little fatigue testing had been performed on resin alone, and the long-term fatigue capability of the resin in many composite applications was a question mark. When composite materials fail in interlaminar shear, it's never really clear whether the failure is due to bonding problems between resin and fiber or to fatigue failure of the resin itself.

A number of different methods have been used to test WEST SYSTEM epoxy in fatigue depending upon specific needs for material design data to support wind turbine blade efforts. While it is difficult to make general conclusions from specific test data, it is apparent that WEST SYSTEM epoxy exhibits good fatigue life and can maintain a reasonable percentage of its one-time to failure load capability after undergoing 10 million fatigue cycles. (See Appendix B for futher details.)

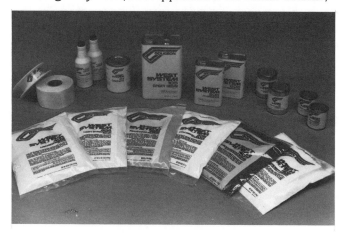

Figure 1—WEST SYSTEM products.

WEST SYSTEM EPOXY

For WEST SYSTEM resin to be an effective moisture barrier, a minimum of two coats should be applied to all interior and exterior surfaces. Areas which will be sanded need at least three coats of resin so that two net coats will remain after finishing. We recommend two additional coatings on hulls which are left in the water year round. All resins eventually break down under direct sunlight, so resin-coated surfaces should be protected with paint or ultraviolet-resistant varnish or, temporarily, with WEST SYSTEM 420 Aluminum Powder or 501 White Pigment additives.

WEST SYSTEM 105 Resin

To make WEST SYSTEM epoxy, 105 Resin is combined with 205 or 206 Hardener. It is a transparent, light-amber, low-viscosity liquid epoxy resin formulated specifically to wet out wood fiber. The excellent coating characteristics of 105 Resin enable it to form a continuous film when mixed and applied with a brush or roller to a properly prepared substrate. Mixtures of 105 Resin and 205 Fast Hardener can be used at wide temperature ranges. In cold weather, follow the special handling instructions discussed later in this chapter. WEST SYSTEM resin is not considered flammable and has little odor.

WEST SYSTEM 205 Fast Hardener

Our 205 Fast Hardener is one of two hardeners designed for use with 105 Resin. It is formulated with medium viscosity polyamines. When mixed in the ratio of 5 parts resin to 1 part hardener, the cured epoxy becomes a rigid solid with very high physical strength. It provides a highly effective moisture vapor barrier. The gel time for 100 grams of 105 Resin/205 Fast Hardener at 70°F is 10 to 15 minutes. Fast Hardener produces a partial cure in 5 to 7 hours at 70°F. Because of its glossier surface cure and faster cure time, 205 Fast Hardener is preferred for natural finish applications.

WEST SYSTEM 206 Slow Hardener

WEST SYSTEM 206 Slow Hardener is an epoxy curing agent which contains a mixture of low viscosity polyamines. When combined with 105 Resin in a 5 to 1 ratio, 206 Hardener produces a strong, rigid, moisture-resistant solid. The combined 105 Resin/206

Slow Hardener has a gel time of 25 to 30 minutes at 70°F. Slow Hardener's longer pot life is helpful in warm weather and for bonding, coating and repair jobs. Partial cure time at 70°F is 9 hours.

WEST SYSTEM FILLERS

These additives are designed to be used as needed to modify WEST SYSTEM resin/hardener mixtures for bonding, filleting and fairing applications. To be sure that resin and hardener are properly combined, stir them together thoroughly before adding fillers. Slowly add fillers and continue mixing to desired consistency. Avoid inhalation of filler particles.

WEST SYSTEM fillers affect the viscosity of epoxy. Epoxy/filler combinations will flow more slowly than standard epoxy and some will have more resistance to sag. Exact quantities of filler depend on application. We suggest that you experiment with filler mixtures until you find the best consistency for a given job. Approximate ratios for very thick, self-supporting "peanut butter" mixtures and for less thick, slow-spreading "honey" combinations, are provided as buying guides. These represent extremes. In fact, fillers may be added to achieve a wide range of viscosities.

We are continually updating our high and low density fillers. The products listed below are subject to change as we find more effective substances for each job. In this book, we refer to high and low density fillers and filler mixtures. Any new products will be interchangeable with the fillers described here.

WEST SYSTEM 403 High Density Microfibers

Our 403 Microfibers are fine cotton fibers used to thicken epoxy for use in general bonding and filling. Resin/microfiber mixtures have superior gap-filling

Figure 2—Application tools for WEST SYSTEM products.

qualities and retain wetting and penetrating capabilities. Microfibers help ensure 100% bonding within joints by preventing areas of resin starvation. Use 5% to 15% by volume of epoxy for coating well-fit joints. To fill gaps or make fillets, add Microfibers to resin to make a putty-like mass. Mix in quantities desired at the rate of 1 pound of Microfibers and 6 pounds of mixed epoxy for peanut butter consistency, and 1 pound of Microfibers and 8 pounds of epoxy for the consistency of honey.

WEST SYSTEM 404 High Density/High Strength Filler

Specifically developed for maximum physical properties in hardware bonding applications where high cyclic loads are anticipated, 404 High Density/High Strength filler can also be used for filleting and gap-filling where maximum strength is necessary. Add it to mixed resin at a rate of up to 40% by weight, depending on viscosity needed. A mixing rate of 20% to 30% by weight makes a thickened resin mixture appropriate to most applications.

WEST SYSTEM 405 Filleting Blend

The 405 Filleting Blend is a mix of cellulose fibers and other fillers. Because it is tan and blends in with light woods, 405 is particularly good for fillets in naturally-finished interiors. A 6 ounce bag of 405 Filleting Blend will thicken 4 pounds of resin/hardener mix to peanut butter consistency.

WEST SYSTEM 406 Colloidal Silica

WEST SYSTEM 406 Colloidal Silica is an extremely fine synthetic silica used to thicken mixed epoxy and prevent its running off vertical and overhead surfaces. The addition of small amounts of Colloidal Silica significantly reduces sag. Added to fairing compounds, it makes a peanut butter-like mixture which does not drag as it is applied. Colloidal Silica may also be used to thicken bonding adhesive for filleting. For a peanut butter consistency, combine 406 Colloidal Silica with mixed resin at the rate of 6 ounces per 3.6 pounds of epoxy. For honey consistency, plan on 6 ounces to 9.4 pounds of mixed resin and hardener.

WEST SYSTEM 407 Low Density Microballoons

These 407 Microballoons are tiny, hollow, brown phenolic spheres. Combined with resin, Microballoons make easily-mixed, easily-sanded, dark-colored filling and fairing putties. They are handy as a thickening additive for epoxy used to bond lower density veneers. Cured resin/407 Microballoon putties are structural materials with reasonably good strength-to-weight characteristics. One 9 ounce bag mixed with 1.4 pounds of epoxy has peanut butter consistency, while a bag combined with 2.2 pounds of resin/hardener makes a honey mixture.

WEST SYSTEM 409 Low Density Microspheres.

WEST SYSTEM 409 Microspheres are hollow, white, inorganic spheres which can be used interchangeably with 407 Microballoons. Microsphere putties are somewhat lighter in weight and have less load-bearing capacity than 407 mixtures. Microspheres drag slightly more than Microballoons and are more difficult to mix and sand. They do not hold a feather edge as well as Microballoons, but they are much less expensive and may be preferable for large jobs. A small amount of 406 Colloidal Silica will reduce drag in Microsphere putties. Mix at the rate of 6 ounces to 1.8 pounds of mixed epoxy for peanut butter viscosity and 6 ounces to 2.9 pounds for honey.

WEST SYSTEM 420 Aluminum Powder

Added to resin up to 10% by volume, 420 Powder helps to shield epoxy from harmful effects of sunlight for up to six months. Aluminum Powder is applied to areas which will not be finished immediately, and it may also be used as a darker base coat to highlight flaws before final fairing and painting. Because 420 Aluminum Powder/epoxy surface coatings have increased hardness and resistance to abrasion, they are more difficult to sand than pigment/epoxy coatings.

WEST SYSTEM 421 Fire Retardant

Our 421 Fire Retardant is a hydrated alumina powder which is combined in a ratio of 1 to 1 with mixed epoxy. We recommend using 421 in engine and galley areas where fire hazards may exist. A 421/resin coating is more fire resistant than epoxy alone, and it will self-extinguish when the source of flame is removed. It should, however, be considered combustible in a major fire.

WEST SYSTEM 423 Graphite Powder

This 423 Graphite is a very fine black powder which can be mixed with WEST SYSTEM resin to make a durable coating material. Graphite/resin coatings do not have the antifouling properties of bottom paints, but they are often used to put smooth, low-maintenance surfaces on rudders, centerboards and the bottoms of drysailed racers. Graphite/epoxy putty simulates tradition caulking in teak deck construction and simultaneously protects resin from sunlight. Add 423 Graphite to mixed epoxy at 10% to 30% by volume.

WEST SYSTEM GLASS FABRIC AND REINFORCING FIBERS

WEST SYSTEM 740-744 Glass Fabric

Boat builders use fiberglass cloth with WEST SYSTEM resin to reinforce laminated and strip-built hulls, cover staple holes and protect areas subject to high abrasion. Our fabric is treated with a silane finish, rather than the volan used with polyester resin. This permits thorough saturation with WEST SYSTEM resin and significantly improves resin-to-glass adhesion. WEST SYSTEM glass cloth becomes transparent after it is wet out, so laminations of 4 and 6 oz. cloth may be used on naturally finished hulls. WEST SYSTEM fabric is available in different widths and weights per square yard. Consult a current product catalog for up-to-date information.

WEST SYSTEM 731-733 Glass Reinforcing Tape

Glass tape is a convenient form of fiberglass cloth used to reinforce high-stress areas such as chines and hull-deck corners. This tape provides extra tensile strength to resist the development of hairline cracks, and it adds resistance to abrasion. WEST SYSTEM Glass Reinforcing Tape is available in 3, 4 and 6 inch widths, with finished selvages and weave equivalent in weight to 10 oz. cloth.

WEST SYSTEM 701 Graphite Fibers

Continuous, unidirectional graphite fibers have a tensile modulus of 33 million psi. They are low in density, but stiffer than steel and aluminum and most other structural materials on a per-pound basis. Epoxy/graphite composites are many times stiffer than fiberglass composites, but are only slightly heavier. Properly-applied graphite fibers can make a structurally-marginal component successful. Graphite fibers are also useful in situations where stiffness is required but the advantage of increased geometry is limited by size and space. WEST SYSTEM 701 Graphite Fibers have been used to stiffen masts, cen-

terboards, rudders and canoe paddles. They are sold in 1 inch wide "tapes," with average tow thickness of approximately .01 inch.

WEST SYSTEM PIGMENTS

WEST SYSTEM pigments are heavy, epoxy-based pastes used to tint resin/hardener mixtures. Colored coatings of epoxy can serve as base coats for final finishing and, because they highlight flaws and imperfections, as guides for fairing and sanding. Pigments can interfere with resin penetration, so they should only be added to resin used for second and third coatings. They do not provide a final surface, but must be covered with other finishing systems.

Because they are thick pastes, pigments can be difficult to mix into epoxy. As long as care is taken to maintain the standard 5 parts resin to 1 part hardener ratio, pigments may be diluted with very small quantities of resin before mixing with desired amounts of resin and hardener. Both 501 and 503 pigments are combined at the rate of about one teaspoon of pigment to 8 ounces of resin. More pigment will increase opacity, but it will also increase the viscosity of the mixture.

WEST SYSTEM 501 White

This 501 White Pigment may be added to epoxy mixtures and used as a base coat for final finishing of interiors. It provides an adequate temporary sunshield when painting must be delayed.

WEST SYSTEM 503 Gray

Our 503 Gray Pigment performs the same functions as 501 Pigment, but is darker in color and therefore only suitable as a base for dark paints. It is easier to sand than 420 Aluminum Powder but less effective as a UV shield.

WEST SYSTEM SURFACE PREPARATION KIT

WEST SYSTEM 860 Aluminum Etch Kit

This two-part chemical etch kit prepares aluminum surfaces for bonding and coating. Treatment improves adhesion of epoxy and fibers to aluminum. Instructions for use are printed on bottle labels.

WEST SYSTEM METERING PUMPS

We sell three types of metering pumps. All quickly dispense both hardener and resin in reliable proportions and conserve epoxy by preventing waste.

Choose among them according to the quantity of epoxy your project requires.

WEST SYSTEM 301 Mini-Pumps

Polypropylene mini-pumps are intended primarily for low-volume users. They are available in three sizes, which screw directly on the various sizes of hardener and resin containers. One stroke of the resin plunger dispenses 5 units of resin and one stroke of the hardener plunger dispenses 1 unit of hardener. Mini-pumps are inexpensive and may be left in resin and hardener cans for extended periods.

WEST SYSTEM 306 Model A Dispensing Pump

This portable metal pump is designed for larger-volume users and is of great help on any project larger than a dinghy. Rigid plastic reservoirs store resin and hardener. A single stroke dispenses hardener and resin simultaneously in correct ratio at the rate of about half an ounce per stroke. We offer cleaning service and rebuild kits for Model A pumps.

WEST SYSTEM 309 Gear Pump

We designed and built this pump for our own use. It delivers about an ounce of mixed epoxy with each full turn of the crank and it can meter up to five quarts per minute. Features such as positive shut-off minimize resin loss and the mess of dripping spouts. Metal reservoirs hold two gallons of resin and one gallon of hardener.

Mixing and Handling

All WEST SYSTEM epoxy mixtures begin with accurate measuring. Combine 105 Resin with either 205 or 206 Hardener in a ratio of 5 parts resin to 1 part hardener. The easiest way to be sure of proportions is to meter resin and hardener with WEST SYSTEM dispensing pumps, but epoxy may also be measured by weight and volume. Get into the habit of wearing skin protection whenever you handle resin and hardener.

There are tricks which will speed up an epoxy cure, but adding extra hardener is not the best of them. More hardener will not make a harder cured epoxy. Over the years a good number of boat builders have tried modifying hardener-resin proportions and many have found that the experiments don't work. We stick with 5 to 1 ratios in all applications. If nothing else, this reduces waste by guaranteeing that resin and hardener containers run out at the same time.

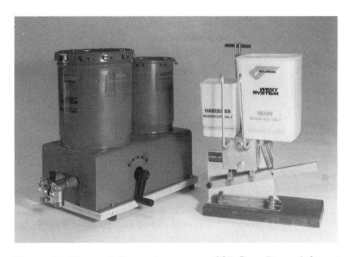

Figure 3—Metered dispensing pumps: 309 Gear Pump left and 306 Model A pump right.

If you weigh resin and hardener, remember to allow for the weight of the container. Use a small capacity scale and check to be sure that it is accurate. Avoid mixing more than a pound of epoxy at one time unless you have a number of helpers. It's a good idea to weigh ingredients separately — first, say, 10 oz. of hardener and then 2 oz. of resin — before pouring them into the mixing cup.

Mixing by volume is less accurate because the densities of resin and hardener are different, but it can be quick and convenient. One way to mix correct ratios by volume is to mark a clean stick at six equal intervals and hold it upright in a cylindrical container. Fill with resin to the fifth line and then add hardener until you reach the sixth. Some boat builders draw proportional graphs to facilitate volume measuring of various quantities.

To prevent contamination, mix resin and hardener in clean, deep containers. Wax-free paper, plastic and metal mixing pots, including orange juice and soup cans, work well. Foam cups insulate the heat generated by curing epoxy and may burn, so use them only in very cold weather. We like reusable WEST SYSTEM polypropylene mixing pots because cured resin pops right out of them. It's hard to mix epoxy and fillers in pots which are too small or very shallow or in square-cornered containers. Use bigger pots than usual if you are mixing putties, and always combine ingredients in a can or pot before pouring them into a roller pan.

After properly measuring resin and hardener, mix them together thoroughly. It's not necessary to churn vigorously, but stir well for about 30 seconds, occasionally scraping down the sides of the pot. Insufficient mixing will result in epoxy which cures irregularly. We use 6-inch-long non-sterile wooden tongue depressors as mixing sticks. When the basic epoxy is mixed, pour in any additives and stir well.

An exothermic polymerization reaction begins when resin and hardener are mixed. Molecules move to build polymers, cross-linking chains, and give off energy in the form of heat as they bond. An epoxy mixture will look the same and be easy to use during its *pot life*. Then, as the reaction accelerates, it *gels,* thickening and changing from a liquid to a solid. The pot becomes warm to the touch as the resin becomes more difficult to apply. When most molecules have formed polymers, the epoxy reaches a *partial cure* and is relatively tack-free. Although residual reaction continues for two weeks, an epoxy-coated surface can often be

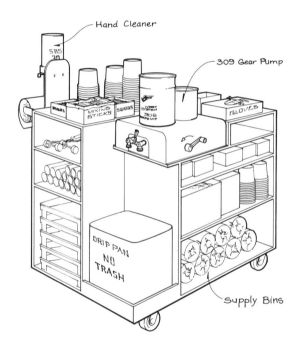

Figure 4—For professionals, or for those of you with large projects, taking the trouble to set up a mixing table can save considerable labor hours. The object is to organize all WEST SYSTEM products and related supplies used in a project on a single table, so that you can use them as easily and efficiently as possible with little wasted effort or time.

The single most important item on the table is, of course, the dispensing pump. Next are the fillers and additives used with the resin to form the various mixtures. These are located around the table in individual areas such as pull-out bins. After resin has been drawn from the dispensing pump, you can select the filler ingredients needed and quickly mix up the resin mixture desired for the specific job at hand. All the mixing and application tools, such as the mixing pots, stirring sticks, brushes, rollers, squeegees and application knives are positioned in the most advantageous locations around the table structure. Related supplies, such as hand soap, rubber gloves, paper towels, cleaning solvents, etc., are also located for easy access. The drawing shows how these items might be laid out, but every situation is different and you may want to change the design of your mixing table to better accommodate your particular situation.

worked and sanded within 24 hours. Best cures are achieved within this schedule.

In some cases, you may want epoxy with a longer or shorter pot life. The easiest way to manipulate gel time is to choose between WEST SYSTEM 205 Fast Hardener and 206 Slow Hardener, which are formulated to cure at different rates. One hundred grams of 105 Resin/205 Fast Hardener will begin to set up in 10 to 15 minutes at 70°F, while 105/206 epoxy takes about twice that time to gel. All other things being equal, it makes sense to use slow hardener when you need working time, as on large coating jobs.

If you have the supplies and pumps on hand, you may consider using 205 Fast Hardener and 206 Slow Hardener in combination to gain some advantage. Hardeners may be mixed as long as the 5-1 resin/ hardener ratio is maintained when they are added to resin. With some experimenting, you may be able to custom-mix epoxy which has a longer pot life than usual with fast hardener.

Boat builders sometimes report that they have used standard proportions of resin and hardener, but that their epoxy has cured either too slowly or too quickly. When this happens, pumps are the first thing to check. If you run into an unpredictable pot life which cannot be explained by ambient temperature, test to make sure that your pumps are correctly metering and dispensing resin and hardener.

Bonding with WEST SYSTEM Epoxy in Difficult Conditions

Most questions about WEST SYSTEM epoxy come up when it is stored and used in difficult conditions. Extremely hot or cold weather can affect cure rates and extreme moisture, in the form of wet wood or high humidity levels, has been known to cause other problems.

Epoxy's sensitivity to heat becomes immediately apparent when, after months of working in the cold, you first mix epoxy on a hot day and find that it sets up much more quickly than you expected. In warm temperatures, reaction is faster, pot life is shorter and cure-up occurs more rapidly than in cold weather. In the same way, if you are used to mixing resin in hot weather and it turns colder, pot life will be longer and cure-up time extended.

The temperature of the workplace affects the speed of the polymerization reaction. Because each molecule needs energy in the form of heat to react, the initial pace of the reaction is set by the temperature of resin and hardener. Heat generated by the reaction accelerates molecular cross-linking until the most active phase of the reaction is complete. When resin and hardener are cold, the reaction gets off to a slow start and can't build up enough heat to cure within normal time limits. On the other hand, the heat of warm resin speeds up the chemical reaction. If cold epoxy is applied to cold wood, or if warm epoxy is applied to warm wood, these effects are magnified.

Cure rates are also determined by what happens to the heat generated by the exothermic reaction. This in turn depends on ambient temperature levels and the ratio of mass to exposed surface area. A quantity of resin and hardener mixed and left standing in an orange juice can will cure quickly in warm weather because the energy produced cannot easily escape into the atmosphere. It insulates itself and accelerates the exothermic reaction. An equivalent amount of epoxy in a roller pan will cure more slowly because its heat dissipates through its increased surface area. Epoxy loses less heat and cures faster in a bonding application with little exposed area than it does in a thin film coating with maximum exposed surface. In general, fillers shorten pot life. The extra stirring needed to blend additives and resin and the relative smaller surface area of thickened resin combine to add and retain heat.

For best results in hot weather, choose WEST SYS-TEM 206 Slow Hardener for its increased pot life. To prevent premature set-up, mix small batches to keep heat production at a minimum, and quicky pour them into a roller pan to increase exposed surface area. Store unmixed resin and hardener in a cool place. If you can't put them in a refrigerator or cooler, at least keep them in the shade and out of direct sunlight.

Very cold weather can present greater problems. Resin viscosity increases and metering with dispensing pumps becomes almost impossible at very low temperatures. Thick epoxy is hard to handle and it may not adequately penetrate wood. During slow cures, coated surfaces may be contaminated, especially by moisture and carbon dioxide, and become cloudy. Cold wood substrate and frozen resin can add to difficulties.

Several measures may be taken to overcome these effects. Use 205 Fast Hardener, and store resin and hardener in a warm place. Using a cylindrical container as a mixing pot, stir the mixture longer than usual, and allow heat to build up for a few minutes before you pour the epoxy into a roller pan. Think about using external heat sources to bring materials up to good working temperatures.

If you have a heat gun, it is handy for warming both epoxy and wood that will be bonded. There is no point in heating materials much over 100°F since excess heat can boil away portions of the epoxy formulation,

so we prefer 750°F hot air guns to more powerful models. Try to avoid blowing air into mixed epoxy, and warm it gently with adequate ventilation. If the mixture foams, it has probably boiled and will no longer be reliable. Heat guns can ignite combustible materials, so be careful whenever you use them.

Heat lamps and regular lightbulbs can be used locally to raise the temperature of joints as they cure and to warm containers of resin and hardener. When we want a small part to cure, we often put it in a "hot box" with a lightbulb. Rigid sheets of foil-backed foam insulation make cheap and easy warming compartments for supplies and set-ups. Lamps present significantly fewer fire risks than heat guns, but should still be used with caution.

If WEST SYSTEM materials freeze in very cold storage conditions, crystals may appear in the resin when it thaws. If this happens, boil a pot of water large enough to hold the container, remove it from direct heat, and carefully put the can of resin in the water bath. Remember to remove the container's lid to avoid danger of explosion. Stir the warming epoxy well with a clean stick until the liquid regains clarity and all crystals at the bottom of the container are dissolved. Then replace the lid and shake the resin well to melt any crystals which might be clinging to the top of the container. If you suspect that resin in your pump has crystallized, pump warmed resin through it to remove the crystals.

We recommend that WEST SYSTEM resin be used only on wood which has a moisture level between 8% and 12% but realize that in emergencies it may be necessary to bond wetter materials. WEST SYSTEM epoxy can be used on wood which has an 18% moisture level, although internal stressing may develop. With damper wood, there is also a possibility that excessive moisture may affect the performance of 205 or 206 Hardeners, which are water-soluble.

In the past, surface coatings with 206 Slow Hardener have occasionally become cloudy in very humid weather, so we usually recommend 205 Fast Hardener for clear coated hulls and components. Recent fine tuning of the formulation of WEST SYSTEM slow hardener has largely eliminated this problem, but surface cloudiness may persist if coatings cure in the presence of some gases and contaminants. Since fast hardener will set up more quickly and is therefore vulnerable to contamination for a shorter time, we continue to suggest its use on surfaces which will be naturally finished. Improvements in its formulation have resulted in a hardener which cures with less surface deposit and is less susceptible to the effects of humidity and low temperatures than either slow hardener or the fast hardener sold before 1985.

Terminology Used in this Book

Throughout this book, we use *epoxy* and *resin* interchangeably to describe epoxy resin. Except where otherwise stated, *epoxy, resin* and *standard resin* refer to WEST SYSTEM epoxy mixed in the ratio of five parts 105 Resin to 1 part 205 or 206 Hardener with no added fillers.

By contrast, *resin mixture, epoxy mixture, thickened mixture* and *adhesive mixture* are combinations of mixed epoxy and fillers. We have for the most part been quite specific about which filler should be used in any given application. A *406 resin mixture* contains 406 Colloidal Silica additive, while *high density resin mixture* and *low density resin mixture* contain high density and low density fillers respectively.

It has been extraordinarily difficult to devise a terminology which accurately describes the exact thickness or viscosity of these mixtures. Our choices of *peanut butter, honey, syrup, cream* and *thick syrup* may seem slightly incongruous. They are, however, universally understandable.

When resin and hardener are mixed in proper proportions, epoxy will usually gel, or begin to harden, in less than thirty minutes. At this point, the resin is *uncured*. Some operations like trimming fiberglass joints are best undertaken when epoxy is *partially cured,* 3 to 8 hours after application, depending on the temperature. At this point, the epoxy is no longer liquid or rubbery and not yet brittle. It's important that the cutting operation does not peel fiberglass away from the hull. Although residual exothermic reaction continues for up to two weeks, we consider epoxy to be *fully cured* three or four days after application, depending on ambient temperature. In many cases, coatings of WEST SYSTEM epoxy will be sufficiently cured for subsequent operations after 12 to 24 hours.

Chapter 8

Safety

Boatbuilding should not be hazardous to your health. While we don't feel that it's necessary to discuss all aspects of woodworking safety, we do think it important to set guidelines for safe use of WEST SYSTEM* Brand products.

We are particularly concerned about health problems associated with epoxy resins, solvents, wood and dust, and with the acute fire hazards these substances create when used in careless combination. The following discussion concentrates on these issues. We hope that you will take the time to inform yourself about other potential shop hazards, including those presented by power tools of all kinds.

We urge you to read this chapter in its entirety, but realize that shop safety simply isn't a terribly lively topic. We have therefore organized our information so that the most important is presented first in the form of general rules and then in greater detail.

You have a right and a responsibility to make informed decisions about the materials you use. Although a very small percentage of the population is unusually susceptible to the effects of WEST SYSTEM epoxy, most people have no problems with it. If you are allergic to a number of substances, or if you recognize yourself as someone who may be extra sensitive to resin, hardener, solvents or wood dust, be sure to observe the special handling procedures later in this chapter.

WEST SYSTEM Epoxy

Epoxy resins and particularly hardeners have long had a reputation as skin sensitizers. In selecting the ingredients for WEST SYSTEM epoxy, we have searched for a balance between necessary physical properties and lowest possible toxicity.

Personal susceptibility to epoxy depends on three factors: degree of contact with the material, individual body chemistry and state of health. Individuals who are prone to allergies, hay fever or asthma are more likely to become sensitized than others. People with light complexions may be more sensitive than people with darker complexions. If you are suffering from fatigue, a virus infection, a cold or a sore throat, you may be unusually susceptible to sensitization.

By itself, WEST SYSTEM resin rarely causes sensitization. The 205 and 206 Hardeners are both skin irritants and sensitizers. Their toxicity is greatly reduced as they are mixed in a 5 to 1 ratio with 105 Resin, but adequate handling precautions must still be taken. We recommend that the following safeguards be strictly observed.

(1) Maintain good health by eating and sleeping right and exercising regularly. Don't smoke. If you are tired or have the flu, go to sleep and let that bonding job wait until you feel better. Keeping your body in shape will lower chances of accidents and sensitization.

(2) Avoid all direct skin contact with resin, hardeners and mixed epoxy. Wear plastic gloves whenever you handle WEST SYSTEM materials. Barrier skin creams provide good additional protection if you have sensitive skin, allergies or a lot of messy work to do.

(3) Never use solvents to remove epoxy from your skin unless absolutely necessary. Waterless skin cleaner works well in most cases. Always wash well with soap and water immediately after skin contact with solvents.

(4) If you spill moderate amounts of epoxy on your clothes, change them immediately. Use skin cleaner to remove the resin from you and your clothes.

(5) Use epoxy only in areas with good ventilation. In close quarters, such as boat interiors, be especially careful to provide both exhaust and supply of air.

(6) Provide maximum ventilation and wear a dust mask when you sand epoxy, taking extra care if it has cured for less than a week.

(7) Protect your eyes from contact with WEST SYSTEM resin, hardeners and mixed epoxy by wearing safety glasses or goggles. If contact should occur, immediately flush eyes with liberal quantities of water under low pressure for 15 minutes. If discomfort is present, seek medical attention immediately.

(8) If you develop a skin rash while working with WEST SYSTEM epoxy, stop using the product until the rash disappears, usually three or four days later. When you go back to work, improve your safety precautions and prevent any skin contact

52

whatsoever with hardener, resin, epoxy and their fumes. If problems persist, consult a physician.

(9) Watch and handle pots of mixed epoxy carefully. Never throw epoxy waste into the trash before it has solidified and cooled.

Solvents

Almost all solvents are poisonous if swallowed or inhaled in sufficient quantities. Solvents can irritate the lungs, respiratory system, eyes and skin, and some may cause damage to other organs, including the heart. Several solvents have been linked to types of cancer.

Because solvents dissolve and leach out the skin's protective oils, the most common result of low-level direct exposure is dry skin. The drying effect of solvents on air passageways is known to interfere with the lungs' natural ability to clean themselves of impurities. When inhaled in high concentrations, solvents may cause depression of the central nervous system. Symptoms of overexposure range from nausea and irritability to something which resembles alcohol intoxication. Continued inhalation of particularly toxic solvents can lead to loss of consciousness, permanent brain damage or death.

Flammable solvents are a common cause of shop fires. Nonflammable solvents may break down into dangerous gases, notably phosgene and hydrogen chloride, when exposed to very high temperatures.

For these reasons, it is essential to observe the following rules whenever you use solvents:

(1) Always select the least toxic and least flammable solvent which will get the job done. Avoid all solvents if your overall health is not good.

(2) Do not smoke or use cutting torches and other burners in the presence of solvents or near solvent storage areas. Store solvents in tightly capped, approved containers in a safe place away from smokers, heating devices and small children.

(3) Avoid all skin contact with and inhalation of solvents by wearing appropriate safety equipment — gloves, goggles and respirators — when handling them.

(4) Use solvents only in well-ventilated areas. Bring fresh air into your shop and evacuate solvent-laden air. In closed surroundings, wear a respirator with cartridges. If you can set up a ventilated hood or booth, use it for all operations which involve solvents.

(5) Take special care in hot weather, when solvent fumes and wood dust may combine to pose a high fire risk.

(6) Do not operate power machinery or climb ladders if you have been working with solvents in a confined area. If you feel tired, nauseated, "high" or irritable while using solvents, move immediately to a well-ventilated room or go outdoors. First aid for unconsciousness resulting from overexposure to solvent fumes is fresh air.

Wood Dust

Modern woodworking equipment generates high concentrations of wood dust. Inhalation of any dust in excessive quantities will cause bronchial congestion. Chronic irritation of the upper respiratory tract is common among woodworkers, who also share higher-than-normal rates of nasal, sinus and larynx cancer. After working for years in the lumber industry, some people develop an occupational asthma.

Some woods cause specific diseases, and direct contact with the dust, sap or oil of certain trees may bring on skin irritation and other allergic reactions. While tropical woods present the majority of problems, splinters from some North American species — Douglas fir is a prime example — seem to infect almost immediately. Toxicity is somewhat reduced by seasoning because as lumber dries it loses some of its irritating extractives.

Personal susceptibility to wood and wood dust follows general patterns of susceptibility to other toxic substances. Reactions are more common in warm weather, expecially when dust settles on sweaty skin, more frequent among members of high risk groups and more often found in individuals with light complexions. Respiratory problems are far more likely to arise among smokers and others whose lungs are already under strain.

Reducing exposure to wood dusts, sap and oil will minimize their ill effects. Basic shop rules should be enforced. Following are suggestions for sensible shop rules:

(1) Take special precautions before handling wood if your general health is not good, or if you suspect that you may be particularly sensitive to wood.

(2) Sand only in areas which have adequate fresh air intake and ventilation. If dust levels in your shop are high, or if you are sanding in a confined space or for a long time, wear a comfortable dust mask.

(3) If your shop is dusty, make sure everyone, not just the person sanding, wears a mask.

(4) When you have a choice, use a cutting tool, a chisel or plane, rather than an abrading tool, a polisher or sandpaper.

(5) Use wet, rather than dry, sanding techniques whenever possible.

(6) If you must sweep your floor, wear a respirator and use sweeping compound. Vacuuming and mopping are preferable because they send less dust into the air.

(7) Use dust collectors on major dust-making machinery.

(8) Take precautions to prevent fires. Store solvents safely, use heat-generating equipment cautiously and establish rules about smoking.

Boat Shop Safety — Detailed Information

In the past twenty years, increasing interest has been focused on safety in the work place, and especially on the effects of on-the-job exposure to chemicals. Although artists and craftspeople rely on many of the materials and processes used in major industry, they haven't been as concerned about health effects as industrial workers. As you read this, realize that even if you only build your boat in your home on a part-time basis, you should be attentive to basic safety issues. You owe it to yourself to maintain the highest levels of industrial hygiene in your workshop. No one else can do this for you.

The human body is constantly assaulted by potential hazards in the physical environment. Bacteria, insects, molds and other biological stressors try to invade. Toxic chemicals contained in air pollution and a wide variety of everyday compounds may enter our systems. Other stress comes from repetitive motion, or lack of it, as when the body is forced to sit or stand or hold something too long. Too much or too little heat, light, vibration or noise can cause various types of damage.

We usually survive these attacks. Pain is a good warning signal: if something hurts, we often stop doing it, and so prevent serious problems. At times, however, because we don't know that a substance is hazardous or toxic, or because the cumulative stress on our defense systems is extreme, our bodies are overwhelmed. When this happens, our health may be permanently impaired.

Personal susceptibility to stress in general and toxic materials in particular depends on several factors. The first of these is the total burden the body is asked to bear. Combinations of different kinds of stresses — say a bacterial infection on top of exposure to a toxic solvent — will increase the likelihood of adverse effects. The amount of exposure to any substance will also determine reaction. If you use a lot of solvent, and do it very frequently, eight hours a day, you will have a

greater reaction to it than if you use only a little for a few minutes every week or so. Finally, reaction depends on the toxicity of the specific material. Several solvents are so toxic in small amounts that they simply should not be used.

Some people belong to high risk groups and run higher-than-average chances of ill effects from exposure to various kinds of stress. Young children, especially infants, and older people have much less resistance than young adults. Asthmatics, smokers and individuals who have or are susceptible to lung, kidney and heart disease are less resilient than healthier people. People who have histories of allergies may react more strenuously than non-allergic people, just as workers who have been repeatedly exposed to wide ranges of chemicals may be more than usually prone to problems. Pregnant women may have increased susceptibility to a number of materials. Their unborn babies may be damaged by substances which pass to them through the placenta.

Potentially hazardous stressors enter the body by three routes: direct skin contact, inhalation through the lungs and ingestion through the mouth and digestive system. Exposure may harm the eyes, ears, skin, lungs, heart, liver, kidneys and central nervous system. The extent of damage depends, again, on personal susceptibility and on the toxicity and dose of the stressor. The site of damage is to some extent determined by method of exposure and by the material itself.

Certain individuals, most notably pregnant women and very young children, simply should not use some materials. Others, including members of other high risk groups, must take precautions to make sure that stressors cannot enter their bodies. Smokers can lower their total stress levels by giving up the habit. We can all eliminate health hazards by cutting off exposure by skin contact, inhalation or ingestion and, at the same time, by controlling the toxicity and exposure levels of the materials we choose to use.

Whenever possible, choose the least toxic material which will do the job, and use materials in their least toxic forms. Store your supplies in properly labeled, covered containers. Keep flammable materials in appropriate cans in areas where open flames and smoking are prohibited. Replace bottle caps after pouring solvents and wipe up spills immediately. Buy a fire extinguisher which will be effective on the kinds of materials you have on hand. Safely dispose of rags and chemicals.

Dust and fumes can cause damage. Take steps to control them by setting up a good ventilation system with both supply and exhaust built into it. Figure out a way to rig up a local exhaust fan in an enclosed area and confine sanding operations to this enclosure. Install dust collectors on all stationary power tools. Wherever possible, choose wet over dry processes — wet sanding is far preferable to dry sanding. Clean your shop regularly, before clutter and sawdust pile up. If you sweep your floor, wear a dust mask and use sweeping compound. In general, vacuuming and wet-mopping are preferable to sweeping because they are less dusty procedures.

Personal hygiene is an important element of overall shop safety. Separate work and non-work clothes for storage and laundry, especially if you are using fiberglass. Never smoke or eat as you work, and wash thoroughly after work, before eating and before going to the bathroom. Take measures to prevent contact between materials and your hands and face. If you splash yourself, wash immediately with soap and water. If you need to see a doctor, remember that the materials you use may have some effect on your general health and be sure to talk about them.

Finally, make sure that you have personal protective gear to match your jobs. Wear appropriate safety glasses or chemical workers' goggles to prevent eye injury, wear gloves when handling solvents and epoxy to prevent skin contact, dust masks when sanding and respirators when solvent-washing to prevent inhalation. If you operate loud power machinery wear ear protectors to prevent hearing loss. These devices protect only the wearer. Remember that everyone in the shop may need a dust mask even if only one person is creating dust.

How to Use WEST SYSTEM Epoxy

WEST SYSTEM 205 and 206 Hardeners and, to a lesser extent, 105 Resin, may affect you in two major ways. Hardeners are corrosive primary irritants and may cause varying degrees of chemical burns on direct contact to eyes and skin. Alone and when mixed with resin, they are also sensitizers: a poison ivy-like rash may appear on areas, usually the hands, arms, and face, which have been repeatedly exposed to them. We advise that you take extreme measures to avoid eye and skin contact with any of these materials.

Your skin may be irritated any time you carelessly handle hardeners or mixed epoxy. By contrast, sensitization usually occurs only after multiple exposures. These chemicals cause proteins to change in such a way that the body begins to produce antibodies to fight them off. Once sensitized, you will remain allergic to epoxy and hardener, and possibly to similar materials, for life. While dilution in resin reduces the toxicity of hardeners, mixtures should still be handled with adequate precautions.

The leading cause of sensitization, is, of course, direct exposure to resin, hardeners, mixed epoxy and their fumes. It follows that the best way to prevent it is to avoid all direct contact with and inhalation of these substances. Without exposure, antibodies simply will not develop and irritation will not be a problem.

Wear plastic gloves and eye protection whenever you handle WEST SYSTEM materials. If for some reason you can't wear gloves, use a protective skin cream. We prefer disposable plastic gloves to creams because they are less likely to wear through, and because when your work is done you can just peel them off and throw them away. If you have a particularly long bonding operation, wipe off the excess resin on your gloves or remove it with an industrial hand cleaner before it cures.

If, in spite of all your care, you drip some epoxy on your skin, remove it quickly with paper towels and waterless skin cleaner. Resin sets up faster on warm skin than on wood, and it may cure in minutes. Harsh detergents and solvents dry skin and make it more susceptible than usual to irritation. If, as a last resort, you decide to remove WEST SYSTEM resin from your hands with a solvent, choose one with low relative toxicity. Use it sparingly, and wash immediately with soap and water. Repeated exposure to solvents causes problems of its own, so do not rely on them as skin cleaners on a regular basis.

For big jobs, or if you are a member of a high risk group, apply cream to your forearms and face and put some on your hands under plastic gloves. On particularly messy projects, wear disposable, low-cost shop aprons and sleeves. Resin can soak through clothing and bond to your skin. If you spill epoxy on your garments, take them off immediately. Use paper towels and skin cleaner to remove WEST SYSTEM resin before it cures from both your skin and clothing.

Always wear protective clothing and a dust mask when you sand "green", partially cured epoxy. When it is fully cured, 7 to 30 days after application, depending on environmental conditions, WEST SYSTEM resin loses much of its toxicity. Until then, however, epoxy and its dust may cause skin rashes if you have been sensitized or have a sensitive body chemistry. This reaction is greatest when dust settles on skin which is already wet with perspiration. Inhalation of uncured epoxy dust may also cause asthma-like symptoms in sensitized individuals.

Good ventilation will help control dust, and it will also assist in eliminating the irritations which can be caused by resin, hardener and mixed epoxy fumes. Although these fumes usually present few problems, they can trigger reactions during large jobs or when epoxy boils as it cures. People who have been previously sensitized may develop rashes or constriction of the bronchial air passages after even minimal exposure to these vapors by skin contact or inhalation.

If epoxy is left around to cure in mixing pots in hot weather or in very large quantities, it may sometimes create a fire hazard. When too much heat is generated by the polymerization reaction, containers can melt and fires can start. When pots of leftover mixed epoxy are thrown in the trash before they've cured, the results can be dangerous. We therefore recommend that you move epoxy waste outdoors to a nonflammable surface where it can get plenty of air. Be careful not to burn your hands whenever your mixed resin and hardener appear to be heating up.

As a rule, it is easier and safer to dispose of small quantities of resin and hardener by mixing them together in their containers and allowing them to solidify. Solid waste disposal regulations vary from area to area and by quantities and use. Contact local officials to verify procedures in your town. Never pour WEST SYSTEM materials into areas which may cause pollution.

Solvents

Solvents are indispensable to the average boat builder. They can also be among the most hazardous substances in the boat shop. In recent years, both government and industry have taken increasingly critical looks at a wide variety of commonly used solvents. Some have been found to be so dangerous that they have been removed from the marketplace.

Most solvents are also extremely flammable. By themselves, in paints and other formulated products, they are frequent causes of industrial fires. It could be argued that the fire hazards posed by solvents are their greatest threats, to both human health and property.

For these reasons, it is imperative that you follow basic shop safety rules whenever you use solvents. Carefully study tables of flash points and permissible exposure levels before you use solvents, and then be sure to keep exposure down, ventilation up and open flames far away. Figure 1 lists important relative information about a number of solvents used in boatbuilding.

Boat builders typically use solvents irregularly, sometimes in questionable working conditions and almost always without sophisticated means of monitoring exposure levels. You might work with them for occasional cleanups, for 15 minutes at a stretch, or perhaps for as long as two or three hours during a solvent washing or painting operation. Although some solvents give odor warnings when exposure levels are high, these signals may be hard to recognize if you've been confined with the smell in an interior for a few hours or if you have a cold. Official organizations provide figures for the parts per million of solvent you may safely inhale over a forty hour work week, but if you are working twelve-hour days, seven days a week on a personal project and have no way of taking air samples, these numbers are of limited value.

In the absence of more precise ways of establishing safe solvent levels in your working environment, you must become an educated consumer and err on the side of safety. Although they are not intended as relative indicators of toxicity, established permissible expo-

Figure 1 — *Comparative toxicity profile of selected solvents*

Solvent	TLV (ppm)	Odor Threshold (ppm)	Anesthetic effect ppm/time	Evaporation rate (Butyl acetate = 1)
Acetone	1000	200-400[1]	N.S.[3]	7.7
Methylene chloride	200	310	900-1200 20 min. 2000 5 min.[4]	14.5
Methyl ethyl ketone (MEK)	200	25[2]	300 N.S.	4.6
Toluene	100	200[2]	200 8 hr. 600 3 hr.	1.5
Turpentine	100	No data	No data	.38
Xylene	100	No data	No data	.75

[1] 200-400 ppm was detected only upon initial contact; over 700 ppm cannot be detected. *Industrial Hygiene and Toxicology*, p. 1729.

[2] *Industrial Hygiene and Toxicology,* Vol. II, F.A. Patty, Ed., Interscience Division of John Wiley and Sons, New York, 1965.

[3] Not specified.

[4] Peak exposure limit in any 2 hour period. OSHA.

sure levels (PELs) provide some useful information if they are considered in conjunction with evaporation rates.

Acetone, which is used very frequently, has a very high safe exposure level, as measured by PEL, but a relatively high evaporation rate. This means that it will reach fume levels more rapidly than, say, xylene or turpentine. These two solvents evaporate slowly and have low acceptable exposure levels. Problems with them arise in one of their more common uses — spray painting. Because fumes can build up so quickly during this kind of application, avoid spraying paint unless you have a specially-designed ventilated booth or forced air respirator.

Evaporation rates and permissible fume levels can only partially guide you in choosing solvents. Fire hazard, as measured by flash and lower explosive limits, should also influence your decisions. A comparatively low flash point temperature indicates a comparatively hazardous substance. As Figure 2 indicates, the flammability of acetone is one of its major drawbacks. Some solvents are nonflammable and will neither ignite nor explode.

In order to run a risk of explosion, solvent fumes must reach fairly high concentrations. This is unlikely to happen in typical boatbuilding operations, where solvents are primarily used for cleaning, but danger increases as the amount of solvent used in a given time period increases, assuming little or no ventilation. Washing the entire interior surface of an enclosed hull with a quickly evaporating solvent such as acetone could raise fume levels to a point where explosion is a real possibility. Spray painting in an unventilated area may also invite trouble.

The highest danger of explosion occurs with a mixture of solvent fumes and wood dust in hot weather. Wood dust by itself has a dangerous explosion potential, and it lowers the concentration of solvent fumes needed to cause an explosion. As temperatures increase, the concentrations of solvents required for explosion drop. One worker, hand sanding, could not propel enough wood into the air to give any cause for worry, but several people operating power sanding equipment could. An open flame can set off an explosion, as can an accidental charge of static electricity or a spark from a malfunctioning sander.

Methylene chloride, a common and effective solvent, has a very high evaporation rate. There is some question about the reliability of its odor warning, so you should stop using it and move to a ventilated area well before concentrations are so high as to cause a strong smell. This solvent is nonflammable and will not explode.

In high concentrations, methylene chloride breaks down into carbon monoxide in the body and may cause variations in heartbeat and heart attacks. High levels of exposure may cause depression of the central nervous system. Controversial laboratory tests suggest that it may cause genetic changes and cancer in animals. Repeated skin exposure may result in irritation. Permissible exposure levels to methylene chloride are also controversial: the current OSHA PEL, 500 ppm over a 40-hour work week, has been questioned repeatedly and is five times higher than the standard advised by the American Conference of Government Industrial Hygienists. In spite of this, methylene chloride is usually considered to be among the least toxic of industrial solvents.

With careful, appropriate use, high concentrations of solvent fumes will not develop. If you follow the rules set forth earlier in this chapter, you should have no problems. If a coworker pays less attention to safety than you do, however, it may be helpful to be able to identify the more dangerous symptoms of overexposure.

Depression of the central nervous system, also called narcosis, is sometimes difficult to recognize. It may lead to loss of coordination, impairment of judgment and, in severe cases, "shrunken brain." Like drunks, people under the influence of a solvent sometimes don't realize the extent to which they have lost good sense.

Wood

Wooden boat shops tend to look alike: they are dusty places filled with piles of lumber and plywood.

Figure 2 — *Comparative flash points and lower explosive limits for selected solvents*

Solvent	Flash point[1] (closed cup test)	%LEL[2]
Acetone	0° F	2.9
Methylene chloride	NF[3]	—
Methyl ethyl ketone	28° F	1.8
Toluene	45° F	1.2
Turpentine	93° F	0.8
Xylene	81° F	1.0

[1] Flash point is the lowest temperature at which flammable vapor is given off by a liquid in a test vessel in sufficient concentration to be ignited in air when exposed momentarily to a source of ignition.
[2] Lower explosive limit is the volume percentage of the vaporized solvent that makes an explosive mixture in air.
[3] Non-flammable.

Boat builders live with the dust that results from sanding and sawing, and cherish odd bits of wood. Sawdust and timber are so "organic" that we assume they're benign. In fact, they aren't. Both can be significant hazards to your health.

Thanks in large part to high-speed abrasion techniques, modern woodworking equipment generates high concentrations of wood dust. It doesn't take a doctor to tell us that breathing this is bad. Inhalation of any dust in excessive quantities will cause bronchial congestion. The world is full of dust, and normally our respiratory systems deal successfully with large volumes of it. Mucus in our lungs attracts foreign particles, which are moved up and out on fine hairs called cilia. We can withstand incredible abuse, but there are limits. Smoking, dry air and high dust concentrations all strain our bodies. If two or three of these stressors combine, the burden becomes too great and significant health problems may develop.

Dust from two North American trees can lead to other respiratory ailments. Redwood dust is the cause of sequoiosis, an acute respiratory disease similar to pneumonia. Symptoms, including shortness of breath, bronchial congestion, dry coughing, chills, sweating and fever, usually appear a few hours after exposure. Repeated attacks can result in permanent scarring of lung tissue. Western red cedar dust can cause asthma or rhinitis, an inflammation of the nasal passages. The causative agent here seems to be plicatic acid, which may also give the wood its well-known smell.

As Figure 3 indicates, the resins, alkaloids, tannins, acids, salts and gums of some wood species are toxic to humans. Direct contact with dust, sap or oil from these trees may cause skin irritations and other allergic reactions. West Indian satinwood and mansonia are considered primary irritants because rashes and blisters will appear after a single contact. Cocobola and other tropical woods are sensitizers: skin inflammation may develop after repeated contact with them.

Reducing exposure to dusts, sap and oil will minimize their ill effects. Follow basic shop safety rules stated earlier in this chapter to prevent any difficulties. Be aware also that molds and fungi which grow in piles of sawdust can cause lung, nail and skin ailments, so clean around your tools regularly. Eliminate wood's final threat to your health by taking adequate precautions to prevent fires.

Figure 3 — *Toxic Woods*[1]

Wood type	Respiratory ailments[2]	Skin and eye allergies[3]
Cedar, western red (Thuja plicata)	X	X
Ebony (Diospyros)	X	X
Greenheart (Ocotea rodiaei)	X	X
Iroko (Chlorophora excelsa)	X	X
Mahogany, African (Khaya ivorensis)	X	X
Mahogany, American (Swietenia macrophylla)		X
Makore (Tieghemella heckelii)	X	X
Mansonia (Mansonia altissima)	X	X
Obeche (Triplochiton scleroxylon)	X	X
Opepe (Nauclea trillesu)	X	X
Ramin (Gonystylus bancanus)		X
Rosewood, Brazilian (Dalbergia nigra)		X
Rosewood, East Indian (Dalbergia lanfolia)		X
Satinwood, Ceylon (Chloroxylon swietenia)		X
Satinwood, West Indian (Fagara flava)		X
Sequoia, redwood (Sequoia sempervirens)	X	
Teak (Tectona granifs)		X

[1] This chart is excerpted from "Health Hazards in Woodworking," by Stanley Wellborn, in *Fine Woodworking,* Winter, 1977, and includes woods that are known to cause allergic, toxic, infectious or respiratory reactions. Although researchers point out that not everyone is sensitive to these woods, they warn that woodworkers should be particularly cautious when sanding or milling them.

[2] Respiratory ailments include bronchial disorders, asthma, rhinitis and mucosal irritations.

[3] Skin and eye allergies includes contact dermatitis, conjunctivitis, itching, and rashes.

A Note on Safety

The object of this chapter has been to acquaint you with the hazards of boatbuilding, particularly those associated with the construction techniques discussed in this book. We hope that we have not scared you away with this candid outline of what we feel are significant threats to your health. With foresight and intelligent precautions, you can easily control them and operate a safe shop.

There are many types of dust. We have discussed only a few of them here. Dusts from minerals such as asbestos and crystalline silica are very dangerous, mainly because the shape, durability and chemical composition of their particles make them, among other things, difficult to expel from the lungs. Fiberglass dust, as might result from sanding and grinding a hull, is also quite hazardous. We strongly recommend that you wear a dust mask when you work with glass tape and cloth. You'll find, also, that gloves and heavy clothing will reduce the number of itchy, irritating cuts that result from handling the material.

WEST SYSTEM fillers and additives present few health hazards. Use all of them in adequately ventilated areas, and, for comfort as much as safety, avoid inhalation. When mixed with epoxy and fully cured, our additives sand to inert dust.

Many other boat shop hazards exist. If you have questions or problems, talk with your doctor. Several recent publications provide excellent safety information for artists and craftspeople. We urge you look for these and to thoroughly research the substances you use.

In this chapter, particularly on the subject of solvents, we have purposely presented extreme cases.

In normal boatbuilding situations you probably run equal chances of overexposure to solvent, fire, and injury from a power tool. It's self-defeating to worry a great deal about solvents if you are careless about using your table saw or sloppy about fire prevention. In the end, when it comes to setting the rules and practices of your shop, your health and safety are in your hands.

To a very great extent, health hazards in any boatbuilding operation rise and fall directly in proportion to the exercise of plain old good sense. If you master basic safety principles, take responsibility for enforcing rules and make decisions well, your shop will be a safe place in which to work.

Chapter 9

Laminating & Bonding Techniques

Our methods of boatbuilding are simple and flexible because they rely on a few very basic skills and procedures: laminating, bonding, scarfing, coating and finishing. Detailed instructions on using WEST SYSTEM* Brand epoxy in each of these applications are provided here and in the following chapters of this book.

In building our boats, we use two basic types of bonding procedures, one for joining structural framework and interior items, and the other for constructing hull and deck skins. This chapter will concentrate on the first of these, and includes instructions for laminating wood, laminating wood with core materials, and applying fillet joints. Chapters 17 through 21 provide detailed information on various methods of laminating hull skins.

We believe that bonding is the most efficient and structurally sound way to join pieces of wood. While our techniques for bonding wood fibers in epoxy resin are somewhat similar to the methods of bonding glass fiber in polyester resin used in fiberglass boat construction, we use much less resin.

Principles of Laminating Lumber

Frames, ribs, keels, stems and deck beams are structural elements that are usually made by laminating several pieces of lumber stock to form the finished parts. The basic reason for laminating these items is to achieve the desired shape of the particular parts as exactly as possible. Traditionally, these shapes were formed by steam bending, by using wood with a natural curve similar to that desired, or by sawing curves on various segments of straight stock and joining them together with fasteners to form the shape desired.

Besides achieving the desired shape, laminating wood has the following side advantages:

(1) High strength with low potential for failure due to defect. Any one piece of wood may be compromised with a defect, but if several pieces are laminated together, a defect in one of the pieces is only a minor problem; thus, the more pieces involved in a lamination, the lower the failure rate due to defects.

(2) A curved lamination made up of many thin pieces of wood relieves most internal stresses prior to the bonding of the parts into one unit. Internal stresses can easily develop in thicker solid stock.

(3) Laminating can also be an economical use of material. You can make use of shorter pieces of stock by incorporating scarf joints, following procedures described in Chapter 10, within a laminate. You can also join smaller pieces to make up the width you want.

The thickness of each layer of stock within a laminate is crucial to its success. Choices here depend totally on the radius to which the piece must conform. Generally, we select a thickness which bends easily around the desired curve, checking it by sawing up a sample and bending it around the form or shape over which we plan to laminate. If it feels a bit stiff and difficult to bend, we plane it down until it's easier to position. When you choose a stock thickness, remember that the stiffness of wood is proportional to its thickness cubed, so if one piece is twice as thick as another piece of the same species, it will be about eight times as stiff. Be sensitive to small changes in stock dimension because they have major implications for the make-up of your laminate.

Thickness of laminating stock will also affect *springback*. Any lamination will retain a slight bit of memory. When clamps are released and a piece is freed from its form, its curve will relax and become slightly wider than the form. This new dimension is sometimes referred to as the *springback shape*. There is less springback in thinner laminations.

Keep in mind that while it may be easy to bend one layer of wood over a form, it will be a little more difficult to bend many layers. If you have a total of ten veneers to bend at the same time, the combined resistance of all of the pieces may be more than you are prepared to handle with the clamping method you have devised.

Don't saw stock thinner than it needs to be. Except for a possible reduction in springback, usually nothing is gained structurally by adding more layers to a laminate. When you use thin layers where thicker ones would work well, you spend unnecessary time sawing, laminating and bonding the increased surface area.

Even when laminating is not needed to achieve a desired shape, we always laminate when the stock

* TRADEMARK OF GOUGEON BROTHERS, INC., U.S.A.

needed exceeds 1 inch in thickness. With lumber stock thicker than this, the potential for internal stresses that may cause problems later on is too great, especially with kiln-dried lumber, which is the most widely available on the market today.

Preparing Stock for Laminating

The major goal when manufacturing stock for laminating is to prepare the most dimensionally accurate stock possible which, when stacked together, will have as few voids as possible, and will therefore require less gap-filling adhesive for proper bonding. Most laminating stock will have to be sawn to size, and we recommend a table saw of at least 1 horsepower with a 10 inch blade so that you can make both accurate and smooth cuts on the surface of the stock being sawn. This is especially important if you do not own or have access to a thickness planer with which to further dress the laminating stock. Check the accuracy of your saw to make sure that the guide is parallel with the blade and that the blade is positioned exactly at right angles to the table surface. Make cuts over 3 inches in depth (depending upon the species of wood) by sawing in from both sides; that is, make a saw cut of several inches from one side, then turn the material end-for-end and saw in several inches from the other side. You should set up ramps both in front and in back of the saw to hold the stock in the proper plane with the saw table surface as it passes through the blades, and set up spring tension guides to hold the stock flush with both the table surface and the saw guide. Even with the best sawing techniques, there will be some discrepancy in dimensional accuracy, but the stock is usually acceptable for most laminating situations.

If you have a thickness planer, pass all of the stock through it. A very light cut will true up any dimensional inaccuracy. Craftsmen who take very good care of their tools sometimes wax the tables of their planers. Since wax can interfere with the quality of a bond, remove any that might be on your planer before you begin.

Forms for Laminating

The block on floor method is most commonly used to manufacture laminated ribs, frames and stems. A wooden floor or a thick piece of plywood serves as the base to which you can affix blocks to form the shape you desire. Transfer the shape to be laminated to this surface from the lofting board. Then saw triangular blocks, as illustrated in Figure 1, and drill several holes in their backs for screws or nails. Fasten an adequate number of blocks along the outside perimeter of the

shape on the floor. Then position a second set of blocks opposite each of these, leaving a sufficient distance in between to insert both the lamination to be clamped and a clamping wedge. If the curve is severe, use the clamping wedge with a pad, which you can place against the stock. Drive the wedge between the blocks on the floor and the clamping pad. You will only

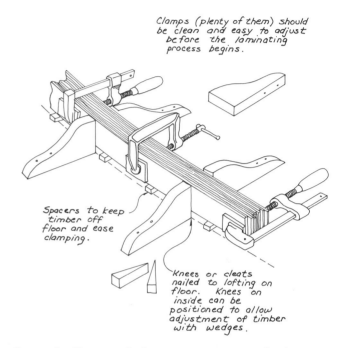

Figure 1—Cleats and clamping arrangement for laminating structural pieces on floor or base board.

Figure 2—Laminating a long structural member for a trimaran cross beam using cleats secured to lofting floor.

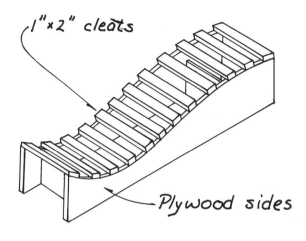

Figure 3—Simple form for laminating wider pieces.

Figure 4—Laminating floor timbers using stringers as the form.

need enough blocks to hold the laminate to its shape because you can use any number of clamps between the blocks to achieve enough clamping pressure on the laminate once you have developed its shape.

Some laminations may be too wide to be handled easily with the block on floor method. In these cases, you can manufacture a simple mold form similar to that shown in Figure 3. Lay out the shape you want on thick construction grade plywood, allowing for the thickness of the lath planking which you will nail across the plywood edge. Cut out two identical pieces of plywood and place them at the desired distance from one another. Then fasten and bond the lath planking into position at desired intervals. Add any additional bracing that is needed to make the structure sufficiently sturdy. Using additional crosspieces to press the lamination material against the form, clamp the laminating stock to this form by positioning a clamp at either edge of the mold form.

Often, the hull framework itself serves as a natural laminating form, and you can save a great deal of time by taking advantage of this. Take special care that no damage occurs to the framework during the laminating procedure. Shield the framework from clamp marks with the use of clamping pads, and protect members against any excess resin with a plastic sheet barrier. Figure 4 shows some frames being laminated using the stringers as a form. Further details on this type of laminating procedure are discussed in Chapter 21.

Allowance for Springback

All laminations will relax from the curve that they have been clamped to. This springback may range from 1/16 inch to several inches, depending upon three factors: the severity of the curve the lamination must take, the thickness of the stock that is laminated and the number of pieces used to make up a lamination. Because of these factors, there are no hard and fast rules you can use to determine the amount of springback that a lamination will have. After manufacturing a few laminations, you will quickly develop a feel for what the springback may be in a given situation. The object, of course, is to try to anticipate what the springback might be and then to overbend your lamination, so that when it relaxes, it will assume the exact shape desired. However, it is rare for a lamination to end up exactly as desired, although you can come very close and then take several corrective measures, which will be discussed later on.

The Dry Run and Clamping Procedures

If you don't have much experience or if you are faced with a complex or unusually shaped form, try a dry run of your lamination. Assemble and clamp your pieces with no epoxy to see if there are any flaws in your approach. Also check at this time to be sure that you have enough clamps. Because there is no epoxy in the way, you will be able to see gaps and take appropriate corrective action, including increasing clamping pressure and re-machining your stock. Once WEST SYSTEM resin is applied, you will have only a short time to correct any mistakes. If something goes wrong, you could lose the whole lamination and all the work and material that goes with it.

To distribute clamping pressure over more area, make up *clamping pads* out of pieces of wood to be placed between the clamp jaws and the stock. The pads will also prevent any clamp marks from occurring on the lamination surface. When you have clamped up the lamination to your satisfaction, it is sometimes helpful to mark the position of each clamp on the stock, so

Figure 5—Cleats are being screw fastened to base board to force laminates into shape required. Clamps in pile in upper right will be used during dry run and final lamination.

that you can reposition it quickly when actual laminating begins. When you remove the clamps from their trial run positions, place them close by so that you won't have to hunt around for them and can position each clamp as quickly as possible.

Clamps are usually heavy and cumbersome, and can take a lot of time to position and tighten. It is extremely important before laminating begins that there be a reserve of clamps close by, that they be of sufficient size and that they be checked for workability (i.e., that no glue lumps are on the threads). Whenever we are preparing for laminating without the luxury of a dry run, we line up more clamps and clamp pads than we actually think will be needed, and place them at various intervals around the laminating area for quick access. For speed, we recommend that you use the adjustable bar-type clamps rather than C-clamps, which take much longer to fit into place. If you do use C-clamps, we suggest that you open them all beforehand to the approximate dimension you will need.

Applying WEST SYSTEM Epoxy

For laminations that are large and are composed of many pieces, you should organize the adhesive application procedure so that it can progress quickly. Cover a bench with polyethylene sheet and nail several sticks across it to keep the laminations from touching the bench surface when they are covered with adhesive and turned over. Coat one surface of the lamination with an adhesive mixture, roll the piece over on the strips and coat the opposite surface. The bottom and top pieces of the lamination, of course, need coating on one surface only. As you coat the pieces with adhesive, assemble them in a neat stack in preparation for insertion in the form. From the time that you first apply

it, you will have about an hour to apply the adhesive to all of the lamination members, insert the members in the form, and apply the clamping pressure. If the temperature is over 85°, you may not have this much time, even when using the 206 hardener. When laminating, adhesive application usually requires the most time, but several applicators working simultaneously can speed up this operation.

We almost always use high density filler to make up the adhesive mixture for laminating, determining the thickness of this mixture according to the quality of our wood. Rough sawn surfaces may require epoxy and filler mixed to gap-filling, thick syrup consistency. With sufficient clamping pressure, the epoxy used to laminate well-planed stock will need little if any filler to guarantee adequate adhesion.

Thoroughly stir your epoxy and filler and pour it into a roller pan. Use a foam roller sawn to desired width — (if possible, the width of the lamination) — to apply the adhesive to your wood. Roll vigorously with downward pressure to control the amount of resin on the bonding surface. When a thicker adhesive mixture is rolled on the surface, it will leave a thicker film, which is usually the desired effect. A thinner adhesive mixture is easier to control and you can roll it on the surface either in a very thin film or in thicker quantities, as you wish. Again, the quality of the laminating material will determine how much resin you need to apply to the mating surfaces.

When you have applied adhesive to all of the mating surfaces (we always coat *both* mating surfaces), you are ready to form the lamination. If you have already done a dry run, the only thing you need to add is polyethylene, which you can wrap around the lamination stack to prevent it from becoming bonded to any of the form members, clamps or the floor. Be careful to prevent any of this plastic from inadvertently becoming lodged between some of the laminations, preventing a good bond. Then apply clamping pressure, taking up the clamps slowly as the adhesive squeezes out from between the laminations. Excess adhesive moves to the edges slowly, and you may have to tighten all clamps or wedges at several intervals of perhaps 10 minutes. A small amount of adhesive escaping from the edges is a healthy sign that there are no voids within the lamination itself. However, if an excessive amount of adhesive is escaping, then you probably applied more than was needed, and with the next lamination you should try applying a little less. There is no need to apply excessive force to the lamination with the clamps; in fact, excessive clamping pressure may create undesirable stresses within a lamination. Good, solid *contact* pressure is all you really need.

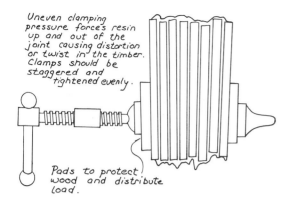

Uneven clamping pressure forces resin up and out of the joint causing distortion or twist in the timber. Clamps should be staggered and tightened evenly.

Pads to protect wood and distribute load.

Figure 6—Pads and clamping pressure.

Fitting to Shape

All laminations, after they are manufactured, will have what we call a *mating surface,* which you will eventually bond to another part of the boat. This surface is usually the shape used to determine the setting up of the lamination forms.[1] When the adhesive is cured, remove the lamination from its form and check the mating surface for accuracy. You can do this with a template made from the body plan, or perhaps by fitting it in the hull or mold set-up where it will eventually be positioned. If springback has been severe, but it is a light lamination that is easily bent, you can probably bend the lamination to the desired position when you install it in the boat and should have no problems. For a heftier lamination with springback which you cannot easily rebend to its original shape, remark and machine it to the proper dimension, using a saw and hand plane. In addition, you may need to bevel the lamination or do other special machining, such as notching for stringers or keel. Usually this work is done when the lamination is fitted into its final position in the boat.

If the laminated piece will be exposed in the finished boat, as ribs and frames sometimes are, plane or sand its sides and face and round its edges as desired. It is far easier to precoat and prefinish at your workbench than inside your hull, so do these jobs before installing your part.

Using Core Materials

Lightweight core materials are often sandwiched between denser, load-bearing skins of materials like fiberglass. These cores may also be laminated between

Frame 7—Laminated frames fit to hull.

two pieces of wood to form rigid, light panels. This is a particularly effective way to build extra stiffness, with little additional weight, into parts which have a lot of surface area, and may be used on cockpit floors, bunk bottoms, bulkheads, partitions, decks, cabin tops and even hulls.

Many materials have good panel stiffness, but many of these are also relatively heavy by the square foot. A

Figure 8—Laminated floors, fit and prefinished, and ready to be installed.

core must be lightweight, and it must have adequate crush and shear strengths. We've found three core materials which bond well with epoxy and produce good results when laminated between wood skins: lightweight wood, such as balsa, in both flat and end grain dimensions; various types of foam; and manufactured honeycomb materials, especially resin-impregnated honeycomb paper.

[1] A lamination can be formed over a male or female form. The female form would be the mating surface for a rib or frame lamination. If a male form is used, the thickness of the rib or frame being laminated should be deducted from the form dimensions to manufacture a lamination with a correct mating surface.

Figure 9—"DN" class iceboat. Hull bottom showing core material and frames. Outer skin has not yet been bonded to this panel.

Balsa is one of the better core materials. When used in its end grain dimension, it makes a core with excellent crush resistance. We've also tried balsa in flat grain, using it both as a core and to improve structural strength by contributing to the overall stiffness and strength of a panel. Unfortunately, balsa is fairly expensive and it is impractical to use in the end grain without a special commercial treatment which makes it even more costly.

We have often used other lightweight woods in flat grain dimension as cores in some framework laminations. Laminated deck beams are good examples of how to save weight higher up in a hull by combining proper proportions of a low density wood, say, cedar, with a high density wood, Douglas fir or white ash. The resulting lamination has adequate stiffness and

strength and is much lighter than one made entirely of high density wood.

We rarely use foam cores. Semirigid varieties, such as Airex™ and Klegecel™, are the only foams which we have found adequate, and even these are not as impressive in strength to weight as light woods. Foams crush and have great impact resistance, and they are better insulators than other core materials, but they are so expensive that they are usually the most costly part of wood lamination. Although WEST SYSTEM epoxy will not chemically react in a destructive way with most foams unless it is applied so heavily that it becomes very hot as it cures, in most situations, given a choice between wood and foam cores, we prefer wood.

Resin-impregnated honeycomb paper, sold as Verticel™, is our favorite core material. At about 50¢ a board foot — (prices vary by cell size, resin content and thickness) — it is the cheapest of the various honeycombs available, and it is easy to bond and apply. We've used Verticel for years and have found its light weight and excellent crush and shear strengths perfectly adequate in most applications. Honeycomb paper is helpful on both flat and curved surfaces. It can be applied to slightly compounded areas such as decks and cabin tops because its cells are able to bend slightly and deform. We recommend 15% resin content Verticel.

Interlaminate application rates of WEST SYSTEM epoxy vary a great deal. Tests on samples of wood hull laminate show an average rate of 12.8 square feet per pound of resin per glueline. The application rate of a medium-density mixture of resin and filler, applied with a notched plastic spreader to bond core materials to plywood skins, is about 18 square feet per pound of resin. A rate of approximately 28 square feet per pound can be expected for mixtures applied over coated surfaces. Factors determining these rates include surface condition of the substrate, pot life of the resin, ambient temperature, work habits, size of the job and quality of clamping pressure.

Bonding Core Materials

Different core materials require slightly different bonding techniques. End grain wood and foam absorb resin at unusually high rates, and allowances must be made for this in order to guarantee good joint strength. The cells of resin-impregnated paper honeycomb bond to wood in a very atypical pattern of small fillets. Normal laminating procedures are sufficient, however, when your core material is low density wood in flat grain dimension.

Large quantities of WEST SYSTEM epoxy will penetrate end grain wood. When too much resin is absorbed by a wood core, there will not be enough adhesive for a strong bond with a skin, and the joint will be starved for resin. To solve this problem, we recommend a two-step application procedure. First, use a foam roller to apply standard resin to the surfaces to be bonded. Your coating should be adequate but not overabundant. Next, apply a mixture of adhesive and 406 filler, in thick syrup consistency, to the core. Use enough of the mixture to fill any voids between the core and the surrounding skins.

This adhesive mixture may be too thick to apply evenly with a foam roller, so use a modified plastic squeegee to apply even, controlled amounts of thicker adhesive, especially over large areas. To make this applicator, cut notches along one edge of a standard plastic spreader, as shown in Figure 10. Experiment to find the notch depth and frequency which will deposit the correct amount of epoxy/filler mix on your wood. An easy way to cut the edge of a squeegee is to use pinking shears.

Foam cores absorb slightly less resin than end grain wood, and their absorption rates are very predictable. When the large pores on the foam's surface are filled, the rest of the epoxy/filler blend will fill gaps between the core and laminate skin. Since the object is to make a bond which is at least as strong as the foam but is lightweight, use low density, gap-filling filler; even if the mixture is heavily loaded with filler, the bond will be stronger than the foam. To be sure that all voids are filled on more porous foams, use additional low density additive to make a thicker adhesive mixture. A notched squeegee will help force thick adhesive into foam pores.

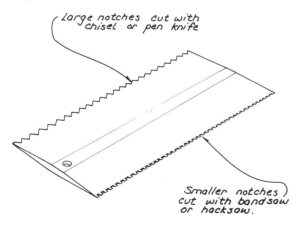

Figure 10—Flexible plastic squeegee notched to apply adhesive.

Figure 11—Applying adhesive with notched plastic squeegee.

Paper honeycomb presents an unusual bonding situation. Because it is made up of cells ranging from ¼ to ½ inch in diameter, this type of core is actually joined to only a small percentage of the total area of the surface skins. Many little fillets form when honeycomb is bonded in lamination. The adhesive "gets legs" as it is applied to the core, and, due to its surface tension, travels up the cell walls a distance of up to 1/8 inch, although 1/16 inch is normal. This process results in a bond which is far stronger than the paper honeycomb.

Take steps to be sure that these little fillets develop. First, use a foam roller to wet out the edges of the honeycomb with a regular 5 parts resin to 1 part hardener epoxy mixture. Don't try to deposit quantities of resin on the edges as you do this — the goal is to saturate cell wall edges in the same way that you apply a first penetrating coat of epoxy to wood. Then, still using the foam roller, apply a thick coat of standard epoxy to the surfaces of the structural skins. If your skins are precoated, this is unnecessary. In this case, follow the directions in Chapter 11 to prepare the coated surfaces for bonding. To avoid the formation of high spots, assemble your lamination before the epoxy on the honeycomb has a chance to set up.

If the fit between a honeycomb core and plywood skins is not close, or if you suspect that your clamping pressure may be inadequate, you may wish to modify this technique. Coat your core with regular epoxy and then coat your wood with a mixture of epoxy and low density filler. The viscosity of this mixture depends on the fit between core and skins. Use more filler if you have a rough fit, less if your surfaces present fewer gaps. If you know that there is perfect contact between your core and wood, you may need no additive, provided that you apply the resin in sufficient quantity.

When you use a honeycomb core, be careful to avoid dry bonds within the laminate. This is usually a result of the wood's absorbing too much resin; if most of the epoxy you apply is absorbed by the skins, there will not be enough on the surface to develop the fillet bond needed for maximum strength. One way to prevent this is to coat the wood, wait an hour or so until the epoxy is tacky, and then bond the honeycomb to the skins.

Whatever the core material and adhesive mixture used, structural strength will be only as good as the quality of the bond that is developed between the components. We suggest that you make a sample laminate of the combination that you intend to use, then destruction test it so that you can assess the quality of the bond. This is a simple and quick way to determine both the ideal mixture and the amount of adhesive needed for a given surface to ensure adequate bonding. Once you have tested several laminates with a given type of core material, you will have gained enough experience to be able to determine the adequate amount of adhesive for a given surface without having to test each laminate.

To perform a destruction test, make two samples, each 3 inches wide by 10 inches long. Place two 2 inch by 2 inch by 4 inch blocks of wood near the edge of a bench, roughly 10 inches apart, and support one test sample on them. Using a clamp in the middle of your sample, slowly deflect the wood toward the bench until it breaks. Study the relationships between the various components to determine where the sample failed and how. Take your second sample, put it in a vise and hit it with a large hammer. This will give you some idea of how well your sample will withstand shock loads.

Forming and Clamping Cored Laminates

Cored laminates are easy to make if their surfaces are flat or in only one plane, a bit more difficult if slightly curved, and very difficult if curved in more than one plane.

To manufacture flat parts such as bulkheads, partitions, doors, counter tops, bunk bottoms and floors, look for a flat area which is at least as large as the part to be laminated. This can be the floor or a bench. If you are planning many flat laminates, it is worth building a special form. Your work area must be perfectly even, with no twists or warps.

Assemble components, usually two outer skins and a core, on your surface, apply adhesive, and then use weights for pressure over the surface area of your assembly. Almost anything which is easy to handle and weighs from 3 to 10 pounds can be used as a weight. Many common items, including bricks and small pieces of scrap steel, work well. In our shop, we now regularly use double-wrapped sandbags.

The amount of weight you need depends on your particular lamination. In all cases, it should be sufficient for *contact* pressure between layers. If the outer skins are thin plywood, very little weight is necessary unless the panels are badly warped. Distribute pressure over the entire surface of the skin, using leftover stringer stock, scrap lumber of equal thickness, or thicker pieces of plywood or particle board to spread the load.

You can apply some clamping pressure to the lamination with staples. Usually, cored laminations have an outer perimeter that is made up of a solid wood material which we refer to as *core framing*. This material is made up beforehand from stock the exact thickness of the core material, and can be used wherever desired in conjunction with the core material within the laminate. Some cored laminates may be designed to have a great deal of core framing within the laminate so that only staple pressure is needed for assembly. However, staple assembly is usually successful only with thicker plywood skins because of their increased panel stiffness. In most cases, even with the use of staples, weighting will still be needed to ensure a good bond between the laminate components.

We usually plan our cored laminate layout right on the plywood panel from which we will cut one of the exterior skins. Once the perimeter of the laminate is determined, you can lay out the exact positions and dimensions of the core framing right on the panel. Then cut the laminate skin slightly larger than size (to

Figure 12—Deck constructed using light beams and Verticel as core materials. See Chapter 25 for a full description of this deck construction.

facilitate final fitting), and make a duplicate that will become the second skin on the opposite side of the core material. Saw the prepared core framing to length and position it around the perimeter of the laminate and wherever else desired within the interior of the laminate. When the core framing is fitted, bond it into position on the marked skin surface using either temporary or permanent staples to hold the pieces in place until the adhesive can cure. Then fit the core material around the core framing and apply the adhesive. With all of the parts to the cored laminate in place, you can complete the laminate by bonding on the second skin.

You can make *slightly curved cored laminates* using techniques similar to those used for flat laminates, but you must build a special curved form. This curved form

Figure 14—Cockpit sole with curved shape using core laminates. This was accomplished by laminating a curve in core frames before they were bonded in place.

must be a fair arc over which the components of the laminate will bend easily. A proper form will help ensure that the curve in the laminate is fair and will require fewer clamps and weights for good contact pressure between the components. A slight curve can also facilitate clamping. Position several long boards of adequate stiffness across the laminate at given intervals and clamp them down to the form at each end.

Cored laminates with compound curves are very difficult to manufacture unless you use enough core framing material within the laminate to allow for a good deal of staple pressure. Even then, you should not make these cored laminates of solid panels, but should mold them with veneers or strips of plywood over a form, as discussed in Chapter 18. The most successful compounded cored laminates have been manufactured using vacuum bag techniques. Unfortunately, preparations for this method require a great deal of time and it is uneconomical when only one laminate is to be manufactured.

Bonding with the Fillet

The fillet has become one of the most versatile wood bonding methods, especially for joining parts at or near right angles to each other. Basically, a fillet is a continuous bead of thickened resin mixture applied to the angle between two parts to be joined. It increases the surface area of the bond and serves as a structural brace. Filleting requires no fasteners of any kind and can result in a joint that is as strong as the parts being joined together. The use of fillets in conjunction with fiberglass tape is fully explained in Chapter 22.

There are some limitations with filleting, however. The fillet cannot join two materials end-for-end and is

Figure 13—Cockpit seats showing matching panels and core framing. Core material can be fit around the framing. In this case, framing itself was adequate to support plywood panels.

most successful for joining parts at roughly right angles. The fillet also works best when joining thinner wood material, such as plywood up to ¼ inch thick. At this size, it is relatively easy to manufacture a joint that is equal to material strength. As the material joined becomes thicker, the fillet size must increase accordingly. The large fillet becomes less attractive because of material costs (wood is much cheaper than WEST SYSTEM resin) and application difficulties (a large fillet becomes very unwieldy as its mass increases, due to the consistency of the material in the uncured stage).

A fillet is especially effective when joining parts that meet at difficult angles. A good example would be a bulkhead that meets with the hull skin at varying angles along its perimeter. Traditionally, a wood cleat would be laboriously laminated and fitted to join hull and bulkhead, requiring many hours. However, a fillet of the proper size may be just as effective structurally and can be installed easily and quickly. Other interior items, such as cabinets, bunks, partitions, seats, counters and floors, can also be quickly installed in the hull with the use of the fillet. Some of these items, such as shelves and cabinets, may be installed with small fillets that, although not up to material strength, may be adequate because they serve no critical structural purpose.

We often use the fillet to reinforce existing joints. The fillet can be a simple and fast way to increase the bonding surface area between two parts. For example, you can give a frame or stringer more contact bonding area with the hull skin by installing a fillet on either side of the member. The alternative might be to choose a thicker stringer or deck beam than is really needed for the sole purpose of developing more bonding area; the fillet can solve the problem with considerably less weight.

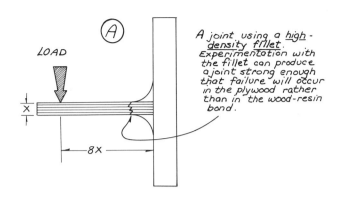

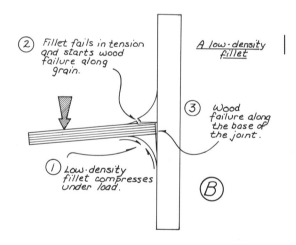

Figure 16—Test results and failure modes for samples using low- and high-density fillets.

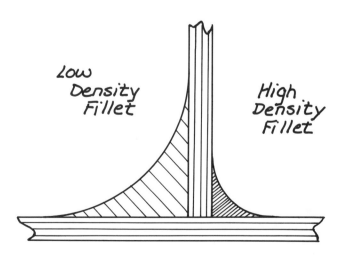

Figure 15.

To make up filleting mixture, use WEST SYSTEM resin and various fillers. The object is to make the best joint at the least weight and therefore to use the lowest density filleting material possible. At the same time, your joint must have enough strength so that any joint failure will occur in the wood rather than in the fillet itself. Our 406 Colloidal Silica filler is stronger and heavier than our low density filler. For high-strength applications, we use 406 filler mixed with resin to a peanut butter consistency. This produces a material which spreads easily but does not sag under its own weight.

In many situations, a high density fillet is not needed because its physical properties are far above the grain strength of wood, so we make up a lower density material using a combination of 406 and low density fillers, varying the proportions depending on the strength required. WEST SYSTEM 405 Filleting Blend may be added to mixtures that will be used for exposed fillets on certain woods. Its color will blend well with some woods to make fillets less conspicuous.

Figure 16 shows the results of tests we performed using various plywood thicknesses, fillers and fillet sizes. These results apply only to the specific plywood we tested and might be different if another wood was used. Because of the many variables involved, we cannot advise on the sizes and types of fillets needed for every application. You can easily perform your own testing to determine the exact fillet you need. This type of testing will also quickly give you a feel for the strengths and limitations of the fillet as a joining method. When you have gained knowledge through use, you will find many places in your project where fillets will both improve your structure and save your time.

Make a test sample similar to the one in Figure 16, using the material you plan to join. Take an educated guess about the filler and fillet size needed to develop material strength. Make a fillet on your sample and allow it to cure for at least 24 hours, or less if you apply heat. Put the control part of your test piece in a vise and load it. The load should be exerted a distance of about eight times the thickness of the material, measured from the base of the joint.

If your sample breaks clean, leaving the fillet intact, you have achieved *material strength,* the breaking strength of the material as a cantilevered beam. This is considered strong enough for most engineering in boat construction. If the break occurs within the fillet or the wood fiber of the control piece, make a new sample with a larger fillet. Repeat the test until the fillet performs to your satisfaction.

Applying the Fillet

There are five steps in the process of applying a fillet:
(1) fitting and marking the parts to be joined,
(2) administering epoxy/filler mixture to the joint,
(3) forming the fillet to the size and shape desired,
(4) cleaning up of the fillet,
(5) sanding and coating.
If the fillet is to be a practical joining method, you must learn to apply it with both ease and speed. At the

same time, you will want to make fillets that are pleasing to the eye so that they will not detract from the beauty of your boat. Your first try at filleting will probably be awkward and slow, but fortunately it doesn't take long to develop reasonable skills.

Fit all parts as carefully as possible. Reducing gaps between pieces reduces mechanical loading on the filler and improves joint strength potential. When you are satisfied with your fit, make several surmarks up and down the joint and across both pieces so that you can remove and accurately replace them later. To save mixing and preparation time, fit and mark a number of parts and then bond them all in one large filleting operation.

If the parts to be joined are uncoated, it's a good idea to apply a initial coating of resin to the area of the joint. When fillets are made on bare wood, the substrate may absorb too much resin from the filleting mixture. Then, the mixture thickens and becomes almost impossible to work with. If the wood has been precoated, as described in Chapter 11, you will need only to sand the joint area to be sure of an adequate bond.

When the parts are ready, mix epoxy and appropriate fillers. Good smooth fillets depend on the correct thickness of the filleting mixture, and with a little experience you will quickly learn what works best for you. The viscosity of this mixture becomes more crucial with larger fillets. As the mass and weight of your epoxy/filler combination increase, so does its tendency to sag.

One solution to this problem is to make the mix even thicker, but this results in fillets which are difficult to apply and which will require a lot of clean up later. Very thick filleting mixture may not properly penetrate the substrate and so may result in weak bonding. We find that a two-step installation procedure, applying

Figure 17—Disposable syringe used for applying adhesive bead.

70

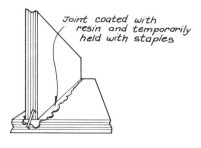

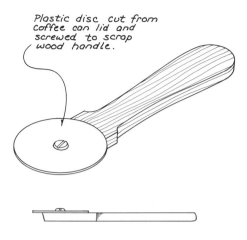

Figure 19—Simple plastic filleting tool.

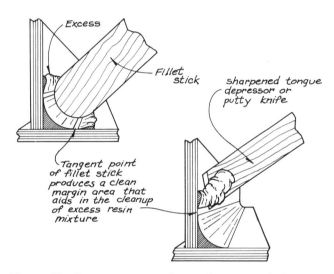

Figure 18—Proper sequence for application and cleaning of fillet.

about 60% of the joint on the first pass and the remainder when this stiffens up, is effective in this situation.

Begin making your fillet by applying a liberal amount of fillet mixture to the mating edge of the joint. Then position the part so that its surmarks line up exactly, using staples, small nails or clamps as appropriate to hold it temporarily in place. Much of the epoxy/filler mixture you use here will squeeze out and become part of the fillet; the rest will fill any gaps between the two parts.

Next, apply fillet mixture all along the line of the joint in the quantities needed for the fillet size desired. A flat stick with a rounded end is a good tool for moving adhesive from pot to joint. Continue using your stick to smooth out the fillet and to remove excess material and redeposit it where needed. Applying just the right amount of epoxy/filler blend to a joint is one of the keys to filleting success. It is better to add just a little more than to end up short because it's more difficult to add material later than to remove a little excess.

In the past we have recommended a variety of tools for fillet application. Disposable cake decorating bags are clean and accurate for laying down a bead of fillet mixture, but they are very difficult to find. Syringes, too, make good applicators, but they require time-consuming loading and cleaning. While it may seem to be efficient to use your finger to apply and smooth fillets, don't do it. A splinter in the joint may cut through your glove and into your finger, and this can be quite painful.

To finish your joint, take a piece of thin stock a little wider than the fillet itself and round off one end. Cut the radius of this curve to match the desired radius of your fillet when the stick is held so that it bisects the joint. Because this dimension is very important in controlling fillet size, round off several sticks and experiment with them. With a *fillet stick* of any given radius, you can further control fillet size by changing the angle of your passes. When you hold the stick at a 10° angle to your joint, your fillet will be flatter, while if you hold it at a larger angle, it will be curved.

The experienced applicator can form a perfect fillet with only one pass of the fillet stick over a properly applied fillet mixture. It is not unusual, however, to need several passes to form and smooth the fillet to the desired state. Always make the final pass with the fillet stick with some firmness so that the excess fillet mixture will be deposited on either side of the fillet. The pressure on the fillet stick is important because it creates a gap between the excess material and the fillet so that you can clean away the excess without disturbing the fillet. Figure 19 shows a plastic-tipped filleting tool that has worked particularly well to form very smooth surfaces on the fillet.

Clean up of the fillet begins with careful removal of any excess material. Usually a 1 inch putty knife or sharpened stick of about the same width is used in conjunction with a paper cup or can. Carefully scrape away the excess from either side of the fillet, and then deposit it in the container by wiping the side of the knife on the container edge. Repeat this procedure until all of the excess has been removed.

After the fillet has begun its cure and started to stiffen (anywhere from 30 minutes to 2 hours, depending on fillet size and temperature), you can do some further smoothing of the fillet surface with more passes of the fillet stick. A rough fillet surface or protruding edges can be smoothed considerably, especially if you catch the fillet at just the right stage in the cure cycle, and this saves a lot of sanding later on.

When the fillet has achieved a full cure, you can, of course, sand it as smooth as desired, but this is hard work, especially with the high density fillet of 406 filler. Fortunately, a properly installed fillet should need very little sanding to achieve adequate smoothness. Usually we use hand held 80 grit sandpaper for smoothing fillets, being careful not to damage any wood grain on either side of the fillet. When the fillet is completed, we always apply one coat of standard resin over the entire fillet surface. You can do this when you apply a coat of resin to the general area.

Chapter 10

Scarfing

It's very difficult to buy lumber and plywood in the right lengths for boat construction. When we do manage to find wood which is long enough, it is usually too expensive to consider. As a result, we've developed our own *scarfing* procedures, and use them to make long boards, panels, plywood and veneers out of shorter ones.

Scarfing is a basic and essential boatbuilding skill. When a well-made scarf is bonded with WEST SYSTEM* Brand epoxy, it can be as strong as the material it joins. Desired lengths of lumber and plywood may be built up with no increase in the width or thickness of the material at the joint. It may seem that this procedure does not merit a full chapter of this book, but since we are continually asked questions about scarfing, we fully explain it here.

Although there are several different kinds of scarf joints, we use only one, the simplest and most reliable. We machine identical bevels at the ends of pieces to be joined, fit these *matching bevels,* and then permanently bond them with epoxy. In many boatbuilding situations, we use a ratio of 8 to 1 to determine the size of the bevel, so that a 1 inch thick board will have a bevel 8 inches long. When high-density, high-strength wood is used in a critical area, a mast for example, 12 to 1 proportions may be required. For extra strength and safety, we increasingly recommend 12 to 1 scarfs for lumber.

The main object of the bevel is to develop enough surface bonding area to exceed the strength of the wood itself. If you have any doubts about the amount of surface area needed with the wood you intend to use, you can manufacture a sample joint and destruction test it. The sample does not have to be large: ½ inch thick x 1 inch wide is sufficient. Machine 8 to 1 bevels on two pieces and join them with an adhesive mixture. When the resin has cured, support the ends of the sample (well beyond the scarf joint) and then apply force in the middle of the scarf joint until it breaks. If failure occurs within the bond of the scarf itself, you will have to increase its surface area by increasing the scarf angle to a higher ratio for the stock thickness.

The *direction of the load* on the scarf joint itself is of little significance in comparison to the development of

bonding *surface area to withstand that load.* To develop maximum surface bonding area *with minimum waste of material,* you should bevel the side of the lumber with the largest dimension. For example, if you had a piece of 2 inch x 4 inch stock, no matter what the load direction, you would make the 8 to 1 beveled joint on the 4 inch side rather than the 2 inch side.

Although the principles of scarfing lumber and plywood are the same, the actual procedures differ. In this chapter, we first discuss methods of scarfing boards and then move on to a discussion of plywood scarfs. We rarely scarf veneers for boats, but when we do, we follow the basic steps used with plywood.

Scarfing Lumber

Making bevels by hand: Depending on the size and type of lumber, you can use a variety of hand tools to cut bevels. Other methods of beveling are faster, so we make bevels by hand only on large stock or when we have just a few pieces to work on.

Check to make sure that the end of your board is sawed square with its length. Then plan bevel dimensions carefully and mark them on the end of the board. Measure the length of the bevel in from the squared edge and, using a square, draw a line parallel to the edge. This will represent the end of the bevel; it is usually referred to as the bevel line. Draw diagonal lines on each side of the board to connect the bevel line with the squared edge on the opposite side.

Now remove excess stock to get close to the lines you have drawn. There are many ways to do this: you can make a careful cut with a sharp handsaw, sawing as close to the marks as your skill will allow, or you can use a wide chisel and mallet, a large plane with a deep-set blade or a power plane. When you have rough machined the bevel close to its marks, use a sharp block plane to finish it, watching the marked lines as you proceed.

At this point, place the stock on a flat surface such as a workbench, with a block under the feather edge of the bevel which can support the edge but will not interfere with the hand planing. Continually check the bevel for flatness in both directions, so that when you plane the bevel to its final marked lines, you leave a fine feathered edge at the very end of the stock. When

* TRADEMARK OF GOUGEON BROTHERS, INC., U.S.A.

you have completed the scarf bevel, check to make sure that it is flat in both the length and widths planed (we just set the edge of the plane on the bevel surface for a quick check) to ensure a totally flat surface which will mate properly with another scarf bevel to form a dimensionally accurate and strong scarf joint.

The scarfing jig: To save time, you can easily build a jig on which to mass produce accurate scarf bevels on various sizes of straight lumber. Our basic scarfing jig design, shown in Figure 1, operates on the same principle as a miter box. A typical miter box is really only useful for cutting bevels on the very thin planks needed for strip-built canoes, but the jig can produce the angles of cuts needed for 8 to 1 and 12 to 1 bevels.

The final dimensions of the jig are determined by the stock to be beveled, but we always have made ours a little larger, so that we can bevel a reasonable variety of stock sizes on one fixture. Construct the jig by bonding two upright fences onto a flat base, making the fences and base long enough to support the stock being cut. Cut a mortise into the bottom of one of the fences of the jig to receive a wedge, which will hold the stock firmly against the opposite fence. Then lay out the bevel angle accurately and mark it on the jig, being extremely careful to make sure that the *sawing line* is perpendicular to the jig floor, so that you will produce square bevels. Make the first saw cut into the jig, using a back saw or a carefully controlled panel saw. This first cut is crucial to an accurate jig. Test its accuracy by manufacturing several beveled joints and checking them for squareness. Now you can use the jig to manufacture scarf bevels by placing stock in the jig and using a back saw or panel saw to make the desired cuts. You may need to finish the bevels with a sharp block plane.

You can also set up this scarfing jig on the table of a radial arm saw. Clamp the jig to the table so that it is angled slightly to the travel of the saw to produce the exact bevel desired as you pull the saw blade through. Clamp lumber in the jig and proceed to cut the bevel. Although the set-up with the radial arm saw takes longer, it vastly increases the speed at which you can machine bevels. It is not unheard of to manufacture over a hundred accurate bevels per hour, when you are well set up and organized.

The router method: Another method of making bevels is to use a router in conjunction with a guide fixture. This has one advantage over the scarf jig, in that it has the capacity to cut bevels in stock of a wider dimension range. The disadvantage is that the basic fixture takes a little more time to engineer and construct, and is not so portable because it must be aligned with a flat surface

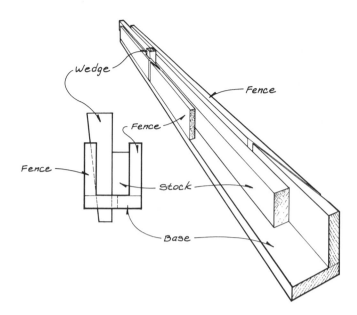

Figure 1—Scarfing jig.

in order to be of value. Usually this fixture is permanently attached at the end of a long, flat surface, such as a workbench, and used when needed. Figure 2 shows the basic components of this fixture and how it might be assembled. There are a number of variations on this design, but the basic principle, which is to provide guides which direct the router across the stock and machine the proper bevel, is the same. Move the router back and forth across the bevel face, cutting as much stock as the fly cutter bit and power of the router will allow. With a sharp bit and accurate guides, you can produce a very smooth and even bevel surface. An electric plane can be substituted to perform in the same manner as the router.

Bonding scarf joints: A beveled scarf joint is only as strong as the bond developed between the two mating pieces. Therefore, the bonding and structural capacity of the adhesive you use is absolutely crucial to successful joints. Over a long period of time, WEST SYSTEM adhesive mixtures have shown the ability to produce strong scarf joints if proper bonding procedures are followed.

The quality of the fit between mating surfaces is another important factor in successful scarfing. Although it is possible to correct minor irregularities with a thickened, gap-filling adhesive mixture, it is better to keep working a joint until it fits well. To check a fit, clamp the two pieces of stock together in a trial run. If the bevels mate poorly, gaps will be immediately apparent and you can fix them. Even if the bevels do mate properly, sight down the joined pieces to make sure that there is no bend at the scarf to indicate that the bevel angles do not match. When you are satisfied

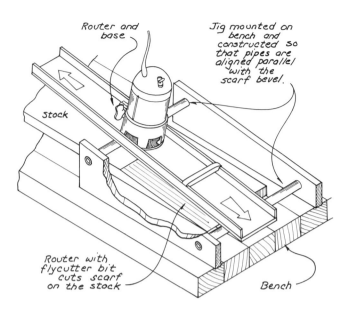

Figure 2—Jig for cutting scarf bevels with router.

with the joint, you are ready to apply an adhesive mixture to the bonding surfaces of both parts.

Beveled scarf joints present a unique bonding problem because you are dealing primarily with *end grain* wood. Most bonding in wooden boatbuilding is between side or *flat grain* wood, where tight cell structure limits the resin penetration into the wood fiber. End grain wood, in comparison, can be penetrated deeply by the bonding adhesive. This penetration of adhesive far into the wood in itself makes the joint stronger. However, deep penetration can cause difficulties if so much adhesive is drawn into the wood fiber that an adhesive-starved joint develops. Then, serious voids can occur between the mating surfaces which may compromise the structural integrity of the joint. Once you understand this problem, you can easily take preventive measures when applying the resin.

There are several ways to apply epoxy to a lumber scarf joint. The method of choice, outlined here, not only helps to fill gaps, but also minimizes the chances that the epoxy you've applied to fill gaps will be drawn into the end grain during the curing process.

To bond lumber scarfs, mix a batch of WEST SYTSTEM epoxy and apply it, with no fillers, to both bevels. Let this coating sit for five minutes, and then add either Colloidal Silica or high density filler to the epoxy in your pot. The consistency of this mixture depends on the quality of your joint. Apply desired quantites of thickened resin to both bonding surfaces. The first coating will penetrate into your wood, increasing the likelihood that the second coating will remain close to the scarfed surface to bridge any minor voids.

Clamping scarf joints: To make accurate scarf joints, you need a long, flat surface, such as a workbench or the floor, on which you can assemble and clamp the bevel joints. After you have applied the adhesive, bring together the two pieces of stock you are joining so that their bevels slowly meet, using slight pressure with your hands. Then press them together firmly, squeezing out any excess adhesive. Make sure that both pieces are flat on the surface, but pressed well together, so that there is neither over-nor under-matching of the bevels (See Figure 4.) Determine straightness in the *edge* dimension by feeling the edges of the scarf with your fingers, or set up a straightedge on the flat surface against which you can assemble the two pieces of stock, thus ensuring straightness in both dimensions. When you have lined up the scarf joint perfectly, locate a staple along the edge of the scarf joint on one surface, turn the stock over, realign the joint, and locate another staple on the opposite surface in the opposite scarf edge. These temporary *locating staples* hold the scarf joint in proper position until you can apply clamping pressure.

It is important that you clamp the joint firmly, so that good contact is made between the surfaces. However, excessive clamping pressure is not needed and should be avoided because it may pre-stress the joint unnecessarily. Before you apply any clamping pressure, remove any excess resin which has squeezed out of the joint to facilitate cleanup. Then wrap the scarf joint in wax paper or light polyethylene film to prevent inadvertent bonding of the scarf joint with clamps or the flat surface. Apply clamping pressure with any number of clamps desired, or make up simple clamping fixtures

Figure 3—Coating bonding surface with a roller.

utilizing wedges to apply even pressure over the entire scarf joint. Often we insert a clamping pad between the clamp and the stock being clamped to distribute clamping pressure over more area and prevent clamp marks from appearing in the face of the stock.

When manufacturing the planking, stringers or ribbands for a mold or hull, you will bond a great many scarf joints in a short time. Just as we have developed higher production methods to machine scarf bevels, so have we developed techniques which vastly speed up the scarf bonding procedure. When making numerous scarfs with the same size stock, we prepare and temporarily line up the joints and then, rather than clamping them individually, apply adhesive and clamps to a number of scarfs in one operation. The number of joints which you can assemble at one time is limited by the assembly life of your epoxy and the dimensional capacity of the clamps or clamping fixtures you are using. While we have clamped up to twenty scarf joints at once, it takes a great deal of care to keep this many from shifting.

Production bonding needs to be well organized, and requires the cooperation of at least two people. First, pre-sort the stock to be joined and lay out the individual pieces on a flat surface opposite one another, with each of the beveled surfaces facing up and pointing toward its mate. No doubt you will want to make up varying lengths of scarfed material, and you should do your planning at this stage to minimize waste when you are actually assembling the scarfed stock on the boat.

When you have laid out and organized all of the stock, establish a separate assembly area close by on a flat surface and prepare the clamps and a staple gun which shoots ⅜ inch wide crown staples. On the floor, lay out wax paper or polyethylene sheet that is somewhat wider than the scarf joints themselves to prevent inadvertent bonding. Then make up the adhesive mix-

ture and administer it to all the upward facing beveled surfaces following the application procedure previously described.

Move two matched pieces of stock to the prepared assembly area and align their beveled bonding surfaces, using the procedure previously described. After you have inserted the locating staples, turn the stock up on edge with the side of the scarf joint resting on the wax paper or polyethylene sheet that you have laid on the floor. Before you move another pair of stock into the assembly area, wrap a roll of wax paper over the standing surface of the scarf you have just lined up; this will create a barrier between it and the next scarf joint when they are placed side by side. Then lift this roll of paper up the side of the second scarf joint, so that you can nestle the third scarf joint beside the second without any bonding occurring between them. Continue weaving the roll of wax paper back and forth between all the ensuing scarf joints you line up.

When you have lined up all of the joints in this manner and they are sitting on edge, position heavy pieces of stock about twice the scarf length on each side of the stack. These serve as clamping pads to distribute pressure evenly. Position clamps at either end of the pads to keep the joints from sliding apart when pressure is applied to the scarf area. Use enough clamps to apply sufficient pressure over the scarf joint area to ensure good bonds. When clamping a large number of joints

Figure 5—Stringers being prepared for bonding and clamping. Scarf bevels have been cut on both ends. This set-up groups scarfs close to each other to minimize number of clamps needed.

Take care when bonding thin stock or more than one scarf to avoid gaps in the joint (A) or scarf misalignment (B). Both situations result in a weaker, more unsightly joint.

A

B

Use wire brads or staples to prevent slipping during scarfing.

C

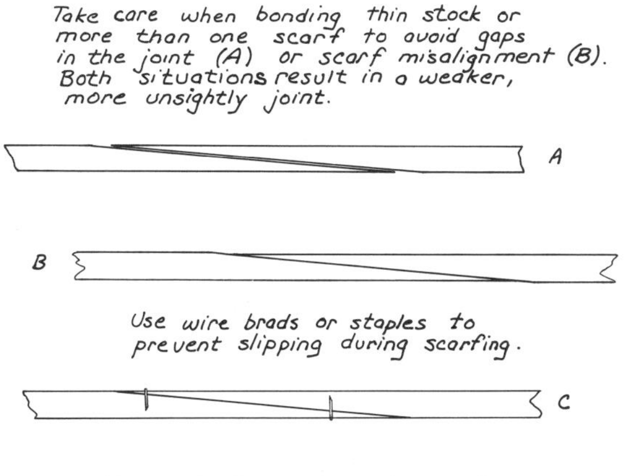

Figure 4—Precautions during clamping.

at one time, you may need to tighten the clamps at several intervals as excess adhesive slowly squeezes out of the joints.

Fairing up scarf joints: A scarf joint is almost finished when its adhesive has cured. The final steps in scarfing are always fairing and cleanup. Excess resin inevitably squeezes out around the joint and must be removed. If you have any misalignment within your scarf, you will need to fair into the overall dimensions of the stock. We suggest that you take care of these matters when your epoxy is partially cured — 5 to 8 hours after application the joint should be strong enough to allow you to remove clamps — because at this stage the epoxy is easiest to sand and plane. After 5 to 7 days the work will be much more difficult.

Remove the temporary locating staples before you begin fairing. Hand held block planes are the basic tools for fairing scarf joints. Using two of them, each at a different blade setting, speeds up the fairing process when you have a lot of scarf joints to do. Set the blade on the second block plane for a finer cut to remove the last bits of material. Then use an 11 inch sanding block with 60 grit paper to smooth out any plane marks and to final fair the joint.

Scarfing Plywood Panels

There are major differences between scarfing lumber and scarfing commercially manufactured plywood panels. One significant dissimilarity is dimension: a 6 inch or 8 inch wide scarf joint in lumber is considered large, but a 4 foot or even 8 foot wide scarf joint in plywood is standard. Plywood is usually much thinner than lumber and therefore plywood bevels are usually shorter. Unlike bevels in stock, which consist entirely of end grain wood, plywood bevels have both end and flat grain. Because plywood differs from lumber as a material, the methods used to cut plywood bevels and bond plywood scarf joints are somewhat different from those used with lumber.

Plywood is such a commonly used material in modern wooden boatbuilding that the ability to join plywood panels with a sufficiently strong joint is of major importance. The average boatbuilding project also uses enough plywood so that plywood scarfing requires a significant number of labor-hours in relation to the boatbuilding project as a whole. We recognized this problem long ago in our own shop and developed a guide which could be assembled on a table saw to direct a plywood panel across the table saw blade and

* TRADEMARK OF GOUGEON BROTHERS, INC., U.S.A.

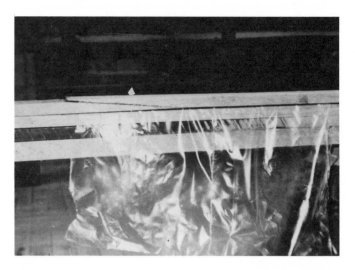

Figure 6—Plastic sheeting woven back and forth between stringers to prevent bonding due to resin runout. When placing this plastic sheet, care should be taken to prevent pinching the plastic in the scarf joint, as this will weaken the finished joint.

create a perfectly sawn bevel edge in a short period of time. The only difficulty with this fixture was that we had to use the table saw for many other things and, therefore, had to set up and remove the fixture frequently. The set-up procedure required at least 20 minutes, so unless we had a lot of bevels to cut on plywood, we usually planed them by hand.

The SCARFFER* Attachment: To solve this problem, we adapted our table saw device, and attached the guide to the bottom of a hand held circular saw. What we liked best about this tool was that we could leave it in place on the saw, ready for use at any time, with no set-up required. The combined cost of a saw and attachment was so low that we could well afford the luxury of keeping the device permanently attached to an extra saw. Eventually, because we found it so useful, we added it to our line of WEST SYSTEM products.

The SCARFFER circular saw attachment, shown in Figures 7 through 9, is inexpensive and can be bolted to the bottoms of most 7¼ inch hand held circular saws. It comes with a manual which provides step-by-step instructions for attaching it to a saw, setting up plywood panels and sawing bevels. The SCARFFER attachment is ideal for work with plywood up to ¼ inch thick, and with minor hand finishing may be used on panels up to ½ inch thick. We feel that it is an investment which quickly pays for itself in labor savings, even on small projects. Bevels cut with the SCARFFER attachment can be more accurate than hand-cut joints, especially when you have little experience making scarfs by hand.

Making bevels by hand: A prime requirement for hand beveling is a flat table or bench of sufficient size and with an edge which will support the plywood edge you are beveling. Position the plywood so that the edge to be beveled is lined up perfectly with the edge of the table or bench, and clamp it down. Draw a bevel line along the length of the plywood just as you would with lumber stock. Usually you would have an 8 to 1 bevel, so if you were using ¼ inch plywood, you would draw the bevel line 2 inches from the edge of the plywood. Because of the length involved, and the fact that plywood edges are usually straight, we usually use a marking gauge to transfer this distance for the bevel line.

The basic tools you will need for hand beveling are a block plane and a smoothing plane. Using a power plane can save a lot of time in roughing the scarf bevel down close to its intended dimension, but without this luxury use a smoothing plane with a sharp, deep-set blade to remove a majority of the stock as quickly as possible. Then use a more finely set block plane to finish off the scarf bevel, being careful to keep the bevel straight and *flat* as you proceed. Keep the plane blades sharp at all times. Otherwise, the alternating grain in the plywood edge will begin to cut at different rates, causing unevenness in the bevel face. This problem means you also have to use sandpaper with extreme caution, because it will sand the two directions of grain at different rates, also causing unevenness. The only real defense against the grain problem is to sharpen the plane blade frequently. The plane will lose its fine cutting edge quickly when you plane plywood, due to the adhesive between plies. The lines created by the various plies in the plywood give a good indica-

Figure 8—Running saw with SCARFFER attachment along the straightedge.

Figure 9—Plywood panel showing bevel cut with saw and SCARFFER attachment.

tion of progress you are making when planing the bevel. Any humps or unevenness in the bevel usually shows up as a crooked line when you sight down the glue line between the laminations.

Hand beveling can be tedious and difficult, but it is like a lot of other boatbuilding jobs in that it is a learned skill and your quality and speed improve with time. If you have never done hand beveling, we suggest that you practice on a few scrap pieces of plywood. Occasionally, plywood bevels get messed up beyond repair,

Figure 7—Setting up a straightedge for the SCARFFER attachment.

but a mistake does not usually mean disaster. Simply mark in a new bevel line an inch or so beyond the old line and start the whole procedure over again.

You can save a good deal of time when hand beveling by setting up several panels in a stack for simultaneous planing. For instance, assume that you want to plane bevels on four ¼ inch panels all at once. Draw 2 inch bevel lines which represent 8 to 1 bevels across all the panels, and stack all four of the panels on top of one another on a flat table. Place the edge of the bottom panel flush with the edge of the table. Then place the second panel with its edge matching the bevel line of the first panel, and the third panel with its edge matching the bevel line of the second panel, and so on. Clamp the whole stack to the table, and plane one continuous bevel over all of the panel ends. (See Figure 13.)

However you cut the bevels, we do add one note of caution about laying out the bevels if you plan on natural finishing. It is not uncommon to receive plywood panels which have a higher quality veneer on one side than the other. Be sure to lay out the bevel angles on the *proper side* of the plywood, so when you join the plywood panels the good surface is always on one side of the joined panels.

Bonding plywood scarf joints: Plywood panels, beveled by hand or with the SCARFFER attachment, are more difficult than lumber to line up and join for bonding. You can quickly learn to assemble small scarf joints with nothing more than your sense of touch and several clamps. Long plywood scarf joints, on the other hand, are troublesome to fit and may require complex clamping procedures. Because the possibility of aggregate error is high, we recommend against clamping a number of wide scarf joints in a single operation.

To prepare plywood scarf joints for bonding, first line up the bevels to check them for mating accuracy.

Figure 10—Use a power plane for roughing out scarf bevel.

Figure 11—Planing narrow plywood strips with a block plane.

This requires a flat working surface: either a floor or a bench that is large enough to accommodate the two pieces being joined. You will need a steel straightedge about 1 foot long to lay across the face of the scarf joint to help sight it from above. Mate the two beveled surfaces by pushing them into each other, tapping them a fraction of an inch at a time. Between taps, press the bevels from the top with your hand, holding both plywood panels flush with the underlying surface. Then place the straightedge across the joint; if the bevels are meeting correctly with no overlap, the straightedge should be touching both surfaces evenly. If there is an overlap of the bevels, the straightedge will rock slightly on the feather edge, and stand high on one side or the other of the panels. If there is a gap between the beveled surfaces, simply sighting the edge of the scarf should indicate this. Occasionally there may be an advantage in tapping the panels together until the straightedge indicates that a slight override exists between the bevel surfaces. Then, draw the two panels from each other in very small increments until the straightedge again reads that a flat surface exists between the two panels. With long scarf joints, line up the bevel carefully on one edge and then insert a temporary staple. Then line up the opposite edge in similar fashion and insert a staple in it. If you have machined the bevels straight on both panels, the mating between the two in the center portion of the panel should follow the accuracy that is developed at either end. When the panels are in perfect alignment, make surmarks across the faces of both panels, so that when you apply adhesive, you can reassemble them in the exact position. Make the surmarks across the scarf joint edge at approximately a 45° angle. Make at least two surmarks, one at each edge of the panel, and insert as many as you need in between.

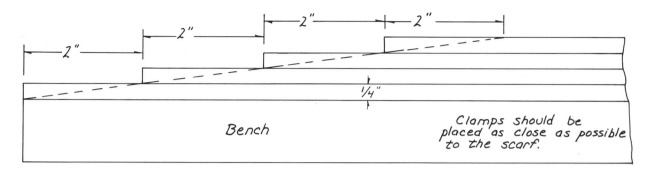

Figure 12—Stacking panels to cut several scarfs simultaneously.

Apply the adhesive to the beveled plywood faces using either one of the methods described for use with lumber. Lumber bevels are composed entirely of end grain wood, but at least one third and perhaps as much as two thirds of the joint face of plywood will be flat grain. This will not absorb the large amounts of resin that end grain does, so you can apply less epoxy and still be sure of a sound bond between panels.

Clamping plywood scarf joints: The potential problem with the plywood scarf joint is achieving proper clamping pressure. A basic requirement for clamping is a large, flat work surface of the size used to fit the joint, but with one additional provision. The work surface must be of a material which will receive staples or small nails. If needed, you can position several sheets of ¾ inch thick sheathing grade plywood over your floor or the workbench to receive fasteners readily. Cover that part of the work surface which will be beneath the scarf joint with wax paper or polyethylene sheet. Apply the bonding adhesive, position the panels on the flat surface and join the bevel surfaces together so that the surmarks line up. Then position a locating staple in each edge of the joint to prevent any movement of the two panels while you are clamping. Cover the top of the joint with wax paper and place a strip of plywood over the paper at the scarf joint. This plywood strip should be about the same thickness as the material being spliced together, and should be wide enough to cover at least the entire area of the splice. Drive a sufficient number of staples or nails through the strip and the scarf joint into the receiving material below, drawing the two beveled surfaces firmly together.

You can create adequate pressure with staples when clamping plywood up to ¼ inch thick. With thicker panels, nailing is recommended. When using nails, we usually use a much thicker clamping strip, of perhaps ¾ inch stock, so that fewer nails are necessary for even pressure over the entire surface area. A piece of curved stock, held in place with clamps as shown in Figure 14, will help distribute clamping pressure evenly across your joint.

Because you may be bonding wide panels, it is extremely important to fair up these joints while the adhesive is still in its partial cure stage. Use the same tools and procedures to clean up and fair plywood scarf joints as you would use with lumber scarf joints. It works best to do the cleanup and fairing operations while the plywood is still lying on a flat surface; this is especially important with thinner plywood.

Scarfing in Place

Very often in a boatbuilding job you may need a scarfed panel of very large dimensions (for example, a complete deck surface) which is impractical to install in one piece. To solve this problem, we have developed a technique to scarf together plywood panels right in place on the hull as they are being installed. This scarfing in place procedure adds two difficulties in the basic plywood bonding operations: (1) the measuring, marking and fitting of the bevels on the two panels to be joined will require a great deal of extra planning if the scarf joint is to be made over a solid portion of the hull framework; and (2) the two plywood panels will require more clamping because they will be bent over a curved surface, rather than laid on a flat surface. The degree of curvature involved will determine how much clamping pressure is needed to overcome the natural

Figure 13—Cutting scarf bevels on stacked panels.

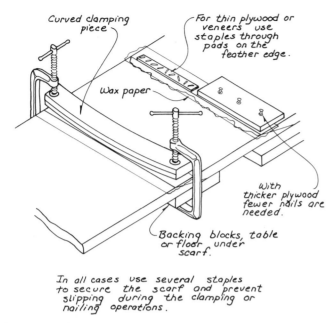

Figure 14—Several methods for clamping or securing scarfs during bonding.

tendency of the plywood panel to resist the bending forces.

In most situations, it is easier to place the scarf joint over a solid member of the hull framework when you are scarfing in place. This may be a frame, bulkhead or stringer large enough to receive staples, nails or screws of sufficient length and numbers to generate the needed pressure. Plan the scarf joints carefully so that the bevels will center themselves directly on this solid point when you install the panels. Even with careful measuring, you may have to sacrifice some plywood in order to locate the scarf joint properly because of the existing hull or deck framework location. Follow the normal procedure for clamping; however, you may need to generate much more pressure to pull the joints properly in place for a cure to take place. To generate maximum pressure use temporary steel screws in conjunction with washers and insert them in pilot holes which are drilled through the clamping strip and through the scarf joint into the receiving solid member in the interior framework. Scarfing in place is commonly done in constructing hulls and decks with sheet plywood. Chapters 22 and 25 give more detailed explanations of the measuring and installation procedures.

Scarfing to Reduce the Scrap Rate

In the past, the scrap rate could reach close to 40% of materials purchased for a given project. You can reduce this figure substantially by the proper use of the scarf joint. When you consider that longer lengths of both plywood and lumber are sold at premium prices, it is easy to understand that being able to use shorter lengths of material can be extremely cost-effective. Quality plywood is not only expensive, but much of it may be wasted because of its limited length. A typical example is the use of plywood for laminating strips when molding hulls. On a larger boat, the lengths you need may vary anywhere from 9 to 14 feet, depending upon the area of the hull where you apply the strips. With this variation, no matter how careful the planning, significant waste will occur. However, you can cut the waste to less than 5% by making up extremely long panels (as long as your working space will allow), from which you can then cut carefully measured lengths. It is not uncommon for us to make up 50 foot long plywood panels of perhaps 1 foot in width, from which the major waste might be at most several feet at the end. The smaller scrap pieces become, the less value they have because of the increasingly limited areas in which they can be used. So joining several smaller pieces together to make up a larger piece can be time well spent. When making up stringers, planking, sheer clamps or keels, a little planning can pay big dividends. Try to determine ahead of time, within a foot or two, the exact lengths of each member required, then plan a combination of stock and scarf joints that will come closest to the desired length. For instance, you could join two 18 foot boards into one 35 foot length; if needed, make a shorter 26 foot length by joining one 18 footer with half of another 18 footer. Then use the other half of the 18 footer to join with yet a smaller 14 footer to form a plank 22 feet in length, and so on. If you have made up a list of all plank lengths needed for your project, you can methodically begin to make the best use of your stock by developing those lengths most easily made. Then make up those lengths where you may have to accept a higher scrap rate, which at some point is always unavoidable. The point is that prior planning will enable you to make the best use of the stock you have on hand.

Chapter 11

Coating and Finishing

In Chapter 5, we explained the theory behind sealing wood in WEST SYSTEM* Brand epoxy. Here we provide detailed practical instructions on applying resin coatings and on finishing coated wood surfaces. We like to keep boatbuilding simple, so in our shop we continually try to make these necessary jobs as quick and efficient as possible. Readers of earlier editions of this book will note that we've modified some techniques and tools and have found better ways to do several tasks.

One of the best things about WEST SYSTEM resin is that it's easy to finish. A properly coated wood surface has a hard, durable, stable and moisture-resistant base for painting and clear coating. Special finish preparations are rarely necessary because most finish systems readily adhere to resin-coated wood. Since the moisture content of the wood beneath the final epoxy coating is under control, paint and varnish tend to last longer.

In most roller and brush coating procedures, use the standard application sequence which is detailed in this chapter. Apply an initial coating of resin as evenly as possible, and let it cure. Lightly sand high spots, "fuzz" and bumps until they are smooth, fill staple holes, and apply a second coating. Proceed in this manner until

Figure 1—Coating exterior of an IOR ½ ton racer. This boat has a natural finish. All fairing, finish sanding and coating were done prior to removing hull from mold.

* TRADEMARK OF GOUGEON BROTHERS, INC., U.S.A.

you have applied as many coatings of WEST SYSTEM epoxy as you think necessary, and prepare your surface for final finishing. For protection against moisture and moisture vapor, you should have at least two net coats of resin remaining after sanding and finishing.

An alternate technique for coating with epoxy is somewhat quicker than standard roller-brush methods but can be used only on flat or almost-flat surfaces. *Flocoating,* also described in this chapter, is particularly handy in areas where you want to build up a thick coating of epoxy quickly.

General Coating Guidelines

Boat pieces and parts may be coated with WEST SYSTEM epoxy at various times during construction. There are no firm rules, so plan out what seems to be a convenient schedule early in your project. Sometimes, especially with exteriors, it's a good idea to wait until the hull is completely assembled and then to coat the entire structure at once. Usually, however, you can save a great deal of time by coating individual interior components before installing them. *Precoating,* as we call it, at the workbench is much easier than coating and sanding in difficult and awkward positions in a boat.

Consider labor savings when you think over the timing of your coating. Finish work can be a surprisingly large part of the total labor in a boat, as professional builders are painfully aware, and any increase in efficiency is worthwhile. When work is easier, it goes more quickly. Gravity is against you when you coat and sand the ceiling of a cabin roof after it is in position, and the job can be strenuous. Resin will drip from overhead surfaces and may create difficult clean-up problems. If the same plywood surface is coated and sanded before installation, you will save time and irritation, and you will probably do better work.

Complete final fairing and shaping of all wood pieces before applying an initial resin coating. Shaping and fairing are very difficult after epoxy has been applied because cured, epoxy-coated surfaces are many times harder than bare wood.

Inspect the final shaped and faired wood surface to check its moisture content. It should be as dry as local humidity — preferably not more than 85% at 70°F. —

will permit so that higher-than-normal moisture levels will not be sealed in. Because WEST SYSTEM hardener is water soluble, excessive amounts of water in wood may alter your resin-hardener ratio and impede epoxy cure. If your wood's moisture level is above 12%, you may have problems with resin penetration. If its moisture level is in the range of your wood's saturation point, resin may not penetrate enough to maintain grain strength. Moisture content below 12% has little effect on resin absorption, so unless its cells have been damaged in overzealous kiln operations, wood that is too dry is preferable to wood that is too damp.

If in doubt about the moisture content of a thin plank, sand it with 80 grit paper. If you can't produce a dusty cutting, the wood is too wet. This trick does not work with thick boards, which tend to dry out on the surface while remaining green inside, so if you have any questions, wait until a less humid day, or until your pieces are drier, for any bonding or coating. Apply resin to wet or damp wood only under emergency conditions when there is no alternative.

Your wood should be clean and free of contamination because oil, dirt, dust and solvent residue will prevent proper bonding. Remove oil and grease with solvent — we've found that alcohol is very effective — and sand your wood to eliminate the possibility of solvent interference with epoxy adhesion. If you use rags, be sure that they are clean and that they do not dissolve in your solvent and leave a deposit of material on the substrate.

The temperatures of your shop, wood and epoxy are important to the quality of a coating job. We find that a range between 60 and 70°F. is best. Both epoxy and wood should be at room temperature or warmer before coating. At colder temperatures, the viscosity of resin increases and it becomes difficult to apply. Warm resin, on the other hand, even when applied to cold wood, will remain thin long enough to easily penetrate. Warming the substrate and allowing it to cool a little before coating also enhances resin absorption. Warming both the epoxy and the wood is a little more work, but worthwhile in cold conditions. You may also, with slightly less satisfactory results, apply cold resin to a cold surface and then heat both simultaneously with a hair dryer, heat gun or light bulb.

Try to maintain constant temperatures as your epoxy cures. If freshly-coated wood warms up — as, for example, when cold wood is brought into a warm shop, or when coated plywood is taken from a cool shop into hot sunlight — expanding air in the wood will form bubbles on the coated surface. In the same way, if a coated surface is taken from a warm shop to cure in

cold conditions, it may become cloudy or contaminated, especially by condensation.

Use WEST SYSTEM epoxy, mixed in the standard ratio of 5 parts resin to 1 part hardener, for both bonding and coating. We suggest 205 Fast Hardener for coating applications at 70° F. or less, and 206 Slow Hardener in hotter weather. Fast Hardener cures more quickly, with less chance for contamination, and is therefore better where a clear finish is desired. Under normal conditions, you can sand a 205 Hardener coating 24 hours after application and a 206 Hardener coating within 24 to 48 hours, depending on ambient temperature.

Use epoxy without fillers or additives for most coating jobs. When you need a mixture which will not run easily, add small amounts of 406 Colloidal Silica. Mix a 4 ounce batch of resin, and add more small batches to it in the roller pan as needed. Don't thin WEST SYSTEM epoxy with solvents because doing this may compromise the moisture resistance and physical properties of the resin.

The most practical way to apply a WEST SYSTEM epoxy coating usually is to roll it on with a high-density urethane foam roller. After a good deal of experimenting, we have settled on WEST SYSTEM 800 Roller Covers, which have 1/8 inch thick foam on stiff fiber backing. Covers with porous, low-density foam or with foam thickness greater than 3/16 inch will add an undesirable amount of air to epoxy during application and reduce control of coating thickness. We therefore advise against using them. Roller covers are inexpensive and almost impossible to clean, so we always discard them after use.

We have weighed our roller covers before and after using them and have found that they sometime absorb over 2 ounces of epoxy. Two ounces can be a significant waste factor in small jobs, so organize your work and try to coat a number of components at one time with one roller cover. Foam will deteriorate as resin begins to cure because increasing epoxy viscosity causes increased drag. To extend the life of your roller cover, mix small batches of epoxy and roll your cover dry before adding additional resin to your roller pan.

There are many areas in a boat which can't be reached with a standard 7 inch wide roller. One of our solutions to this problem is to saw roller covers into shorter sizes and mount them on an adjustable frame. In other tight situations, we use small, cheap, bristle brushes for coating. For firmer action and greater control, we usually cut the bristles on our brushes short.

WEST SYSTEM resin is a dense material which requires a good deal of roller pressure. This pressure, combined with vigorous rolling action, leads to an even surface coating over a large area, but it also often produces a surface stipple of air bubbles. If you remove this stipple before the resin cures, so that the surface is smooth, sanding and finishing are quicker. Factory-made foam brushes can be used to eliminate stipple, but they are expensive and a little too flexible to be ideal.

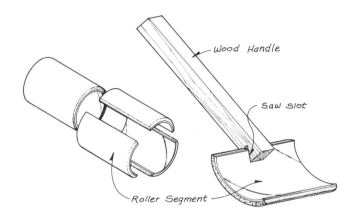

Figure 2—Cutting roller cover to make foam brush.

We make our own, cheaper, brush-like foam tools from WEST SYSTEM 800 Roller Covers. Cut a roller cover in half crossways, and then slice each half longitudinally into three pieces. These cuts will serve as brushing edges, so they must be straight and clean. Then make a handle by sawing a slot in a stick and insert a segment of roller into it, as shown in Figure 2.

Although, as a rule, they are not particularly effective for applying resin and they cost a lot more than rollers, we sometimes use bristle brushes to smooth out and touch up epoxy coatings. It's hard to brush an even and consistent coating over a large area and, once the job is done, harder still to clean the brush. WEST SYSTEM epoxy can be cleaned from bristles, but because resin's catalytic action continues even after drastic reduction with thinners, this procedure is much more time-consuming than standard paint cleaning. If you use brushes, store them in a covered coffee can full of solvent.

It may be possible to spray WEST SYSTEM epoxy, but we strongly recommend against it. Leaving aside the practical difficulties — our resin is a high-density material which is very difficult to atomize, and reducing it with thinners will lower its physical properties — the possible health hazards are enormous. If a sensitized or potentially sensitized individual were to come into contact with atomized resin, the health effects could be very serious.

Initial Coating With WEST SYSTEM Epoxy

When you apply a first coat of WEST SYSTEM epoxy to bare wood, it will penetrate the wood's surface and adhere to its cells, replacing air in voids and fissures. The amount and depth of this penetration are affected by several variables: the density of the wood, its grain alignment and its moisture content. The purpose of an initial coating is to encapsulate the wood. Very deep penetration is actually undesirable.

Wood density is the most important of the factors which determine resin penetration. Cedar will absorb more resin than mahogany. Grain alignment affects penetration because end grain absorbs much more resin than flat grain. Grain runs exactly parallel to length in few boards, and most have some run out, so it is very common for resin to penetrate unevenly in a single board. End grain is also a major avenue for moisture absorption, so relatively deep resin penetration here is needed.

Individual wood cells are very resistant to all types of liquids, including water, and are not easily penetrated by any liquid unless they are submerged for long periods of time. When you apply an initial coating of WEST SYSTEM epoxy, it will penetrate the voids and fissures within the cells and will travel only into cells which have broken walls. This is what you want to happen. Were the resin to thoroughly saturate the wood, its weight and brittleness would increase faster than any benefits.

In most woods, in fact, resin absorption is desirable only to the point at which wood grain strength is reached. Whenever a resin-bonded joint breaks, the fracture should be in the wood rather than in the bonding line. This is obviously important for bonded joints, but it is just as important for coatings. If a coating adheres so tenaciously that you only have to worry about the integrity of the wood itself, you eliminate a great deal of concern. It has long been considered almost impossible to find a coating which adheres to a wood surface in a difficult marine environment over a long period of time. Polyester resins and most types of paint have produced at best mediocre results.

A large percentage of the volume of a piece of wood is air. If it cannot escape during coating to allow resin to take its place, this air can be a major deterrent to good penetration. When you apply the first coat of resin to bare wood, you often see many small air bubbles on the surface. These appear when the epoxy and the air exchange places.

In most cases, this transfer occurs easily. Sometimes, however, difficulties can develop. Air passage can be restricted when cold, thick resin is applied in a heavier-

Figure 3—Building up resin coating on deck of proa SLINGSHOT. Note that topsides and bottom have been coated with grey pigmented resin.

than-usual coating. In this situation, there appears to be a standoff, with the air unable to pass from the voids and the thicker resin unable to move in until the air escapes. The obvious solution to this is to work in a heated area, but if that is impossible, there are several other techniques which will help. For information on these, see the Guidelines section of this chapter.

During the inital coating process, recoat areas that look dry as the resin penetrates, rolling on fresh epoxy as necessary. End grain will soak up a great deal of resin. Don't apply too much in the first coating as an excessive film can impede good air transfer. Instead, roll a second coat over the first after a few minutes. Casually inspect your surface for 15 minutes after applying an adequate initial coat, and reroll areas where excessive penetration occurs.

Because wood grain expands as it absorbs resin, cured inital coatings are often fuzzy and rough. Sand your surface until it is smooth before applying a second coating of epoxy or a layer of fiberglass. Major voids, staple holes, nicks and dings can be filled after a second or third coat, but we usually take care of them after the initial coating, so that the filled areas will be covered with resin. After puttying these spots and allowing them to cure, fair them smooth with sandpaper on a block. Then you are ready to apply a second overall coating.

Second and Subsequent Coatings with WEST SYSTEM Epoxy

Use a foam roller to apply the second coat of WEST SYSTEM resin. The important goal now is a smooth

coated surface and for this you need long, vigorous strokes. Roll the resin in several directions to maintain as even a film as possible. If you inadvertently apply too much epoxy to an area, it may run. Cold epoxy is difficult to apply in a uniform film, so use only warm resin on second coatings. Use a brush to remove any air bubbles or stipple, following the guidelines mentioned earlier in this chapter.

Apply at least one penetration coat and one secondary coat to every surface inside your boat. It is possible to remove one or more coats of resin during sanding, so areas which require a lot of abrading will require a minimum of three coats of resin. You can apply more coatings and they will provide greater resistance to the elements, but you reach a point of diminishing returns in both practical and economic effectiveness with more than three net coats of WEST SYSTEM epoxy.

The smoother the surface coating, the less sanding you will need for a really smooth finish for final painting. In many cases, you can leave the second or third coating as-is in interiors and other areas which have no need of a decorative coat of paint or varnish. Make provisions for final finishing your exterior early, however.

Samples coated at our shop show a coverage rate of 40 square feet per pound of applied mixed resin. Since 2 ounces of resin can be wasted in a roller cover and some film may remain in a roller tray or mixture pot, actual coverage may be reduced by up to 25%. A fair average application rate for estimating material costs and weights for initial and secondary coatings of WEST SYSTEM epoxy is 35 square feet per pound of mixed resin.

WEST SYSTEM Pigments and Other Additives

Pigments and other specialized additives may be added to the epoxy used in secondary and final coatings. Since they may affect penetration, we advise against using these materials in initial coatings. See Chapter 7 for detailed information on these products.

WEST SYSTEM white and gray pigments cannot, of course, be used on naturally finished hulls. However, if you plan to paint your boat, they can be quite helpful. During coating applications, pigments aid in maintaining visual control of film thickness, and during sanding they can prevent the removal of too much substrate. Pigmented epoxy can also serve as a colored painting base, so fewer coats of final finish are needed to cover a hull.

Both pigments and WEST SYSTEM 420 Aluminum Powder provide protection from sunlight. Epoxy resins break down under prolonged exposure to ultraviolet light; if you do not plan to coat your hull with a finish system immediately, add either pigment or powder to your last coat of resin. This is a temporary measure which does not replace a final paint finish. Aluminum powder is more difficult to sand than pigment, so we suggest using it only on areas which are already fair and smooth.

WEST SYSTEM 421 Fire Retardant and 423 Graphite Powder are used in specific areas in specialized coating applications. Mix fire retardant into epoxy for secondary coatings of high-risk areas; it is usually only necessary on surfaces in galleys and near engines. Graphite powder/epoxy coatings are occasionally applied to rudders, centerboards and dry-sailed racers.

Flocoat Procedures

Flocoating is one of the most efficient ways to coat wood. If you use a flocoat, you can achieve a very

Figure 4—Bottom of proa SLINGSHOT has been coated with grey aluminum flake pigmented resin and sanded in preparation for painting.

smooth surface, with thickness equivalent to at least three individual coatings, in a single operation. The disadvantage is that the technique relies on epoxy's tendency to level itself, so it only works well on reasonably flat surfaces. Flocoating is not effective on vertical surfaces or on inclines which are so steep that the resin runs to a lower area.

In the past few years we've gradually modified our flocoat technique, and now use several different procedures, depending on the desired weight of the part we're working on. The instructions which follow represent a slight change from earlier editions of this book.

To apply a flocoat, begin by spreading resin over your plywood with a regular plastic squeegee. This coating should be very light. Use only enough epoxy to get out the wood and allow for some initial penetration. You do not want to build up a film.

About an hour after you have spread the first coat, pour a large quantity of resin directly from your mixing pot over your plywood surface. Use a serrated plastic spreader to distribute this epoxy as evenly as possible. The serrations on your tool will form little ridges which will help control the thickness of your coating.

Next, immediately begin rolling your surface. Use light pressure with your roller, and stroke slowly in two directions with a couple of passes each way. Check again for an even surface, and finish up by brushing your flocoat smooth. Within 10 to 15 minutes, your resin should self-level to a glass-like finish.

We usually sand the entire panel to desired finished smoothness when the flocoat has cured. Then we cut out whatever parts we need. In many cases, this sanding is in preparation for final varnishing or painting, which takes place only after the entire boat is assembled.

Flocoating can work to save labor in some other, non-flat areas, and it can also be used occasionally to level off uneven surfaces. We have used the technique to coat centerboards, rudders, deck areas, floorboards and cabin tops, but in many of these applications we used less epoxy than we might have, had the surfaces been perfectly flat. You can add low density filler to the resin used for flocoating to make a mixture which runs less than epoxy alone. Apply a flocoat of this fortified resin to level off a panel.

We usually use a total of about 2 pounds of mixed WEST SYSTEM epoxy for flocoating one side of a single 4 x 8 foot sheet of plywood. This amounts to approximately 1 ounce of resin per square foot of surface area, and includes the epoxy used to initially penetrate the wood. Quantities of mixed resin needed to apply the first coating will vary somewhat even within a given species of wood, so account for this variable factor by mixing a little less or a little more epoxy as needed. For your first effort, try mixing 6 to 8 ounces of epoxy for the initial coating.

Cleaning and Sanding Coated Surfaces

WEST SYSTEM resin will bond to cured WEST SYSTEM epoxy-coated surfaces. No sanding is needed. Take care, however, to make sure that the surface does not become contaminated between coatings. It's good practice to wipe all cured resin surfaces with a clean rag and water.

Sometimes a greasy substance appears on cured surfaces. This is amine blush, a by-product of the resin/hardener reaction, and it should be washed off with a water-dampened cloth before any further coating. If left in place, amine blush will clog sandpaper, and it may also jeopardize good bonding. This residue has been known to attract indetectable amounts of moisture, which then prevent proper adhesion of subsequent coats of epoxy. Amine blush is most evident when a coating is cured in cooling temperatures, so maintaining constant environmental controls as resin cures will, to some degree, prevent its development.

In other situations, surfaces may be contaminated by substances which are not water-soluble or by water itself. To remove non-soluble materials, use a good cleaning solvent with a clean rag or sand them away. In high humidity, moisture may collect on a surface. This will act as a contaminant and interfere with bonding between coatings. Condensation may cause clouding in an epoxy coating. When water is a problem, be sure to use fast hardener, as this cures more quickly and has less "green" time in which to collect moisture, and try to maintain more constant temperatures. If for some reason you are working outdoors in the rain, cover freshly coated areas with a tent of plastic sheeting.

To eliminate any potential contamination problems between coating, it's sometimes easiest to recoat while the previous coat of epoxy is still "green." This can be anywhere from 1 to 3 hours after the earlier application, depending on temperature and hardener. When the resin begins to cure and becomes tacky, you can immediately roll on another coat without having to worry about running. We have applied as many as three coats in a single day, with only short intervals between them, with no sagging. Since you can't sand between these coatings, your final surface may be rougher than desired, and this may be a disadvantage of this system. On the other and, we have found that the self-leveling ability of successive coatings is sometimes as good as, if not better than, a single coating.

When you have applied the proper amount of epoxy, your next step is to smooth the surface for painting or varnishing. In many cases, especially in the interior, you will have sanded most of the parts before installing them in your hull. It is usually most efficient to sand exterior surfaces on the completed hull after all coatings have been applied.

General sanding of a cured resin surface can be a lot of hard work, especially if you are working towards a high gloss final finish. There are, fortunately, some labor-saving shortcuts. We use a foam disc grinding pad on a light duty power circular polisher to rough and smooth sand 90% of the hull's exterior surface areas. Usually, we use 80 to 100 grit sandpaper with the sanding pad to first rough sand coated surfaces, and then use 120 to 180 grit for power finish sanding. Many boatbuilders find this surface adequate. A further wet sanding by hand with 220 to 320 grit paper will produce an extremely smooth surface for a high gloss finish for either varnish or paint.

Primers

We find that we rarely need primer paints when we coat hulls with WEST SYSTEM epoxy. Primers can't, of course, be used on naturally finished hulls, but even on painted surfaces they don't seem to result in any particular saving in finishing time.

Primers are not usually needed to help bond a paint film to cured WEST SYSTEM resin. Most finish coat-

Figure 5—Finish sanding grey pigmented resin on deck of SLINGSHOT. Orbital finish sanders can be used effectively for such finish sanding.

ings readily adhere to a well-sanded epoxy-coated surface, although interfacing primers are required with some specialized bottom paints. If the instructions on your paint or varnish recommend a specially primed surface, sand your resin coating until it is no longer glossy or shiny, and follow the directions given for fiberglass preparation. Test the product in an inconspicuous area to be sure that it will bond to epoxy. If any product fails to dry within the period specified on its packaging, try a different brand or use a primer.

Primers are sometimes used to make sanding quicker. The theory is that they are easier to sand than resin, and while this may be true in some situations, you must weigh the benefit against the time needed to apply the paint and to achieve an even surface. Since primers are difficult to apply evenly with a roller or brush — because of the safety issues involved, we automatically rule out spraying primer paints — application time may well exceed any extra resin sanding time. Primers definitely do not flow as well as WEST SYSTEM epoxy, so you need a good deal of sanding just to get the primer as smooth as the original rough-sanded resin surface.

A colored base coat will facilitate final fairing by serving as a guide to prevent oversanding, and will also, to some extent, reduce the number of coats of paint needed to cover an unpainted surface. When we plan to paint a hull, we therefore often add WEST SYSTEM pigment to our final coat of epoxy, and use this instead of primer as a tracer coat.

Surface Glazing

While primers don't significantly reduce finishing time, glazing or surface compounds often do. These commercially available products are much thinner than standard puttying fillers, so you can apply them quickly in a thin film over large areas. We recommend using a wide putty knife or squeegee to apply surfacer. This technique results in a relatively smooth surface which is not difficult to sand to a fine finish. Since small particles of dirt can interfere with your finish, be sure your wood is clean before applying these products.

Surfacing compounds have an advantage over primer paints in that they are high solids materials and can be used to mechanically force-fill small voids and depressions. Imperfections in a overall cured resin surface can be filled quickly and efficiently, assuming that they are reasonably small or shallow. Often, the choice is between sanding away small air holes and valleys or filling them. The extra sanding takes time and may involve the removal of more protective resin coating than desirable, so surfacing compounds present an attractive alternative.

All major paint companies market these compounds with instructions for their use. Be sure to select compatible surfacer and finishing systems since some finishes use very active solvents which can lift surfacing materials. Also check your instructions to be sure that you use the recommended thinner when your compound is too thick to apply in a controlled thin film.

Be particularly aware of the consistency of your glazing compound as you apply it. If it is too thick, it will be difficult to apply in a controlled film, and if it is too thin, you will lose filling power. It's better to err on the thin side because you can always apply a second coat and this is much quicker than sanding away excess. You may have to add thinner at regular intervals to make up for its continual evaporation as you work.

Paints

Over the years we have tried many different paints manufactured by many different suppliers, but we haven't tried them all. Some paints and varnishes do not cure well over WEST SYSTEM epoxy. Paint behavior can be unpredictable and we can't test all of the many brands on the market, so we urge you to experiment with your planned finishing system before you make a major investment in it.

Recently developed linear polyurethane (LP) paints are without question vastly superior to any others we have used. We recommend LP systems highly as the best for use over WEST SYSTEM resin. They have excellent resistance to sunlight, salt spray and other

Figure 6—Rolling on two-part linear polyurethane paint.

weathering agents, and because they are as hard and resistant to abrasion as polyester gelcoat, they are used almost exclusively for recoating fiberglass hulls. Linear polyurethanes bond extremely well to properly prepared WEST SYSTEM epoxy coated surfaces.

LP paints may be sprayed, rolled and brushed. Hand application is slower than spray painting, but requires less preparation so there is not a great time difference between the two methods. In some situations brushing may be quicker. In all cases it is far safer.

Hazardous solvent fumes escape from any type of paint as it is applied, and care must be taken to provide adequate ventilation during all painting operations. Linear polyurethanes present additional health hazards because they contain 1 to 2% isocyanate, a highly toxic material. When LP paints are sprayed, isocyanate is atomized and may be inhaled. Most LP manufacturers recommend that spray painters wear forced air respirators while working, but we recommend that you simply do not spray LP paints. Roller and brush application of linear polyurethanes substantially reduces the problem.

Clear Coatings and Natural Finishes

Clear coatings, commonly called varnishes, are attractive, durable and fairly easy to apply. Their major drawback is that they break down under exposure to sunlight and therefore require more maintenance than pigmented coatings. We share the desire of wooden boatbuilders to show off the beauty of the material, but because a major goal of our philosophy is to keep things practical, we prefer to use clear coatings in interior and other areas where the effects of ultraviolet rays are minimal. See Chapter 24 for a discussion of varnishing interiors.

Two things happen when a clear-coated surface is subjected to too much sunlight. The first and most obvious is that the varnish itself gradually degrades. At the same time, in a less well understood process, slight chemical and physical changes take place in the surface wood cells through the varnish. These changes may contribute to coating failure by promoting the physical separation of an already-weakened coating from the ultraviolet-altered wood.

With the limitations of present technology, all clear coatings on wood may be expected to break down in the presence of sunlight. The time this takes depends on the formulation of the specific coating, the number of hours it is exposed to sunlight, the location of the varnished item on the boat and the surface under the clear coating.

Some clear coatings have longer life spans than others. Those which last the longest contain expensive

ultraviolet shields. Sold by most marine paint manufacturers, these are usually called spar varnishes; one of the easiest ways to recognize them is their high cost. Most spar varnishes have a phenolic resin base mixed with tung and linseed oil, a combination which is less hard and durable than LP paint but which has the best track record among clear coatings for withstanding sunlight. There are now several clear linear polyurethane paint systems formulated with UV filters.

Varnish will last longer on hull topsides than on decks. Decks receive direct exposure to sunlight, but hull sides take only glancing blows and are usually partially shaded. The early morning and late afternoon sun that shines directly on topsides is not nearly so destructive as midday light because its rays are well filtered by atmospheric interference. For these reasons, two coats of spar varnish over WEST SYSTEM resin on a deck might last only a summer in our Michigan climate and twice as long on the hull sides.

You can cut down on labor and extend the life of your varnish considerably by adding a new coat every year. At the beginning of every season, lightly sand your clear coated areas and apply a single coat of material.

Using WEST SYSTEM resin as a base for varnish appears to lengthen the life of a clear coating. We feel that the reason for this is the very tenacious bond which is made between the resin and the wood fiber. It seems to be more difficult for wood to separate from a well-bonded epoxy coating as it alters under UV rays than from a standard varnish.

Any natural finish which is exposed to sunlight will require more maintenance than a colored coating. All decisions on bright finishing should be made with full realization that more upkeep will be necessary in the future. Repair of dings and gouges is much more difficult on a naturally finished hull and may require rout-

Figure 7—Bright finish on GOLDEN DAZY.

ing out a whole outer layer of veneer. On the other hand, one advantage of a clear coated hull is that should you decide that a natural finish is not practical for your situation, you can paint it. It's much more difficult to change from paint to a clear coating than to change from clear coating to paint.

There are many excellent clear coatings on the market. Different brands may react differently to heat, cold and humidity, so experience with a given brand is perhaps the largest single factor in a successful job. Test all coating materials on a small sample of your surface before applying them. Buy a small quantity of your proposed finish, apply it following manufacturer's instructions, and if it doesn't dry within an appropriate period, try a different brand.

Cost

In general, the costs of paint, varnish and related materials are a very small portion of the total cost of a boat's paint job. Surface preparation and coating application require an enormous amount of time, so an expensive but long-lasting paint is usually a better value than a short-lived, inexpensive coating. When you make decisions on paint, consider the quality and reputation of a product as well as its price. A coating which costs twice as much and lasts twice as long as its competitor is probably a better buy because it will save you considerable labor.

We suggest that you gather all available information about the paint or varnish you intend to use. Most manufacturers publish complete technical bulletins on their specific coatings and coatings systems as well as application and mixing instructions. Experience with one brand will help you to predict its behavior in different situations, but in all cases we recommend testing paints and varnishes before applying them to large areas.

Applying Paint and Varnish

We are always reluctant to spray paint or varnish because of the health hazards involved in the application method, and have usually relied on the roller-brush method of painting and varnishing. With some experience and the benefit of a good material, this technique can rival a quality sprayed finish, but you must develop your skills. We hope that the following comments will help. See Chapter 24 for details on applying varnish and paints to interiors.

Before you begin coating, prepare your final sanded surface. It must be free of all dust, dirt, sanding residue and contaminants. We suggest using a four-step surface preparation procedure:

(1) Wipe down the hull using a large sponge, continually rinsing it out in a large bucket of water. Try to keep it as clean as possible as you remove the majority of the loose material from the hull surface.
(2) Wipe the wet hull dry with soft, clean rags or paper towels.
(3) Wipe the hull down again, using soft, absorbent rags slightly wetted with a solvent (enough to wet the hull as you are wiping it down).
(4) Use a tack rag to remove any remaining dust or dirt from the hull surface. (Use a tack rag again just prior to applying paint to the surface.)

Dust control can sometimes be a difficult problem in a wooden boatshop. Usually, you should discontinue all wood sawing or machining operations well in advance of the actual painting operation. It is a good idea to wet down the entire boatshop floor with a light spray of water. This will not only help keep dust down on the floor, but will also attract dust from the air.

Use the same foam sponge rollers to apply the paint film which you used to apply WEST SYSTEM resin, and for the same reason: control. This type of roller does an excellent job of applying a *controlled* film thickness over a large area in a minimum amount of time.

The primary uses of a brush are to smooth out the stipple finish which the roller leaves and perhaps also paint those areas which are difficult for the roller to reach. Even application of paint to a surface is difficult with a brush because of the problem of controlling the film thickness.

The painting job is best split up between two people, and this is without question the fastest method. Arm one man with a roller and roller pan and the other with a wide brush (3 or 4 inches) and a small container of paint. The "roller" begins application of the paint, using long, steady strokes to cover a specific area before the roller is again filled in the paint tray. It is important to learn early the approximate surface area you can cover with a roller full of paint as you apply it to the hull surface. Once you have developed a feel for "area," you will be able to plan the rolling application better. Then you won't get in trouble with too much paint collected in a given area and no place to move it to. A common error is to discover that you are a little light on paint film in one area, but in correcting the situation you make it much worse by applying much more paint than the area can handle without running. The solution is to learn how to get just a little paint out of the roller pan with the roller, just as you might control the amount of paint on a paint brush by scraping it against the sides of a paint can. It's harder to do with the roller, but can be done.

Immediately after the paint is rolled on, the "brush person" follows with a slightly wet-out brush, stroking the surface vertically or horizontally with only enough pressure to smooth the coating. Finer brushes will produce the smoothest surfaces with the best chance for flow out, and we suggest that you use only high quality brushes. The "brusher" should follow the "roller" as closely as possible without getting in his way, so that the time span from initial roller application to final brushing is as short as possible. This gives the paint film the best chance to flow out before the solvent content of the paint film begins to evaporate. Paints are usually composed of 40 to 60% solvents, most of which will evaporate before the paint film cures. These solvents play a key role in the successful development of the surface finish. Immediately after you apply paint to a surface, the solvents it contains will begin to evaporate and a cure or drying out of the paint film begins. The *rate* at which the solvents evaporate is crucial to the roller-brush application process. If the solvents evaporate too fast, the paint film will not have a chance to flow out smoothly. Brush or roller marks will remain visible. If too much solvent is used, the paint will have less viscosity, resulting in a thinner paint film which may not have the coverage or the gloss which is desired. The object, of course, is to use just enough thinner to promote good flowing of the paint and no more. Hot, dry conditions will require that you use more thinner, due to faster evaporation. Manufacturers also offer fast or slow thinners to help with the evaporation problem.

As the painting progresses, the "brusher" will have the best feel as to how the paint is working. If it is dragging under the brush, add more solvent for proper flowing. Usually, you can add this right into the roller pan and immediately stir it in with the paint. On hot, dry days evaporation will cause a rapid loss of solvent out of the roller pan, causing a paint to become too stiff for proper flowing. You can solve this problem with small applications of solvent to the roller pan at frequent intervals to match the amount of solvent lost by evaporation. Again, the "brusher" will be the first to feel that the paint is getting too stiff.

Usually, two coats of paint are required with the roller-brush method for sufficient color coverage. You can use the application of the first coat to gain experience in application methods. If you get some runs, dull spots or actual misses, you can correct them before you apply a second coat. Runs are usually the most difficult problem, but it is common to sand a little between coats anyway, so they aren't regarded as a major disaster on the first coat. However, with the sec-

ond coat, you're pretty well stuck with them. If you do develop runs on the second coat, hopefully you will discover them before the paint film begins to stiffen. The only chance to deal with a run and make it better is to stroke the immediate area of the run lightly with a small brush that is as dry of paint as it is possible to make it. The object is not to add any more paint in the area of the run, but, in fact, to remove some with the brush.

With linear polyurethane paints, we have found that it is not necessary to sand between coats to get good adhesion, provided that recoating is done within a 36 hour period. Of course, to achieve the optimum final finish, a light sanding between coats with fine paper is desirable because this removes any dust or imperfections which might exist in the first coat surface and provides the best possible surface for the final coat.

Figure 8—Bright finish on IOR ½ ton yacht HOT FLASH.

Chapter 12
Synthetic Fibers and
WEST SYSTEM Epoxy

There are many areas in wooden boat construction where we and many others have successfully used synthetic fibers to augment wood structures and increase their overall capability. Synthetic fiber augmentation has been particularly effective in areas where constrained geometry is necessary. Centerboards, rudders and masts are all components where denser, high-strength fibers can be incorporated with wood to improve performance.

For hulls, the fiberglass-covered, wood strip composite process described in Chapter 20 has proved to be an excellent mating of wood and synthetic fibers. In more typical wood/WEST SYSTEM* Brand epoxy construction, synthetic fibers are regularly used to increase exterior hull and deck durability by providing a denser outer surface to resist abrasion and impact loads. This is usually accomplished by sheathing exterior surfaces of a boat with a woven fabric which is bonded to the wood with epoxy resin. Glass fiber is by far the most important and popular synthetic because of its low cost, ready availability in many different weaves and ease of handling. However, carbon and aramid fibers are used increasingly in areas where weight or stiffness is critical.

The decision to use fabric sheathing and structural synthetic fiber augmentation should be made carefully, with particular attention to the extra cost and weight involved. There are a potentially infinite number of ways to assemble combinations of wood, synthetic fibers and epoxy into a structure. Be aware when specifying an assortment of materials into a composite matrix that a wide variation in material properties can result. A combination which has high specific stiffness, for example, may have very low impact strength. A potentially high-strength laminate might have poor crossgrain and interlaminar shear properties.

Unfortunately, for most composite material combinations, there are no scantling rules and limited test data is available to serve as a guide. Some results of static and fatigue testing of various wood and fiberglass laminates are provided in Appendices B and D. These data can be used in the development of composite laminates, but we suggest that seeking the help of materials experts and direct testing of specific laminates are very worthwhile before final decisions are made on scantlings for a given craft.

A Survey of Synthetic Fibers and Cloths

Both synthetic and natural fibers may be used with WEST SYSTEM resin in boatbuilding. Excellent results may be obtained when synthetic fibers are applied to wooden structures at room temperature with minimal bonding pressure. The performance characteristics of the wood, however, will dominate the composite. Synthetic fibers can be easy to maintain and most have good strength-to-weight ratios, but they can be difficult to machine with typical woodworking tools.

Fiberglass, Kevlar™ aramid and graphite are popular modern structural materials which have applications in boat construction. Fiberglass, available in E(lectrical) and S(tructural) grades, is denser and has less stiffness and tensile strength than either Kevlar or graphite. It has more impact strength than graphite. Kevlar 49 has higher impact resistance and tensile strength than fiberglass and graphite, and it has the highest strength-to-density ratio of the fibers, but it is relatively weak in compression. Graphite, also called carbon, has the highest stiffness-to-density ratio of the three.

Since fiberglass, aramid and graphite have clear strengths and weaknesses, it's fairly easy to decide among them. Lightweight fiberglass, which is white and opaque, will become transparent when it is wet out with resin. Kevlar and graphite are yellow and black respectively and therefore are not appropriate for sheathing boats which will be naturally finished. Kevlar's high tensile strength and impact resistance can be exploited, but it should not be relied upon for high compression loading. Kevlar is impossible to fair and it becomes fuzzy when it is sanded. Although it is moderately priced compared to graphite, aramid is considerably more expensive than fiberglass. Graphite can be especially helpful in building small or intricately shaped components which must be quite stiff, but its brittleness and price restrict its use in other applications.

Three other synthetic fibers have been used extensively in boatbuilding. Dynel™ acrylic, polyester and polypropylene fabrics are low modulus materials which stretch much more than glass fibers to resist a load. One popular theory is that this may be an advantage if a hull is damaged by a sharp object — an outer skin of fabric might stretch rather than tear and serve as a bladder to keep the boat afloat. Meanwhile, under normal conditions, these fabrics are parasitic: they con-

* TRADEMARK OF GOUGEON BROTHERS, INC., U.S.A.

tribute weight, but very little strength or stiffness to the structure. An alternative is to use Kevlar, which can pay for its weight in added strength and stiffness, when fiberglass cannot provide sufficient impact resistance. Kevlar will, however, significantly increase the cost of a hull.

Dynel, polyester and polypropylene are quite inexpensive compared to the other reinforcing fibers, but some aspects of their application can be difficult. In some cases, they do not become transparent when they are wet out. They tend to float in resin, and this may cause an irregular surface which requires additional fairing. These fibers do not abrade well, so this process can be difficult.

All of these synthetics are available in many forms. Fiberglass, for example, is sold as chopped fibers, chopped strand mat, roving and cloths woven with twisted and untwisted yarns. Woven cloths are sold by weight — a square yard of 6 oz. cloth weighs 6 oz., and a square yard of 17 oz. cloth weighs 17 oz. Weave patterns affect the feel and handling of the cloth and can detract from its physical properties, particularly in fatigue, because of stress where the yarns cross. Woven cloth is better than matting insofar as it permits precise alignment of fibers. Twisted yarns tend to be weaker than untwisted yarns because filaments can be fractured in spinning. "Knit" unidirectional cloths provide the best alignment of fibers under load.

Most fibers, synthetic and natural, are treated with sizing to protect them from moisture and to facilitate processing. Various finishes are used on fiberglass, and some of these are more compatible with epoxy resin than others. Amino silane finishes promote bonding with epoxy, while the more common volan finishes promote bonding with polyester resins. WEST SYSTEM epoxy will bond with volan-treated glass, but substantially better results are obtained with the proper silane-finished variety.

Combinations of wood and reinforcing fibers may be used to take advantage of the strengths and weaknesses of the fibers. If, for example, you sheathe a hull with Kevlar for impact strength, you may also have to add an exterior layer of fiberglass to prevent abrading the aramid during fairing. As we explain more thoroughly in Appendix D, two or more layers of synthetic fibers can be laid together on a wood laminate, or they can be interspersed between layers of wood. In an attempt to increase impact resistance it may be more efficient to laminate a layer of Kevlar near the interior of a hull, where loads will be in tension and fairing problems minimized. Then a fiberglass skin can be added on the exterior.

Fatigue Behavior of Synthetic Fibers

As we were testing fatigue behavior in wood, another NASA program investigated fatigue resistance in several glass fiber composites. From this, several conclusions can be drawn about both glass fibers and the resin used to bond them.

Resin played a significant part in high cycle fatigue resistance. Polyester-bonded samples were about 8% stronger in one-time, load-to-failure static capability then epoxy-bonded samples. In high cycle fatigue, however, the roles reversed: the polyester laminate retained less than 19% of its original one-time static strength. (For more detailed discussion, see Appendix B.)

Failure occurs in glass laminate in two distinct ways. Early on, even in the first few cycles, a matrix cracking and debonding occurs, primarily because of glass's low elastic modulus. At about 100,000 cycles — or, if a boat is subjected to cyclic load increases associated with waves every 3 seconds, after about 83 hours of sailing — the glass fibers, having relieved themselves of small discontinuities, become the dominating factor through to final failure. At the early low cycle matrix debonding stage there is significant loss of residual mechanical properties, including stiffness. This is probably what causes some fiberglass racing boats to get soft and lose their competitive edge. The effects of sea water on the fatigue performance of fiberglass are not yet fully understood. It appears, however, that fiberglass laminate material properties may be significantly reduced by exposure to salt water.

Common Uses for Fiberglass Cloth

Glass cloth is regularly used for protection in high abrasion areas. We use it on interior surfaces of centerboard trunks and cases for retracting rudder blades and cover the centerboards, daggerboards and rudders which move in these cases with cloth for abrasion resistance and increased strength. The end grain in plywood joints can be protected with cloth or tape. Joints in high traffic areas receive more abuse than others, so we often use glass tape on them. In Chapter 22 we discuss the use of glass tape on plywood chines.

Although we do not always use fiberglass cloth on high quality marine grade plywood, an exterior layer of cloth is necessary for finishing soft or rotary-peeled plywood. Fiberglass can make Douglas fir ply much easier to work and more reliable over time. Cloth sheathing will also prevent the surface checking which is so common with fir plywood. Boats built with Western red cedar provide a surface which is relatively soft.

A layer of cloth serves as a *screed* and helps to maintain an adequate thickness of resin coating, creating a more durable surface. Without the cloth, it's easy to sand away a lot of epoxy and leave little to protect the wood surface.

Glass cloth is also useful for structural purposes. In strip composite construction, it increases hull strength and stiffness. In other types of hulls, it can improve local strength and stiffness, especially in areas where loads do not coincide with the orientation of the wood grain or when extra support is needed to balance uneven numbers of layers of wood. Additional wood will also increase hull strength and stiffness, and it is often cheaper and lighter to use, but in some areas constrained geometry doesn't allow enough room.

Layers of cloth can rapidly turn 5-ply panels into 7-ply panels, and do so in such a way that a layer with a higher modulus of elasticity is further away from the neutral axis. When fiberglass cloth is applied to a curved panel, it is neutral while the wood below it is prestressed. The cloth helps the entire panel retain its shape, and it can reduce the number of stringers needed for longitudinal support. When fiberglass is laid away from the neutral axis between layers of a wood laminate, it can help control springback. In other applications it restricts crossgrain shrinking, swelling and splitting.

We often use lightweight, 4 oz. to 6 oz. woven glass to cover the many hundreds of tiny staple holes on the exterior surfaces of hand-laminated hulls. To do this, we coat the hull, let the resin cure and sand it lightly. The epoxy seals the end grain in staple holes so that they will not absorb too much resin as the cloth is applied. Then we apply the fiberglass in the normal manner.

On naturally finished hulls, lightweight fiberglass cloth can be particularly useful. Just as cloth covers staple holes, it will cover some smaller flaws and the fabric will hold clear resin in small voids until it cures. Flaws and voids may also be filled with tinted resin, a technique used on major imperfections, but the results are unsightly by comparison. Suggestions on the best ways to treat larger flaws are provided later in this chapter.

Although it is cheaper than Kevlar and graphite, fiberglass is more expensive than wood and its application is time-consuming. To decide if a sheathing material is warranted for a project, make test panels out of the wood you plan to use. Judge the effectiveness of any fabric according to weight increase per square foot, relative increase in stiffness and strength, resistance to abrasion and impact, difficulty of application and cost.

Surface Preparation for Reinforcing Fabrics

Before applying any cloth, roll an initial coating of WEST SYSTEM epoxy over the bare wood surface following instructions in Chapter 11. Then fill all depressions and voids with resin thickened with low density filler. The initial coating doesn't need to be completely cured, but if putty is applied while the epoxy is still fluid, it may disturb the surface and result in more sanding later. Some builders prefer to allow the initial coating to cure completely and then to sand it lightly or scrape it with a cabinet scraper before filling. The smoother surface may allow for a more precise puttying operation which requires less sanding.

On bright finished boats, we try to fill voids as attractively as possible, ignoring very small nicks and relying on the cloth to hold enough resin in place to fill them. Sometimes we mix resin with fillers and other ingredients to make putties which blend in with the color of the surrounding wood and use these to fill larger voids. At other times, we mix about 2 oz. of epoxy, usually with slow hardener, and let it stand for about 45 minutes at 70°F, or until it is a thick, clear paste which can be directly applied to voids. To keep it from sagging, we cover the paste with a small piece of polyethylene, pressing the patch smooth to fair it into the overall surface. Then, when the epoxy has cured, we remove

Figure 1—Applying fiberglass to deck of 60 foot proa SLINGSHOT using the dry method. Glass cloth around daggerboard slot has been wet out.

the plastic and sand the surface fair. We always try to avoid sanding through the initial coating of surfaces which will be naturally finished because sanded areas will show up noticeably lighter after recoating. (Much of this discoloration will modify with time.)

When the initial coating and puttying applications have cured, begin sanding or scraping the resin coating very lightly. Then do a more thorough job on all puttied areas until you have removed the fuzzy feel of the cured epoxy and the filled spots are fair and smooth. We usually use a 2,000 r.p.m. electric polisher with a 7 inch soft foam disc pad and 80 grit aluminum oxide paper for this job, but a sanding block and 50 or 80 grit paper will also work. Vacuum or sweep the surface to remove all residue. Particles the size of sand granules can help trap air between substrate and cloth and cause serious bonding problems.

Applying Fabric

All fabrics are applied in about the same way. Whenever possible, we use the *dry method*. This will not work on overhead and vertical surfaces, however, so in those areas we reluctantly rely on a *wet application method*. WEST SYSTEM Fast Hardener is preferable for areas which will be naturally finished, but it may not provide enough time for wet method fabric application. In this case, slow hardener is preferable because it allows more working time.

If the surface is fairly flat, lay the cloth cut over it and smooth all wrinkles. Use staples or masking tape to hold it in place, slightly overlapping any cloth joints. When the material is in position, pour mixed epoxy directly on the fabric. Begin by mixing small quantities of resin, and increase batch size as you gain more experience. Use a squeegee to spread the resin and to remove any pools which form. Firm pressure is neces-

sary, but don't press so hard that you shift the cloth.

The dry method has clear advantages. The resin is easy to control and, because you use limited quantities at any time, there is no rush. With this technique, the epoxy never starts to cure before you are finished with the squeegee. With the wet method, on the other hand, speed is of some importance. The wet operation can be tricky, and may require the organized efforts of three people.

If you are working on a vertical or overhead surface, lay out and fit the fabric and then roll it back on its tube for easy handling. Mix resin and hardener, apply a coating to the substrate, and wait until it thickens. Then lay the cloth into the epoxy, sliding it into position. Surface tension will usually hold the cloth where you want it, but when you are installing heavy cloth overhead you may need staples to prevent drooping. We find that the entire process is much more successful when one person holds the tube of cloth and two others position it and smooth out wrinkles. As soon as any part of the cloth is positioned where you want it, roll on more resin. Wet out the cloth completely and remove any air bubbles, using a squeegee as you would with the dry method.

With the wet method, application area is limited by time and number of workers. If you use slow hardener, you will have only about an hour from the time you first coat the surface to complete the procedure. This is usually adequate, but if you are inexperienced or have problems convincing friends to share in the fun, start with smaller areas and work up to big surfaces as you become more capable.

Whether you use the wet or the dry system, the point of the squeegee process is to saturate the weave of the cloth and then to remove any puddles of excess epoxy which might cause the fiberglass to float from the surface. Squeegeeing also helps to loosen air which might be trapped in the cloth/resin matrix. A properly squeegeed surface has a rather matte finish and its weave should be only about two-thirds filled with resin. Don't try to fill it completely at this point — later coatings will take care of the problem. As you work, watch for areas of cloth which haven't received enough epoxy. Dry spots may be difficult to see, but they usually look dull and slightly white. It's especially important to prevent them on surfaces which will be naturally finished because the cloth will remain visible if it is not wet out completely.

Take special steps if you are applying fiberglass to a naturally finished hull and want it to be clear and transparent. Lighter weight fabric will be clearer than heavier fabric. Four ounce cloth will be virtually transparent when it is wet out, and some glass strands may

Figure 2—Applying polypropylene cloth to a 45 foot outrigger hull using the wet method.

be visible with 6 oz. cloth. Avoid excessive handling or folding of the fabric and, to prevent fractured strands, squeegee as little as possible. After laying the cloth on the hull, use a vacuum cleaner to remove any loose fibers. If strands of glass fiber accumulate in the resin as it is spread, it may become frothy, so apply small quantities of resin at a time to minimize the use of the squeegee. If you are having a lot of trouble, try rounding off the edges of the squeegee. If globs of milk-colored fractured strands develop, pluck them from the wet surface.

Figure 3—Wetting out the fiberglass cloth on a wing mast for 60 foot proa SLINGSHOT. In this case, 4 oz. fiberglass was draped over spar and wet out with rollers.

Milkiness in a finish may be caused by aeration of the resin as it is moved around during the wet-out process. The resin begins to cure and thicken quickly and, as its surface tension increases, minute bubbles are trapped in it. To prevent aeration, mix small batches of epoxy and apply them with a squeegee rather than a roller.

The resin/cloth matrix is easiest to trim when it is only partially cured, 2 or 3 hours after application with fast hardener. Excess cloth is much more difficult to cut when the resin is fully cured, and it can be hard to peel it from a surface where it is not wanted. Use a sharp blade to cut away overhangs of resin-soaked cloth, keeping the blade clean with solvent.

We usually lay cloth on one half of a hull in one operation, lapping it a couple of inches past the keel. An irregular overlap can cause fairing problems, so we even off the fabric parallel to the keel before the resin has cured. To do this, we hold a light batten parallel to the keel, cut along it with a sharp knife, and peel away the excess. Then, when we apply cloth to the other side, we lap it two inches past the centerline for a total overlap of about 4 inches, and even it off. The extra layers of cloth help to protect the keel, which takes a good deal of abuse. There isn't much reason to overlap cloth anywhere else on the hull.

Running out of cloth and starting a new roll halfway down the hull can cause some problems. An overlap will create a bump which will require filling and sanding, but it can be hard to butt two pieces of cloth against each other. We've found that the best solution is to fit the two pieces carefully, with as little overlap as possible, and squeegee them in place. Then, when the resin is partially cured, we slice down the middle of the overlap and, working on each side in turn, lift the fabric from the hull, pull away the excess and replace the fitted portion. A little more resin may be needed to rewet the surface.

You can recoat the cloth with foam rollers when the resin is tacky. The first roller coating will probably not fill the weave of the fabric completely. Allow it to cure and then sand the surface lightly with a power sander and soft foam disc pad, taking care not to oversand any areas. Don't try to achieve a totally smooth surface — just remove the high spots so that the next coating will flow out more evenly and less sanding will be needed later. We usually apply two more coats of resin in quick succession before final sanding, but one is adequate in some cases. Coat the cloth heavily enough to make sure that final sanding will not expose any bare fiber and reduce the moisture vapor barrier provided by WEST SYSTEM epoxy. Then coat and finish the hull as described in Chapter 11.

Applying Unidirectional Graphite Fibers

WEST SYSTEM unidirectional graphite fibers are useful in masts, rudders, centerboards and other applications where high strength and stiffness are necessary but space is limited. They are packaged in tows, 1 inch wide unidirectional arrangements of approximately 40,000 fine black hairs. Lengths are wound with paper on reels for easy handling.

To prepare a surface for graphite fibers, check to see that it is clean and apply an initial coating of WEST SYSTEM resin, following instructions in Chapter 11. When this has cured, fill surface voids with a putty-like mixture of epoxy and Collodial Silica and allow this to cure. Sand filled areas flush with the surface and then lightly sand the entire substrate to guarantee that no contaminants remain to affect adhesion. Before applying graphite to an aluminum mast, use a WEST SYSTEM aluminum etch kit to prepare the substrate.

Defects and holes in aluminum may be filled with a mixture of epoxy and Colloidal Silica and sanded, but an initial coating of epoxy is unnecessary.

Next, apply a liberal coating of epoxy to the surface. This should be thick enough so that the graphite fibers will be partially saturated when they are laid out. Place the fibers as desired on the wet resin. If you are dealing with long pieces of graphite, use a dowel as an axle through the reel, unrolling with one hand and positioning with the other. Apply more epoxy and lightly work it into the fibers with a squeegee. When they are saturated, gradually increase the pressure. Then tap resin in between the filaments with a stiff-bristled brush. This process is easier if you warm the resin with a hair dryer as you work. When the graphite seems to be thoroughly saturated, carefully inspect it, probing with a corner of a squeegee and moving the fibers very slightly.

Use a modification of this technique to bond graphite to vertical and overhead areas. After coating, filling and sanding as usual, apply a second, light coat of epoxy to the surface. Then, before laying them in, wet out the fibers. Use the paper in which they are packaged as a temporary backing and spring clamps or masking tape at the ends of the graphite to keep them in place. When the fibers are wet, press them and the paper in place. Run a hand or a plastic spreader along the paper to be sure that the tow is in position. Peel off the paper, apply more epoxy and work it lightly as described above until the graphite is saturated.

For additional strength, it's possible to apply several layers of tow on top each other. In this situation it's best to step-taper the tows like a leaf-spring, applying the longest piece first and then successively shorter pieces. This way, you can feather each layer when you sand it and avoid cutting through full-length fibers.

Chapter 13

Lofting

Before you can actually build a boat, you must loft its lines to full size. This means taking the small scale plans of the design and projecting them to actual boat size. Most boat hulls are complexes of curved surfaces. Lofting guarantees that these curves flow smoothly into one another with fair, even lines. Because lofting determines the exact shape of the mold stations, success in lofting means that the stringers and planking can be easily applied to the molds and the resultant hull will be fair and look and perform as the designer envisioned. On the other hand, a poor job of lofting will result in parts not fitting and a shape which is hard to plank. Sometimes, poor lofting can lead to dissatisfaction and abandonment of the project.

This process of drawing the lines that describe the shape of the boat full size is necessary to correct the errors that creep into the small scale lines drawing that the designer uses to develop the shape of the hull. For example, if a boat were designed using a scale of 1 inch equals 1 foot, for a 30 foot boat you would have a 30 inch lines drawing. You would need to expand this 30 inch drawing 12 times in all directions, and in doing so you would also have all the errors that were drawn into the lines drawing multiplied by 12. This would result in inaccuracies that would detract from the even, smooth curves of the hull. Properly done, lofting corrects these inaccuracies. Making the corrections on the lofting floor rather than after construction has begun saves a great deal of labor and is necessary to produce a fair hull.

If you have never lofted a boat before, accurate lofting will be time-consuming. In many ways, it allows you to mentally build the boat before sawing any timber. Thought and head scratching expended at this stage will surely save frustration and errors after the actual construction has begun.

Lofting is a process which is hard to visualize or understand until you actually do it. To explain it abstractly is difficult. Furthermore, each loftsman has his own tricks for making the job easier, quicker and more accurate. We recommend that you look over this entire chapter before you begin. If you are daunted by the idea of starting out full-size, loft a simple boat on a large piece of paper. This will help you get a feel for what you're doing.

The following is a general discussion of the proce-

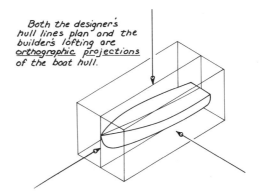

Both the designer's hull lines plan and the builder's lofting are orthographic projections of the boat hull.

The amateur builder will find the building project much easier if he takes the time to study the plans and attempts to see the boat in the lines.

Figure 1.

dures involved. More detailed explanations can be found in Howard I. Chapelle, *Boatbuilding* (W.W. Norton & Co., New York, 1941), Allan H. Vaitses, *Lofting* (International Marine Publishing Co., Camden, Me., 1980), and Robert M. Steward, *Boatbuilding Manual, 2nd Ed.* (International Marine Publishing Co., Camden, Me., 1980). If you have access to a computer and want to use it in the lofting process, consult Steward's book.

Hull Lines Drawings

The lines drawings will show three different views of the boat. Figure 6 shows a simple set of lines. The *profile* is the shape of the boat from a side view. The *half breadth plan* is the top view from the deck. The *body plan* is the end view of the boat from either bow or stern.

There are four types of lines in the drawings: the station lines, buttock lines, waterlines and diagonal lines. Together they form a three-dimensional grid. Each line represents an imaginary plane passing through the hull. (See Figure 6.)

Station lines: The imaginary planes of the station lines run vertically and athwartship. The shapes of the stations are shown stacked atop each other in the body plan view, half on one side of the centerline, half on the other. Station lines are almost always numbered.

Buttock lines: The imaginary planes of the buttocks pass through the boat vertically, fore and aft. The planes are spaced, generally at regular distances, off the centerplane that divides the hull in half. The centerplane is seen as the profile.

Waterlines: For these lines, the planes pass through the hull horizontally, at certain distances from the baseline.

Diagonal lines: The imaginary planes of the diagonals always run fore and aft, but are neither vertical nor horizontal. The intersection of a diagonal with the profile plane forms a line that is parallel to and some specified distance above the baseline. The height and the angle are chosen by the designer to facilitate fairing of the hull and usually intersect the body plan station lines at angles as close to 90° as possible.

For any set of lines, in at least two views the station lines, buttocks, waterlines and diagonals are represented as straight lines, and this forms the grid. On the third view, these lines are shown as curved or sectional views which represent the intersection of the plane with the surface of the hull.

The profile view will include the sheer line, keel and stem. The buttocks appear on the profile view as section views of the boat in the same plane at specific distances away from the centerline. In the half breadth plan appear the deck line and all the waterline sections. The diagonal sections also appear on this view. The body plan is made up of section views of the areas of the hull that the station lines intersect. The section from the bow to the widest point amidship will show up on one side of the centerline, and from the stern to the widest point amidship will be the other side.

Because most boat hulls are symmetrical, you only need to loft one half of the boat. However, some multihull designs have asymmetrical hulls and in these cases, obviously, you would have to lay out both sides of the hull.

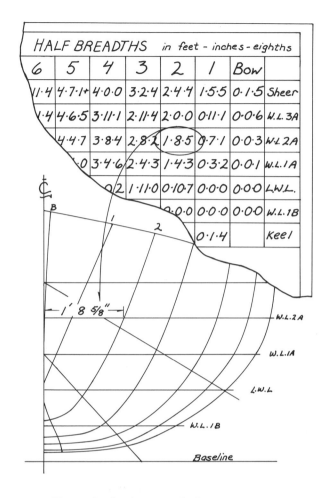

Figure 2—Application of offset dimensions.

give you the deck line and half breadth section views of the waterlines. Another set of offsets will give you the diagonal sections from the centerline. The diagonal sections are viewed at right angles to the diagonal lines on the body plan.

The Table of Offsets

The table of offsets provides the dimensions needed to loft the hull lines. It is arrived at by the designer by measuring the hull lines drawings with a scale rule. Above the table of offsets will be noted the units of measurement employed, for example, "offsets in feet, inches and eighths." A plus or minus will indicate a measurement slightly over or under that indicated, for instance, 1/16 inch. Thus, 1-8-5 in the table in Figure 2 would be 1 foot 8⅝ inches. The offsets for the profile view will be shown in heights above baseline or, in some cases, below baseline. Included in these offsets will be the profile view of the boat, which would be the keel, stem and sheer line, and the profile view of the buttocks sections. A second set of offsets will be the half breadth view measured from centerline, which will

Materials for Lofting

The lofting floor: The first thing needed is a place to loft the boat. Ideally, this space should be about 6 feet longer than the overall length of the boat, and about 4 or 5 feet wider than the widest or tallest point of the boat, whichever is greater. For a multihull, these dimensions usually apply to the biggest hull. Some multihulls, however, have cabins and wing structures that must be lofted and these need half of the total beam plus some working clearance. With the multihulls we have built here, we have been able to loft the hulls separately and then fade in the connecting structures where convenient on the lofting board. This enabled us to use a much smaller lofting board which could be narrower than half of the true overall beam of the craft.

For us it has been easiest to loft on a wood floor. If

you have a plywood floor in good condition, you can loft directly on it. If you want to save the lofting, or if the floor is in slightly rough condition, lay down a cheap grade of plywood of sufficient size to do the entire lofting. Coat this plywood with two coats of white semi-gloss paint and lightly sand it with 120 grit sandpaper. You can draw on the surface with lead pencils as well as ball point pens, and the white color makes everything easy to see.

Steel tapes: It is ideal to have a steel tape which will measure the full length of the boat and a shorter steel tape, say 12 feet long, that can lock in position. The shorter tape is handier for doing smaller layout projects.

Straightedge: You can purchase one or make it yourself. It should be at least a few inches longer than the distance from the baseline to the uppermost part of the boat to be lofted. If you are constructing a straightedge, clear pine is a good material. To check the straightedge for accuracy, joint one edge straight and check it by placing it down on the floor and drawing a line along the straightedge. Then turn the straightedge over and slide it up to the line. If there is no error, the straightedge will just touch the line in both positions. It is very important that this tool be as accurate as possible.

Square: For a smaller boat, you can use a steel carpenter's or framing square. On larger projects, you will have to construct a square to fit the job. Clear pine works well. We usually make the square out of 1 inch x 4 inch wood, with the longer arm the same length as the straightedge and the shorter arm about half that length. Check the two usable edges of the square in the same way you did the straightedge to make sure that they are perfectly straight. Put in a diagonal brace to maintain a perfect 90° angle. It is a good idea to glue the square together, making sure that any gussets or fasteners used will allow you to lay the square flat on the lofting board on either of its sides. This will make the square more versatile.

Although your square should be perfect, don't count on it for precise 90° angles in lofting. Wherever a true perpendicular is required, take the time to construct it using a bar compass.

Bar compass: You can make one yourself with slotted pieces of wood, bolts, washers and wing nuts, or you can buy one at a drafting supply house. It is used to construct perpendicular lines.

Bevel square or adjustable sliding T-bevel: This is used to transfer angles from the lofting board to various parts of the boat.

Weights, or hammer and nails: These hold the battens in position as they are used to fair the curves of the boat. Drafting weights are available at some drafting supply stores and are, of course, the handiest to use; however, a few dozen flatirons or padded bricks will do, or you can use a hammer and a pound or two of No. 6 nails.

Battens: These are thin pieces of wood or plastic which are bent around nails or weights so that you can draw curves. They are among the more important lofting tools. You can purchase sets of plastic battens of varying flexibility from drafting supply houses, or you can manufacture wooden battens yourself. The plastic battens are usually used to lay down the body plan where the curves are tighter, whereas wooden battens are usually used to fair waterlines, diagonals, buttocks and profile lines.

Spruce or clear white pine of the straightest grain you can find seem to be the best materials out of which to make battens. Most hardwoods are not too satisfactory because they tend to take and hold shape when left curved. An exception to this is that you can use a thin ash batten to lay out the station sections of the body plan or sharp curves in the stem and buttocks.

We usually lay in several 1 inch x 4 inch boards of clear pine for battens and rip them up to varying sizes depending on what we need. As the lofting progresses, different batten sizes may be desired, so a little extra material to make specialized battens comes in handy. Make one main batten that is 5 or 6 feet longer than the length of the boat. It should be about ¾ inch square for a small boat, and about 1 inch square for a larger boat. We use a 20 to 1 scarf in making up battens because the longer the scarf, the less likely it is that the scarf will cause a hard spot or kink in the batten. The main job of the batten is to allow you to sight the expanded lines of the boat and find areas of error. A crooked or kinky batten will make this job difficult.

The process of fairing will be much easier if you paint your battens flat black. The black is in sharp contrast to the white lofting floor and eliminates color variations in the grain of the wood. Using non-glossy paint will minimize harsh glare spots, as will the use of indirect lighting over the lofting floor.

Pens and pencils: You will need several ball point pens with different ink colors, several hard lead pencils and a pencil sharpener, and a felt tip pen. Be sure to use waterproof pens and markers; there are few things more irritating than finding that your wet feet have blurred your carefully drawn lines.

Kneepads or a movable foam cushion: The lofting process will be far more comfortable if you have something to kneel on.

Stock for measuring sticks and pick up sticks: Have on hand some scrap lumber or a few pieces of 1 inch x

4 inch stock which can be ripped into strips. You will need to make up approximately 15 sticks, half of them as long as your boat is high from the baseline, and half of them about as wide as its biggest half breadth dimension. Ideally, the sticks should be slightly wedge-shaped in section so that one edge makes a point.

Stock for blocks: Have enough 1 inch x 2 inch material on hand to make 6 inch long blocks. You will need one block for each station line in your lofting.

Cable and string: Lengths of cable and string will be used to lay out your lofting grid and must be at least as long as your lofting floor. The cable will have to stand up to about 500 pounds of tension and should be about 1/16 inch in diameter.

Laying Out the Grid

The first step in lofting is to lay out the *grid* for the three views. The grid is the general name denoting all of the straight lines that represent the locations of the buttocks, waterlines, diagonals, centerlines and station lines. You can easily recognize the grid from the lines

drawing by the fact that all the grid lines are straight, running either parallel with or at right angles to the baseline. The only exceptions are the diagonals, which in the body plan are lines coming off from the centerline at various angles. In small scale drawings, most designers draw separate grids for the profile, half breadth and body plans to help eliminate confusion. When the boat is lofted to full size, all these views are generally superimposed to save space, as in Figure 3. A common line then serves as the baseline of the profile view and the centerline for the half breadth and diagonal views. Sometimes a separate grid is laid down on a portable board for the body plan, so that it can be moved to different areas of the shop in order to build molds from it. Usually, however, the body plan is superimposed on the other views and the mid-station line of the profile view serves as the body plan centerline.

The grid is not difficult to lay out, but it is important that you do it with precision. If an error goes undetected it may not show up until many hours later, at which time there will be little to do but get out the

Figure 3—A lofting grid laid out for superimposed hull lines. Also pictured, various tools useful for lofting.

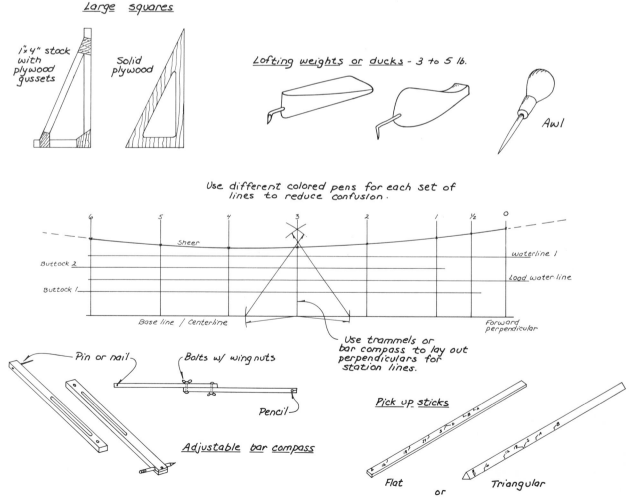

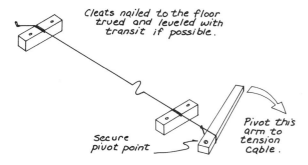

Figure 4—Arrangement for tightening baseline cable.

semi-gloss paint and start over. The grid lines will be permanent, and after careful checking they are drawn in ink.

The baseline: Because you use the baseline to lay out all the dimensions for the grid, you must lay out this key line very accurately. Our method is first to stretch a *locating cable* alongside where we want the baseline. We locate the baseline close to one edge of the lofting board, being sure that there is enough room to loft the boat above it.

To place the locating cable, we anchor it flush to the floor at one end with a heavy nail or screw, and run it over cleats to a lever at the other end of the floor. This lever — a flat board — pivots horizontally on a screw that passes through it and into the floor, and we anchor the cable on the underside of the lever between the pivot and free end. Using the free end as a handle, we then pull the lever until the cable is in about 500 pounds tension and nail the free end securely to the floor to maintain tension. (See Figure 4.)

We transfer the location of the cable to the lofting floor using the small tool in Figure 5. This tool is designed so that the thin (1/32 inch) tongue slips under

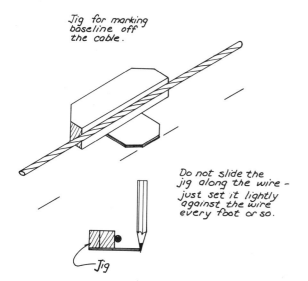

Figure 5—Jig or gauge for transferring baseline to lofting board.

the wire without disturbing it, and the raised portion butts into the wire. We put a pencil tick at the end of the tongue on the lofting, repeating this every few feet.

Station lines: The next step is to draw in the station lines. In laying these out you will want the first and last stations about equal distance from the ends of the lofting floor, so that you have some working room at each end of your lofting. Using a full length steel tape, mark and label in light pencil all the station points on the baseline.

We distrust the first inch of a steel tape. To be sure of accurate measurements, we slide the tape to its 1 inch mark and tick the surface at the 5 inch mark Then we retract the tape so that its 4 inch mark lines up with the tick on the board. Everything is again at zero. Some people slide the tape to the 1 inch mark and add the inch to all dimensions, but we have managed to saw things an inch too short too many times using this system.

Because an accurate lofting depends on the accuracy with which you lay out the foundation or grid, always double check grid dimensions before going on to the next step. It is important to note at this time that you must lay down all of the grid dimensions, i.e., station spacing, waterline spacing, buttock spacing, etc., exactly as the designer specifies. They might be hard to scale from the lines drawing, but the designer generally specifies the distances between all of these lines somewhere on the plans.

Next, erect the station lines perpendicular to the points you have marked on the baseline. We use the following procedure. First, construct a perpendicular line at the forward station, using a bar compass. Work to as high a degree of accuracy as possible. (See Figure 3.) Using the straightedge, draw the line in ink and extend it a few inches above the highest point of the boat to be lofted.

Using the square, then draw in lightly with pencil the station line at the opposite end of the lofting. Extend it a few inches above the boat's highest point. Next, measure from the baseline up these two station lines to the height of the boat plus a few inches so that you have a point of equal distance from the baseline on each station line. Then stretch a string between these two points, the string being, of course, parallel to the baseline. Starting at the station line which was geometrically constructed and drawn in ink, run a steel tape parallel to the string and mark the locations of the upper points of the station lines.

After checking the station line dimensions, use your straightedge and draw in all the station lines in ink. Be sure to check the station line which you drew in with the square using light pencil, as the square might have some slight inaccuracies. Using the felt tip pen and making a fat, easy-to-see line, label the tops and bottoms of the station lines with the station number. It is good to keep this labeling below the baseline and above where the lines of the boat will intersect the station lines.

To make it easier to lay out the rest of the grid, nail a block (1 inch x 2 inches and about 6 inches long) at each station line. Position the blocks on the lofting floor so that they are below and just touching the baseline and are approximately centered on each station line. Don't nail the blocks down too firmly; several may have to be temporarily removed when you fair your battens. You will now be able to use *measuring sticks* that will follow the station lines and firmly butt against the blocks, saving you from having to crawl down to the end of the station line each time to make sure that the measuring stick is exactly on the baseline.

Waterlines: The next job is to lay out all of the waterlines in the profile view. These will run parallel to the baseline and the distance between them will have been specified by the designer. In order to save time and eliminate potential errors, we use a measuring stick to mark the locations of the waterlines, rather than relying on a steel measuring tape at each station. Marking a measurement of, for example, waterline 2 at 3 feet 4 3/16 inches, once on a measuring stick is much less trouble than having to look this measurement up on the plans and lay it out each time with a steel tape. The measuring stick is nothing more than a stick which has the locations of all the waterlines from the baseline up. Lay the steel tape along the measuring stick and accurately mark and label the heights of all the waterlines above the baseline. Then lay the stick along the station line and butt it against the block nailed to the baseline. Make a light pencil mark on the station line at the location of each waterline. Repeat this procedure at every station line. Then, using the straightedge, connect all the parallel dots and draw in all the waterlines using ink. You can use the same ink color that you are using for the baseline and the station lines. Label each waterline on the ends.

Buttock lines: The next job is to lay out the buttocks. In drawing the buttocks, you will be using the baseline as a centerline and drawing the buttocks as straight lines as they are represented in the half breadth view. Make a measuring stick for locating the buttocks, following the same procedure that you used to lay down the waterlines. Use a different ink color in order to distinguish the buttocks from the waterlines. Label each buttock. If a buttock and waterline coincide, label the lines as both.

The body plan: The last job in completing the grid is to lay out the grid for the body plan. As mentioned before, some loftsmen use a separate portable board on which to draw the body plan, but we draw the body plan right on the lofting floor, using a station line near the center of the boat as the centerline of the body plan. The following directions are for drawing the body plan on the lofting floor.

Determine which station line you are using for the centerline of the body plan. On one side of the centerline you will be laying out the body plan from the stern to the widest part of the boat, and on the other side from the bow to the widest point. The waterlines you have already drawn will be passing through the body plan at their proper places and will need no further work. However, you will have to draw in the buttock lines. Because the body plan represents a view from the ends of the boat, the buttocks will be vertical lines parallel to the centerline and at the same distance out from the centerplane as they have been drawn in the half breadth plan. Take the buttock measuring stick you have already made and place it at right angles to the centerline of the body plan. The upper and lower waterlines are convenient places to position it for marking. Draw in the buttocks on both sides of the centerline and parallel to it. Ink in the buttocks using the same ink color that you used for the buttocks in the half breadth plan.

The next job is to lay out the *diagonals* in the body plan. If the boat has diagonals, these lines will be represented in the lines drawings of the body plan as straight lines extending out from the centerline at various angles. The designer feels these angles will be advantageous in fairing the shape of the hull. A study of the body plan usually shows the diagonals starting at the intersections of the waterlines and the centerline, and somewhere out in the body plan crossing an intersection of lines, possibly that of a waterline and buttock. If this is not the case, you will have to use whatever other information the designer supplies to develop the diagonals. This may be an angle measured in degrees. Once you have located these diagonal lines on your body plan and have double checked them, ink them in. Use a different ink color from that used for the other lines, and be sure the color you pick will be easily distinguished from the color you are using for the waterlines. Later on, waterlines and diagonals will be coming close together at low angles in the half breadth view of the lofting and you need to take care not to get them confused. The grid is now completed.

The Sheer Line

Although some expert loftsmen lay down several

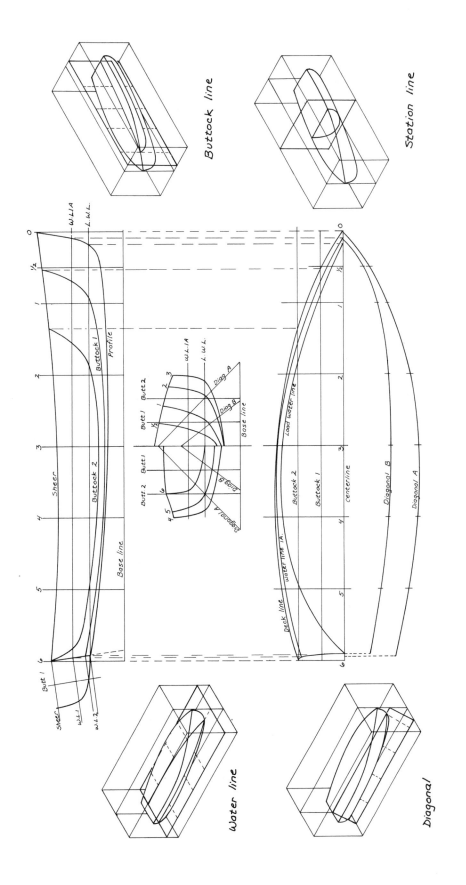

Figure 6—A simple set of lines showing the three views: profile, body plan and half breadth. The diagonals are drawn in at the bottom using the half breadth centerline. Isometric drawings around edge show hull lines as they intersect a rectangular prism. (These drawings are for illustration only.)

lines at one time, we find it less confusing to lay down and fair one line at a time, making sure it is correct before going on to another.

The first curved lines we put down in lofting a hull are the lines which outline the profile of a boat. Usually we begin with the sheer line. Go to the table of offsets for the profile view, given in distances from the baseline. Then at each station line carefully measure the dimensions from the baseline given in the offsets. Then lay a fairing batten on these points.

To fair a line: Select or mill a batten that will bend into a curve between the points to be faired. The object is to get the right flex — not so stiff that the batten breaks or moves the weights, nor so flimsy that the batten waves and makes it difficult to lay down a fair curve. First, lay the batten so that its edge is on the marks where the sheer line meets the foremost and aftermost stations, allowing equal overhang at each end. Hold it there using either lofting weights or small nails. If you use nails, put them *beside* the batten so the batten can slide lineally when you make any corrections (i.e., never nail the batten to the lofting). Then go to the mid-station and push the batten until its outside edge is on the mark and secure it in position. Continue moving the batten at the station marks, making the batten touch every point if possible.

If there seem to be any errors at this point, i.e., the batten is ½ inch or more off a mark, we first check to see if we have made any errors in taking the measurements from the offsets. If not, we then check the lines drawing with a scale rule to see if the offsets are correct. If it appears the designer has made a major error in transferring the measurement from the lines drawing to the offsets, we measure the lines drawing as carefully as possible and transfer the new measurement to the profile view. We also correct this in the table of offsets.

Once we have checked for major errors, we move the battens off the measurement points the minimum amounts to attain a fair curve. There is no scientific formula for the fairness: the curve should be pleasing to the eye and it should have no humps or flat spots. The best way to check a curve is to get your eye down level with the batten and sight along it looking for deviations.

Take your time sighting the batten to correct any errors in the curve. Move the batten the least amount possible to establish a fair curve and sight along the batten again. Once you are satisfied, draw the sheer line in ink. The color used in drawing the buttock lines in the grid would be good for the sheer line and other profile lines.

Other Profile Lines

The other lines which outline the profile of the boat are the keel line and the lines for the stem. Lay these out in the same manner as you did the sheer line, taking the measurements from the table of offsets and using a batten to fair the lines. Ink in the lines when they are fair.

In boats which have planking that ends in deadwood, there will be a rabbet line. This usually shows the shapes of the inner keel and stem and should be laid out too. We don't have a rabbet for the planking in our method of construction because we laminate the deadwood and outer stem on the hull after planking.

The Deck Line

The next line we lay out is a half breadth, or top view, of the deck line. The offsets for this line appear in the table of offsets shown in half breadth from the centerline. Transfer the measurements and fair this line as you did the sheer line. Double check any major errors and then move the batten just enough so that it forms a fair, even curve. Draw in the deck line in ink. The lines that you have drawn so far are final and it won't be necessary to change them during the lofting process.

Body Plan Sections

With the drawing of the grid, profile lines and deck line, the primary lines of the lofting are complete. The next step is to lay out the body plan, which is the section view of the stations. The profile lines and the deck line, drawn in ink, will give you the height of the keel profile above the baseline and the height and width of the sheer at any given station. The first job is to transfer these dimensions — as faired, not as given in the table of offsets — from the profile and half breadth views to the body plan using *pick up sticks*.

Pick up sticks do just that: they pick up a dimension from one area of the lofting and transfer it to another area or view. They are much easier to use and provide less chance for error than a steel measuring tape.

Pick any station to start with in transferring the profile and sheer points to the body plan. Lay the pick up stick along the station line so that it is touching the block at the baseline and the fine edge of the pick up stick just touches the station line. In using the pick up sticks, always label what station line, waterline or other information you are transferring. In this case, you would write the station number and baseline on the end of the sticks touching the baseline. Then you would mark and label the keel profile height, the sheer height and the deck width. Then take the pick up stick to the body plan grid and lay it along the centerline, touching the baseline block in the profile view. Mark the height of the keel profile and sheer on the centerline. Lay out the stations on the body plan on the same side of the centerline as the designer has drawn them in the plans.

To locate the half breadth deck point, draw a line out at right angles to the centerline at the height of the sheer. Most loftsmen use the adjacent station to lay out the sheer height and connect the two points with the straightedge, drawing in a light pencil line. Then, measure out from center on this line for the sheer point. This is slightly more accurate than using the square off the centerline. Once these points are located for a particular station, label them according to the station they belong to. Then lay out the rest of the stations in the same manner. These points are permanent and won't change until planking thickness is subtracted.

The next job, and it is a fairly big one, is to use the table of offsets plus the points that you have already located to lay out the body plan, which consists of a half section view of each station. Some loftsmen at this point lay out all the offsets for the body plan, measuring directly on the body plan grid with a steel tape. Other loftsmen prefer to lay out all of the dimensions on measuring sticks and then transfer the information to the body plan with these. Neither method offers a big advantage, although it may be easier to work in one spot with a table of offsets to mark the sticks than to climb around on the lofting board dragging the measuring tape and the offsets with you as you go. Whatever system you use, label everything carefully.

If you use measuring sticks, you can put the information for an entire station section on one measuring stick as long as this will not result in too much confusion. To do this, start at one end of the stick and use this end as a centerline from which to lay out the waterlines. Then use the other end of the stick as the baseline to lay out the buttocks, using a different ink color from that used for the waterlines. To mark the diagonals, choose the end of the stick which is less crowded for the centerline and use a different ink color. Then take the marked stick over to the body plan grid and transfer all of the information to the appropriate waterlines, diagonals and buttocks. Remember that the deck and profile have already been faired and won't appear on the measuring stick.

When you have laid out all the points, bend a thin batten around them, trying to make it touch them all. Hold it in place with small nails — on either side of the batten, not hammered through it — or weights. If you find gross errors, go through the checking process explained earlier. Adjust the batten, moving it as little as

Figure 7—Lofting weights and flexible plastic batten being used to fair after sections on an IOR racer.

possible from the points, until you have a fair, even curve, and then draw in the line in pencil.

Lay out the rest of the station sections in this manner. We suggest laying down the points for only one station section and rough fairing that station section before you go on to another. Some station section lines will cross each other and if points exist for several sections, this can get somewhat confusing.

It will help a little bit when it comes to final fairing if you use some consistency while rough fairing the section lines of the body plan. For example, if you move station 3 out slightly on the load waterline and station 2 needs correction in that area, make the correction on station 2 by moving it out slightly at the load waterline rather than moving it in on waterline 1. By the time the body plan is laid down, although the boat is by no means fair yet, it is quite easy to envision the shape. Unless a major error is found, the section of the after-

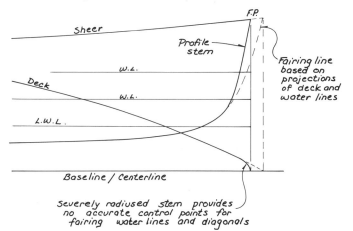

Figure 8—Profile fairing line for longitudinal hull lines.

most station in the body plan usually remains unchanged.

On the forward half of the body plan there is sometimes a line close to the centerline, but not necessarily parallel to it, which represents the thickness of the boat at the point where the planking ends, but before any rounding of the stem has taken place. You need to draw this line in also. It will later be used to determine the distance from center of the waterlines at the point where they run out past the stem. Some designers draw a light line in the profile view called a *fairing line,* which will appear to be some distance ahead of the stem, for the sole purpose of determining where the waterlines and diagonals, if slightly extended, would intersect with the centerline. (See Figure 8.)

At this point on some hulls we subtract planking thickness. This procedure is discussed later in the chapter.

Fairing the Longitudinal Lines

The next job, and it is a long one, but the essence of the lofting process, is to check the fairness of the body plan sections using the waterlines, buttocks and diagonals as tools. *This process will require continual readjustment and fairing of all the lines until the measurements and intersections correspond in all views.* The offsets will no longer be used except to check gross errors. Instead, the dimensions will be picked up from the lines already laid down in the lofting.

We usually start the fairing process at the load waterline. Select a pick up stick that is longer than the widest point at the load waterline of the boat. Place it with its sharp edge touching the load waterline and one well-squared end touching the centerline of the body plan. Label the pick up stick "load waterline" and label the end that is touching the centerline "centerline." Being careful not to move the stick, transfer the widths of the load waterline at each station to the stick. You will, of course, need to lay the stick on both sides of the body plan in order to pick up the dimensions of the load waterline at every station in the boat. Then take the stick to the half breadth view and use it to lay out the waterline widths on their respective stations.

In the profile view, the load waterline will intersect the stem or fairing line, and this intersection needs to be transferred to the half breadth view. Place your square perpendicular to the baseline on the point where the load waterline intersects the stem. Project this point down to the half breadth centerline. This will give you the end point for the waterline in the half breadth view. Go back to the body plan and measure the width of the stem at this point and transfer it back to the half breadth plan.

Then you are ready to fair the load waterline in the half breadth plan, following the procedures discussed earlier. Move the batten the minimal amount off the points until the curve looks fair and then draw in the line using light pencil. Then remove the batten and make a quick survey to see at which stations you had to move it from the marks in order to fair it. Use a clean pick up stick to transfer these corrected load waterline widths to the appropriate station sections in the body plan. You now need to redraw the station sections in the body plan to conform to the new waterline widths. For this job, use the thin batten. Change the station shape the minimal amount to obtain a fair curve that touches the corrected load waterline widths. Be sure that all station sections that need correction are corrected before going any further.

Usually we then pick up another waterline about halfway between the load waterline and the sheer. Use the procedure described above for this waterline and again make all corrections to the stations. It may be that these corrections to the station sections are significant enough to affect the already fair area of the load waterline. This type of discrepancy can appear throughout the lofting process. There are no hard and fast rules as to which lines should be adjusted if you find such an inconsistency. Check your measurements and study the relationship between your lines in the three views. As mentioned before, visually compare the station sections for similarity.

A good choice for the next line to fair would be a buttock that is halfway between the centerline and the widest point of the load waterline. If you look at the half breadth view, you will see where the buttock intersects the deckline up forward and either the deckline or the transom aft. Using the square, transfer the intersection point of the buttock and the deckline to the sheer on the profile plan. This is the forward fixed point of the buttock. If the buttock runs out before it gets to the last station aft, use the same process in the stern to transfer the buttock point to the sheer. If the body plan shows that the buttock intersects the last station, it is just a matter of picking up the distance from the baseline to where the buttock intersects the last station section and transferring that to the last station in profile.

Then place a clean pick up stick along the buttock line in the body plan so that one end touches the baseline and the sharp edge is touching the buttock line. As with the waterline, label what buttock line the stick represents and label the end of the stick that touches the baseline as "base." Mark all the heights of the station sections, labeling which mark represents which station, and transfer all of these distances to their

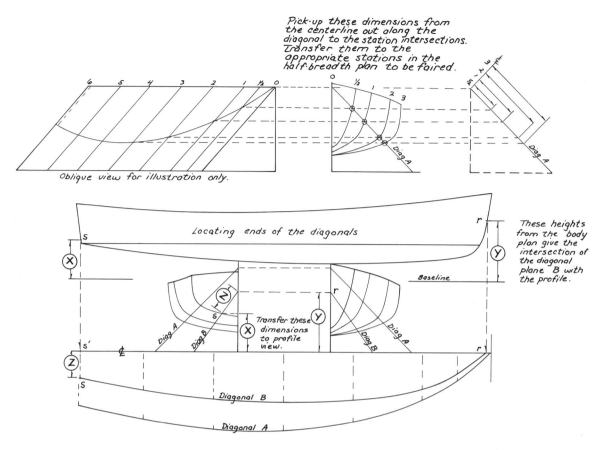

Figure 9—Laying off diagonals.

respective stations in the profile view. Now place a batten on the profile view touching the buttock mark at each station and sight it for fairness.

On most buttocks, bending one batten around the shape of the buttocks may be a problem. On most hulls, buttocks tend to run with just slight curve in the mid-section of the hull and swoop up sharply towards the bow and the stern where the buttock runs out on the sheer. We usually fair the middle of the buttock line first, using the same batten that we used to fair the sheer, and draw a light pencil line along it slightly past the point where the buttock starts to swoop up sharply. Then we remove this batten and use a smaller batten to fair the buttock where it curves more sharply, carefully fairing it into the straighter portion of the buttock. You will find, especially in long, skinny hulls, that as the buttock swoops up sharply, that area of the buttock loses most of its effectiveness in fairing the hull due to the low angle at which it intersects the sections in the body plan.

Use the same process for fairing the buttock that you used on the waterline. If, when the buttock is faired, it is off points that you have picked up from the body plan, you must then change the body plan to coincide with the new location of the buttock line at that station.

Again, make all of the changes on the body plan before going any further. If there is any major change that will highly distort the body plan in order to make it conform with the buttock, then the buttock will have to be changed again. What you are looking for is that all of the lines that you put on the half breadth and the profile view are fair and, when the distances from the center or baseline to these lines are transferred to the body plan at each section, the body plan is also fair.

The next line we would pick to fair would be a diagonal that intersects the hull somewhere between the load waterline and the keel. This diagonal section view will also use the half breadth baseline as its centerline. At this point, some loftsmen like to draw a line parallel to the baseline and intersecting the station lines, but on the opposite edge of the lofting floor, using this line as a centerline for the diagonals to keep the diagonals separate from the waterlines. Because diagonal sections are sometimes very similar in shape to the waterline sections, using a common centerline might become confusing. However, we usually use the baseline as the centerline for the diagonals because later on it will be quicker to pick up information necessary for manufacturing various parts of the boat.

Laying out a section view of the diagonal is similar to

laying out a waterline. The diagonal will intersect the stem and transom at certain heights above the baseline. For the stem, this might be on a waterline, making things very easy. Just follow that waterline to the point where it intersects the stem in profile. If it is not on a waterline, as in Figure 9, take the measurement height y from the baseline to the intersection of the diagonal and the centerline in the body plan (point r). Take this distance y to the profile view and mark off the intersection with the stem (point r). Then use the square to drop a line vertically down to the baseline to locate the point at which the diagonal starts (r).

For fairing the transom intersection you need to use the point where the diagonal intersects the outside edge of the transom (point s). In our example this would be at height x above the baseline. Transfer this distance x to the profile view and determine where it intersects with the transom (point s). Then project this point down to the half breadth view (s^1). Pick up distance z from the body plan (measured along the diagonal from centerline to transom line). Mark distance z perpendicular to s^1 in the half breadth plan to get the point s representing the intersection of the transom's edge and the diagonal B. You will fair the diagonal to this point.

Now lay the pick up stick with its sharp edge just touching the diagonal on the body plan and one end touching the intersection of the diagonal to the centerline. Label the stick according to which diagonal it is and which end touches the centerline. Then, mark the distance from center of each of the stations on the stick and label. Do this, of course, on both sides of the body plan so that all stations are included on the pick up stick. Then transfer these distances to their respective stations in the half breadth plan, labeling them in light pencil as you transfer them.

Now follow the standard fairing procedure of placing a batten on the marks and checking for fairness, moving the batten the minimal amount possible so that it forms an even, smooth curve. Draw in the line in light pencil, and make corrections to the body plan at the stations where the batten had to be moved from the marks to lie fair. If several sections of the body plan have to be grossly changed in order to conform to the diagonal section, the diagonal may have to be readjusted in that area in order to fair the hull.

Now it is just a matter of going through this fairing process with the rest of the diagonals, buttocks and waterlines that shape the hull. Since everything is still being drawn in light pencil, take care in labeling all the lines to keep track of what's what. As mentioned before, there will undoubtedly be some necessary changes that will affect some of the lines that have

already been faired. An example would be in fairing a diagonal that is close to a buttock that is already faired. In order to get the diagonal to lie fair, you may have to change a couple of station sections, which, in order to keep the station sections fair, might necessitate altering one of the buttocks lying close to the diagonals. This sounds like work, and it is. Any adjustment may necessitate re-fairing of other lines, but at this point the changes will be quite small to make everything fair. Care in lofting will pay off in ease of planking.

In some respects, lofting reminds us of sanding a hull and getting ready to paint it, in that a decision has to be made as to when to stop. Most people are quite happy if they achieve plus-or-minus 1/16 inch accuracy in the lofting. In special boats built to a rule, we usually carry it out finer than this, trying to be as accurate as possible so the boat will fall within the designed specifications of the class in which it is racing.

Once you have completed the fairing process to the accuracy desired, ink in all of the waterlines, buttocks and diagonals. Use the same ink color that you used to represent these lines in the grid and label all of the lines so that they are easily identified. Also ink in the body plan, although the stations that will be used to make mold frames or bulkheads, etc., will go through a planking thickness deduction process.

Lofting Hull Components

When the basic fairing of the hull lines is finished, the lines on the lofting board very accurately describe the shape of the hull at any given point. In addition to giving the shapes for the permanent frames, bulkheads and temporary molds, the lofting can be used to develop special patterns for the stem and keel, jigs for laminating, hardware, etc. There are a number of references to such uses of the lofting throughout this book. If this is your first boatbuilding project, we recommend that you read the entire book and note the references that apply to your boat. This will ensure that you make maximum use of the lofting. Using the lofting as a tool, you can now develop the shape of parts so that you can manufacture them to fit accurately in their respective areas of the hull.

For instance, if a bulkhead falls between stations 3 and 4, erect a perpendicular line from the baseline at the location of the bulkhead. Place a clean pick up stick along this line with one end touching the baseline and the sharp edge of the stick just touching the bulkhead line. Using one ink color, pick up the keel profile height of each buttock and the height of the sheer above the baseline. Using another ink color, pick up the distances from the centerline to the deckline and to all of the waterlines. You should, of course, be labeling all of the marks as you are making them. Using another ink color, pick up the distances of the diagonals from the centerline. Then take this pick up stick to the body plan and transfer all the information as you have done previously to develop the station sections. Using a thin batten, draw in this new section, which will represent the shape of the hull at the location of the bulkhead before planking thickness is subtracted.

To summarize, it is just a matter of drawing a perpendicular to locate the part which you want to develop, and then picking up distances from the centerline or baseline to the waterlines, diagonals and buttocks which will best help develop the shape of the part.

Developing an Angled Flat Transom or Bulkhead

If the boat has a flat transom or bulkhead that is at an angle from the vertical, you have to take a few extra steps to develop the shape of such a part. Figure 10 shows the revolution and development of a flat raked transom, but it could represent an angled bulkhead for chainplates or stay tangs.

The first step is to locate the intersection of the waterlines, sheer and keel with the transom in the profile view. Using a big square, project the lines at right angles to the transom profile at the points (a,b,c). It is a good idea to check the spacing for accuracy at the

outboard end of these projections, which you can do quickly and easily with a pick up stick.

Using the transom profile (or a line parallel to it, as in Figure 10) as a centerline, draw in lines to represent buttocks as they appear in the body plan grid (Buttock spacing R). You will now have a grid that resembles the body plan, with the waterline spacing expanded.

Now pick up the distances from the centerline out to the intersection of the waterlines (and sheer) and the transom line (A,B,C). These measurements can be made on either the half breadth (as shown) or body plan views. Set off the measurements on the corresponding waterlines in the transom grid (A', B', C').

Next locate the intersections of the buttock lines and transom in the profile view. Project perpendiculars from these points on the transom profile out to where they intersect their corresponding buttocks in the expanded transom view. Take care to project these points accurately.

You will now have a set of points (a', b', c', d', e', f', g') that describe the true size of the transom. Pick up the flexible batten that you used for the other station sections and, using weights or small nails, make it touch all the points marked on the temporary grid. The profile point at the keel will be where the special station line intersects the profile line. Slight inaccuracies may have crept in during the development of the section, in which case you may have to move the batten slightly in

Figure 10—Developing a raked flat transom.

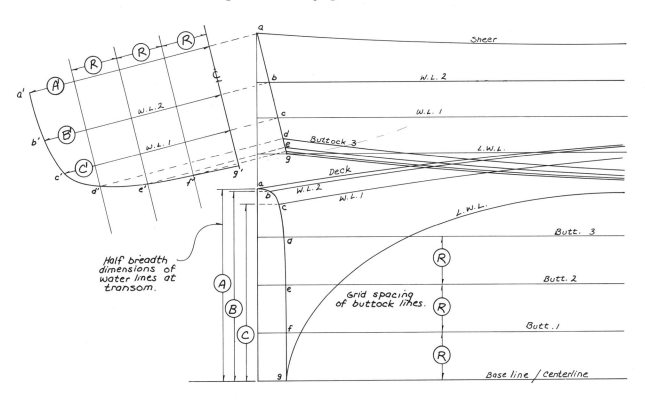

order to make the section fair. If there is a major error, go back and check through the development process. When everything is right, this transom or angled bulkhead will look similar to the vertical stations on either side, although it will be expanded or more drawn out.

Curved Transom Development

It is quite common with bigger boats to have a transom that is both curved and raked, either forward or aft, at an appreciable angle. To develop transoms of this shape is a little complicated, but the following instructions and Figure 11 provide a fairly standard method.

The basic principles involved in the development of the curved raked transom are most easily understood if you consider the transom as being part of a cylinder. As with the cylinder, it is curved in one direction (athwartship) and straight in the other (fore and aft or vertical). Looking at the lines plan, you will see that the buttock planes intersect the transom as straight lines, these being elements of the cylinder. You will use these buttocks as you expand or roll out the transom from its curved shape to a flat one.

The first thing to do is to project an auxiliary view of the after sections of the boat and deck line at a line of sight parallel to the centerline of the transom in profile. (See Figure 11.) Begin by extending the centerline of the transom in profile up clear of the other views. As close to the other drawing as possible, draw in an auxiliary grid centerline at right angles to this extended line. Tangent to this intersection, swing an arc of the radius noted on the designer's plans for the transom. This is the curve to which the transom will be laminated when it is built. Measuring out from the auxiliary centerline, draw in the buttocks parallel to this centerline, spaced as they are in the half breadth plan (a, b, c, d). Then project the points where the auxiliary buttocks intersect the design arc of the transom down from this auxiliary view to the corresponding buttocks in the profile view.

It is also necessary to determine the true intersection of the sheer and the transom in this auxiliary view. To do this, first project the intersections of the aft two (or three) station lines with the profile sheer up into the auxiliary view. These projections will intersect the auxiliary centerline at 90°. Pick up from the half breadth plan the distance from the centerline to the deck line for the aft sections. Then transfer these dimensions to the auxiliary view, from the centerline out along the station projections. Fair a batten through these marks. This sheer line will intersect the arc of the transom.

Next, prepare the grid for the expanded transom. You can use the transom centerline in the profile view as the centerline for the grid, or draw a centerline parallel to it but a little away to keep things clear. Lay a batten *around* the arc in the auxiliary view and pick up the buttock spacing (a',b',c',d') and the point where the arc intersects the deck line. Then transfer these distances, laying the batten straight and at right angles to the expanded transom centerline. Draw in the buttocks parallel to the centerline, and also lightly draw the line (parallel to the buttocks) that represents the intersection of the deck line and the transom (e'). This gives one half the true width of the transom if it were laid flat. Go back and identify in the profile view the points where the projections of the buttocks from the auxiliary view intersect the buttocks. Project these points (m, n, o, p) out to the expanded transom grid, where their intersections with their respective buttocks will outline the shape of the transom.

If more points are needed for accuracy in developing the shape of the outside edge of the transom, add more buttocks to the *body plan* in between the standard buttocks. Using a pick up stick, transfer the heights for the last three stations to the profile view. Then follow the process used with the primary buttocks to get the additional points.

It will be necessary to know the amount of deck crown, so this, too, should be projected in. Some designers give the amount of deck crown as a percentage of beam at any point, while others give a centerline that runs above the sheer line to show the amount of deck crown. We generally allow slightly more material on the transom than is necessary for the deck camber by lightly drawing a line parallel to the sheer, but above it, at least as high as the deck camber will be at the stem. Draw this line far enough to intersect the projected profile centerline of the raked transom. From this point of intersection draw another line to the intersection of the deck line in the outer corner of the transom. Give this line more curve than would appear on the standard profile plan to allow for plenty of fairing material on the transom.

Looking at the previous work, note that the buttock lines projected down from the auxiliary view intersect the top of the transom in the profile view. Project these intersections out to the respective buttocks on the grid for the expanded transom. Connect the dots with a flexible batten. This will allow more than enough material for fairing. Later on in construction we make a template of the exact deck crown at the point where the transom meets the deck line. This, along with the other deck beams installed in the boat, allows us to use a batten to accurately fair the edge where the deck meets the transom.

Further reading on transom development, as well as on other lofting specialties, can be found in the sources

Figure 11—Developing curved raked transom on a modern racer.

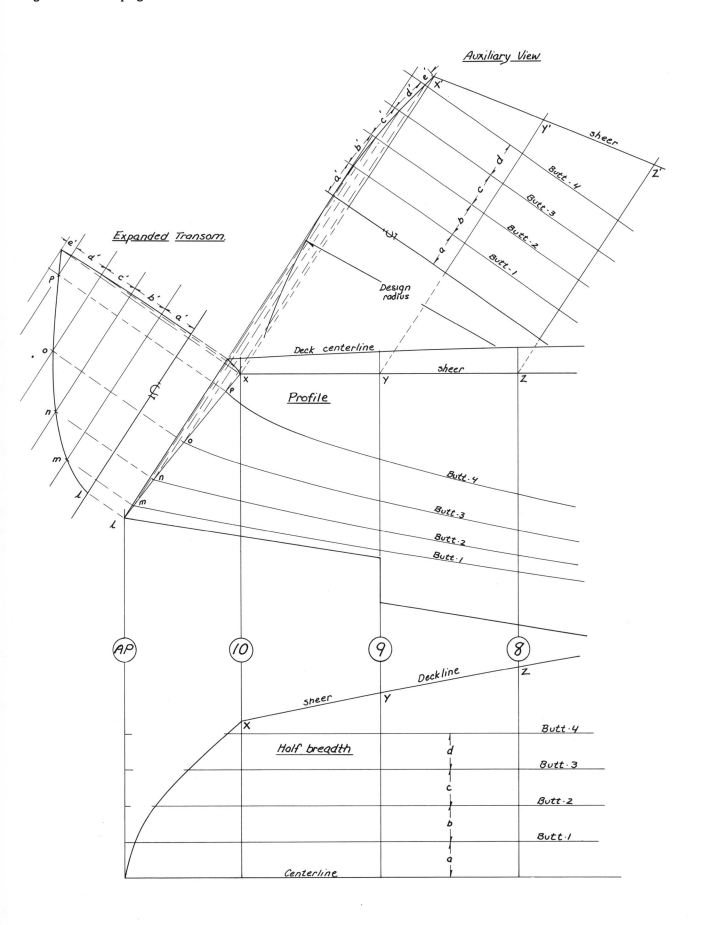

listed at the beginning of this chapter.

Subtracting Planking Thickness

Boats are lofted to the outer thickness of their planking. Before you can build any interior frames or molds, you need to subtract this planking thickness from the body plan and special bulkhead layouts. We usually do this as we lay down the body plan and before we fair in its lines. This system demands a little more work but ensures that any parts made from the lofting will already have the planking thickness subtracted from them. Slight inaccuracies creep in as you subtract planking thickness. However, if the process takes place before the diagonals, buttocks and waterlines are used to check and fair the body plan sections, these inaccuracies will be faired out. The end result is a slightly fairer, more accurate shape when the molds and the bulkheads are set up.

In some hulls, however, such as wineglass section hulls, you might feel more secure if you subtracted planking thickness after the hull has been faired to eliminate any complication that might arise in fairing the deadwood into the hull.

The procedure for subtracting planking thickness is the same whether you do it before or after fairing the body plan. If you decide to subtract the planking thickness before you fair the body plan, take the steps outlined below after you have laid down the body plan but before you have picked up any waterlines, buttocks or diagonals to fair it.

On long, thin hulls, such as multihulls with their thin skins, there is no problem in subtracting the actual planking thickness directly from the molds and frames. However, on boats with thicker planking and/or more abrupt curves, some problems can arise if the same amount of planking thickness is subtracted from all of the station sections. If you take a station somewhere in the middle of the boat, it intersects the planking at very close to right angles. If you measured the planking across the angle at which this station intersects it, it would measure the same as the actual thickness of planking that is used. However, if you measured a station close to the bow, where the planking comes across that station at a considerable angle, say 20°, you would find that the measurement would be considerably more than the thickness of the planking. This extra amount would have to be subtracted from the station at that point so that when the boat is planked, the outside dimension will be the same as the final loftings. Although there are different ways of subtracting planking thickness, all of them require that you find the bevel angle of the station and measure the distance through the planking stock at that angle. The distance measured across the angle of the planking stock is the amount subtracted from the station section at that point.

The first step is to make a *master bevel board*. This is a tool which you can keep around the shop and use for various projects, so it's worth making a good one. Take a square piece of plywood about ¼ inch thick, with its sides at least as long as the greatest station spacing on the boat you are lofting. We usually make it a little bigger so that it will fit most projects, and recomend a 3 foot square as a good size. Place a point of the bar compass in one corner of the square and draw a 90° arc of the largest radius possible. (See Figure 12.) Next, divide this arc or quadrant into 90 parts, each representing one degree. Accurate work is important. Start by dividing the arc into three parts of 30°. Then divide one 30° arc into six parts of 5°. Then divide one of these 5° parts into 1° marks. Make a quick template, using the construction you have just done, to divide the other two 30° sectors into six parts of 5°. Then divide all the marks into 1° marks. Now you need a straight stick which will reach diagonally across the square. Draw in and label the lines every 5°. Because this bevel board will be permanent, use a ball point pen.

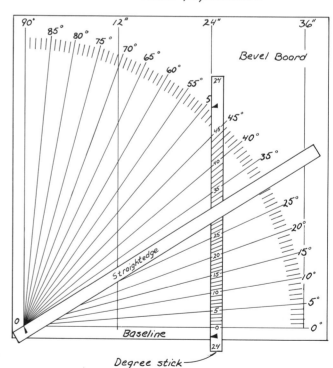

Figure 12—Master bevel board.

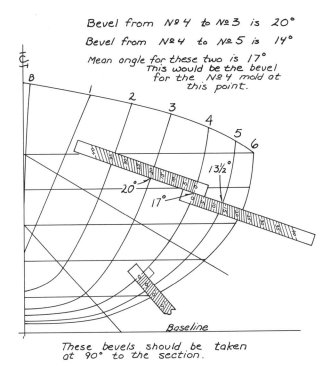

Bevel from № 4 to № 3 is 20°
Bevel from № 4 to № 5 is 14°
Mean angle for these two is 17°
This would be the bevel
for the № 4 mold at
this point.

20°

13½°

17°

Baseline

These bevels should be taken
at 90° to the section.

Figure 13—Determining mold bevels using a degree stick.

The side of the square that goes from the center to the 0° mark will be the baseline. Mark off the station spacing from the center along the baseline, and at that point construct a perpendicular line. Draw the line in, using light pencil. Next, mill up a piece of wood that is longer than the greatest distance between station sections on the body plan, making it about ⅛ inch thick and the exact width of the thickness of planking that will go on the boat. Lay this stick on your bevel board so that one edge touches the vertical station line and the bottom of the stick touches the baseline. Use a couple of small tacks to hold it in place. Then, using a small straightedge, transfer all of the angular lines across the stick and label them. Be sure to mark the edge of the stick that is touching the station line.

Now take the stick to the body plan as shown in Figure 13. Let's say you want to deduct the planking thickness from station 4 at a point on the topsides. Lay the stick so that its base touches station 4 at this point and it is projecting at right angles to station 4, and read the degree line closest to station line 3. Let's say that it is 20°. Now, place the base of the stick on station 4 so that it is projecting at right angles and read the degree line closest to station 5. Let's say it is 14°. The bevel at that point on station 2 would be the average of these two readings, 17°. The planking thickness deducted would be the distance measured across the stick at that 17° angle. (Remember, the stick is the same width as the planking.) Figure 14 shows two methods of sub-

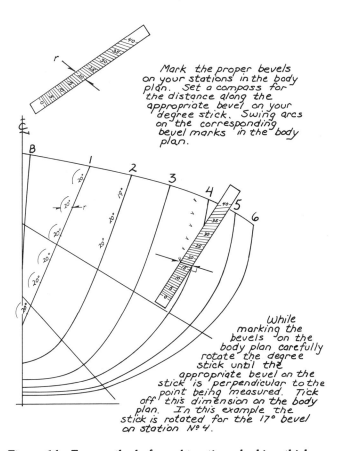

Mark the proper bevels on your stations in the body plan. Set a compass for the distance along the appropriate bevel on your degree stick. Swing arcs on the corresponding bevel marks in the body plan.

While marking the bevels on the body plan carefully rotate the degree stick until the appropriate bevel on the stick is perpendicular to the point being measured. Tick off this dimension on the body plan. In this example the stick is rotated for the 17° bevel on station № 4.

Figure 14—Two methods for subtracting planking thickness from body plan sections.

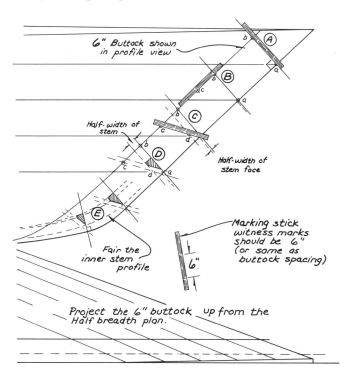

6" Buttock shown in profile view

Half-width of stem

Half-width of stem face

Fair the inner stem profile

Marking stick witness marks should be 6" (or same as buttock spacing)

6"

Project the 6" buttock up from the Half breadth plan.

Figure 15—Determining bevels and planking thickness deduction for inner stem.

tracting this dimension.

In detail A we adjust a compass to the distance and swing an arc off at the labeled bevel as along stations 1 and 2 in our example. In detail B we rotate the stick as we mark the bevels and carefully tick off the distance using the stick itself. The measurement, of course, is made at right angles to the section line.

If two station sections are close to parallel all the way from the sheer to the keel, you can subtract the same thickness from the station everywhere. Otherwise, in just about every hull shape, a calculation made for planking thickness subtraction about every 6 inches is adequate. In the few midship sections you will find the bevel angle so low that there is very little difference between true planking thickness and the amount that has to be subtracted, so most loftsmen don't bother to calculate extra planking thickness deduction at very low bevel angles in the midship sections. You can write the bevel angles down on the stations at the same time that you do the planking thickness deduction work. After you have finished marking the planking thickness deduction from the station, place a batten on the tick marks and draw in the reduced station shape.

Subtracting the planking thickness from the stem is slightly trickier. At this point, if you are subtracting planking thickness before the longitudinals are faired, you need to draw a buttock on the body plan 6 inches from the centerline and pick up the distances for the forward third of this buttock. Then lay it out on the profile view. If you are subtracting planking thickness after having faired all the hull lines, this buttock is most easily projected up off the half breadth plan. (See Figure 15.) Draw a line at right angles from the profile

stem at a point where the stem intersects a waterline, extending the line aft to the point where it intersects the profile of the 6 inch buttock (as in detail A). Then draw a line perpendicular to this first line at the point where it intersects the buttock. Measure out 6 inches and make a mark (as in detail B). At the point where the first line and the stem intersect, measure out the half width of the stem at right angles and put a mark (see detail C). Connect this mark with the upper mark. You should now have a reasonably accurate sectional view of the stem. If you lay the stick which is equal in width to the thickness of the planking beside this line and draw a parallel line, you will have the shape of the stem minus the planking thickness. (See detail D.)

Next, fair a profile line for the new inner stem, using the points established in the stem section views you have just completed. (See detail E.) If you are subtracting planking thickness before fairing the hull lines, you will now have a view of the inner stem to which you can fair the waterlines.

The only other area where there might be some confusion in subtracting planking thickness is in the last station aft, where there is not another station with which to average the angle. For planking thickness subtraction, the one angle will be close enough. If you want to bevel the last station from the lofting, you will have to allow for a few degrees because the planking will be curving as it comes into that station.

This completes the basic lofting. You should now have the exact shapes of the desired stations from which you can cut the mold frames, permanent frames, bulkheads, transom and other manufactured parts.

Chapter 14

Mold Frames and Permanent Frames

Boat construction begins when lofting is complete. The first steps, building frames for each lofted station and setting them up on a foundation, are discussed here and in Chapter 15. Since you may wish to approach these jobs simultaneously, we recommend that you read through both chapters before you start. As you do this, note that most wood composite boats, even very large ones, are built keel up and sheer down.

Although we refer to *station frames,* and assume that you are placing your frames along the station lines, you may in fact use any regularly spaced lines along your hull. We use station lines because they are already drawn in the lofting and are therefore convenient. In cases where a permanent frame is close to a station, you may use it instead of a station frame and need an extra mid-station mold frame to support planking. If at any time in the set-up process you decide to add a mold frame, draw it into your lofting as you would a station line. An auxiliary grid with only a few lines is a good place to do this sort of special work.

There are two basic types of frames. *Mold frames* are assembled to make a form over which to bend the planking or stringers of a mold or hull. When they are used in a mold, mold frames become permanent parts of it. Mold frames are removed from the finished hull, and so are sometimes referred to as temporary or dummy frames. *Permanent frames,* on the other hand, are attached to the hull skin during the manufacturing process. They are incorporated into the finished hull and are not used to construct molds. Bulkheads, ribs and other components which are installed in the set-up are considered permanent frames.

Some hulls are built over mold frames only and the ribs, bulkheads and other transverse pieces are fitted and installed afterwards. Other boats are built over permanent frames only. Quite often, however, combinations of mold and permanent frames are used. Many hulls built using WEST SYSTEM* Brand epoxy and laminating techniques do not have enough transverse structural members to constitute a mold and some temporary mold frames have to be used. We always aim to build as many transverse elements as practical into the mold frame set-up. This requires less labor

than installing the items after the hull skin has been formed, and the results are usually better.

Planning Permanent Frames

With careful planning, you can substitute many permanent parts for temporary mold frames. Among the transverse pieces to be permanently installed in a hull are such things as bulkheads, sides of lockers, supports for berths, ribs for engine bed support, laminated floors for through bolting ballast keels — any pieces that run athwartship or at right angles to planking or stringers.

Make a list of all such items while your project is still in the planning stage, and judge which ones can reasonably be jigged into the set-up and how. You will probably find that few, if any, of the pieces are positioned on a station line, so you will have to loft most, if not all, as extra stations. However, they may have to be lofted anyway, whether you put them into the set-up or fit them after you lay the planking.

Full bulkheads are probably the easiest parts to include in a set-up because they outline the entire hull perimeter, just like a full mold frame. If the bulkhead happens to be reasonably close to a station, you can omit the mold frame for that station if you judge that the planking will be properly supported and will form fairly. If the bulkhead is more or less dead center between two stations, then you will probably have to include the mold frames for both stations.

As you plan permanent frames, give some thought to jigging design. All pieces in the set-up, permanent or temporary, will be supported by vertical legs. Your job will be to arrange these legs so that they don't get in the way of each other. You can cut out the centers of mold frames to allow bracing to pass through them, but you cannot hollow out bulkheads. Instead, plan to run diagonal braces for bulkheads through companionways and other cutouts.

Another point to consider if you are putting a bulkhead in the set-up is whether it protrudes above the sheer (such as one that might form the back of a cabin above the deck line). If so, the set-up will have to be high enough off the floor or strongback to leave room for this.

Many other items that can be included in the set-up

are smaller than a bulkhead and will only span a portion of the hull perimeter. In these cases, you cannot allow these pieces to substitute for an entire mold frame, though it may be possible to build partial mold frames that can provide complete support in conjunction with a partial frame member.

Other considerations that are necessary if you are going to install permanent structures in the set-up will be discussed later in the chapter. First, however, will come a discussion of mold frame construction.

Mold Frames

Our favorite mold frame material is particle board, also known as chipboard or pressed wood board. It's inexpensive, dimensionally stable and has no grain. Four foot x 8 foot sheets of ¾ inch chipboard are readily available because they are widely used as subflooring in residential construction, and a single sheet is usually large enough to make both halves of a mold frame.

Mold frames may also be made of ¾ inch lumber, 4 to 10 inches wide. If you use stock, you will generally have to cut station line shapes out of several pieces and then join them together with plywood gussets.

The main job of any mold frame is to hold the shape of the boat. So long as it is strong enough to do this, a dummy frame may be open in the center, like a large horseshoe, or closed, with material more or less solidly arranged across the station. Once structural considerations are met, the only difference between frame designs is that it may be easier to attach legs to solid frames than to open ones.

Transferring the Shape

Unless a designer specifies otherwise, you will need to cut out mold frames for every station in the lofting. The shape of the frame for each particular station is the shape represented in the body plan of the lofting. Some designers may specify extra mold frames in areas of acute planking curve. These are usually referred to as *half mold frames* and are located midpoint between stations.

The body plan shows only a half shape of each station, so you will have to cut out each station shape twice and then join the two halves together to form the full station. *However, cut only half of each mold frame by the line transfer methods we are about to describe. Cut out the other halves using the original halves as patterns.* The reason for this will be explained later under the subject of *controlling edges*.

Whichever type of frame you use, remember to sub-tract planking thickness from your lofted station lines before transferring them to your mold stock. It may also be necessary to subtract the thickness of mold planking. These deductions from your lofting may be substantial — to build a ½ inch thick hull on a mold with ¾ inch thick ribbands, you will use half mold frames which are 1¼ inches "thinner" than your station lines — so pay close attention to the planking thickness deduction procedure outlined in Chapter 13.

The trickiest part of making mold frames is transferring the station line shape from the lofting floor to the mold frame material. As far as we know, there are four ways of doing this. One method of transfer is to loft the body plan on a portable board and then saw the board up into templates. Naturally, this won't work if the station lines cross each other or even if they are very close together. We can only recommend this method if you loft the body plan twice, giving one lofting to cut up and leaving one for reference.

A second method is to use tracing paper through which you can see the lines. Spread the paper on the lofting floor and trace the station lines either freehand or with a batten. Then move the paper to the mold frame material and make pick marks through it onto the frame stock. The easy way to do this is to use a pounce or tracing wheel, but you may also use a pin or a nail. Connect the pick marks into a line with a batten.

The third and most popular method of transferring lines is the nail method illustrated in Figure 1. For this, you need thick-shanked nails with small, sharp-edged heads. Small box nails work well. Position these on their sides on the lofting floor, so that the shanks are at right angles to and the edges of the heads rest on the station lines. Hold a nail by its point and tap the side of its shank with a small hammer until the shank is flat in the floor and close to half of the head is buried. Sink nail heads in this way at several points along the station lines, adding more in critical areas such as sharp curves or chines, until you have a good outline of protruding nail heads. Then, place your frame material over the lofting and gently walk on it to press the nail heads into the stock. Remove the mold material and use a batten to connect the nail head impressions into a line.

We have developed a fourth method, shown in Figures 2 and 3, of marking mold frames. This technique requires making special battens and batten holders, and therefore takes a little extra time, but it gives fast, accurate results. The holders are screwed or notched onto long, thin battens, which are anchored in place on the lofting. We can push mold frame material under this assembly for marking.

You may need more than one batten, especially if the sharpness of your curves varies considerably from station to station. Make each one out of a straight, flexible wood such as ash. Batten thickness depends on the degree of curvature of your station lines: each batten should flex comfortably along the lines on which it will be used.

Next, cut eight or so pieces of wood to approximately 1½ inches x 1 inch x 18 inches. These are your batten holders. Drill one or two holes for nails at one end of each piece. You can use any long, thin nails you have on hand, as long as they slip through these holes easily with no slop, so be sure that your drill is the same size as the shank diameter of your nails. Cut a thin wedge out of the bottom of each stick, beginning where the piece will attach to the batten and rising over its length to within an inch or so of your nail hole or holes. This trimming will allow the batten to drop down onto the frame stock.

Finally, decide how you will attach your holders to your battens. If you want to use roundhead wood screws, drill holes in the tapered end of each holder and every six inches along the length of your battens. Place flat washers under the screws as you insert them

and tighten only enough to eliminate slop. If you choose to use notches, cut them in the holders to fit your various battens. Each holder can be notched twice, once for a thin batten and once for a thicker one.

When this is done, your device is ready to use. Start by attaching batten holders every foot or so along your batten. Try to align the inner edge of the batten along the station shape, and anchor the holders outside the line with nails through the drilled holes. Don't drive the nails flush: you want them to give a little, and you will have to pull them out to move on to the next station anyway. Add more holders as needed until the batten is accurately lined up.

Once you have properly aligned the batten and set the nails, you are ready to insert the mold frame material. You usually have to roughly trim the mold frame edge so that there is no excess material in the way of the nails. When the frame material is in the best position, let the batten back down and trace the station shape by running a pencil along the *inside* of the batten. Make sure the pencil is sharp so that you can mark the line right up to the batten.

Figure 1—Nail method for picking up mold sections from the lofting.

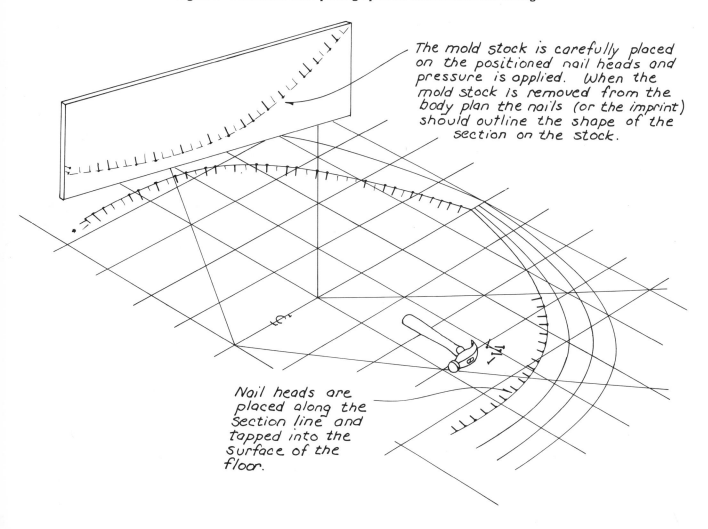

The mold stock is carefully placed on the positioned nail heads and pressure is applied. When the mold stock is removed from the body plan the nails (or the imprint) should outline the shape of the section on the stock.

Nail heads are placed along the section line and tapped into the surface of the floor.

118

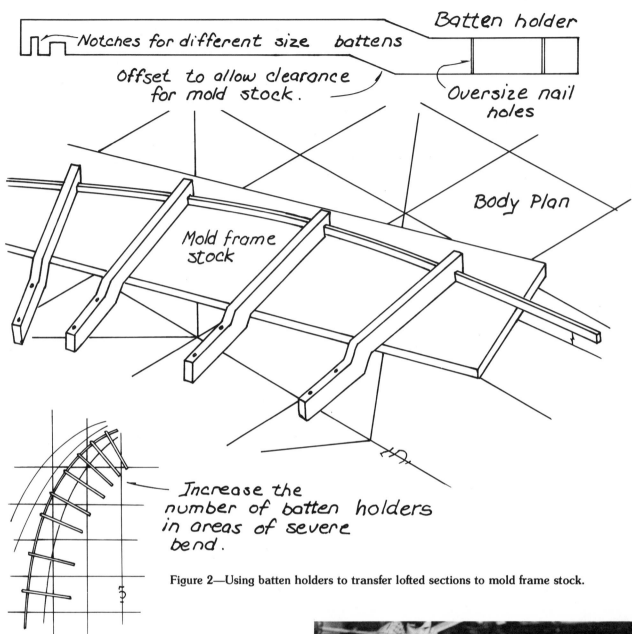

Batten holder

Notches for different size battens

Offset to allow clearance for mold stock.

Oversize nail holes

Body Plan

Mold frame stock

Increase the number of batten holders in areas of severe bend.

Figure 2—Using batten holders to transfer lofted sections to mold frame stock.

Controlling Edges

After you have drawn the lines on the frame stock, but before you begin cutting, label the piece with its station number. Use a felt tip pen, and make sure that you mark on the side on which you've drawn the lines. This is the *control* side of your frame. The edge of this surface is the *controlling edge* of your frame.

The reason for establishing a controlling edge is straightforward. It is difficult to keep a hand held saw blade perpendicular to the material it is cutting at all times. When the blade cants, the top and bottom surfaces of the piece have different outlines. It's therefore

Figure 3—Transferring deck camber for a bulkhead from lofting to plywood stock using batten and holders.

best, when sawing, to concentrate on following a line on one surface. This way, you can cut one side of the material true to form and there's no confusion about which lines to rely on. Marking helps to keep track of which side is the control side.

When it's time to set up the frames, control sides are aligned with station lines drawn on a floor or with notch marks on a strongback. To facilitate beveling, the thickness of the mold frame material and the width of the anchoring blocks below go on the side of the line towards the bow or stern, whichever is nearer. At the center station the mold frame material goes on whichever side you have chosen to put the anchoring blocks. This changeover point usually occurs at the widest part of the boat. With this arrangement, anchoring blocks and mold frame material end up on one side of the station line, with the legs that connect them on the other side. The controlling edge of the mold frame is then in a vertical plane above the station line.

We must mention that some builders do just the opposite of the above by placing the anchoring blocks and mold frame material on the inside of the station line and the legs on the outside. In this way the mold frame edges do not have to be beveled to let the planking down to the controlling edge. We believe, however, that beveling mold frames is better, especially if the planking is stiff and, in bending, will put a lot of pressure on the frame. If a thin edge is all that there is to resist the pressure, a certain amount of local crushing is bound to occur, and the crushing in effect will result in a distortion of the true edge. Unfortunately, the crushing is unlikely to be uniform throughout the set-up, and so the planking may not be as fair as it could have been if the mold were beveled, which gives the planking support over the width of the frame material.

Mold Frame Halves

Cut out the mold frames with a hand held saber saw, a band saw or any hand saw which can follow a curved line. After you have cut out all the first halves of the frames, take them back to the lofting floor and place them on their respective stations to check for any discrepancies. Make sure that you have a frame for each station and that each is properly numbered. You will inevitably need to hand trim edges. Block planes, sharp files and coarse sandpaper on a block all work well for this. Use the controlling edges of these frame halves as patterns to mark the material for cutting the other halves.

Earlier, we stated it was imperative that only half of each station mold frame be cut out by transferring the

Figure 4—Fitting and assembling frames for double chine trimaran hull on lofted sections.

line from the lofting floor. The reason for this is that the control sides of the second halves have to be mirror images of the original sides. Except in the case of the tracing paper method, in which paper can just be turned over, it is not possible to get both a straight image and a mirror image with any of the line transfer methods. Therefore it is necessary to use the original half-mold as a pattern for the other half in order to get the control sides on the same sides when you truss the halves together.

Once the second halves are cut out, mark them for control sides and number them. Check them against the lofting or the original halves for accuracy and numbering.

Assembling the Mold Frames

The two halves of a mold frame are held together with a plywood gusset in the area of the keel, and with a spall. A spall usually spans the mold frame at the highest waterline of the station. We find that it's most efficient to prepare these pieces in advance and bond and mark as many as possible in a single operation on the lofting floor.

You can make the gusset out of ¼ inch or ⅜ inch plywood. Cut it out in the approximate shape of the lower 12 inches of the station. The gussets should be of generous size, so that they give plenty of support. It is best not to place them up to the edge of the mold frame, but to keep them an inch away from the edges. You will eventually bevel the edges and there is no good reason to include the gussets in the beveling operation.

Spalls are usually made of either 1 inch x 4 inch or 1 inch x 6 inch boards, well seasoned so that they will not shrink or swell at some point after installation. Every spall must have one long, straight edge, for in addition to functioning as bracing members, spalls are applied so that one edge serves as a set-up reference line. Although it makes no difference in many cases, it's usually better to place a spall with its straight edge facing up in the set-up. This way, you can set a level on top of it for reference and better see the edge when you measure. Keep the ends of a spall in an inch or ½ inch from the edges of the mold frame so they do not interfere with the fairing of bevels.

The greater the distance a spall must span, the greater the chances of its becoming unstable. Instability will destroy its usefulness as a reference line. If the boat you are building has a great deal of beam, you should probably support the spall toward the center with trus-ses running at an angle to the mold frame. An alternative is to position the spall slightly away from the reference waterline and to stretch a string across the waterline marks. You can then use the string for reference during setting up.

To truss the two halves of the mold frame together, place the frames *control side down* on the lofting floor. Only one half will fit into the body plan lofting. The other half, being a mirror image, goes on the other side of the lofting centerline. To locate this half in symmetry, you have to measure the offset of the highest waterline (the distance from the centerline to the body plan line) and transfer it out in the opposite direction.

Figure 5—Typical mold frame with legs and spall installed and reference lines marked.

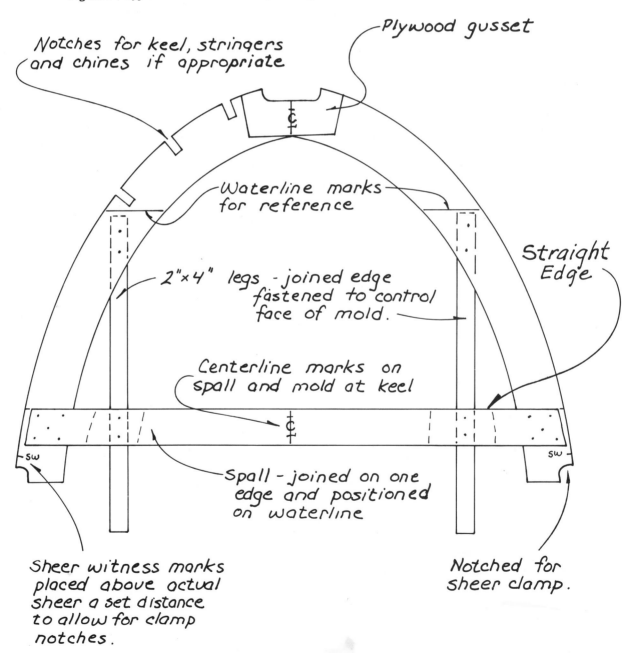

Figure 6—Bonding gussets to permanent frames.

Make a tick mark or drive in a small nail and locate the mirror half out to this mark. Also butt the two halves at the keel.

Then apply the gusset to the non-control side of the mold frames. Bond the gusset in place with adhesive, using screws, nails or staples as fasteners. Recheck the position of the two halves, and then you are ready to apply the spall. Before the spall goes on, however, you must draw a line against which to align the straight edge of the spall. Use two small squares and place their edges sitting vertically on the waterline on the lofting floor. Then use the spall itself as a straightedge and push it gently against the two squares. When it is in position, draw against the spall's edge, across the face of the mold frames. Use this line to reposition the spall when you permanently install it with adhesive and fasteners.

The fasteners become extraneous as soon as the epoxy cures, but we recommend using them nevertheless to speed things up. If you use fasteners, you can put together the two halves of a mold frame, move the unit out of the way, and immediately go on to the next pair of mold halves. Without fasteners, the assembly will be fairly fragile until the resin sets up. Handle all mold frames gently until they are cured.

Note that if you build mold frames in the way we have described, you may have to destroy them to get them out of the finished hull. When stringers and sheer clamps are notched into mold frames and covered with layers of planking or veneer, the frames can be difficult to remove. If you are building a one-off boat, you probably won't care about saving your frames, but if you plan to use them again or give them to someone, put them together with screws and through bolts rather

than epoxy so that they can be disassembled after the hull is planked.

After bonding the gusset and spall, and before moving the mold frame from the lofting, make reference marks. The edge of the spall is one reference. Label it with the number of the waterline it represents if you plan to use different waterlines at different stations. Also mark the centerline. To do this, place a straightedge over the lofted centerline and use the two small squares, set on edge as before, to transfer the line from the lofting to the straightedge. Use the straightedge as a guide to draw a line across the spall and the gusset.

Finally, you have to mark the sheer, but you can do this on the edge of the mold frame, next to the lofting floor. You do not need to raise these marks to the non-control side of the material. As soon as you pick the frame up off the floor you can draw the sheer mark around onto the control face. In fact, it is necessary to mark the sheer lines on the control side, for if they were raised to the non-control side, they might be out of position.

The sheer marks, unlike the waterline and centerline references, are not used when setting up. They come into play much later, during installation of the sheer clamps. For this reason, the sheer marks should be quite durable and easily identifiable so that there will be no trouble finding them later on.

General Advice

If your boat will have longitudinal stringers notched into its mold frames and these are marked on your lofting, pick up the marks and bring them around to control faces as you did with the sheer marks. Stringers rarely run on waterlines, so picking them up on the non-control side of a mold frame may result in distortion. On all but long, narrow hulls with little angle change, we suggest waiting until after the frames are set up to cut notches. If you choose to cut them earlier, plan carefully and make them a little small.

If your design calls for notching out the apex of the frames to receive a keel, your gussets should be large enough that they will not be weakened by the loss of the notch material. Also, you will have less grief if you keep nails and screws out of the way of notch sawing lines. You can remove all nails or screws once the adhesive cures, but inserting them so that they are out of the way in the first place minimizes the difficulty.

Attaching the Legs

Two inch x 4 inch legs are big enough for virtually any boat, and you can use smaller stock for smaller boats. Legs don't have to be made out of the best lumber in the world, but every piece should be joined straight and cured well enough to ensure that it will remain reasonably straight. Fasten legs to the control side of the mold frame with nails or screws and epoxy. You can bond the legs in place whether you plan to save the frames or not. If your molds disassemble along the centerline, the legs will not get in the way when you remove the frames from the planked hull.

The best procedure is to apply legs as parallel to the centerline as possible so that you can use them during set-up for plumb references. The control face of a mold frame is rarely flat, so it may not be a particularly good place to set a level to see if the frame is plumb. However, if the sides of the legs are straight and true and parallel to the centerline, you can position the level against them.

When you have the legs and adjacent frame material in vertical alignment, brace them with jigging. Straighten up the mold frames when you install your sheer clamp, stringers, keel and other transverse members. Once these pieces are in place, the controlling edges will be close enough for practical purposes.

Attaching legs is no problem if you are using closed, solid mold frames. It is easiest to do this when your foundation centering cable is in place. Erect lines parallel to and at equal distances from the mold frame centerline on either side of this centerline. Space these so that when the legs are attached, the centerline of the mold frame will line up with the centerline of the foundation and the legs will butt against the anchoring points.

You will probably not be able to attach legs all the way up and down the control surface of an open frame. Secure them to what mold frame there is and then also to the spall. Since the spall's surface is not in the same plane as the control face, add shims to the spall on the same side as the mold material in the area where the legs will cross it. Scraps of frame stock are, of course, the perfect thickness for this. Erect the leg position lines, in segments, across the mold frame and the shims, and then apply the legs.

The height of the legs is arbitrary, but it must be uniform throughout the stations. Choose a leg length that will result in the hull being a convenient height to work on. When the set-up is going to be on a floor, rather than on a strongback, you need to cut off the legs of all the mold frames so that the reference waterline marks on the frames (if the same waterline is used as reference throughout the stations) end up a uniform distance above the reference cable. If you use differing waterlines for reference on differing stations, you will have to make allowances for these distances in measur-

ing the legs for cutoff.

On strongback set-ups, where there is clearance below the anchoring blocks, you can allow the legs to run past, but you should mark the distances to the top surfaces of the anchoring blocks on the legs, provisionally, as a starting point when setting up the frames on the strongback.

Permanent Frames

Earlier in this chapter we recommended that the thickness of the mold frame material be placed outside the station line so that you can bevel it to the contour of the planking. We also pointed out that you have the option of placing the mold frame material inside the station line, eliminating the need for beveling, if you feel the controlling edge is strong enough to withstand pressure without distorting.

With permanent members there is no option. All edges have to be beveled carefully so that planking fits to them all across their thickness. The process we use for marking bevels with battens and a hand saw is described in Chapter 15. This will work well on dummy frames and permanent pieces alike, but we do suggest a more cautious approach to the bevel on a permanent part.

In a set-up which includes both mold and permanent frames, make the bevels on all of the mold frames first, cutting bevels on permanent frames to an angle slightly less than you know they'll need. Even if you began with a power plane, it's a good idea to use a hand plane to bring the bevel on a permanent frame to its final angle. The use of battens across the set-up to check bevels periodically as you are planing helps develop accuracy.

One reason to be careful as you bevel permanent members is that if you cut too deeply, you may make more work for yourself. If you over-bevel mold frames, you can build them back up with thickened resin, plywood strips or whatever. It doesn't make much difference what a temporary frame looks like. The appearance of a permanent frame, on the other hand, is important, and a good fit between it and the planking is necessary for both structural and aesthetic reasons.

Appearance also counts in installing spalls and legs on permanent frames. These are positioned in exactly the same way that they are on mold frames, but it may be necessary to use fasteners instead of epoxy to hold them in place during construction. Attaching legs to permanent frames requires some extra attention. If the job is not done neatly, the permanent members may bear permanent, visible scars.

While WEST SYSTEM epoxy can be relied on to fill

Figure 7—Bonding cheek pieces to permanent bulkhead.

Figure 8—Building a laminated transom with cheek pieces.

gaps and span voids, your boat will be lighter, it will look better, and it will be cheaper if you work your wood until you have good fits. If you over-bevel, however, and the choice is between throwing out your frame and building it up with epoxy, you can use resin to bridge gaps. A good solution to larger mistakes is to bond in shims of wood and reshape to desired bevels.

To lay out a permanent transverse member, such as a bulkhead or floor timber, loft a line to represent the surface which is nearer the boat's widest station. When you cut out or laminate this piece, this is the controlling edge. Locate the position of this line in the foundation as described in Chapter 15, and place anchoring blocks accordingly.

Plans usually specify that bulkheads, locker sides and berth supports be built from a given thickness of sheet plywood. It's unusual to find a major bulkhead, say of ¾ inch plywood, held in place in the hull just by bonding its edge to the planking. In most cases, cheek pieces are positioned on one or both sides where the plywood meets the planking. The cheek piece is bonded to both the bulkhead and the planking to increase joint surface area.

We find that it's best to laminate the cheek piece, bond it to the bulkhead and then put both pieces in the set-up as a unit. If the cheek piece is on the changeover side of the bulkhead, make it larger that the controlling edge so that there will be enough material after beveling for a good joint. If possible, however, bond cheek pieces to the non-control side of a member so they will be somewhat easier to bevel.

Problems with Rough Fairing Permanent Frame Items

In the first stage of fairing, where you place the battens over frames that have not yet been beveled, a difficulty arises when permanent frames are included in the set-up. When there are mold frames only, all of which are of the same thickness of material, the *non-controlling edges* are all in the same relative position to their corresponding *controlling edges,* and so the rough fairing works rather well. In other words, if the mold material is, say, ⅝ inch thick, the non-controlling edges will all be more or less in line with the controlling edges and ⅝ inch from them. The controlling and non-controlling edges of permanent frames also will be in line with each other, but they may be something other than ⅝ inch apart. If this is so, fairing roughly over non-control edges is much more difficult.

The solution to this, in the case of pieces that are thicker than the mold frame material, is to do a preliminary bevel. Assume, for example, that a bulkhead together with its cheek piece is 2 inches thick and that the mold frames are ⅝ inch thick. The technique is to draw a line on the bulkhead-cheek piece ⅝ inch from its controlling edge so that the fairing batten can rest on the line. All of the material being removed is material that would have to come off eventually anyway, so the operation will cost little in time. Because the piece will now have its ⅝ inch line exposed to contact with the batten, you can rough fair the piece in with the rest of the frames in the set-up.

Pieces that are less than the thickness of the mold frame materials — and thankfully there will be few, if any, of them — have to be shimmed to a thickness equal to that of the other frames. Suppose the piece is ⅜ inch while the mold frames are ⅝ inch. You will have to find or mill something that is ¼ inch and apply it to the piece's non-controlling edge to build it out to ⅝ inch. A movable piece, applied with two clamps that you can shift around as you shift the batten, is probably the best.

Precoating and Prefinishing

It's easier to fabricate parts on the shop floor than

124

inside a hull. Accordingly, we suggest as much prefabrication as possible. If you are working on a bulkhead, for example, you might cut and frame companionways before installing it in the set-up. Precoating with WEST SYSTEM epoxy, discussed in Chapter 11, is usually quicker, and the results are generally better, than coating after a piece is in place and the hull planked. Do all the jobs you can before the piece goes into the set-up.

We have difficulty convincing builders of the merits of precoating and prefinishing, and we think that this is because prefinishing does not work in other boatbuilding methods. In conventional construction, where paint and varnish are used to coat surfaces and something else is used as an adhesive, the various substances may be incompatible. When you use wood/epoxy construction techniques, however, with WEST SYSTEM resin as both a coating and an adhesive, the problems of incompatibility never arise. If you precoat

Figure 9—Prefinishing permanent frames for 60 foot trimaran.

Figure 10—Permanent frames ready for set-up. These frames have legs and spalls attached. They have been prefinished and notched for stringers.

a bulkhead or rib with epoxy, and then use the same epoxy to bond that piece in the hull, it will form a homogeneous encapsulation and joint. It does not matter that the resin coating on the surface has cured at a different time than the bonding adhesive.

Precoating saves time and it also protects pieces from minor nicks and gouges. Cured WEST SYSTEM epoxy is very hard. It will resist a certain amount of errant hammering and banging of jigging lumber. The coating is not indestructible, however. It can be damaged, so try to avoid hitting it.

If you have put a precoated bulkhead in the set-up and adhesive squeezes out and runs down onto it as you plank the hull, wipe off the excess resin, smooth it out or form it into a fillet before it cures. A beaded run down the bulkhead will be unsightly, so wipe it up before it sets. If a drip does cure, it isn't a disaster; you will just have a little extra sanding to do later.

Chapter 15

Setting Up

Setting up, the process of lining up frames on a foundation so that they outline the lofted shape of the hull, is one of the more exciting parts of boatbuilding. If your lofting and frame construction are accurate, you will finally begin to see the shape of your boat.

Begin setting up by choosing a foundation sturdy enough to hold components in place until they are fastened to each other and the hull is lifted away. This may be the floor or it may be a *strongback*. Position frames over the foundation, but not touching it. For accuracy, you must locate frames exactly parallel to each other and perpendicular to a centerline which you will erect, the *centering cable*. When the frames are in position, fasten their legs to anchoring blocks, assemble permanent bracing between them and the foundation, and bevel and fair the set-up to receive planking.

The Foundation

If you are building on a dirt floor, you have little choice but to build a strongback. If you have a wood or concrete floor, on the other hand, you can use a strongback, but it's not necessary unless the floor is in poor condition. A strongback is required if a concrete floor is so cracked and heaved that it's impossible to draw on it, or if a wooden floor is of questionable strength. Otherwise, the floor itself can serve as a foundation, and all you have to do is sweep or vacuum it.

A strongback usually looks something like a ladder, with rungs at every station line. All strongbacks are pretty much alike except for the size and spacing of their timbers. Your plans may include specifications, or you may have to design your own. The following is a general outline for construction.

To make a strongback you need four timbers of equal width and thickness. Two of the pieces — the longitudinal members — should be slightly longer than the overall length of the boat, and the other two — the cross members — should be about two thirds of the boat's beam. Stock about 2 inches x 12 inches is heavy enough for most hulls. It helps if all four timbers are reasonably straight. Since they will be anchoring points for a cable drawn to several hundred pounds of tension, the shorter timbers should be fairly stiff. You will also need 2 inch x 4 inch boards for the cross pieces at the station lines.

Build a rectangle by boxing the ends of the two longitudinal timbers with the shorter ones. The pieces should be on their edges. If you are working on a concrete or wood floor, screw lag bolts through the cross members into the longitudinals. If you are working on a dirt floor, you will be using stakes to hold the side pieces, so you don't need any fasteners. The 2 x 4 station line cross members will be installed later.

Place the strongback on the floor, seating the bottom edges of the timbers so they won't rock, shift or settle as the weight of construction bears on them, and level it. Although adjustments can be made later, when jigging is attached to the timbers, you will save time by making sure that the edges are level and at the same height at this stage. Check for irregularities on a wood or concrete floor and bond blocks in place as needed to support the entire length of the strongback. If you are working on dirt, scrape away high spots until the pieces sit firmly and then drive sharpened 2 x 4's as far as possible into the ground beside the ends of each timber. Nail these stakes to the strongback to keep it upright and to forestall settling.

Figure 1 shows the strongback and mold frames for a small canoe. Note that it's possible to raise a small strongback up off the floor to a convenient working height.

The Centering Cable

Before setting up the frames and jigging, run a cable the length of boat to represent a centerline. This will be

Figure 1—Strongback and molds for canoe.

the reference for aligning frames and measuring station lines. If you are building a large boat and can borrow or rent a transit, consider using it to make sure that your cable is accurately laid.

A string will work for a centerline, but we prefer to use 1/16 inch or 3/32 inch diameter wire rope stretched to about 500 pounds tension. The cable stays taut and will not break or stretch if you trip on it. If your foundation is the floor, run the centering cable an inch or less above it. If you are using a strongback, run it above the cross pieces. Anchor the centerline on guides outside the bow and stern of the boat. For longer hulls you may want to add slotted support blocks at intervals along the length of the cable. Both guides and blocks should be indestructible. Set them so that even the clumsiest feet can't move them after you've begun setting up.

The centerline must be level so that frames can be set up perpendicular to it. Use a line level, available at a hardware store, to check it before finally fastening it off. Hang the level in the middle of the cable and raise or lower one end of the cable until it's level. Turn the line level 180° to check in the other direction. If it's level, you're done.

When the cable is centered, put down the lines over which to erect frames. Mold frames are usually positioned on station lines, spaced as they are in the lofting grid. If you are including permanent frames such as bulkheads in the set-up, draw lines to position them.

Space the lines over which the frames are to be set up exactly as they are on the lofting floor. You can use the big lofting square to establish the lines perpendicular to the centerline. Line the square up with the centerline at each mold frame or permanent frame position and mark the floor or timbers on each side. If you are not using a strongback, draw the lines directly on the floor. If you have a strongback, draw lines on it to represent the station lines. These may not be at perfect right angles to the timbers if the timbers are not parallel or if they are warped, but they must be parallel to each other, spaced from each other just as they are in the lofting and perpendicular to the centerline.

Anchoring Blocks

When you have marked the lines and checked them for accuracy, make and install *anchoring blocks* or *cleats*. These can usually be cut from 2 inch x 4 inch

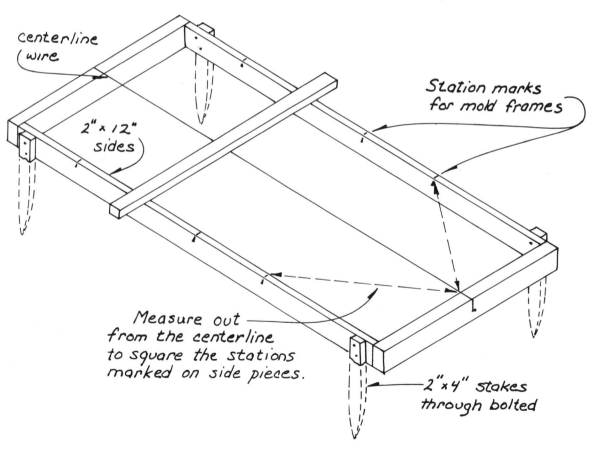

Figure 2—Strongback arrangement for a dirt floor.

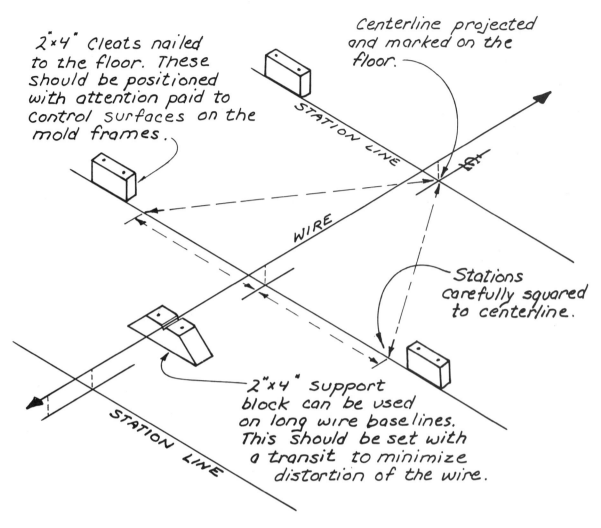

Figure 3—Centering cable and anchoring blocks.

stock, although a larger boat may require larger blocks. If you are using a strongback, install the 2 x 4 cross pieces, broad side down, at each station line to make cross members which extend beyond where the legs will intersect. If you are not using a strongback, fasten the anchoring blocks directly to the floor. It isn't necessary to put down lengths of 2 x 4 — you can use two short pieces at each station, placed broad side down at the point where the legs will meet the floor. Leave the blocks a little long, so there will be a margin for error and adjustment. With either type of foundation, place the anchoring blocks flush beside the lines marked for the frames. When you install the legs, they will butt against the sides of the blocks.

Always place anchoring blocks on the side of the line toward the bow or the stern, whichever is nearer, with a *changeover point* at the widest part of the hull. For the forward half of the hull, the blocks go forward of the line, and for the after half they go aft of the line. Blocks on the station line at the changeover point can be placed toward either the bow or the stern. If you use

pairs of blocks, they must both be on the same side of the line.

Fasten blocks to a strongback with nails and epoxy. Then fillet their edges with a thick mixture of epoxy and high density filler. Make fillets on two or three sides of the block only, leaving open the side where the jigging leg will be attached. Since most load is straight down through the legs to the floor, little side load comes onto these blocks at any time during construction. If your foundation is the floor, edge filleting with no further bonding will keep the blocks in place. The advantage of fillets is that you can heat them with a propane torch to remove them when the project is finished.

Setting Up

The process of setting up frames has four objectives: to locate the controlling edges of the frames over the corresponding station lines marked on the strongback or floor; to make the centerlines of the frames plumb, fore and aft and athwartship; to line up the centerlines on the frames perpendicular to the centering cable; and to locate waterlines on the mold frames at specific heights above the cable.

You either need two spirit levels or one spirit level and one plumb bob to do a set-up. The plump bob and level method is the more accurate and should be used on any boat large enough to have accommodations. With small boats, two levels can be used.

Three foot levels are long enough, but you should check them for accuracy and compensate for any error. To check a level for horizontal accuracy, place it against a wall, with the bubble between the reticles, and draw a line the length of the instrument along its edge. Then turn the level end-for-end and place it back along the line. If the bubble is still in the reticles, the level is accurate. If not, move the level until the bubble comes into position and draw a second line along the edge of the level. This line will intersect the first and the error is one half the angle of the intersection. In other words, if the lines are ¼ inch apart 3 feet from the intersection, the error is ⅛ inch for 3 feet. If you continue to use such a level, write the amount of error and its direction on the instrument itself. Check vertical accuracy in a similar manner, but do not turn the instrument end-for-end. Instead, just flop it over so that one side is against the wall, and then flop it again. If a level has several spirit tubes, check each one. One or two may be accurate and you can mask any inaccurate ones.

Some levels have adjustable spirit tubes. To make these accurate, draw the two lines as above, and then adjust the bubble into the reticles on a line which bisects the angle formed by the original lines.

Use a straightedge to measure the heights of the mold frames during set-up. It can be quite light, but it should not be easily bent. In most cases, 1½ inch x ½ inch stock is adequate. The straightedge must be long enough to reach from the highest point in the set-up to the centering cable. A little excess length is desirable, but more than an extra ¼ inch or so — however much the cable clears the floor or strongback — gets in the way as you work.

To set up the heights of the mold frames, you need the waterlines on the mold frames and the centering cable on the foundation as reference points. Take all of these points off the lofting body plan. If you have not drawn the cable location on the lofting floor, do so now. Then place the straightedge along the centerline of the body plan and mark it for the cable location and the waterlines. Because all of the mold frames may not have the same waterline as a reference point, you need to mark the straightedge with all the waterlines that come into play.

To set up the first station, clamp the straightedge ⅛ inch to the side of and parallel to the centerline of the mold frame face. Then adjust the straightedge up and down until the appropriate waterline mark on the straightedge is aligned with the reference waterline on the frame.

Spring clamps are handy and effective for holding the straightedge to the frame. Apply the clamps at the vertex of the frame and at the spall. If the straightedge is put on the control face, you will have to put a shim of scrap mold frame material between the straightedge and the spall as a spacer to hold the straightedge parallel to the control surface. If the straightedge is put on the opposing non-control surface, you will need a shim of scrap spall material to fill a space between the straightedge and the vertex so that the straightedge is parallel with the controlling edge.

In Chapter 14 we suggested that you install the spalls so that their edges are the reference waterline. If this has been done, recheck the edges for straightness. An alternative to using the edge of the spall is to stretch a string, held by spring clamps, across the waterline marks on the frame and to adjust the straightedge mark to the string.

Putting up the Frames

In constructing the frames you have already cut the legs to a uniform height or marked this distance. When you set up the frames, the cable and its corresponding mark on the straightedge will be very close to the same height as soon as the mold station is set into position. Place the station so that the straightedge is next to the cable but not touching it. Put clamps over the legs and anchoring blocks and tighten them at least enough to keep the frame from falling over. Screw type C-clamps are more satisfactory than sliding, quick-action clamps because they do not fall off when you make adjustments. Then put a temporary diagonal brace in with

Figure 4—Setting up first frame. Note anchoring blocks on floor.

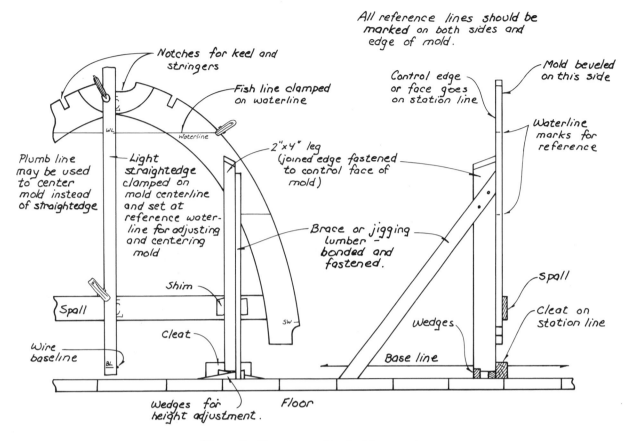

All reference lines should be marked on both sides and edge of mold.

Notches for keel and stringers

Fish line clamped on waterline

Control edge or face goes on station line

Mold beveled on this side

Waterline marks for reference

Plumb line may be used to center mold instead of straightedge

Light straightedge clamped on mold centerline and set at reference waterline for adjusting and centering mold

2"x4" leg (joined edge fastened to control face of mold)

Brace or jigging lumber - bonded and fastened.

Shim

Spall

Cleat

Wire baseline

Spall

Cleat on station line

Wedges

Base line

Wedges for height adjustment.

Floor

Figure 5—Two views of typical frame set-up.

clamps as you plumb the station fore and aft with the spirit level. You can loosen the clamps on the legs enough to allow the legs to slip on the anchoring blocks while adjustments are made.

To position the stations, you can use either a *plumb bob* or the *two level method*. As mentioned earlier, the plumb bob ensures greater accuracy. To use the plumb bob, attach it at the station vertex on the centerline with a spring clamp and enough string so that the point of the bob barely clears the centering cable. Place the bob on the opposite side of the station from the straightedge so they are not in the way of each other.

Next, adjust the position of the station until the following conditions simultaneously exist:

(1) the plumb line is over the centerline of the frame, with the point of the bob over the centering cable;

(2) the frame is plumb fore and aft and free of twist, that is, the frame is exactly perpendicular to the centerline;

(3) the cable mark on the straightedge is level with the cable.

To detect twist, hold the spirit level in a vertical position in various locations on the station face. If you have applied the legs precisely parallel to the centerline, you

can use the legs as the arbitrarily chosen points to be made plumb. To eliminate twist, you usually need to adjust the diagonal, or to install a second, and sometimes even a third, diagonal.

If the set-up is on a floor, you can use wooden wedges, tapped under the legs with a mallet or manually, for minute increments of vertical adjustment. If the set-up is on a strongback, you can make these adjustments in the clamping of the legs to the anchoring blocks. Vertical adjustment usually necessitates adjustment of the diagonal(s) to bring the station back to plumb and the taking up or letting out of line to the plumb bob. Keep working until the station position is accurate. One adjustment may necessitate others.

If you are using the *two level method* instead of a plumb bob, you will need a second spirit level. Clamp this horizontally along the spall. The straightness of the spall edge is obviously very important. With the two level method, bringing the bubble of the second level into the reticles takes the place of bringing the plumb line over the station's centerline. Bringing the straightedge to the cable then performs the function of aligning the centerline onto the cable. The other level is used as before.

Orient the level that is clamped to the spall in the same direction on all the frames. In other words, if the frames are being set up in a north-south direction athwartship, mark one end of the level "N" or "S" and always position it accordingly. In this way, any error in the level will always be in the same direction and the result will be that all of the station centerlines, though they may not be perfectly vertical, will at least be in the same plane, which is all that really matters.

Before applying any filleting, it is a good idea to go to the lofting floor and measure and make notes on the distances for each station of the cable to sheer and the cable to the top of the mold frame. After a station is in position, check the measurements in the set-up before applying the filleting. The check is good for revealing any gross errors in manufacturing or setting up the frame. Such errors would reveal themselves rather soon in any case, but it is better to discover them before it becomes necessary to chisel away the filleting material in order to correct them.

When you are sure that the station is in perfect alignment, you can fillet the legs to the anchoring blocks and the floor. Use a high density resin mixture that is roughly the consistency of peanut butter. The strength and holding power of this mixture is adequate to support the legs throughout hull construction if you make generous fillets along all the lines where the legs

Figure 7—Straightedge clamped at centerline of frame.

Figure 6—Frame set-up showing straightedge, string on reference waterline and levels.

and the block meet. There is no need to put adhesive between the surfaces or to otherwise support the legs if the fillets are formed on clean, oil-free surfaces.

Nailing and Screwing Legs

If you have plenty of clamps, you can just fillet around them and leave them in place until the filleting material cures. This allows you to proceed immediately to the next station. You can patch in the remainder of the fillet later, after the clamps are removed.

If you don't have enough clamps to go on to the next station, you can use nails and/or screws driven through the legs to the anchoring blocks to hold the frame in position while the filleting cures. Drive the nails and screws while the clamps are on. After you remove the clamps, recheck the position of the station. Nails and screws can allow small amounts of movement. Therefore, do not rely on nails and screws as a permanent measure to prevent movement. You should always apply fillets, if only because they show telltale signs of movement so slight that they otherwise might go unnoticed.

Figure 8—Setting up frames. Note wedges on floor under the legs. Frame in foreground is clamped to its anchoring block and the diagonal bracing. Straightedge is clamped along frame's centerline and just touches centerline cable at floor level.

Permanent Bracing

The temporary diagonals, which are only clamped until the filleting material on the legs cures, must be replaced by permanent diagonals. Some thought must go into location of the permanent diagonals, especially if you are placing some bulkheads in the set-up. Bracing will have to be kept out of their way.

If it is necessary to release the temporary diagonals before you apply the permanent ones, you will have to replumb the station, fore and aft, and recorrect twist. Handle both of these operations as before by holding a spirit level vertically on the face of the mold frame. Since the legs will have been permanently secured by this time, you need not worry about any other aspect of the station positioning. When everything is aligned, fillet the permanent diagonals in place.

When all of the frames are set up, we usually place a batten in various positions across the frames to see how the whole thing fairs. Since the frames will not have been beveled at this time, this fairing check will be crude, but it will nonetheless reveal any sizable mislocations. Should a frame appear to be out of place,

check its position, as well as those of the frames on either side of it, by measurements from the lofting. Be sure you know exactly where an error is before changing things.

Warping or curling of mold frame material will cause an appearance of error, especially toward the ends of the set-up. If the long batten shows a discrepancy, check for warp or curl in the stations, as well as for station position.

Beveling

Frames are beveled so that planking can bend evenly, with smooth curves, over them. Begin this operation by rolling flat black paint on the edges of the frames. Most of this paint will be planed away; the object is to leave a thin line of black on the controlling edge so that you know it has not been disturbed.

Use a batten which spans at least three stations as a guide for beveling. Lay it over three frames and nail down its ends. If your mold frames are only ¼ inch thick, you can just hack away excess stock from the middle frame. If they are thicker, take a hand saw and cut marks on the edge of the middle frame on either side of the batten parallel to it as it crosses the frame edge at an angle. Cut no deeper than the black control edge. Move the batten up and down the frame, sawing or hacking every foot along its edge. Check for fairness. When you have finished one frame, move on to the next.

When all larger frames are marked, chisel away the wood between the kerfs so that you have a series of notches. Check again for fairness, and then scribble

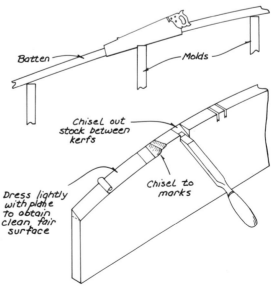

Figure 9—Beveling mold frames.

across the bottom of each notch with a pencil. Using the pencil marks to guide you, plane the entire edge of the frame. We use power planes to rough cut bevels, but advise against them unless you have some experience with these machines. Hand planes do just as well, though at a somewhat slower rate.

Fairing

Once you have rough cut the bevels so that only a thin line of black remains on the controlling edges, you are ready for final fairing. As in lofting, the eye and artistic sensitivity are the main tools. The object is to make the long batten touch all the controlling edges under it and form a curve free of lumps or flat spots in all positions on the length of the set-up.

To accomplish this, it may be necessary to cut below the marked black control edge in some areas, and to build up above the edge in others by bonding on strips of wood or not beveling to the full depth of the saw cuts. Accurate work in lofting, picking up, cutting frames, constructing them and setting them up will hold errors that have to be corrected in this manner to

a minimum. Minute errors in each of these operations are practically unavoidable, but for the most part they cancel each other out. In some areas, though, the errors will all add up to something that has to be corrected.

In final fairing, the batten tacked across the mold frames sometimes looks wrong or irregular because of the way in which it is positioned. Do not undertake any corrections on the basis of a single batten position. Move the batten all about the set-up, and make an overall analysis of what has to be done. Carefully mark errors on the frames in the exact area where you observe them. As you place the batten in various positions (this is especially a problem in areas of difficult curves) the error in one area may read differently, creating some confusion, and you have to make a judgment between conflicting dimensions as to which one is the real error. Sometimes a compromise between measurements results in the best fairness.

When you are certain what corrections are needed, make them by planing below the marked control edge or bonding on shims. Work until the set-up is fair, without any humps or flat spots.

1

2

3

4

5

6

7

8

9

10

11

12

14

13

15

16

17

18

19

20

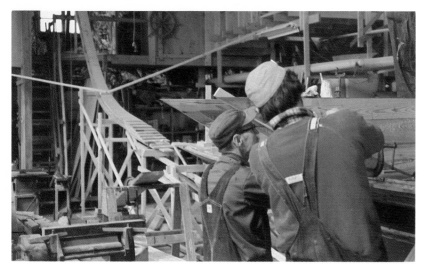

21

22

23

24

25

26

27

28

29

30

31

32

33

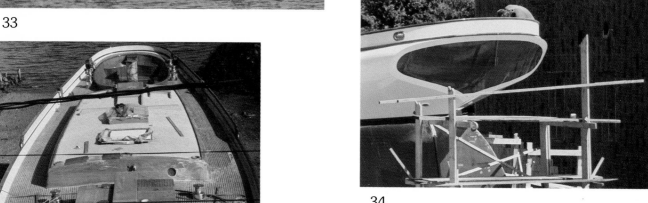

34

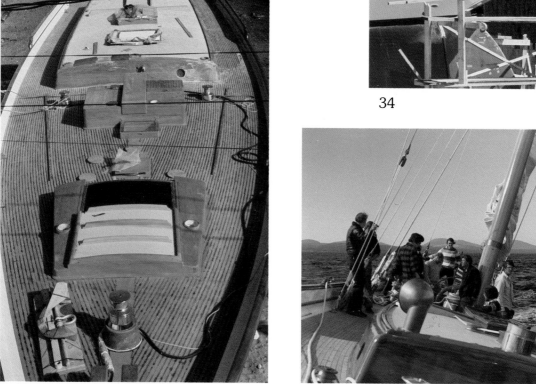

35

36

37

38

39

40

41

42

43

44

45

46

47

48

50

51

52

53

54

55

56

57

58

59

60

61

62

63

64

65

Chapter 16

Keels, Stems and Sheer Clamps

In traditional construction, the keel is the backbone or major structural element of a boat. It's usually large and strong, and ribs and frames attached to it to form the skeletal framework over which planking is laid.

In the composite construction methods we use, however, the integrity of the hull structure is less dependent on the keel. Loads are distributed so efficiently throughout the boat that keels are sometimes almost unnecessary. The stem, a second critical element in older designs, has lost its importance to a lesser extent. Strong stems protect hulls when they strike objects at sea, so we continue to use them to minimize damage.

In addition to describing keel and stem construction, this chapter discusses keelsons, centerboard and daggerboard cases and sheer clamps. With the methods for laminating hulls detailed in later chapters of this book, we plan these components and some interior features before planking.

The Keel/Stem Assembly

The keel, which serves as a natural joining point for the planking on either side of it, is often the key to making modern construction methods practical. A keel also contributes to overall hull strength by distributing high point loading over large areas of skin. This function may be more valuable out of the water than in it: when a boat is hauled, a strong keel may help to support its entire weight at several points.

The size and shape of both the keel and the stem vary widely from boat to boat and depend on structural needs and construction techniques. We usually build the two parts separately, join them with a scarf joint to form a keel/stem assembly and then install the unit in the set-up. A boat with very gentle curve in the stem could conceivably have a stem and keel made in one lamination, but we have never found this to be practical. We make them up separately because keels generally have only gentle curves which can be formed with a few layers of wood and stems often have at least one severe curve which requires many laminations. Laminating an entire unit with many layers to accommodate the curve in one area of the stem would waste time and material. Most boats have transoms, so stems are only required at the bow. A double-ender will need stems at both ends of the keel, however, and in this situation a three piece keel/stem complex may be necessary.

If the keel and stem are to be anywhere near as strong as the hull skin, special attention must be paid to their construction. The keel/stem unit usually joins the two halves of the hull skin and while it is unlikely that this joint will be as strong as the skin, high grain strength is needed to prevent splitting along the boat's centerline. Keels which are less than 1 inch thick can be built of solid lumber, but we prefer to laminate both keels and stems, following procedures described in Chapter 9, because of the structural advantages of the laminate.

There are several ways to prevent splitting at the keel. Graphite or glass fibers may be bonded between layers of planking where they meet. We usually add plywood strips to our keels. On keels less than 1 inch thick, we begin with solid lumber, and then bond plywood to what will be its interior surface in the boat, as in Figure 1, Section B. In large, thick keels, it's wiser to distribute thin layers of plywood through the lamination than to rely on a single strip of heavier ply. Birch plywood is particularly effective in this application because it is strong in tension and it bonds well with epoxy. Three-ply ⅛ inch thick plywood is adequate in most cases.

In traditional designs, stems and keels are usually *rabbeted,* notched to accept planking and allow it to lie flush with the outside of the keel or stem. Rabbeting is time-consuming, and it requires skill and patience. To gain more bonding area we have eliminated it. Instead of rabbeting, we laminate the keel and stem and then shape them to accept the planking, which generally covers all of the keel and most of the stem. The planking is eventually covered with laminated hardwood cap, illustrated in Figure 1. The cap becomes an extension of the keel and performs the functions of a rabbeted keel. Our technique is fast, accurate and potentially less wasteful of materials, and it produces a joint which is structurally superior to a rabbeted joint.

Planning the Keel/Stem Lay-Up

A good deal of thought must go into planning the keel/stem complex. Determine the finished size of the lamination so that you can laminate together enough stock to form a blank from which to cut, shape and fair the final piece. Keel laminations can become complex because they may have different widths and thicknesses along their lengths, depending on the hull shape and the requirements for bonding surface area. Some keels will be very simple, and their entire length can be made out of one size of stock. Other keels may be considerably wider in the middle than they are at the ends, or much thicker at some points than others. Stems also may be much wider at the deck intersection than they are at the waterline.

To develop all of these dimensions you need to go to the lofting board and develop the keel shape at each station. If the designer does not specify an exact keel size, begin by drawing the section view of the keel into several stations on the body plan. The basis on which we develop keel shape and/or size is *surface bonding area*. Wider keels develop more bonding surface and therefore are usually more desirable, but they usually have to get thicker to get wider. When trying to develop sufficient bonding area at various station posi-

tions, you will find that the flatter areas in the middle of the hull permit the use of a thinner keel section, while the finer bow area will require a much thicker keel section to provide the same bonding area. Stems may have to be two or three times thicker than keels because the sharpness with which the planking joins the hull at the stem limits bondable area.

When you have developed the keel shape at a few stations, you can loft and fair the keel at *all* of the stations on the lofting board. It is important to remember that you need to subtract the cap thickness from the outside lofted profile of the hull in order to define the keel and stem profile. The stem is sometimes difficult to project properly in the lofting. See Chapter 13 for a detailed discussion of this procedure. Chapter 13 also gives instructions for the development of all stem dimensions.

Also lay out the area, usually near the forefoot, where the keel and stem meet. A 10 or 12 to 1 scarf bevel is needed for adequate strength, so the joint may be quite long. Because its two parts may curve slightly, a keel/stem scarf joint can be difficult to manufacture.

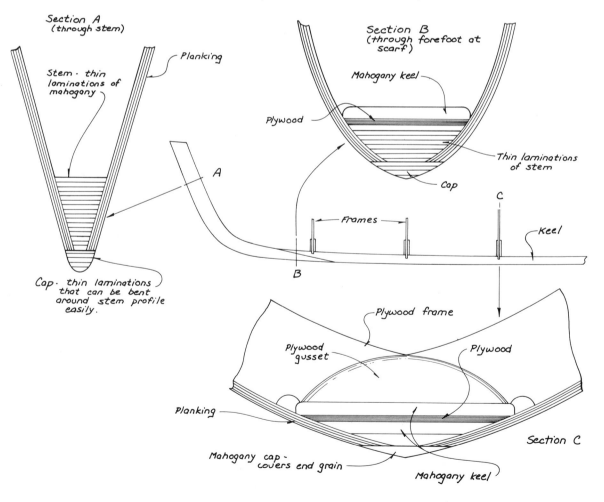

Figure 1—Sections through the hull on 60 foot trimaran ROGUE WAVE. Note plywood laminated into main keel. The cross grain in this lamination counteracts the splitting forces of keel or centerboard.

There are no hard and fast rules about the direction — stem over keel or keel over stem — the scarf should run.

After lofting the stem and keel, locate the scarf. Then draw in the *bearding line,* which shows the inside intersection of the planking and the stem or keel. Make a pattern or template of the area where the stem and forward end of the keel join. The easiest way to do this is to use the nail method of transferring lines described in Chapter 14. It's best to pick up all pertinent profile, sheer, scarf, station and bearding lines at the same time. Check all measurements and label all lines clearly. Cut out the template and carefully trim it to the profile shape on the lofting.

If you are planning to build your boat using the mold method for laminating hulls, the process of installing a permanent stem in your mold may involve a few extra steps. An inner mold stem may be necessary. Loft and shape this piece before you begin work on your keel/ stem unit, following instructions in Chapter 18.

At this point, you should have a reasonably clear idea of the shape and dimensions of the keel and stem so you can prepare stock to laminate the blank for the stem and keel. You can laminate the stock to the exact thickness desired, but you should always add a little extra width to allow for trimming after the blank is completed. While it is possible to save some stock by varying the lengths, widths and thicknesses of the stock in the laminate, this is normally more complicated than it's worth because of the great amount of planning and work involved in cutting out and properly lining up all of the different size pieces. It's more practical to control the thickness of a keel or stem by *step tapering* the wood along the length.

Make the keel and stem blanks a little longer than you will actually need them. The scarf joint will use up some of this surplus, so plan for it. Since the forward tip of the stem blank is usually fastened securely to the floor or strongback in the set-up, extra stock beyond the sheer line may be necessary. The keel blank should extend a short distance beyond the transom to facilitate fairing.

Springback may complicate construction of both the keel and the stem, and it can make proper alignment difficult. In keels, springback can sometimes be so slight that you can push the piece back into position. Stem laminations are usually thicker and may present greater springback problems. If it's impossible to push a stem into shape, you may have to laminate extra stock onto one side and plane away wood from the other to regain the designed curve.

Figure 2—Laminated stem for proa SLINGSHOT. The extra blocking on side of stem is for the slight flare in the bow. Note the set-up cable on the floor and the notch in the stem for the cable in the extreme lower left.

Laminating Forms

The stem may be the largest and most difficult laminated piece in your hull. It's also usually one of the first laminated components you'll need. Practice with a dry run before applying WEST SYSTEM* Brand epoxy to the stem blank.

We usually lay out and bond stem blanks on the floor, using triangular blocks to make a form as described in Chapter 9. Take care to avoid any twisting in the laminate. The stem is aligned along the centerline of a boat, so any distortion will complicate marking the centerline and positioning the stem in the set-up.

Triangular blocks may also be used to laminate keel blanks. We often laminate keels right on our set-ups, using mold frames as forms. The difficulty with this is that the laminating stock is usually wider than the trimmed keel will be, so the lamination must be completed before any notches for the keel can be cut in the permanent or mold frames. The trick is to work out an adequate form without damaging the mold frames.

We recommend the following procedure in this situation. Measure up from the bottom of the marked keel notch enough to clear the notch. Draw a line across the frame parallel to the base of the notch. Mark all frames in this way and saw them off flush with these lines.

Screw or clamp 1½ inch square cleats or blocks to the control sides of all mold frames. Clamp them to permanent frames. These will be points which you can clamp to the keel blank. Include limber holes at the frame/keel joints by cutting notches a little wider than needed for the keel blank. Be careful not to remove so

Figure 3—Set-up for 42 foot GOLDEN DAZY. Keel can be seen on sawhorses beyond molds. The slight rocker in this hull allowed use of a solid keel.

much stock that the frame becomes too weak to support and outline the hull shape. On thick keels, limber holes which do not extend the full depth of the notches can work effectively.

You may need temporary jigging aft of the transom and up around the bow for laminating to help coax the keel blank into bending as it approaches these areas. This jigging can consist of a temporary addition to a bow frame and a partial frame just aft of the transom. Because of springback, it's often a good idea to slightly overbend the keel toward the bow and stern.

When the keel lamination is in position, clamp it securely at each station point, covering each station with polyethylene sheeting to keep resin from dripping onto permanent members and accidentally bonding the keel to the mold forms. Use clamps at each edge of the keel to hold it to the blocks on the mold frame. To be sure that there is adequate clamping pressure on the laminate between stations, use hand clamps with clamping pads to spread the load. Remove any epoxy which squeezes out of the lamination.

Joining Keel and Stem Blanks

Mark centerlines and station lines on the stem and keel blanks while they are still in the set-up. To mark the interior of the stem, hold a plumb bob under the stem and drop it to the centering cable. Mark the location from which the plumb bob falls straight to the cable at intervals along the stem and draw a line with a batten to connect the marks.

Use a level to lay out station lines and any other frame locations perpendicular to the centerline. Then mark the widths of the keel and stem on their respective blanks. Rough plane the side edges of the blanks to these dimensions, but wait to taper any thickness until after the pieces have been joined. Place the keel/

stem template on the blanks or take them to the lofting. Transfer all reference lines and marks for the scarf.

Cut scarf bevels on both blanks and then join them in the set-up to check for proper alignment. If the angles don't match almost perfectly, work with them until they do. We usually allow a little extra length in scarf joints to allow for this bit of fitting: if the bevel does fit the first time, we remove the excess.

We generally bond the scarf joint in the set-up, with both keel and stem lined up in position. Once the bevels are cut correctly, you can clamp the joint anywhere, but to avoid any longitudinal distortion be careful to make sure that the centerlines of the two pieces line up.

When the keel and stem are a single unit, prefinish the portions which will show on the hull's interior. Plane and sand the surface smooth and round any edges. Then apply two or more coats of WEST SYSTEM resin to the prepared surface and lightly sand it before installing it in the set-up.

The final step in making the keel/stem unit is machining bevels on the surfaces to which planking will be bonded. It's possible to do this using lofted measurements, but the job is easier in the set-up, where the controlling edges of mold frames can act as guides in determining angles.

Notching Frames

When the keel and stem are joined and shaped, cut notches in the frames to receive the unit. The width and depth of the notch in any frame is determined by the dimensions of the keel/stem at this station. Lay out these measurements on the frames and cut the notches

Figure 4—Laminated ash stem scarfed to solid mahogany keel. Note stringer bonded to stem.

as accurately as possible. The bevel of the notch will be the same as the bevel of the frame in the area of the notch.

Good fits between the keel/stem and mold frames are essential wherever the assembly is attached to permanent frames. In areas where the keel is a single thickness, use a long batten to check the fairness of keel notches in the mold frames. We often insert the keel/stem in position to check the notches for depth and width. The stem usually crosses only one or two frames. After that, it's unlikely that it will be notched in place. Instead, it will sit on top of a flattened area which is machined at the correct height on the mold frame.

Installing the Keel/Stem in the Set-Up

Join the keel/stem to the frames at every station in the set-up. Bond the unit to permanent members with a thick mixture of epoxy and high density filler. Draw the pieces together with clamps, if they reach easily around the frames, or drill holes and run screws through the keel and into the frames. If you use screws, remember to remove them so that they won't be in the way of beveling. Fill the drilled holes during finishing. To reduce sanding, remove any epoxy which squeezes out of the joint.

Figure 6—Laminated keel for ROGUE WAVE bonded to frames. Keel is ready to be faired. Frame across centerboard slot will remain uncut through planking process to prevent any distortion of keel due to stresses created during planking. Centerboard case is installed after boat is turned over. In this case, it was taller than the set-up allowed.

To anchor the keel/stem to *mold frames,* use blocks and screws in somewhat the same manner as described earlier for using the set-up as a laminating form. Screw square blocks of appropriate dimensions to the control side of the mold frames, making them even with the bottom of the notched-out area and holding them in place with several screws and perhaps some adhesive if needed. Drill each of these blocks for one screw (although you can use several if necessary) and insert the screw upward through the block and into the interior side of the keel. Use a washer to keep the head of the screw from pulling through the block. Do not insert the screw so far that it will interfere with machining that will be done on bonding surfaces. Later, when the hull is completed, you will need to remove these screws so that the keel and hull will come free from the mold frames.

You will need jigging to position the tip of the stem so that it will not move during beveling. You can use the excess length that has been left on the stem blank beyond the sheer line as an attachment point for this jigging. After the planking has been applied, you can saw the stem flush with the sheer line measurement.

Beveling the Keel/Stem to Receive Planking

After the keel and stem have been securely positioned in the set-up, mark them for beveling. We usually use a hand saw for this procedure. Saw into the keel, using the saw blade to represent a fair extension of the control edge of the mold frame. Make another similar saw cut an inch or so away and remove the

Figure 5—Keel/stem assembly fit to molds for 32 foot HOT FLASH. Molds are notched so keel lies flush with control face of mold. Note blocking used to secure keel/stem assembly to molds.

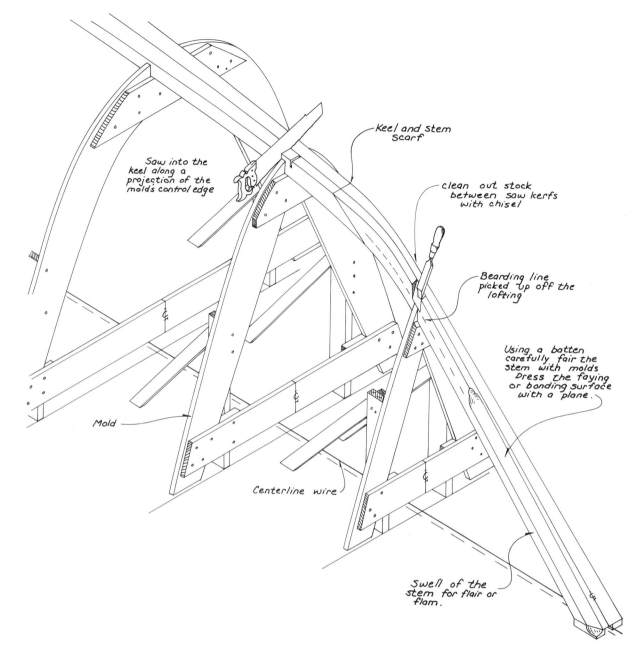

Saw into the keel along a projection of the molds control edge

Keel and stem scarf

clean out stock between saw kerfs with chisel

Bearding line picked up off the lofting

Using a batten carefully fair the stem with molds Dress the faying or bonding surface with a plane.

Mold

Centerline wire

Swell of the stem for flair or flam.

Figure 7—Set-up for typical IOR racer. Control lines have been drawn on stem. Notches are cut in keel at molds to determine bevels. Stem is blocked up to allow centerline cable to pass freely underneath.

material between these cuts with a chisel. Then fair the bevel up with the mold frame itself. Repeat this procedure at every station on each side of the keel. Use a long plane to cut away the stock between the mold frames until the keel is planed down to the bevels already cut at each station position. For large keels, a power plane can save a lot of time and work. Take great care not to develop any hollows between stations, and lay a batten along the length of the keel to make sure that you are maintaining overall fairness. If you do develop any low spots or you find that the keel lamination was a little shy in some areas, you can bond

another layer of veneer or thin plywood in this low area and then fair it to the desired level.

Stems are a little more difficult to bevel for several reasons. First, you can only rely on one or two mold frames to act as guides for beveling. Secondly, the bevel is usually a much more severe V-shape that requires considerable removal of stock. To complicate matters, only that area of the stem close to the waterline may in fact be V-shaped. Higher up in the hull (or close to the sheer line) the stem may become flat on the forward surface. The flat on the stem will be extended to its final dimension with a laminated cap that covers both the stem and planking as shown in Figure 1.

The cross section of the stem blank is more rectangular than the desired final shape. When you jig the stem into position, locate it by positioning the centerline on the back of the stem over the centerlines on any stations or jigging that it crosses. When the stem is positioned accurately, mark it with all of the dimensions needed for beveling. Usually, the most important measurements are the control lines drawn on the face of the stem. The control line(s) may be just a centerline, or, if the stem will have some flare, two lines delineating each corner. See Chapter 13 for detailed discussion of how the stem dimensions are developed.

Begin by cutting the bevels on each side of the stem down to the lines drawn on the front face of the stem. Use a fairing batten to check the angle of the bevels as you progress. For accuracy, lay the batten on the controlling edges of the mold frames three to four stations back from the stem. When the batten lies flush on the stem bevel and meets the control lines drawn on the bevel face (this may be a perfect point along the centerline), the stem is completed. Stem bevels can be tricky, because there is often a large angle change in a

short distance, so you should make frequent checks with a fairing batten along the entire stem dimension to avoid any over-beveling which could cause a crooked stem. Sighting the stem from above the set-up or sighting along its length from the floor can help you detect any unfairness that might develop as you work. Also lay a short batten along the stem to check for hollows.

The Keelson

Keels can take many shapes and forms. The design shown in Figure 8 is one of the more successful solutions to the problem of distributing high point loading, as might be generated by a ballast keel, over maximum area. This type of keel and keelson assembly is basically a relatively lightweight I-beam, with two faces separated by blocking along the length of the boat. Laminated floors and frames distribute load athwartship.

Keelsons are usually made of dense woods with high strength. Ash, for example, is a good choice. We generally install keelsons after removing hulls from their set-ups. The keelson is laminated over the floor and core blocking to form a single unit.

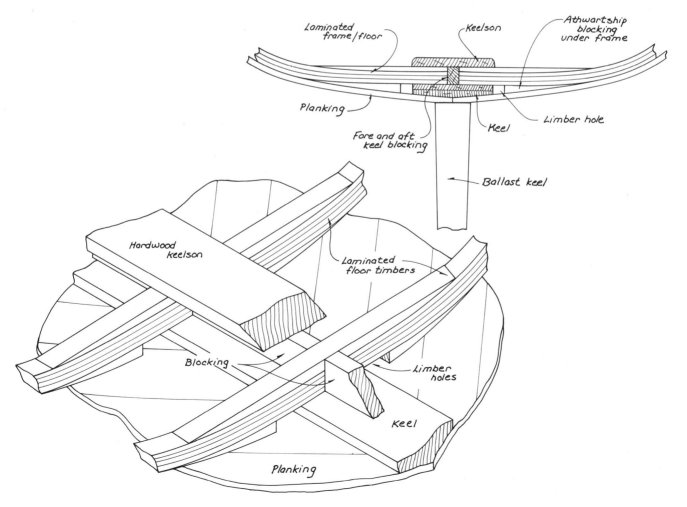

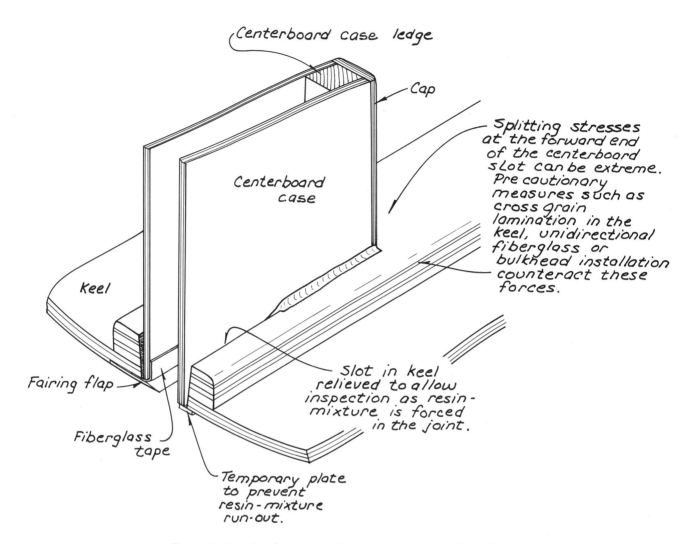

Centerboard case ledge

Cap

Centerboard case

Splitting stresses at the forward end of the centerboard slot can be extreme. Precautionary measures such as cross grain lamination in the keel, unidirectional fiberglass or bulkhead installation counteract these forces.

Keel

Slot in keel relieved to allow inspection as resin-mixture is forced in the joint.

Fairing flap

Fiberglass tape

Temporary plate to prevent resin-mixture run-out.

Figure 9—Details of centerboard case construction and installation.

The structural advantage of this keelson concept is excellent longitudinal stiffness and strength at a light weight. The major advantage, however, is the large safety margin that this method of construction can provide if you ground with a modern fin-type ballast keel. Grounding on a rock can produce severe loading on the entire keel complex as the aft portion of the ballast keel is forced upward into the hull. The beauty of the keelson concept is that the complex is capable of absorbing a great deal of energy by putting the bottom keel and hull skin in compression and the keelson in tension, which is wood's strongest property. Often, a severe grounding will cause the keelson to break in tension. It will absorb tremendous amounts of energy in the process, with the positive result that no other part of the boat is damaged. The keelson is relatively easy to repair by simply scarfing in another piece in the area that has been fractured, and the repair costs little in materials or labor hours. Another structural advantage is that you can make the lower keel itself much smaller than normal, permitting laminated floors or ribs

of the maximum size to pass across the keel with the minimum amount of notching. This provides excellent athwartship load distribution and provides maximum usable headroom space in the process. The keelson represents a very efficient use of material and takes relatively few hours to manufacture.

Centerboard and Daggerboard Cases

Centerboard and daggerboard cases are, in effect, extensions of the keel that provide a cut-out for either a centerboard or daggerboard to pass through. They are also points of extreme high loading and it is very common for damage and leaking to occur in these areas of the boat. Because of this, you should carefully build up the keel in the area in which you install a case. To do this, you might make the keel much thicker at this point, using more cross grain plywood laminations to provide added resistance to splitting. Because a vast majority of the loading on a case is generated in the front, where the slot protrudes through the keel, this area can become one of the highest load points in the entire boat structure, so you should make the front of the slot especially strong to distribute this load over as much area as possible.

Figure 9 illustrates our technique for building and installing centerboard and daggerboard cases. Begin by cutting a slot in the keel a little larger than the perimeter of the case. Lightly bevel the slot, shaping it into a wedge which tapers from a slightly wider top to a narrower bottom. Insert the case into the cut-out so that it is flush with the bottom of the keel, plumb and lined up with the centerline.

Next, work out a way to make sure that any epoxy you apply will not drip immediately out of the keel/case joint. Block the bottom of the case with a piece of wood or tack a bead of epoxy along the joint line and allow it to cure. We usually wrap thin plywood in plastic and staple it to the keel, as shown in Figure 9, and find that this not only prevents oozing but also helps to hold the case in place. Because the plywood is wrapped in plastic, it's easy to remove when the joint has cured.

When the anti-drip device is positioned, pour a slightly-thickened high density adhesive mixture around the outer edges of the case to the full thickness of the keel. Allow this to cure. To finish the case, radius its angles and apply a cap. Fiberglass cloth can be added as desired. We recommend that you apply it to the corners where the boat and the case meet.

The method will result in a perfect structural fit between the case and the keel, and this will effectively transfer all loads to the keel. The chances of failure of the joint between the case and the keel have been minimized, so the possibility that the boat will leak when it is in the water is greatly reduced.

Laminating Sheer Clamps

We generally build up sheer clamps from two or three long pieces of stock in much the same way as we laminate keels. Any sheer clamp which is over 1 inch thick should be laminated. The sheer clamps on many monohulls curve more than their keels and have more twist over their length, a combination which results from the flare of the hull toward the bow and leads to reasonable concern that the clamp might split.

Use the set-up mold frames as a form for laminating the sheer clamps, just as described for laminating the keel. Firmly attach temporary cleats to both sides of all the mold frames at the sheer so that you will be able to clamp at each station. The cleats should be strong enough to support the weight of many clamps all along the sheer. (Clamp weight works in your favor on a keel

Figure 10—Laminating sheer clamp over outside of mold frames. No notches have yet been cut in molds. When it has cured, the sheer clamp is removed, dressed and prefinished. Then it is fit to notches in molds.

lamination, but against you when clamping a sheer clamp at about right angles to the floor.) If there is severe twist in the sheer clamp, you may have to brace up the mold frame to keep it from distorting.

It's fairly easy to control unusually severe twist in a sheer clamp by clamping a large stick perpendicular to it. This gives you leverage on the sheer clamp. You can block the outside end of the stick up or down to position the sheer clamp at the desired twist, thereby removing a great deal of stress from the mold frame.

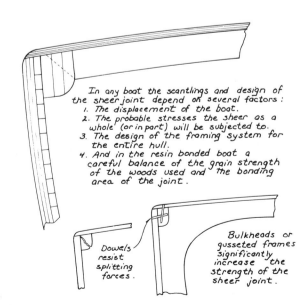

In any boat the scantlings and design of the sheer joint depend on several factors:
1. The displacement of the boat.
2. The probable stresses the sheer as a whole (or in part) will be subjected to.
3. The design of the framing system for the entire hull.
4. And in the resin bonded boat a careful balance of the grain strength of the woods used and the bonding area of the joint.

Dowels resist splitting forces.

Bulkheads or gusseted frames significantly increase the strength of the sheer joint.

Figure 11—Considerations in the design of the sheer clamp.

Figure 12—Sheer clamp laminated on inside of hull. **The hull forms the mold. Note clamping pad on outside to protect cedar planking.**

When the sheer clamp lamination is completed, plane and sand all of its interior surfaces and apply two or more coats of WEST SYSTEM epoxy. Then notch the mold frames and install the sheer clamp in the set-up, following the procedures described for installing keels.

With the stringer-frame and strip plank methods of laminating hulls, the sheer clamps are usually installed in the set-up before planking. With the mold method and sometimes with smaller strip-built boats, sheer clamps are not generally necessary for hull construction and you can install them later, when the hull is completed. When you do this, be sure to use wood clamping pads to prevent damage to the hull.

Chapter 17

Laminated Hulls — A General Discussion

There are many ways to build a wooden boat. A hull may be constructed traditionally, with lapstrake or carvel planking. It may be laminated, with layers of wood laid over a permanent or temporary mold. Finally, depending on its shape, a boat may be built with sheet plywood. Many books have been written on traditional boat construction. Our focus has always been on laminating and plywood methods, and it is these which we will discuss at length in the following chapters.

In the process of shopping for a design, you also shop for a boatbuilding method. Most designers specify exactly how their boats are to be built, if not explicitly, then in their detailed drawings. When you buy your plans, you therefore choose your building technique. For reasons outlined in Chapter 2, we caution against substituting one method for another without consulting your designer.

Laminated Hulls

A laminated hull is basically a piece of boat-shaped plywood. Layers of veneer are bonded together to form a monocoque or partial monocoque structure, so that most of the stresses to which the boat is subjected are absorbed by its outer skin. This method of hull construction is a distinct departure from traditional boatbuilding techniques, and to be successful requires some understanding of both wood and engineering.

As we discussed in Chapter 5, wood is a unidirectional or anisotropic material with exceptional resistance to fatigue. It is strong parallel to its grain, but weak across it, so its fibers must be carefully aligned to receive and transmit loads. When it is correctly arranged, wood grain will maintain its strength through millions of cycles of loads.

To maximize the strengths of wood, you must identify the loads and load paths of the structure in which it is used. Sometimes this is easy. For example, the loads imposed on a mast are primarily in one direction, so you can orient wood fiber along its length to achieve adequate structural strength. Determining the loads on a hull, however, is not so simple.

As they sail, boats are subjected to longitudinal, athwartship and diagonal stresses. For centuries, boat builders have oriented wood fiber in alternating directions, with longitudinal planking on lateral ribs or frames, to make structures capable of withstanding these various loads. In a laminated hull, by contrast, wood fibers run in all directions. No single piece of veneer must take an entire load in cross grain, but, instead, different layers share it. Because the laminated hull is better designed to receive stress, it requires less framing support than a traditional boat.

Laminating allows use of unidirectional material to build an isotropic monocoque. Unanticipated loading is far less threatening when a structure has strength in every direction. Wood is lighter than other materials, so a wooden hull can be thicker, for the same weight, than a hull built of other isotropic materials.

Hot and Cold Molding

Laminating techniques depend on adhesives. Over the years, methods and technologies used to laminate boat hulls have at least in part developed around the specific requirements of glues. Different adhesives require different amounts of clamping pressure and different cure temperatures. Some require tight fits, while others can span voids. These factors in particular have determined the history of laminated hulls.

Early laminated hulls were made by *hot molding,* the process by which most plywood is made today. This technology developed rapidly during World War II, when steel was in short supply. Adhesives then available required heat — often in excess of 300°F., hence the name hot molding — and, frequently, 75 psi of pressure to bond properly. Laminating was complicated because large autoclaves were needed to provide these temperatures and pressures. Capital investment for pressure vessels and molds was very high, so hot molding remained strictly within the economic range of "big business."

For 10 to 15 years after the end of World War II, some leftover hot molding equipment was used in production runs of various sizes and types of boat hulls. Luders 16 and Thistle class sailboats and small Wolverine outboard-powered runabouts are examples of hot molded laminated hulls. Just as the autoclaves and tooling were wearing out, the fiberglass boat industry came into its own with lower production costs and a more marketable, lower-maintenance product. Hot molded hulls couldn't compete against this com-

Figure 1—The 30 foot, IOR ½ ton racer, ACCOLADE, is the largest boat we have built using the mold method.

Figure 2—Beautiful dinghy built by Steven Loutrel using mold method.

Figure 3—Molded dinghy built by Peter Unger. This size and style is ideally suited to the mold method.

bination, and soon the industry died out.

In the early 1950's, adhesives which required neither heat nor pressure came onto the market. Hot molding gradually gave way to *cold molding*. Cures could be reached at room temperature with contact pressure, so the expense of pressure vessels was eliminated. A simple mold or form and staples were all that was needed to hold laminated parts together as they cured. Since a minimum number of tools and little capital were necessary, small builders could practice the laminating procedures which had been limited to large enterprises.

While our hulls may be considered cold molded, we prefer to think of them as *laminated*. Our methods are a direct outgrowth of hot molding technology as it was applied to both boats and aircraft during the World War II period. WEST SYSTEM* Brand epoxy, our contribution to this string of developments, has no special clamping or temperature requirements. Its gap-filling capabilities are an advantage when clamping pressure is limited, and with it careful fits are not of paramount importance. Our wood/epoxy laminating techniques can produce far better results, and longer-lived, lower-maintenance boats than were previously possible.

Methods of Laminating

At the Gougeon Brothers' shop we have used three basic hull laminating methods: the *mold method*, the *strip plank method* and the *stringer-frame method*. Within each of these, endless variations provide flexibility in different situations. Each of the three has advantages and disadvantages, and it is these which we will discuss briefly here. More detailed instructions on each hull laminating technique follow in later chapters.

The Mold Method

A *mold,* or plug, is a form over which to laminate veneer or plywood to the desired hull shape. It provides a solid base on which to exert the pressure necessary to hold layers together until the epoxy has cured. This pressure is usually supplied by staples, but techniques which rely on a vacuum to secure layers are becoming popular, especially in production situations.

If you build a relatively strong mold, you have a firm base on which to build. The biggest advantage of this is reproducibility: you can make any number of identical hulls from a single mold. The major disadvantage of the mold method is that it is difficult to absorb the time and materials required to build a mold when you only want one hull. The larger the boat, the larger this problem becomes, unless you are able to find other people willing to rent or purchase the mold to build their own hulls. Another objection to the mold method, particularly for bigger boats, is that there is no practical way of installing interior frames, bulkheads or stringers in the set-up. You must build all of these structural elements into the interior after you remove the mold from the hull.

In general, we recommend the mold method for boats under 25 feet which have hulls thick enough to require little support from interior framework. Smaller hulls in general are ideal for monocoque construction. Small dinghies, for example, are lightest when built with the mold method. This construction technique is often used for day sailing dinghies and small offshore boats. Although the mold method can theoretically be used on any size hull — the largest mold we ever built was for a 30 foot boat — quicker, more efficient and more cost-effective methods are available for large boats.

The Strip Plank Method

Because of the expense of the mold and the labor needed to install interior members, it's often hard to justify the use of the mold method on larger, one-off hulls. To get around these extra costs, we thought about using the mold as part of the hull, and from this developed the strip plank method of laminating. Most molds are strip planked anyway; with this technique, the planking becomes part of the structure and does not remain part of the mold. Strip planking is efficient and economical for bigger custom boats.

Hulls have been planked with edge-glued strips of wood for many years. Strip planked and fiberglass hulls appeared at about the same time. Larger strip planked boats rely on intricate interior framework for athwartship strength and stiffness. The alternative to

Figure 4—The 42-foot, IOR 2 ton racer, GOLDEN DAZY, built using strip plank method.

interior support, sheathing the planking with fiberglass cloth as is done with stripper canoes, does not provide enough strength for large hulls. We discovered, however, that we can build an exceptionally rigid and strong monocoque by using the basic strip planked hull as a form over which to laminate diagonal layers of veneer. The layers of exterior veneer eliminate most of the interior framework associated with larger wooden boats.

With the strip plank method, it is advantageous to install many major bulkheads in the boat during the set-up and to form the hull right around them. This saves time later because it is usually much easier to install bulkheads before planking than to tediously fit them in a finished hull. In a large, one-off project, including internal structure in the set-up can significantly reduce labor. Too many interior members may, however, get in the way of sanding interior planking.

Strip planked hulls have thick, load-bearing wooden skins. They are reasonably light, with high strength-and-stiffness-to-weight ratios. As a bonus, the thickness of a strip planked hull provides excellent insulation from noise and temperature, and it may also reduce condensation problems. Practical considerations generally limit the use of the strip plank method to boats of perhaps 30 feet or more, but some heavier displacement, shorter oceangoing cruisers have been built with this technique.

Hull thickness is in fact a major consideration in successful use of the strip plank method. The mold must be stiff enough to support layers of laminated veneer, so at least ½ inch planking is usually used on larger boats. For support with minimal interior framing, we recommend that this be covered with no less than three layers of ⅛ inch veneer. The resulting ⅞ inch hull will weigh a bit over 2 pounds per square foot, and this may be too heavy for smaller boats. While the edges of thicker planks can be aligned with dowels or nails, thinner planking may be stapled during edge gluing. Whichever method is used, the strip plank method is not particularly quick when compared to other laminating techniques.

The Stringer-Frame Method

The stringer-frame method is probably the most popular of the three hull laminating methods. Like the strip plank method, it does not require a mold. Interior members such as bulkheads and frames may be installed in the set-up. The biggest advantage of the stringer-frame method, however, is that you can use it successfully with just about any size boat, from a 10 foot pram to a 60 foot oceangoing racer.

One reason that the stringer-frame method is so widely used by both amateur and professional boat builders is that it is the quickest, least labor-intensive way to laminate a one-off hull. This method also has the potential to produce the best strength-and-stiffness-to-weight ratio hulls, particularly in situations where there is little compound curvature as there is in catamaran and trimaran hulls.

The stringer-frame method does have some disadvantages. The most obvious of these is that you have to begin laminating the hull skin with what, in reality, is an inadequate mold: you will have a good, solid molding surface only after you have applied two layers of

Figure 5—The 32 foot, ½ ton racer, HOT FLASH, was built using stringer-frame method. This type of construction is popular with racing boat designers and builders.

veneer or plywood. Because stringers are set at 5 inch to 8 inch centers, sizable quantities of care, skill and work are necessary to be sure of good molding as you apply the first two laminations. For the beginner, therefore, this method has the highest potential for error of the three types of laminated hull construction.

Another shortcoming of the stringer-frame method is that it results in a cluttered interior. Both mold method and strip plank hulls have smooth, uncluttered walls, but the stringers and frames which are part of the stringer-frame method take up valuable interior room and are difficult to keep clean. This kind of interior may also be less pleasing to the eye.

The idea of load-bearing skins supported by stringer-frame systems was first applied to aircraft in the 1930's, when designers found that they could greatly improve strength-to-weight ratios by substituting wood panels for fabric skins. The load-bearing skins became significant in the development of modern aircraft design. The marine industry borrowed the concept and, with a few modifications, used it to build lightweight hull and deck systems. Boats require somewhat thicker skins than planes, but they are not as limited by weight.

Stringer-frame hull skins are much less thick than mold method or strip plank hull skins. While the other methods produce monocoque structures with totally self-supporting, load-bearing skins, stringer-frame hulls are partial monocoques, able to bear loads only when held in proper position and column by supporting framework.

A true monocoque skin is most effective in areas with a great deal of compound curve — an eggshell shape, for example. A stringer-frame supported, partial monocoque skin is most effective with surfaces which are either flat or curved in only one direction. Most successful multihulls, with their long, flat runs, have used the stringer-frame concept to best advantage, since it produces the strongest and stiffest hulls for a given weight. Because monohulls usually have significant compound curvature, they are built very successfully with any of the three methods of laminating, and the decision between methods depends on the individual project.

Figure 6—Looking forward in main hull of 60 foot proa SLINGSHOT. Stringer-frame method is easily adapted to fairly sophisticated designed boats of any size.

Wood for Laminating

The exact sizes and combinations of lumber, veneer and plywood you will use in laminating a hull depend on the method of hull construction you choose. In the following chapters, we discuss the specific materials required for each laminating method. The general considerations here pertain to all three. As you select your wood, also keep in mind the advice on buying wood in Chapter 6.

All wood used in laminating must bend easily over a hull's severest curves. You may be able to use stock up to ⅝ inch thick on very large boats, but on smaller projects you may find that only 1/16 inch veneer can negotiate a tight radius. If you rely exclusively on staples for pressure, ⅛ inch is usually the practical minimum laminate thickness. One-sixteenth inch veneers require more staples for equal pressure over a given surface, and therefore require extra labor for stapling and staple removal. Very thin veneers may also occasionally be pulverized by staples.

The amount of compound curvature in a boat hull determines the width of stock you can use in the laminating process. A short, fat boat requires narrower pieces, while a long, skinny boat can use very wide ones if they are available. The narrowest stock we've used was 4 inches wide. It's unusual to have to use a width less than 6 inches. Most common in boatbuilding are 8 inch veneers.

Length of stock is not critical, but you can save time if your wood is long enough to reach around one half of the hull at a diagonal angle. Scarfing shorter pieces together reduces waste and provides the right lengths, but at a cost of time. You can also in certain situations butt veneers during molding, a technique which is discussed in a later chapter.

You can cut laminating stock yourself, but you may run into problems. It's difficult, even with a large table saw, to resaw stock which is more than 4 inches thick and, as will be explained, it takes a lot more time to fit two 4 inch wide pieces than it does one 8 inch piece. Another problem is waste: if you are making ⅛ thick veneers, you will lose at least 50% and perhaps as much as 70% of your stock to sawdust. If you can use thicker planking, ¼ inch or more, your lumber yard may be able to cut wide pieces on a resaw machine. This relatively efficient equipment wastes only 30% to 40% of the wood.

We usually buy sliced veneers, and have found that they are cheaper than those we saw ourselves. Slicing production methods result in almost no waste and are very fast and efficient. Commercially sliced veneers are available up to 18 inches wide and 17 feet long, although a more common size is 8 to 10 inches wide and 12 feet long. It's difficult to slice wood thicker than ⅛ inch without checking and shattering, but an ⅛ inch veneer limit doesn't seem to be a real disadvantage with smaller boats. Longer hulls of 50 feet or more can use thicker stock if it is available. In these cases, the use of thin veneer involves increased labor for extra laminations, and this may be a major concern.

Commercial plywood is often used in laminating. There are many areas, as will be described in later chapters, where it is a good, practical choice. Plywood has already been laminated, so its dimensions are stable. It is readily available. Thin plywood will not split as readily as veneer when it is bent over tight curves, and it is easy to prefinish, especially for interiors on stringer-frame hulls. Plywood does, however, have some disadvantages. It is expensive and does not have the potential strength of veneer. At least one third of its grain runs at right angles to the remainder of it, so some compromises may be necessary when you arrange it on a hull.

Whichever of the three methods is used, the skin of a laminated hull is strong enough to survive most loads. Because it is made of fatigue-resistant wood, it will maintain its strength over time. The next chapters deal in greater detail with the three laminating procedures. Appendix C gives the scantlings for some hulls which have been successfully laminated with wood and WEST SYSTEM epoxy. These may serve as a guide for scantlings for each hull laminating method and may be useful for comparison with your project.

Chapter 18

The Mold Method: Building the Mold

The strengths and weaknesses of the mold method of laminating hulls result from the mold itself. The process of building a mold is time-consuming, and materials may be expensive. Permanent parts, except for the keel and stem, cannot be installed in the set-up, so the technique is practical only on smaller, thick hulls with little interior framework. When a hull is finished, there may be a choice between cutting up the mold and storing it for years. On the other hand, the mold method is hard to beat if more than one boat is to be built. When a number of hulls are constructed around a single plug, its costs are more than repaid in labor savings alone.

Types of Molds

A mold is a form over which to laminate veneer or plywood. It must accurately describe the shape of the finished hull, and it must be strong enough to hold this shape as you work. As long as it does these things, the exact construction details of a mold may vary according to the requirements of an individual project.

Molds may have solid surfaces, or they may be little more than open lattices. The type of mold you need will depend on a number of factors. Molds used for many hulls or relied upon for exact tolerances must be more substantial than molds used for a single boat. In many cases, the kind of pressure used to hold layers of laminate in place as epoxy cures will determine the nature of the mold.

We have used a wide variety of molds. When we built Tornado catamarans, our goal was to turn out many boats to exact specifications. We used vacuum bag techniques to "clamp" our layers of veneer, so our mold had to be airtight. We built a *solid* or *planked* plug, edge gluing strip planks as we might on a boat hull. This mold was rigid and fair, but to be sure that we could move it around the shop without losing the hull shape, we laminated a layer of veneer onto its surface. Few molds are so sophisticated.

A simple *lath* or *stringered* mold is at the other end of the spectrum. With this type, we set up frames and then fasten *ribbands,* long stringers of wood, over the set-up. Gaps between ribbands may be wider than the ribbands themselves, so that only 40 or 50% of the mold surface is solid wood. Because staples can only

be inserted where there are ribbands, we mark the first and second layers of veneer before fastening them. This takes extra time, but since a ribband mold is quicker to build than a planked one, the balance may lie in its favor when it will be used for only one or two boats.

Somewhere between these extremes lies the mold which is adequate for laminating most hulls. The quality of a mold is most important as the first two layers are laminated, when long staples are used to hold the veneers snug against it. Staples may be inserted anywhere in it, so a solid plug has a distinct advantage during this stage. One less elaborate way to build a strong, rigid planked mold is to laminate two layers of ⅛ inch veneer over an open, stringered mold.

Setting Up the Mold

The first step in manufacturing the mold is to set up the frames and forms onto which you will assemble the longitudinal ribbands. The principles of construction and set-up for mold frames are discussed in Chapter 15. The materials used to construct the mold frames must be structurally adequate, cheap and have an edge thick enough to receive a fastener so that you can attach the planking easily. When making the mold frames, remember that you must not only deduct the planking thickness of the hull, but also the planking thickness that you will use on the mold. If the hull is to be ½ inch thick and the ribbands are to be ¾ inch thick, you must deduct a total of 1¼ inches planking thickness from the lofting in order to arrive at properly sized mold frames. Because of this unusually large deduction, you must pay careful attention to the planking thickness deduction procedure. (See Chapter 13 for further discussion.)

Once you have properly set up the mold frames and completed final fairing, you can begin planking the mold. Although it is not always necessary, many molded hulls are built with provisions in the mold to insert a permanent keel and stem which can be removed with the hull from the mold. It is relatively easy to insert a permanent keel into the mold and to attach the veneers permanently to the keel during the molding process. If the keel is to be 4 inches wide, leave a gap along the centerline of the mold slightly over this

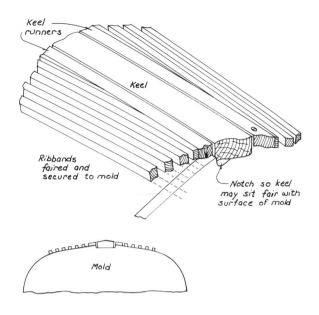

Figure 1—Mold with keel recessed.

width, allowing approximately ⅛ inch clearance between each side of the keel and the mold. We run a permanent ribband, which we call a *keel runner*, along each side of the keel. This then becomes a joining point for all the rest of the ribbands on the mold that would intersect the keel at a diagonal angle. If the keel is thicker than the ribbands, recess the mold frames whatever extra distance is required so that the keel will fair up smooth with the ribbands on the mold surface. (See Figure 1.)

Installing a permanent stem is somewhat more complicated because you must construct the mold using an *inner mold stem* on which the permanent stem will repose during the laminating procedure. You need the inner mold stem as a point on which to attach the ribbands as they approach the bow stem area. This interior mold stem must continue on up to the keel area where the keel runners intersect so that every ribband running in from the hull can either connect with the inner mold stem or the keel runner. No ribbands can be allowed to end at the stem or keel area without being attached to one of these solid points. A difficult part of this installation is to determine the exact location and shape and size of the inner mold stem. To determine this information, you will have to go to the lofting board and work back from the outer stem area. The location of the *permanent stem* itself might be back a ways due to the effect of the planking and stem cap that protrude out in front. Thus, from the outer profile of the boat, you might have to deduct the stem cap and the permanent stem before determining the outer measurement of the mold stem assembly. (See Figure 2.)

Even for molds where you will not be inserting a permanent stem, you will still need to recess the actual mold stem back further than the permanent stem would be, and you can easily deduct these measurements from the lofting board. You're going to need some room for stem assembly, whether it remains attached to the mold or becomes a permanent part of the laminated hull. For example, if you're using ¾ inch square ribbands and they meet at the bow on a mold stem that is shaped to a perfect point, the ribbands alone will still project a frontal flat area of 1½ inches. Thus, you will have to add some material anyway, regardless of whether it will become a permanent part of the mold or the hull. This is a practical consideration to be thinking about when looking at the lofting board and determining your positioning of the mold stem piece. You should also keep in mind that a permanent stem should be large enough to offer sufficient surface area for a properly bonded joint. Thus the size or depth of the permanent stem will affect the location of the mold stem.

Planking the Mold

The planking on both solid and stringered molds must bend in even, fair curves as it is laid over the mold frames. Knots and severe grain run-out will cause wood to bend unfairly or even to break, so use high quality lumber for stringers. When you consider the waste which results from irregularities in lower grade stock, high quality wood is really not significantly more expensive. We usually use clear redwood, cedar or white pine for planking molds, but many other species work well.

As soon as you have finished your lofting, and before you set up your mold frames, decide the thickness of your ribbands. Subtract this measurement from the frames just as you subtracted planking thickness. Most commercially available lumber is already planed to ¾ inch thick, so we usually use ¾ inch square ribbands. If they will not bend easily over all curves, we laminate stringers from thinner pieces or shift them around until they lie well. If long boards are not available, we scarf the ribbands before fitting them. Ribbands may be joined with butt blocks, but we prefer scarf joints because they take only a little more time and do not result in hard spots.

We begin planking the mold by identifying its most difficult curves. Some of the latest IOR racers, for example, have unusually curved shapes to fit a particular rule. Since these may be unnegotiable if approached from the wrong angle, we save time and trouble by running our first stringer so that it best negotiates all of them. This is the *master ribband,* and from it we align all of the other ribbands along the hull.

As you progress up and down the hull, ribbands aligned with the master ribband may have to be reoriented to conform to other shapes. If your planking runs primarily fore and aft, this problem is magnified by the difference between the girth of the hull's fat middle and its thinner ends. Much more planking is needed in the middle of the hull than at its ends.

A simple solution to this is to leave larger gaps between ribbands at the center than at the ends of the hull. Slight variations in the distances between stringers will very slowly change the direction in which they run. This permits a gradual directional transition and allows the planking to bend more easily around more difficult

Figure 2—Lofting and set-up of mold stem assembly.

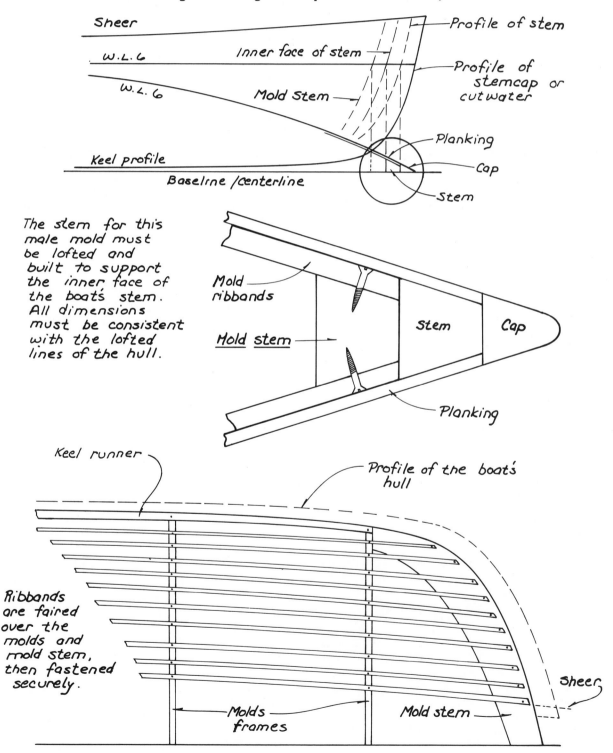

curves. Be careful not to overdo this, however, because too much space between ribbands reduces potential stapling area and may compromise the rigidity of the mold.

It's easy to reinforce a mold when it seems to be too flexible. Short stringers can be inserted between longer ones, as shown in Figure 4, if the gaps between ribbands are too large. To provide additional support to ribbands midway between station frames, bond and staple 2 inch wide strips of thin plywood to the inside of the mold. If you use extraordinarily thin ribbands, and therefore need additional reinforcement, two or even three of these strips can be evenly spaced between frames. A final and effective way to build rigidity into a weak stringered mold is to cover it with a layer or two of veneer and turn it into a solid mold.

Fastening Ribbands to Mold Frames

We generally fasten ribbands to mold frames with a staple gun and narrow crown wire staples up to 1¼ inches long. Staple guns are fast and easy to use, and air-powered models will jar the set-up much less than hammering nails will. The staple gun automatically recesses staples about ⅛ inch below the surface, so they do not get in the way of fairing. This system successfully fastens planking up to ¾ inch thick.

Nails are the second best fasteners for attaching planking. If you use them, drill your planks first to prevent splitting and to minimize the hammering needed to drive them home. Use finishing nails, recessing them to facilitate fairing.

You may also use screws to attach ribbands to mold frames, especially over sharp curves where additional holding power is needed. Always drill a lead hole with

Figure 4—Ribband mold for IOR ½ ton racer. Note use of shorter ribbands to fill gaps between full length ribbands. The skeg shown was laminated out of veneers beforehand, then secured to mold. The veneer used to plank hull was bonded to the skeg. This was done to save the extra expense and time of molding such an extreme shape during general laminating.

the proper size bit and countersink the screw. Self-tapping screws are the best choice if you are working with chipboard mold frames. We sometimes bond or nail pieces of scrap wood to both sides of chipboard frames, close to their edges, and staple or nail ribbands to these rather than to the chipboard. This technique may be quicker than drilling and inserting screws.

If a mold is to be at all permanent or if it will be moved, we bond the ribbands to the frames with a mixture of high density filler and WEST SYSTEM* Brand epoxy. Occasionally, we do this after installing the ribbands, running fillets on both sides of the joint between the ribband and the mold frame. When we lay veneers over mold frames to make a solid mold, we edge glue them and make the entire mold a rigid, monocoque structure.

If you are building a mold for use with the vacuum bag method of applying pressure, your prime requirement is that the mold be airtight. You must maintain this airtightness even though you have driven staples into the mold and removed them numerous times. You need a few staples to hold the veneers in general position until you can apply the vacuum bag. This means that the mold material must be reasonably thick. We have built ours using edge glued strip planking over which we diagonally bonded one layer of ⅛ inch veneer. This made a substantial mold which held up well after manufacturing many units. For vacuum bagging, you should install a flange on the mold below the actual sheer clamp area, extending out approximately 2 inches around the entire perimeter of the mold. The flange serves as a point where you can seal off the vacuum bag itself, and also provides an apex

Figure 3—The ribbands for this 26 foot mold were run parallel to sheer and butted along centerline of keel.

* TRADEMARK OF GOUGEON BROTHERS, INC., U.S.A.

area where the flange meets the mold surface so that you can install piping with which to remove the air between the vacuum bag and the mold. If any permanent stems or keels are to be inserted into this type of mold, pay attention to these recessed areas to make sure that no air leaks at these points.

Whatever type of mold you build, you must complete final fairing prior to beginning the lamination process. Any unwanted humps or hollows will tend to be duplicated in the laminating process, and you are far better off removing them from the mold than trying to do it later by removing needed material from the hull or adding unwanted extra weight in filler material. Use the same final fairing techniques described for hulls in Chapter 19 to fair the mold surfaces.

Figure 5—Resin/filler mixture applied to mold near bow as fairing compound.

Finishing the Mold

When you have completed the final fairing, it's time to pay attention to several other items. Sheer measurements are still located on the mold frames and ultimately will be transferred to the hull itself. The easiest way to do this is to run a ribband directly on the frame marks which define the sheer. This will be a straight, accurate edge you can use later to scribe the hull before lifting it from the mold. Because laminating pressure will be needed a bit beyond the actual sheer, add ribbands beyond this line. Usually an additional inch or two of stringers is adequate. Leave a ¼ to ½ inch gap between the sheer stringer and its neighbor to make room for marking the hull.

Another method for marking the sheer is to drill small marking holes through the mold at each mold frame sheer measurement point prior to laminating the hull. This procedure leaves a little to be desired if you are trying to maintain exact tolerances, but you can line up these holes and check them on the mold using a lofting batten to see whether they form a reasonably fair sheer line. If they are accurate, drill through the pilot hole into the completed laminate to transfer the sheer measurements and then use the lofting batten to complete the sheer measurement on the laminated hull by connecting all of the drilled holes after you remove the hull from the mold.

If you are going to insert a permanent keel and stem into the mold, you must laminate them (if needed) and saw them to shape. You might even prefinish them on that part that would show on the interior of the completed laminated hull, saving some time later on. It is usual to scarf and join together the keel/stem complex right in the mold and final fair them after they are solidly secured in position. Hold them in this secure position by installing screws from the interior of the

mold, usually through a cleat that is attached to the mold frame. Locate these screws in an easy access area so that you can back them off when the hull is complete and ready for removal from the mold. Final shape and fair the keel/stem complex to the mold surface, using the techniques that we have explained in Chapter 16.

With some types of laminated hulls, it is also possible to include the permanent transom in the mold set-up. You can only do this if the transom does not have any reverse slope or if the hull does not have any reverse slant. Either of these would prevent removal of the laminated hull from the mold. It is rather easy to install a permanent transom by temporarily attaching it to the

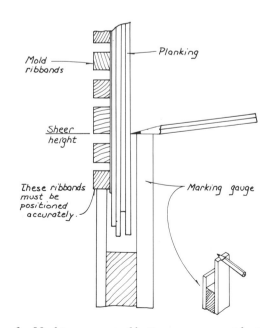

Figure 6—Marking gauge and batten arrangement for transferring sheer from mold to hull.

mold transom, to which the ribbands are already attached. The transom might be prelaminated or might simply be a sheet of plywood. You may have laminated on some additional cleats to create more bonding area, which should not cause any problems. Once you have positioned the transom, fair it off flush with the general mold surface, just as was done with the keel/stem complex. When permanent transoms are not set in, it is usual to extend the mold transoms an inch or two to allow a little extra length for trimming.

Prior to beginning any laminating over a mold, take steps to ensure that you will be able to remove the laminated hull from the mold when it is complete. To prevent any bonding of the laminations to the mold, we generally cover the entire mold surface with a layer of polyethylene sheet, usually 4 to 6 mil thickness, using a new sheet for each hull produced. For molds which do not have any permanent keels, stems or transoms inserted, it is a simple matter just to cover the entire mold with plastic, but for molds which do have these permanent inserts, you must insert the plastic around these structural members so that permanent bonding between the laminations and the permanent members can take place. Usually you can tuck the polyethylene sheet film in between the slight gaps which will exist between the permanent members and the mold itself. If this is somewhat difficult, relax the screws holding these permanent members in place just a bit so that you can insert the plastic under or beside them. This will provide the necessary barrier so that you do not bond the lamination members to the wrong part. When you have completed this step, you are ready to begin the process of building the laminated hull with the mold method.

Chapter 19

The Mold Method for Laminating Hulls

When the mold is faired, it's time to begin planking. Your plans will specify the number of layers of veneer or plywood the hull requires. Although this count may vary from project to project, laminating techniques do not. A hull may be made of sliced veneer, plywood or stock which you have sawn yourself. In this chapter, for simplicity, we use the term *veneer* to refer to all of these materials.

The general procedure for laminating hulls with the mold method is not complicated. If your wood doesn't have a single straight edge, you will have to cut one. Then spile each piece, trimming it so that it lies true against its neighbor at a desired angle, apply adhesive and staple it to hold it in place until the epoxy has cured.

The first layer of a laminated hull is the most fragile. Edge glue its pieces and staple them directly to the mold. Carefully remove excess adhesive and staples, using thickened WEST SYSTEM* Brand epoxy to laminate a second layer of wood at an angle to the first, and staple through the first layer to the mold. Continue laminating in this way, stapling subsequent layers to each other but not to the mold, until the hull is as thick as you want it. Fair it, finish it and remove it from the mold.

* TRADEMARK OF GOUGEON BROTHERS, INC., U.S.A.

Preparing the Stock

You can use any of several different types of wood to laminate your hull. In most cases, boat builders use ⅛ inch commercially sliced veneer, but you may choose plywood or saw the lumber yourself. The first step is to make sure that *every* piece has one straight and true edge. Later in this chapter, when we discuss spiling, the reasons for this will be apparent.

Plywood has a manufactured straight edge accurate enough to require no further trimming. Veneer, however, usually arrives with rough sawn edges which must be straightened. Over the years, we have developed a quick and easy way to work on a number of pieces of veneer, up to 17 feet long, at one time. We set up our cutting jig on three sawhorses and store it away when it's not needed.

Lay four to eight pieces of veneer on a 2 inch x 12 inch plank so that their rough edges are slightly inboard from the plank's edge. Make a straightedge from a piece of clear ¾ inch x 8 inch stock, carefully dressing the edge for overall straightness. Position this on top of the veneers to serve as a guide for a hand held circular saw. Try to waste as little wood as possible, but place the straightedge far enough back from the edges of your veneers to guarantee that you will be able to transfer a straight line to all your pieces. Sandwich the

Figure 1—Method for cutting a straight edge on veneers.

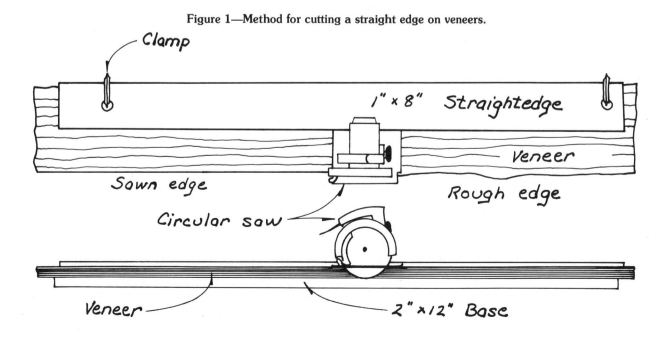

Figure 2—Veneers in intermediate layers of this laminated hull are butted randomly. This reduces scrap and eases layup without sacrificing the strength of the hull. Note the final layer of veneer being laid fore and aft at lower left.

veneers between the straight edge and the plank and hold the assembly with large clamps at either end. Tighten the clamps so the veneers can't shift.

Set your circular saw blade deep enough to cut through all the veneers. A little overcut into the plank is acceptable. Then run the saw along the stack, as shown in Figure 1. When your pieces have one accurate edge, cut parallel straight edges on their other sides. The easiest way to do this is to run the veneers through a table saw.

Some very long veneers taper significantly from one end to the other. Truing these up results in a lot of waste, especially since you can use them for interior layers of the laminate by alternating the tapered ends from piece to piece so that there is no angle change. When we receive tapered veneers, we use our straightening jig on both sides rather than just on one.

Two factors determine the width of laminating material: the amount of compound curve in your hull and how you want your boat to look. You can use much wider pieces of veneer at the ends of your boat, where there is less compounding, than in its middle sections, where curvature is likely to be more severe. Most

people prefer uniform veneer widths on naturally finished interior and exterior surfaces, but this is not particularly necessary. Thin pieces, or less commonly, wide pieces, can be very pleasing to the eye when arranged so that their colors contrast.

Most commercial veneers are between 5 and 12 inches wide after straightening. Wait to saw them into thinner strips until you have experimented enough to know the width which will bend and look best on your hull. It's a shame to saw 12 inch wide veneer into three 4 inch strips when two 6 inch strips may bend just as well with much less labor. You will find out very quickly if your veneers are too wide. If they are, the edges will be increasingly difficult to hold down as the pieces resist bending in two directions at once.

Sort the veneers into piles according to their quality and color. Collect your finest pieces and save them for your first and last laminations, particularly if you plan to bright finish your hull. Further sort this pile into dark, medium and light-toned pieces. Some woods, such as Douglas fir and Sitka spruce, show very little color variation, while others, including Western red cedar and some of the mahoganies, have a great deal. Knotty veneers can be used on all but the first and last layers.

In most cases, 25% of the material you purchase will end up as scrap and only 75% will actually become part of your boat. Most waste is in length because small cut-off ends are almost useless. It makes sense, therefore, to try to reduce your scrap rate by ordering veneer in the most economical lengths for your project. If you do this, however, you may find that your supplier is unable to fill your order. He probably doesn't have much control over the lengths of wood he purchases.

The opposite approach — making decisions based on what is available — is usually more successful. A typical boat hull requires a range of veneer lengths, from very short to very long. These dimensions depend to some extent on the angle at which you laminate. You may wish to work with this angle and your stock until you find the most efficient use of the veneers you have on hand.

You can greatly cut down on scrap by butt-joining or scarfing shorter pieces of veneer. In thick laminates, butts are perfectly acceptable as long as they are staggered across and through the structure. Wood is many times stronger in tension than it is in compression, and a properly bonded butt joint can transmit 100% of all compression loads. Wood's excess tensile strength permits the use of butt joints with a good degree of safety in a hull with many laminations.

Figure 3—Ribband mold for ½ ton racer showing alignment markings for various veneer layers.

When a hull has only two or three layers of veneer, however, we recommend that you choose 8 to 1 scarf joints instead of butt joints. Use the SCARFFER* attachment and the plywood scarfing techniques described in Chapter 10 to cut your bevel. Assemble and bond the joint right on the mold. For accurate fits of both butts and scarfs remember to cut the ends of your veneers exactly flush at right angles to their straightened sides.

* TRADEMARK OF GOUGEON BROTHERS, INC., U.S.A.

Figure 4—Stapling patterns.

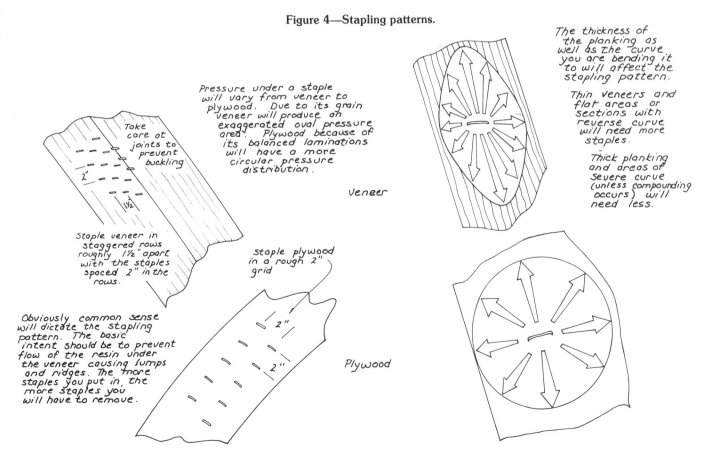

Take care at joints to prevent buckling

Staple veneer in staggered rows roughly 1½" apart with the staples spaced 2" in the rows.

Obviously common sense will dictate the stapling pattern. The basic intent should be to prevent flow of the resin under the veneer causing lumps and ridges. The more staples you put in, the more staples you will have to remove.

Pressure under a staple will vary from veneer to plywood. Due to its grain veneer will produce an exaggerated oval pressure area. Plywood because of its balanced laminations will have a more circular pressure distribution.

Veneer

staple plywood in a rough 2" grid

Plywood

The thickness of the planking as well as the curve you are bending it to will affect the stapling pattern.

Thin veneers and flat areas or sections with reverse curve will need more staples.

Thick planking and areas of severe curve (unless compounding occurs) will need less.

Inserting and Removing Staples

Successful lamination is closely related to expertise with a staple gun. Staples are used on every layer to hold veneers in place until the epoxy has cured, so you will shoot and remove a great many of them. Master several easy techniques before you take aim at your hull.

There are several things to think about as you staple layers of veneer: the orientation of the staple with respect to the grain of the wood, the pressure pattern applied by each staple, and if and how you will extract the staple. As you work you exert pressure, which the staple maintains.

For maximum holding power, always insert staples so that their legs are parallel to the grain of the wood. This will also reduce any damage the staples may do to wood fiber, so it will save some filling on the last layer. Staple holes parallel to the grain are much less noticeable than those which run across the grain.

When a staple is inserted into a piece of veneer, it creates an oval area of pressure, but when it is inserted into a piece of plywood, the pressure area is more circular. These patterns are caused by the direction of the wood fiber: plywood is bidirectional, so pressure is distributed more evenly than it is in unidirectional veneer. The shapes of these pressure areas determine the most effective stapling patterns to use in laminating. We recommend the patterns shown in Figure 4 for use on the flat sections of a hull. Note that plywood usually requires fewer staples than veneer.

Planking thickness and the curve to which you are bending your wood may also affect the number of staples needed for good bonding. Thin veneers require more staples than thicker planking. At the midpoint of

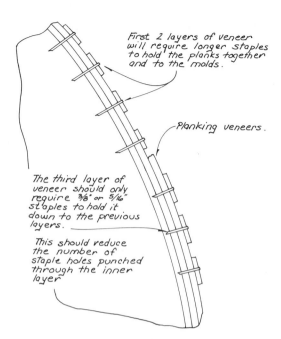

Figure 6—Recommendations for staple length.

a heavily curved hull, a veneer's natural resistance to bending exerts a good deal of pressure, so you can insert relatively few staples. At either side of this sharp curve, however, the veneer will tend to bend away from the mold and more staples will be necessary. Sometimes, for particularly sharp curves, you may want more pressure than can be exerted by the staples you're using. In these situations use longer staples, or hammer nails through a heavy strip of wood to distribute pressure.

We generally begin a stapling pattern in the center of a veneer. Applying pressure here first helps to work excess resin out towards the edges. If you staple edges and then centers on any but the first layer, you may trap pools of epoxy in the center of the veneer, and this may cause it to become unfair. When you apply unusually wide pieces, it is especially important to work out from the center because this is the only practical way to move excess resin from within the lamination.

We usually use ⅜ or ½ inch long wide crown staples to fasten the first two layers of ⅛ inch veneer to the mold. These staples must be removed before new laminations are installed or it will be very difficult to free the hull from the plug. We also often extract staples used to attach veneer to permanent members such as the stem and keel, although these may be left in place. From the third layer on, we use shorter staples, say ⅜ inch or 5/16 inch long for three layers of ⅛ inch veneer, because we are no longer stapling into the mold. Since these staples will not penetrate beyond the first layer and will not interfere with the mold, they do not have to be extracted. We do, however, pull out

Figure 5—More staples are necessary to hold down thin veneers in reverse or concave area near skeg. Also note the reasonably regular stapling patterns employed on planking in foreground.

staples used on the final, exterior lamination.

You can use steel staples, but plan to remove them. If you don't want to pull them out, use staples made of bronze or another alloy. Bronze staples are a specialty item and hard to find, so you may have to use aluminum or galvanized staples. We have left steel staples in our own boats with no problems, but steel staples may rust if the hull or the protective coating around them is damaged. Alloy staples are more expensive than steel, but their cost is more than offset by the reduced risk of corrosion and by the labor savings which result from leaving staples in place.

If you use alloy staples and do not remove them, be sure to adjust your staple gun so that it shoots the staples slightly recessed into or flush with the veneer. Otherwise, difficulties can develop when you try to rough fair or smooth up the surface in preparation for the next layer of wood. If protruding alloy staples interfere with laminating, grind them flush with power tools when you rough fair your hull.

As you build, you will remove a good many staples. To make this job easier, staple through a strip of material, leaving a tail you can grasp to yank out your fasteners. For most applications, we use inexpensive ½ inch wide, .30 inch thick plastic banding tape. We cut this to length, usually 3 to 6 feet, tuck the pieces in our belts, and pull them out as needed, perhaps four or six strips on a 6 inch wide veneer. When our veneers are very long, it's more efficient to cut and handle strips which are half the length of the veneers. The plastic is so strong that even when we staple through it, we only have to tug at it to pull it and many staples free. We remove staples from our banding and reuse it.

At times, particularly on final layers of laminate, other materials serve better than plastic banding. Wooden mixing sticks, scrap veneer, thin rippings from sawn stock and thin plywood can be very good stapling strips. These pieces are heavier than plastic and they distribute pressure over greater area, so fewer staples may be needed. The biggest problem with using them is that they tend to bond to the veneer when resin squeezes out through openings or cracks. When this happens, use an offset paring chisel to carefully peel off the strip.

Wood stapling strips are also useful for preventing damage to veneer. When you use plastic banding, each staple is likely to leave a small, hard-to-sand indentation which may discolor slightly after coating. The process of removing staples can also mar the surface of veneer, and wood stapling strips provide some protection against this.

The special care required for removing staples from the first and last layers of veneer is described in other

Figure 7—Stapling veneer plank to hull's stringers. Note use of plastic strips under the staple heads to ease removal.

parts of this chapter. All staples in all layers from the second layer on may be removed within hours after they are applied. In fact, it's much easier to pull them out when WEST SYSTEM resin is partially cured but strong enough to hold veneers by itself, so we recommend that you attempt this at the earliest possible moment. When your epoxy is fully cured, staples are much tougher to remove and you will spend a lot more time on the job.

Depending on which hardener you use and the temperatures at which you are working, start removing staples 4 to 7 hours after applying a layer of veneer. It's easy to determine the partial cure stage. Check resin which has squeezed up between veneers. If it is generally hard to the touch but you can dent it with your fingernail, it's ready. If you have used banding tape, pull its end directly up and away from the hull. Many of your staples will remain embedded in it.

Staples remaining in the hull often dangle by one leg. Pull these out with a pair of pliers. Some, especially those which are at a bad angle, may tear through the stapling strip and remain in the lamination. These will have to be removed by hand, but since tugging on the strip usually lifts them a little, there probably will be gaps between the hull and their crowns into which you can insert a staple-pulling tool.

Where no gap exists staple removal is a little more difficult, and a well-designed staple remover comes in handy. Although the principles are simple and variations on them are potentially endless, we have been able to find only one effective staple removing tool, a

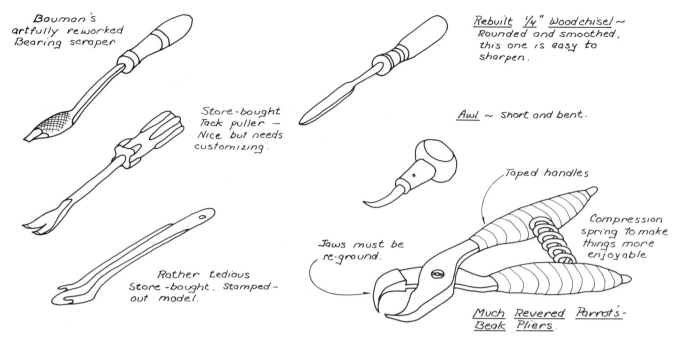

Bauman's artfully reworked Bearing scraper

Store-bought Tack puller — Nice but needs customizing.

Rebuilt ¼" Woodchisel ~ Rounded and smoothed, this one is easy to sharpen.

Awl ~ short and bent.

Rather tedious Store-bought. Stamped-out model.

Jaws must be re-ground.

Taped handles

Compression spring to make things more enjoyable

Much Revered Parrot's-Beak Pliers.

Figure 8—Various staple removers.

model designed for upholsterers manufactured by the Stanley Tool Company. A good tool should have a very sharp hardened steel point which inserts easily under the crown of a staple, and it should have a fulcrum immediately aft of this point which is wide enough to prevent damage to the wood. You should be able to rock the handle to extract the staple with minimal effort. Figure 8 shows some of the tools we have built in the shop with these design criteria in mind.

You can modify a large screwdriver by grinding its end to a sharp wide edge and by grinding a curve on one side so that there is some rocker on the side opposite the edge. If, after grinding, you find that your fulcrum is too small, try bending the screwdriver slightly. A well-hardened screwdriver may not permit this, in which case you can bond a piece of wood or add thickened resin to build up the fulcrum. Your staple remover will receive a lot of use, so it's worth the time it takes to make a good tool which works easily and well.

Applying the First Layer of Veneer

The first layer will become the interior of your boat, so select its veneers with great care and present the finest grain and color you have. We almost always naturally finish interiors because they are beautiful and practical when done this way.

Begin by placing a *master veneer* in the middle of the mold. If you start here, you can plank toward the

stem and toward the transom simultaneously. If two people or teams are available, they can work in opposite directions. Because your angle is in the middle of the hull, it's easier to maintain as you apply veneers. There is no set rule for the angle of the first layer, but 45° is good for starters.

Mark the angle of the first veneer on the polyethylene mold cover. Set your sliding bevel at the desired angle, place it on top of a level and position both tools next to the hull. Move the level until its bubble is centered in its markings and transfer the angle from the bevel square to the mold. Make a mark just long enough to indicate the placement of the first veneer. Then hold the veneer on the mold and draw a line all the way across the mold surface to show its exact position.

If you are installing the master veneer on a mold which has an inset permanent keel, apply a high density epoxy mixture to both the keel and veneer surfaces to bond it in place. Clamp well with staples. Hold the veneer in position on the rest of the mold with as few staples as necessary. To fasten ⅛ inch veneers, we usually use ⅜ inch long wide crown staples and an air-powered, electric-powered or hand-powered staple gun. If these staples won't hold the veneer, try ½ inch long staples.

When the master veneer is in position, fit the veneers on either side of it. Because of the hull's compound curvature, these will not butt perfectly. Your next step will be to trim or *spile* the planks so that they fit well and lie flat without distorting.

Figure 9—Fitting the first layer of cedar veneer for a laminated hull. The plank is secured in the middle. Then the ends are adjusted and fitted to an adjoining plank.

Figure 10—Applying resin to edge of previously-fastened planks.

Spiling

The goal of spiling is to taper the ends of a piece of veneer. The amount of spiling necessary for any hull is in direct proportion to the extent of its compound curvature. Trim and fit your first layer by hand, and remember that your craftsmanship will be on display whenever anyone looks at the interior of the hull.

A typical veneer will taper more at its top and bottom and less towards its middle. A scant ⅛ inch of wood may have to be trimmed from the ends of veneers for a long, thin hull, since its planking will taper gradually in a slight curve toward the middle. A full

rounded hull, on the other hand, may require planking which tapers strongly, so you may have to cut an inch or more off the ends of veneers for this type of design.

To begin spiling, use a staple gun to lightly tack a new veneer as close as possible to the master veneer. The two pieces will usually almost fit at their ends, but there will be conspicuous gap in the middle. The reason for fitting the veneer at this point is to mark it and to make sure that it has a proper *lay*. Figures 11 and 12 suggest guidelines for evaluating this.

Proper lay is especially important when you spile longer veneers. As they get longer, it becomes easier to position them so that one end is tighter to the mold

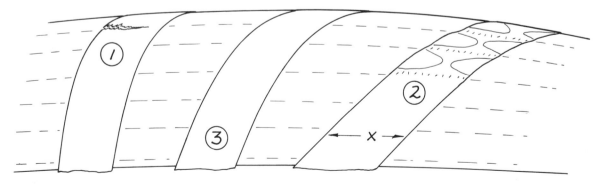

Figure 11—Guidelines for Evaluating the Proper Lay of the Planking: (1) Planking laid too close to plumb will not show compounding, but may break when bent around the bilge. (2) Planking laid at too low an angle will bend easily around the bilge but may develop more severe compounding, resulting in lumps between the staple lines along the stringers. This compounding depends on the relationship between the bend around the curve of the bilge and the bend required along the axis "X" (fore and aft). (3) By experimenting with the curvature at different angles, one can arrive at an angle that will bend easily around the bilge without excessive compounding.

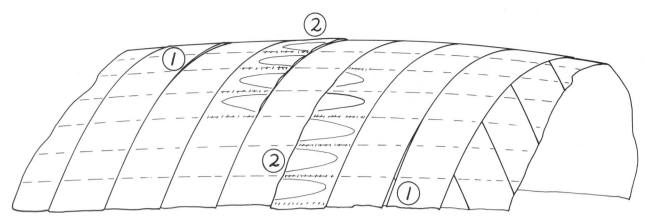

Figure 12—Edge Setting: In some cases during fastening, a person may try to force or *edge set* poorly spiled and fitted planks as in (1). This edge setting subjects the plywood to stresses in such a way as to distort it along the plank's edge, lifting it off the stringer, mold or previous layers of veneer, as in (2) where lumps are formed as the planking is stapled to the stringers. Minor lumps can be stapled flat, but severe ones will not go away. Proper initial fitting is the best solution, as no edge setting is needed. However, if a poor fit finds its way into the planking job, the solution is to fasten the plank flat, ignoring the edge fit and relying on the gap-filling qualities of the resin mixture to fill the void.

than the other. If you mark a plank with an improper lay, the error will show up when you permanently install it. It takes a bit of experience to get the feel of what will and will not work.

If one edge of the middle of the veneer is tighter to the mold than the other, correct the problem by moving the ends until both edges are an equal distance from it. To further check the lay, clamp the middle section of the veneer to the mold with several staples and move the free ends slightly back and forth until you find the natural, neutral position that each will take. Temporarily position the ends with a couple of staples and mark the piece for trimming.

Figure 13—Fitting a veneer against a previously bonded plank.

Use a scriber or a compass, as shown in Figure 14, to mark the veneer. For greater accuracy, especially on heavily compounded hulls, you can make a special spiling marker. Whichever tool you use, set it to the maximum distance between the two veneers, using the edge of the master veneer as a guide. Draw a line of this distance on the temporarily-fastened veneer all the way from keel to sheer. Remove the marked veneer and trim it to the line with a saw and plane.

Finally, trim veneers with a hand held block plane. In instances where you don't have to remove much stock, this may be the only tool you need. If you set the plane blade a little deeper than you would normally, you can remove material very rapidly.

When it is trimmed, position the newly-spiled veneer next to the master veneer on the mold for a final check. You can usually hold it in place with your hands and knee. If you marked and cut accurately, the veneer should fit. Mark any humps or gaps on the edge with a pencil, remove the piece and lightly touch it up with the plane. The first and last layers of veneer will be visible and should fit well everywhere, but you can leave 1/16 to ⅛ inch gaps between interior veneers.

After you have fit the first plank, you will find that spiling the next series of veneers is very similar: about the same amount of wood will have to be removed from the same areas for a good fit. As you become more experienced, you will be able to anticipate the amount of material to be removed. The job will progress much faster as it becomes more repetitive, and you will soon find that you can position a piece for marking in a short time. A straight, true edge on the veneer is important because a crooked edge will mislead you and slow progress.

As you fit veneers for the first layer, staple them to

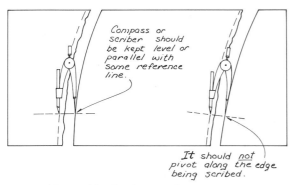

Figure 14—Scribing with a compass.

the mold and bond them to any permanent members just as you did with the master veneer. Be careful not to lose your veneer angle. If you spile too much off the top or bottom of a series of veneers, the angle will change in that direction. Although a few degrees is not worth worrying about, correct any substantial deviation by installing a tapered veneer to restore your original angle.

Although it takes a little extra time, there are good reasons to edge glue first layer veneers. Edge gluing prevents resin from running out between the edges of the first layer as the second layer is applied and in this way contributes to the quality of an interior surface. If the resin hardens, it will be more difficult to sand than uncoated wood and bumpy surfaces may result. Precoating the veneers to avoid unevenness is impractical since many staple holes will have to be coated and filled anyway. A second advantage of edge gluing is that it makes the first layer more rigid, so fewer staples are required to hold the veneers in position.

To edge glue the first layer of veneer, add low density filler to epoxy for a mixture with gap-filling properties. Apply the minimum amount of adhesive necessary to the edges of the veneers. Clamp with staples, using a thin wooden batten or pieces of scrap veneer to distribute pressure over the entire length of the joint. Be sure to cover the stapling sticks with plastic so they won't stick to the veneers.

Applying WEST SYSTEM Epoxy

Structural, gap-filling adhesives make it possible to laminate hulls with little clamping pressure. Low pressure laminating procedures do have a few predictable trouble spots, but you can avoid these by properly applying WEST SYSTEM epoxy and filler mixtures between layers of veneer. If you have not yet done so, read over the laminating section of Chapter 9 to be certain that you understand the procedures outlined there.

No matter how well you staple your wood, you may end up with less than contact pressure in some areas.

Figure 15—Applying adhesive mixture to edge of a cedar plank.

Voids — air pockets between layers of veneer — are therefore an ever-present problem. The key to eliminating them is to use a high-viscosity epoxy mixture and to apply slightly more of it than you really need. If you do this, voids will usually be filled solidly with resin. Cured WEST SYSTEM epoxy can safely span reasonably large areas and make them as strong as any other part of the laminate.

With no fillers, epoxy is too thin and runny to be used in laminating. Increase its viscosity and reduce its density by adding low density WEST SYSTEM filler. This mixture is ideal for use between layers of veneer and also somewhat cheaper by volume than epoxy alone. Filler slightly retards resin penetration and reduces the possibility of a resin-starved joint. A side benefit of this mixture is that it is easier to sand than regular epoxy and so saves time when you clean and fair between laminations.

Mixtures of WEST SYSTEM epoxy and low density filler are almost always well above grain strength, but if you are using veneers from high density woods, you may want to use high density filler. Low density filler may be inadequate for wood with high grain strength.

Stir either filler into epoxy to the consistency of heavy syrup. The mixture should be thin enough to apply with a foam roller or a notched squeegee. It must be able to spread easily within the laminate as you apply pressure and flow to areas where it is most needed to fill gaps. You also want excess adhesive to work its way to the edges of the veneer, where it can escape to the surface.

There is an optimum quantity of adhesive for most laminating situations. If you use too little, there may not be enough resin between the veneers to fill voids and gaps. Too much mixture, especially if it is too thick, may form puddles. When these develop, the veneer may bulge and you may have a bump in the hull which you'll have to fair smooth. Using too much epoxy is expensive and messy.

Two factors determine the quantity of epoxy to apply. The first is the quality of the laminating surfaces. If the veneers are rough and the surface not particularly fair, you will have more voids and more need of gap-filling adhesive. The amount of pressure and the type of curves in the hull also affect application rates.

Usually, a spread rate of about 20 square feet per pound of standard resin, before adding fillers, is adequate for rough surfaces. A rate of 30 square feet per pound is possible with better surfaces and adequate pressure. If in doubt, start out using a little bit too much adhesive, and then adjust downward, using a little less with each veneer until you reach a good rate.

It is essential to apply enough epoxy mixture to the veneer, but it is just as important that this be spread evenly over the entire surface area. Even distribution helps to prevent dry spots. To ensure it, we use both foam rollers and notched plastic spreaders. Techniques for using these simple tools are described in detail in earlier chapters. Although the squeegee is a little harder to get used to and can be messy if you're not careful,

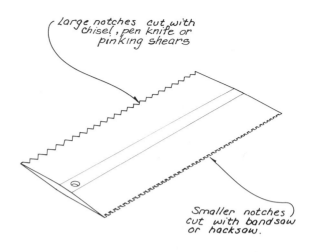

Figure 17—Flexible plastic squeegee notched to apply adhesive.

it is better at spreading a predictable amount of adhesive on a surface. It is also superior if the adhesive mixture is so thick that it is difficult to apply with normal rolling methods.

To make a notched spreader, cut the edge of a squeegee with a pair of pinking shears, a file or a knife. Adjust the notches until the tool deposits the desired amount of thickened epoxy on the veneer. Pour adhesive directly from its mixing pot as evenly as possible along the surface to be coated, and move it around with the spreader until the entire area is evenly covered. Remove any excess epoxy from the wood and transfer it to the next veneer.

If you are using a standard foam roller, you can either pour the resin directly from the pot onto the veneer or put it in a pan first and then pick it up with the roller to apply it. Maintain a relatively even coating thickness on the veneer surface with vigorous rolling. Coating thickness is easy to feel with the roller, but guard against the common tendency to spread the epoxy a bit further than you should.

A good way to check your spread rate is to examine the results. Apply what you think is a sufficient quantity to the surfaces, and staple the veneer in place with the pattern that you plan to follow. Immediately pull all of the staples and carefully remove the veneer. You will be able to see areas on both pieces where contact was made between the two surfaces. Even more apparent will be still-shiny resin on either surface. This indicates no contact and in a real lamination would probably result in a void.

Voids may be caused by too little staple pressure, by insufficient quantities of adhesive and by non-uniform resin application. Check the removed veneer for staple

Figure 16—Rolling thin adhesive mixture on cedar veneer plank with foam roller.

holes in and around the void. It may be obvious that there were too few staples, and therefore not enough pressure, in that area. Significant numbers and areas of voids indicate a general lack of adhesive. If you see no voids at all, but excessive quantities of resin exude from around the edges of the veneer, you are probably applying too much. Reduce the amount on the next try and keep experimenting until you gain sufficient experience.

Applying the Second Layer of Veneer

The laminating process really begins with the second layer of veneer. Start this as you did the first, by positioning a master veneer in the middle of the mold. This veneer usually runs at the same angle as the first layer, but in the opposite direction, so as to form a balanced double diagonal.

When you have decided its position, use a pencil to carefully outline the new master veneer on the first layer, and then remove the piece. Pull out all first layer staples within the marked area and release it from the mold. First layer veneers are roughly perpendicular to second layer veneers, so this staple pulling does not usually disturb their positioning. Staples on either side of the marked area will continue to hold the first layer in place.

Figure 18— Installing second layer of planking.

When you are ready to attach the second-layer master veneer, apply adhesive to both the outlined surface on the first layer and the underside of the new master veneer. Put the piece in its marked position and hold it with your hand while you insert several locating staples at both outer edges, about midpoint along the plank. These staples keep the veneer from moving and help to free both hands for stapling. Then use an adequate stapling pattern for your situation and laminate the master veneer. Remove any resin which squeezes out

Figure 19—Marking and preparing hull for second layer of veneer. Note staples are left in first layer until planks of second layer are spiled.

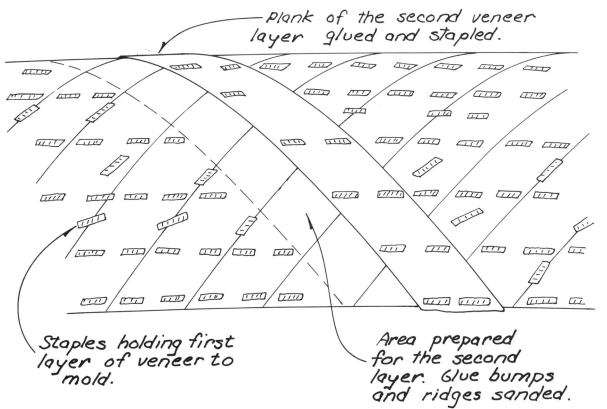

Plank of the second veneer layer glued and stapled.

Staples holding first layer of veneer to mold.

Area prepared for the second layer. Glue bumps and ridges sanded.

at the edges so that uncured epoxy won't interfere with your next task.

An alternate way to apply epoxy to second and subsequent layers of veneer is to sand and coat the preceding layer, and allow it to cure. When you are ready to laminate new veneers, apply a thickened epoxy mixture to both the new pieces and the substrate.

Spile a neighboring veneer just as you did on the first layer, but do not bond it to the mold. We recommend that you wait to apply adhesive to second layer veneers until you have spiled and fitted the entire layer. When they are trimmed, temporarily position pieces with a few staples (it's not necessary that they be held snug against the mold as long as they lie flat and their adjacent edges fit) until you have covered the entire hull surface. Then go back to the veneers on either side of the master veneer and begin laminating.

To do this, remove a piece or two at a time, apply sufficient epoxy mixture to all bonding surfaces and staple the new veneer in place. Proceed down the hull until you have bonded the entire layer. While there is a disadvantage to this method in that you have to tack the wood to the mold twice, the real efficiency comes from being able to laminate all the veneers at one time. This uses both adhesive and labor economically and avoids much of the mess which results from simultaneous spiling and bonding operations.

You can remove staples from second layer veneers before you have installed the entire layer. Try to pull staples out before the epoxy has fully cured. We find that it works best to apply veneers one day and pull the staples the next, but you can begin as soon as 7 or 8 hours after application.

If you find areas where the two layers relax slightly from the mold as you pull out the fasteners, restaple them tightly, with as few permanent, non-rusting staples as possible. This springback is a problem only on hulls with unusual shapes and curves, and its only significance is that the staples may make the hull a little more difficult to remove from the mold. We've never had much trouble with this in our hulls, but we have never had to leave in more than a dozen or so staples. When you remove the hull from the mold, clip any protruding staples flush with sidenippers or wire cutters and sand smooth.

If there is to be a third layer, lightly fair the hull before you apply it. Use a hand plane and a hand fairing block with rough sandpaper to remove any lumps of epoxy between the edges of the veneers and any humps and bumps which have developed during laminating. You can speed this process considerably by using a light duty 2100 rpm polisher with a foam disc grinding pad. We bond a piece of plastic or plywood to the pad, and this combination does a better job of fairing high spots smooth than the foam disc itself. Check general fairness by laying a light batten at various angles to the lamination. Any humps will immediately show up. Quickly mark them for removal with chalk or pencil.

Mechanical Spiling

A major problem with laminating a wooden hull is the tedious spiling required. Proper spiling demands a good deal of time and skill. While first layers, and usually last layers, must be spiled by hand, you can fit and trim the layers in between, however many there are, with a faster and simpler *mechanical spiling process*.

A mechanical spiler is basically a tool which will cut even gaps between veneers. This trimming takes place on the hull, after thickened epoxy has been applied to the bonding surfaces and the veneers are stapled in place. The gaps are filled with standard size *filler veneers* — narrow strips of laminating material. With a spiler, it is possible to laminate an entire hull with minimal amounts of hand spiling. If a hull has enough compound curvature to necessitate a lot of spiling, a mechanical system can be an important time saver.

Unfortunately, no mechanical spiling tool is available in the stores. You will have to make your own, but this is not difficult. There are several ways to make them, but only two basic types of spilers. The first and most common uses a circular saw blade, while the second uses a router with a small fly-cutting attachment. We usually use the saw type and have developed a number of variations on it which work fairly well.

Any machine used for spiling should be able to make an ⅛ inch cut approximately 2 inches away from the edge of a permanently-positioned veneer. This veneer acts as a guide on which the tool rides. It's important, of course, that the machine cut exactly ⅛ inch deep, so it will not cut into the veneer under it. There can be no gaps between veneers wider than the 2 inches the tool can cut. Since typical planks are about ¾ inch apart at the ends and 1¾ inches apart at the middles, this is not a serious limitation. Whichever tool you use, make sure that it is sharp. Otherwise, the blade will tend to follow the grain of the veneers, which, when it runs in the wrong direction, will pull the saw guide away from the true veneer edge.

When we laminate our veneers with a mechanical spiler, we're careful not to shoot any staples in the area where the machine will cut. We cut one veneer with the spiler, using the opposing veneer as a guide. The tapered space between the pieces thus becomes a swath exactly 2 inches wide. We remove the wood that

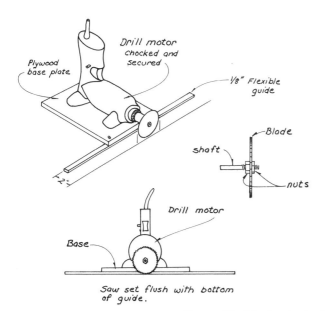

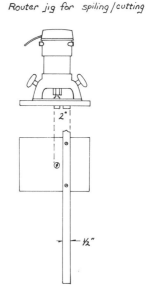

Figure 22—Mechanical spiling systems.

has been cut away and then carefully clean any sawdust and contaminated adhesive from the gap and apply fresh adhesive. Next we fit a 2 inch wide filler veneer, filling up the gap between the two veneers. This procedure is repeated over and over for each space between veneers over the entire hull.

We usually have one team which applies only veneers and moves down the hull quite rapidly, carefully setting each veneer so that a minimum amount of waste is generated in the spiling process. These workers scribe the filler spacing and make a point of stapling outside the area of veneer which will be removed. The spiling team follows, sawing 2 inch gaps and immediately laminating 2 inch veneer strips in the slots which they cut. Fitting and laminating in a single operation is very fast and makes the laminated hull more economically feasible from the standpoint of man hours involved.

We should point out that cutting and removing veneer to make the 2 inch gap must be done before the resin in the lamination has cured. When the adhesive is allowed to set too long, it's very difficult and time-consuming to remove excess veneer and epoxy to prepare the opening for the filler veneer.

Figure 22 shows a simple spiling tool made from a small hand drill. A 10 inch long, ½ inch wide by ⅛ inch thick piece of steel forms a guide. We bend this until it conforms to the hull's more severe curves and follow a veneer edge. We then make our own small circular 2 inch diameter saw blade from the steel blade of an old hand saw, bolt this blade between two nuts on a ⅜ inch diameter shaft of threaded rod, and chuck it in the drill. Finally, we bond a piece of wood to the top of the drill as close to the front and the chuck as possible to

control the cutting depth of the saw blade.

A tool which is easier to adapt but a little bulkier and heavier was the small 4½ inch diameter panel saw. With this, just bolt a simple guide on the base and set the saw depth for ⅛ inch. The modified panel saw works very well in most situations, but it is a little cumbersome to operate when cutting veneers on bigger boats.

You can also use a router for mechanical spiling, as shown in Figure 22. A router cut has a major advantage in that it is not particularly influenced by the grain of the wood and can therefore be more accurate. Its disadvantage is that it makes a good deal of wood debris and this contaminates the area between the two veneers and requires more cleanup before the filler veneer can be installed. Router bits also wear out faster than saw blades. In spite of these shortcomings, some builders prefer router mechanical spilers because of their accuracy.

Applying the Third and Succeeding Layers

After this light fairing, proceed to the third lamination. This differs dramatically from the first two in that you no longer staple to the mold. Instead, you will laminate and staple only to the previous two layers. Begin by placing a master veneer at the desired angle midpoint on the hull as you did with the first two laminations.

Since you do not want to staple into the mold, use shorter staples than you did on the first two layers: for the third layer of ⅛ inch veneer, for example, choose ⅜ or 5/16 inch staples instead of ½ inch ones. You also now have the option of leaving staples in place, thereby saving yourself some time. If you decide against pulling them, use non-rusting alloy staples, inserted so that they are slightly recessed. Otherwise, you may have some trouble when you try to rough fair or smooth up the surface in preparation for the next layer. When you use power machines for fairing, you can grind flush any protruding alloy staples.

Apply all succeeding laminations to whatever thickness in the same way, either leaving the staples in or pulling them out, whichever you prefer. The last layer, however, is applied in a special way and the staples are always removed.

Fair and smooth up the hull before you apply the final layer of veneer, especially if it will be naturally finished. It's better to remove serious humps and fill hollows on the next-to-last layer than to attempt to correct them in the final layer. Aim for a level of overall fairness so that you will need to remove no more than 1/16 inch of your final lamination during final fairing.

If you are seriously out of fair and it appears that a lot of work will be needed, consider removing the staples on the next-to-last layer to speed up fairing. Fill any deep depressions with a very thick, easily sanded and faired low density filler/resin mixture. Remove high spots, using a batten to continually check fairness.

Applying the Final Layer of Veneer

The stapling procedure and lay of veneer you use on the final layer depends on whether you plan to paint or clear coat your hull. A natural finish requires an unblemished surface, and this calls for a little extra care, but the results always seem to be worth the effort.

If you will be painting your hull, apply the final layer of veneer as you did the second layer. We generally use plastic stapling strips on the last layer of painted hulls because they are quicker than the wood strips required for natural hulls. Each staple leaves a small indentation in the wood, but we sand most of these away as we fair and can easily take care of any others during coating and final finishing. Even though you can cover mistakes on a painted surface, it's more efficient to take extra care when applying the last layer of veneer. The jobs of filling and sanding gouges, voids and so on are very time-consuming, so the less you have to do, the faster final finishing progresses.

With surfaces which will be either sanded or painted, take particular care to accurately spile and fit the last layer. Pay attention to the edges of the veneers as you laminate to make sure that they end up soundly bonded together through to the outer surface. We always coat both the flat surface and the edges of the last layer of veneer just to be certain that they won't be dry.

The decision to clear coat a hull exterior is usually based on personal taste. Some naturally finished boats have been done with such taste and skill that they are considered works of art and are talked about and admired. Unfortunately, you have to balance the desire for this type of beauty against the realities of the extra long-term maintenance invariably required to keep a naturally finished surface in top shape.

As we discussed in Chapter 11, sunlight is the major enemy of clear-coated hulls. Natural finishes can break down very quickly, and naturally finished hulls can be much more work to repair than painted hulls if you want to restore the surface's natural beauty.

Early in your project, sort out your very best veneers and save them for the last layer. Personal taste and wood quality will dictate your choices. You can apply this layer either diagonally or horizontally. It may be that more longitudinal fiber is desirable in your hull, in which case it's advisable to run the last layer horizontally. In larger hulls with many laminations, however, the direction of a single outer layer may be of little significance to the overall strength and stiffness of the structure, so personal preference can determine the direction of the veneers.

Hull sides are usually clear coated only to the water line. Boat bottoms are almost always painted, and it is not necessary to continue the veneer orientation used in the bright finish down to the area which will be painted. You can therefore plank the sides of a hull horizontally to its waterline and finish off the bottom with typical diagonal planking. In some boats this may be a structurally advantageous combination.

We hand spile diagonally laid veneers on the last layer of a naturally finished hull, and take particular pains to make excellent fits. We think that a uniform veneer width, usually between 4 and 6 inches, over the entire hull looks better than random widths. Diagonally-laid bright finish is common on boats up to 30 feet, and is rarely seen on longer boats, but as far as we are concerned, tradition is the only limitation.

When we apply veneer horizontally, we always choose a standard veneer size, usually no more than 1½ inches wide. Narrow uniform veneers are pleasant to look at and also bend easily around the hull with little or no spiling. They can be spiled, as planked hulls have been for centuries, but we feel that the extra time is not warranted if it can be avoided. Therefore, fitting the last layer in a horizontal direction is relatively easy because you are able to bend the veneer in two directions at once. We do not scarf the veneers for length, but carefully butt them as we install them, staggering butts down the hull for better appearance and greater strength.

Figure 23—Applying final layer of veneer on IOR 2 ton GOLDEN DAZY. Topsides of this layer were laid fore and aft, and bottom veneers laid athwartship and butted, as in picture. Note that layer of veneer below final layer is of much wider veneers.

Figure 24—Final layer of veneer laid fore and aft on this IOR ½ ton racer.

Horizontal planking usually starts several inches below the sheer at the midpoint of the boat, with the ends of the planking sweeping up to deck level towards the bow and stern. Planking which curves slightly more than the sheer line looks good and, at the same time, makes some room for the planks to straighten out further on down the hull. The goal is to let the planks run no less than parallel to the waterline as it approaches the bottom of the hull. To prevent any "reversing" of the planking, measure from the master veneer to the load waterline. If the distance at the middle is more than at the ends, the planking will tend to reverse or curve the other way, so adjust the master veneer until all the planking will have some curve up toward the deck.

Use a long batten, lightly tacked to the hull, as a guide for positioning the master horizontal veneer. Make sure that the batten outlines a long, gentle arc with no flats or hollows. After you have installed the first plank from bow to stern, remove the batten and

spile planking on either side of it, using the master veneer as a guide for alignment. To minimize both damage to your hull and the number of staples you'll need, use wood stapling strips for the final layer of veneer. These strips should be narrower than the veneer to reduce the chances they will be bonded to the surface. As we pointed out earlier, oozing resin may bond wood strips to your hull, so a plastic barrier is a good safeguard.

When you have completed the last veneer, laminate and install a stem cap. Further layers of wood may be needed to complete the keel profile. In most cases, you can hold these in place with screws until the epoxy cures. For extreme curves, use washers under the screwheads for extra pressure. If this is not practical, make a temporary form in the shape of the stem or keel, allowing for a bit of springback, and laminate the part on this. Then rough saw and bond the piece in position for final fairing.

Final Fairing

Fairing is one of the arts of boatbuilding. We doubt that anyone has ever built a perfectly fair hull, but we've seen some that have been close to it. Up to a certain point, fairness is a necessity, because fair hulls offer less resistance than hulls with humps and hollows. After this, fairness is no longer important as far as movement through the water is concerned, but becomes a point of personal and professional pride.

You should usually complete final fairing and finishing before you remove a laminated hull from its mold. The exception to this is a thin-skinned hull which needs additional support from internal framework. In this case, you would final fair the hull after installing the framework.

Before final fairing, rough fair the last layer of veneer to remove lumps of resin and obvious high spots as you have on previous layers. Block or smoothing planes and slightly flexible sanding blocks with 60 or 80 grit paper are good tools for rough fairing. Don't use air files and other power machines to rough fair hulls which will be naturally finished. Unless you have a lot of experience with power tools, you run a high risk of leaving scratches in the wood and these may show up in the finished surface.

There are two parts to final fairing. The first, *local fairing,* is the process of making the hull smooth to the touch in a specific area. *Overall fairing,* the second job, is more difficult. A hull may be sanded until it is very smooth, but it still may not be fair over all. It's usually at this point that large overall hollows and bumps are visible. It's important that you do everything you can to

Figure 25—This hull is being finish sanded in preparation for resin coatings. Note veneer seam along the bilge. Topsides on this hull were choice veneers, carried from sheer to just below waterline.

be sure of general fairness before you coat the hull because it's very difficult to correct overall fairness problems after coating.

Final fairing involves finding high spots and removing them so they blend in with the overall surface area. The difficulty is in determining exactly where these high spots are before you start planing or sanding. As you work, continually move around and look at the hull from different angles.

A chalk stick works quite well to help find high spots, and can be used to quickly identify them and check your work. Make one from stock between ¾ inch square and 1¼ inch square, approximately 6 feet long. Use the straightest wood available that will also bend in a fair curve. Apply carpenter's chalk to the surfaces of the stick, and bend it around the hull until most of its surface area is firmly touching the hull. Move the chalk stick back and forth slightly on the hull so that it deposits chalk on the high spots. Then concentrate sanding and planing to bring these areas down to fair. You can use the chalk stick as often as you like to monitor your progress until you are satisfied with your hull's fairness.

Always do your final fairing by hand, with 50 to 60 grit paper attached to a block and hand planes with sharp, fine-set blades. Sanding blocks should bend slightly to conform to the contour of the hull. We make ours out of ⅜ inch to ½ inch plywood, although for smaller, heavily curved hulls they may be as thin as ¼ inch. Our sanding blocks are designed for economical use of 11 inch x 7½ inch sheets of sandpaper: we cut them in multiples of 11 inches, up to 44 inches long. The width of the blocks is anywhere from 3 to 3¾ inches, to fit a sheet of sandpaper cut in half

lengthwise, depending on whether we want to attach paper to the block with staples on the edge or put feathering disc adhesive on the flat area. We prefer to use adhesive because more of the sandpaper surface is exposed for use and it's a little faster to change paper. While a 44 inch block may not be necessary in many cases, the 33 inch block is a minimum for achieving overall fairness on hulls 15 feet and up.

If you plan to clear coat your hull, you will want to avoid any deep sandpaper scratches which may show on its surface. When you get to the point where you seem close to a final fairness, switch over to finer grit paper. Begin to direct your sanding strokes in the direction of the grain rather than across it. When you are satisfied with your work, do final sanding with a shorter block. Work in the direction of the grain to remove any cross grain scratches.

Even within a species of wood, sanding can be done at different rates. Lower density wood can be sanded a little easier than higher density wood, and a single piece of flat grain wood has hard and soft areas which can end up rippled after sanding. These factors can contribute to slight, yet difficult-to-remedy, variations in final fairing. Continued sanding sometimes only makes matters worse, as it removes material from softer areas and leaves slight "dishing" in the wood. When this happens, the best solution is to sand with sharp paper, changing it often, and to make liberal use of a block plane with a sharp, fine-set blade. You can usually avoid this whole problem, however, by choosing good, uniform, edge grain veneers for the last layer of a laminated hull.

Figure 26—Molded hull being lifted from ribband mold. Protective plastic sheet can be seen on stern of mold.

Removing the Hull from the Mold

Before you turn over the hull, make the cradles in which it will sit. To fit cradles perfectly, cover the hull with polyethylene and use it as a mold over which to laminate veneer, plywood or fiberglass. This is a very good use of scrap veneer. Form two cradle seats, each 4 to 8 inches wide, which span at least 25% of the half girth. For clamping pressure as the resin cures, use weights or cinch a line around the hull roughly the way you'd cinch a saddle on a horse. When the cradle seats have cured, bond sufficient framework to them to permit the hull to sit close to its lines when turned upright.

It's fairly easy for a group of people to grasp a small, light hull by its sheer and lift it high enough to clear its mold. If your hull is too heavy, or has to be lifted too high for people to handle, use a lifting sling and mechanical assistance. Usually, four pieces of extruded metal U-shaped channel large enough to fit over the edge of the hull at the sheer can be used as lifting points. Each of the pieces might be a foot or more long in order to distribute load over enough area to prevent damage to the sheer. You may want to screw the pieces to the sheer to prevent slipping. Attach a line to them and fasten it to the lifting apparatus.

Figure 27—Hull is set in cradle and immediately trued up with the waterlines. Temporary bracing at sheer stabilizes shape of hull while interior joinery is installed. The ladder at open transom provides easy access to hull.

Lift the hull clear of its mold and set it on the floor. Cross brace the sheers in a few places close to the center of the hull so that they can bear the weight as the hull rolls. Then roll it over into an upright position. With enough people and padding, most molded hulls can be rolled by hand. See Chapter 20 for suggestions on rolling larger hulls.

Chapter 20

The Strip Plank Method for Laminating and Strip Composite Construction

The strip plank method for laminating hulls is a cross between the mold method and traditional strip planking techniques. Mold frames are set up and solidly planked, usually with edge-glued strips of softwood. The set-up is then covered with layers of veneer. The strip planks become the interior lamination of the finished hull. When construction is finished, temporary frames are removed. The rigid, monocoque structures which can be built with this method require substantially less interior framing than other types of wooden boats.

Because the type and number of layers of material which can be laminated over the first layer of strip planking can be infinitely manipulated, this method of construction has endless variations and may be used to construct boat components as well as entire hulls. In this edition of *The Gougeon Brothers on Boat Construction,* we have expanded our discussion of strip planking to include *strip plank composite construction,* one of the more popular and versatile of these variations.

Strip composite construction is probably most widely used in building stripper canoes. It differs from standard strip plank laminating in only one major respect: softwood strips are bent over temporary mold frames, but are covered with fiberglass cloth, inside and out, rather than veneer. Although strip composite construction is a quick and relatively easy way to build strong, light hulls, its use has been restricted to small craft and to parts such as spars and cabin tops. This is largely because no scantling rules have been set for strip composite hulls.

Setting Up for Strip Planking

With the strip plank method, just as with the mold method, we use ⅝ inch thick particle board temporary mold frames to define the shape of the hull. Set up the frames as described for the mold method, and then cover them with strip planking. The only difference is that extra care must be taken to be sure that the bevels on the frames are correct. Hard spots may dent the planking as it is bent over the frames, and this damage can be visible in the interior.

Decide temporary mold frame positioning and spacing during lofting, taking into account the locations of stationary bulkheads, framework and any other internal items which might interfere with a chosen temporary frame location. Usually, setting up a permanent bulkhead means that you can eliminate a temporary frame, but sometimes a bulkhead is situated between two temporary frames and too large a gap would be left if either were removed. Therefore, early on, coordinate the locations of the permanent structural members which can act as mold frames with the locations of the temporary mold frames so that you can provide proper support for the strip planking process with the least amount of set-up.

Planking thickness and the shape of the hull determine the standard spacing between mold stations. For ½ inch thick planking, a 16 inch span between stations is about maximum. Frames which will be covered with 1 inch thick planking might be as far as 30 inches apart. Average spacing for ⅝ inch to ⅞ inch planking is 18 to 24 inches. With any hull, there may be areas of tight, sharp curves which cannot be properly defined by the general station spacing. We usually insert half frames between two normally positioned frames in these areas. If there aren't too many sharp curves, this is much quicker than decreasing the standard frame spacing throughout the hull to accommodate one area of sharp curves.

With the strip plank method, the keel, stem and transom are always included in the set-up to become part of the permanent hull. This means that you will have to make provisions for notching the keel and stem into the temporary mold frames as well as into bulkheads and laminated frames which may also be in the set-up. Hold the keel and stem temporarily in place to each temporary mold frame by inserting a screw through a small block that is attached to the side of the temporary mold frame just underneath the keel or stem area. The screw holds the keel or stem snug against the temporary mold frame until the lamination process is complete. You can then remove these screws easily when it is time to remove the temporary mold frames. Permanently position and attach the keel and stem to bulkheads, frames or any other permanent interior items using alloy wood screws of proper length.

A permanent or temporary sheer clamp must be included in the set-up so that the planks near the sheer can attach to it, especially if the planking will run out, or cross the sheer at an angle. Without hand spiling, it's very difficult to finish planking with strips running exactly parallel to the sheer line. We usually install permanent sheer clamps, although doing this means that we often have to saw temporary frames in order to remove them. This is only a problem if we want to use the frames for another boat.

Precoat and sand exposed interior areas of the permanent sheer clamp, keel, stem, transom, bulkheads and other permanent interior items before installing them in the set-up. Protect all prefinished permanent members by covering them with duct tape or other heavy duty tape which will prevent damage from both dripping epoxy and sanding.

When you have installed all of the permanent members in the set-up and completed final fairing of both temporary frames and permanent members, the set-up is ready for strip planking. During this procedure, you should attach the planking permanently to all permanent members, but avoid any possibility of accidentally bonding the planking to the temporary mold frames. Cover the edges of all temporary frames carefully with strips of 4 mil or 6 mil polyethylene sheet, stapling the plastic several inches back from the edges on both sides of the frame. When you have completed this, you are ready to begin strip planking.

Stock for Strip Planking

Choose the most practical planking size for your project. Most boats will require strip planks between ½ inch and 1 inch thick. Determine the planking size for your hull after considering the following:

(1) the size and width of the boat,
(2) the spacing between permanent or temporary frames in the set-up,
(3) whether the chosen thickness of planking can bend around the most severe curves in the hull, and
(4) the most efficient use of available dimensional lumber.

Planking width is governed by two factors. There is, first, the need to attach one plank to the next with dowels or nails in the process of edge nailing. This is somewhat impractical with anything wider than 1½ inch strips: the widest we've ever used was 1¼ inches. The flexibility of the planking in the edgewise direction is the second factor and is an important consideration for rapid application of strip planking.

If you can select the base stock from which to saw strips, we suggest that you choose slab sawn planks which, when ripped, will show edge grain on interior and exterior surfaces. Edge grain planks are usually more attractive for naturally finished interiors. There

are two better reasons for using them, however: edge grain planks are more stable than other planks and they sand and machine more consistently than flat grain. Fairing up surfaces for final finishing and laminating therefore goes a bit more quickly.

Dimensional accuracy is important when you are sawing and milling the stock for planking. Accuracy is particularly important in the thickness dimension. A plank that is even 1/32 inch smaller than its neighbors will create a depression along its entire length that you will need to fill prior to further laminating. Sawing enough planking for an entire hull is a large undertaking. We always take the time to set up a proper sawing operation by making sure that we have a good feed ramp for easily moving the stock into the saw and a good exit ramp for the stock to lie on as it is exiting from the back of the saw. Whenever possible, we set up spring tensioning to hold the stock down on the saw table and up against the saw guide so that we don't have to rely entirely on hand pressure to guide the stock through the saw blade.

You probably won't be able to buy planks long enough to cover your entire hull. Usually, you have to cut at least one scarf and perhaps as many as four to make up a plank to span all of the hull stations. It is much easier to scarf strips before you apply them, and it can be quite difficult to scarf strip planking in place while bending it over frames, especially in short, wide boats. Do all scarfing carefully and accurately, following instructions in Chapter 10, so that there will be no dog legs or kinks at the scarf or overlaps to increase planking thickness at the joints.

Spiling and Beveling Strip Planks

The concept of planking a hull is at least several thousand years old. The traditional carvel built hull has planks lying edge to edge, and the techniques developed for carvel planking are well known. Traditionally, because boats are fatter in the middle and smaller out at the bow and stern, planking has always been tapered at its ends to adjust for this change in dimensions. Because planks are joined one by one around a curved surface, it's also common to bevel their edges so that they meet flush where they join. Both the spiling and beveling operations are very tedious and time-consuming, and both require a good deal of skill.

With traditional procedures, two workers might be lucky to apply five or six planks a day on a 40 foot hull. To speed up the planking process and make this construction method more practical, we have eliminated spiling and beveling. When these two jobs are unnecessary, two well-organized people can apply up to 25 planks in eight hours.

Instead of spiling, we adjust for dimensional decreases as planks approach the ends of the hull by allowing them to run out at the keel and the sheer as they do when building a mold. Unless the hull is particularly fat for its length, this technique presents no difficulties, provided that the planking is thin enough to bend easily edgewise as it arcs toward the sheer or keel. With a thick WEST SYSTEM* Brand resin mixture, beveling is usually unnecessary for structural reasons. Eliminating it saves a great deal of time. When viewed from the interior, the planking on most hulls always fits tight and looks the same whether it has been beveled or not.

Applying Strip Planking

As might be imagined, locating the first plank on the set-up is of paramount importance because the location of this master plank determines the direction and amount of curve that all succeeding planking will follow as it approaches either the keel or sheer. Improper location of this first plank might cause the planking approaching the sheer to become overly curved to the point where it would be difficult to bend the planks in place, while the planking on the other side of the master plank that is approaching the keel might hardly curve at all. The goal is to locate the master plank about midpoint along the hull, and in an arc that will allow the planking installed on either side of it to bend about the same amount as it approaches the keel or sheer. The simplest method of determining the location of the master plank is to determine mid-frame locations at various points along the hull. Establish these positions by measuring along the perimeter of the frames between the keel and the sheer, starting in the middle of the hull and working out towards the ends. Temporarily exclude the first few stations at the bow and the transom because the shape of the boat is changing abruptly at these points and will not give you a true overall reading of what is happening with the majority of the hull. When you have located a point on the frame at each station which is equidistant from both the keel and the sheer, position a batten along these marks and temporarily nail it in position. Using your eye as the guide, move the batten wherever needed to achieve a fair curve that still intersects the mid-frame marks as closely as possible. You can extend the batten arc to achieve a fair curve over the unmarked fore and aft frames.

With this batten installed, you can get a better idea about how the planking will lie on the rest of the hull. Measure either up or down from the batten at various

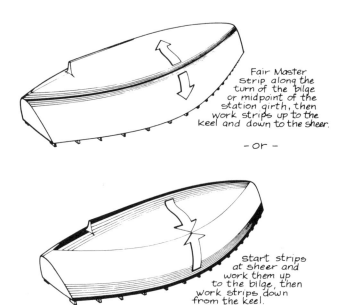

Figure 1—Two suggested methods for strip planking hulls.

points on all the frames to try to get a sense of what the planking will look like as it approaches the sheer and/or keel. As you work out the planking direction, try to determine which are the most severe curves in the hull and establish the best angle for negotiating them. Then compare this with the angle of the master veneer. Another factor which might affect placement of the master plank is the amount of compound curve toward the sheer compared with the compound curve toward the keel. The bottoms of boats are usually compounded more than the topsides, and this may indicate that the master plank should be curved more toward the sheer, where the planks might be more easily bent edgewise due to the lack of compound curvature.

When you have lined up the batten and adjusted it to suit your desire for positioning the master plank, carefully mark its position on each station so that you can install the master plank using these marks as reference. Although it is normally done, it is not necessary that the master plank be located right at this marked mid-point position. You could position the master plank at any point above or below the mid-point marks that you established with the batten, but it must run parallel to and at the same distance from each mark at each station point so that as the hull is fully planked, the planks in the area of the original marks will run true to them.

If you decide that the shape of your hull is not well suited to this type of planking procedure (for example, if the hull is too fat), you can use the *double run* planking system. With this method, you apply the planking parallel with the sheer line up to a point on the hull where it begins to curve excessively. Then apply the next group of planking parallel with the keel, joining it with the planking that has been run parallel with the sheer at a central *joining plank*. Joining the two directions of planking as they run out into each other at some point in the central hull area is difficult without causing a hard spot. This difficulty is not insurmountable, but the double run planking system takes a good deal of extra time in comparison to the run out method, where you have to do little or no fitting at all.

Figure 2—Strip planking a mold.

Applying WEST SYSTEM Epoxy

Assume that you are going to run bottom planking parallel to the keel and topsides planking parallel to the sheer in a double run planking system and that you have accurately marked the set-up to receive the master plank. Install this plank, using screws which are about twice as long as the thickness of the planking to hold it temporarily to the mold frames. We use inexpensive roundhead sheet metal screws with large washers which make it possible to apply more pressure without damage to the wood fiber. Chipboard frames require longer screws than wood frames because chipboard's holding power is not as good as wood's. In areas where you need extra holding power, screw or staple and bond a piece of wood to the side of a chipboard frame and screw the planking into this. Step drill bits, which can cut a pilot hole in the temporary frame and a shank-sized hole in the plank in one operation, save the added step of switching between two different drills or changing bits.

Use alloy screws and epoxy thickened with high density filler to attach planking to all permanent parts of the boat. These screws will be left in the hull. Countersink them enough so they won't interfere with fairing. You will be using two different types and perhaps sizes of screws, one to attach planking to temporary frames and the other to attach it to permanent members. Two electric drill motors set up with two different size bits will save time.

When you have installed the master plank, set up a procedure to easily and efficiently apply the rest of the planking to the frames. Mark the planks with surmarks which line up with a station in the middle of the hull so that you can accurately position them without having to guess if they are centered.

If you are using a softwood such as cedar, use low density additive with epoxy to make a thick syrup. This combination far exceeds the grain strength of most softwoods. If you are working with high density woods with higher grain strength, like mahogany, use the high density filler for a stronger resin mixture.

Support jigs will hold planking upright for convenient epoxy application. We make them of ½ inch plywood, with slots in the tops just large enough for the plank to sit in. We nail these to saw horses and set up as many as are needed to support the plank. About 3 feet off the floor seems to be a comfortable working height.

Applying epoxy to the edges of several hundred planks is a significant part of the work of strip planking a hull. You need a quick, efficient and clean method for mixing and applying the adhesive to plank edges. In the long run, we've found it best to spread the resin mixture with an inch-wide stick. We mix epoxy in a tub, such as the WEST SYSTEM 805 Mixing Pot, making up only enough at one time to fill one third of the tub's volume. Then we stroke it along the edge of the plank with the stick, applying a controlled amount of resin to the surface. If the resin is so thin that it runs easily off the stick, and perhaps off the edge of the plank, thicken it up with more filler.

After you have applied the thickened resin to one edge of a plank, wet out the edge of the strip which has already been installed with a thin coat of standard epoxy. You can do this quickly with a foam roller cut to a good working length. Use the surmark you made earlier to line up the center of the new plank and the middle station. If the hull is very large, it's difficult for one person to install a plank without getting messy. Ideally, two or three people can work together, but if you are shorthanded, make some adjustable stands to hold the edges of the plank at the right height while you fasten its middle to the frames. As fastening progresses out towards the ends of the hull, move the stands inward, and then remove them.

Think of the plank which is being installed as the *glue plank,* and the plank which has already been installed as the *permanent plank.* Begin by fastening the glue plank tight against the permanent plank about midway along the hull. Insert a screw through the new strip into the mold frame. Then skip one or two stations, depending on the size and curvature of the hull, and insert another screw into a mold frame. Hold the glue plank tight against the permanent plank so that there is the best possible fit between them as you insert the screw. After you have fastened it at several mold frames on either side of the mid-hull frame, the glue plank will be under reasonable control and you can fasten it easily to each frame in the set-up. If you have applied sufficient epoxy to the new plank, some should squeeze out. Most of this will be on the exterior of the hull because of the tapered gap between the planks, but some will invariably end up on the interior. Remove excess adhesive from both surfaces before it cures.

Edge Fastening

It is common to have some misalignment between planks in the areas *between* the mold frames. To keep this misalignment to a minimum, you should allow each plank to take a natural curve as you bend it around the hull. You can correct plank misalignment easily by edge nailing with the use of ⅛ inch diameter wooden dowels. While you could use nails instead of wooden dowels, dowels are preferable for several reasons. Because the hull will be laminated over anyway, the extra cross grain strength that nails might provide isn't needed. (Wooden dowels could also provide ex-

Figure 4—Strip planking a 42 foot hull. These strips are being laid from a master plank at the bilge up to the keel.

cellent cross grain strength if they were bonded in place.) Of the hundreds of nails that might be used in a hull, a small percentage will inadvertently break through the sides of a plank. This is a particular problem on the interior of the hull, because the nails are not only unsightly, but difficult to sand smooth or remove. If a wooden dowel happens to run out in the planking, it is easily sanded smooth and is not particularly unattractive.

To align the planking between frames, hold the glue plank and permanent plank between your thumb and forefinger so that they are in exact alignment. Then drill a ⅛ inch diameter hole through the edge of one plank into the next, moving down the plank between each station until you have drilled all of the holes while holding the planking in perfect alignment. The hole drilling depth should be 1½ times the planking width. Depending on the distance between frames, you may need from one to four dowels to hold the planks in proper alignment between stations until the adhesive cures. Drill the hole for the dowel slightly undersize, so that the dowel fits snugly and helps draw the planks together. If available, a second person can follow down the planks as the holes are being drilled, and insert and tap in place the ⅛ inch dowels, while at the same time realigning the planks with his hands to make sure that the predrilled holes line up.

Occasionally the dowels won't have sufficient holding power to hold an errant glue plank snug against the permanent plank. Besides causing an unsightly gap, this problem will cause the planking to get out of fair. To solve this, staple a strip of plywood to the glue plank and then hold it in proper position to close the gap. Staple the other end of the plywood strip to the adjacent two or three planks that you have already positioned.

After installing three or four planks, take the time to

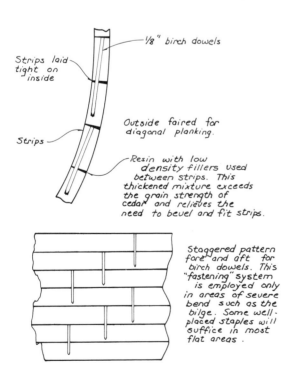

Figure 3—Doweling strips to prevent misalignment.

Figure 5—The keel joint on 42 foot hull shown in Figure 4. Note screw holes where strips are secured to mold.

remove any excess adhesive that has oozed out of the joints from both the exterior and interior surfaces, taking particular care on the interior to keep this surface as clean as possible, saving work later on. After the cleanup operation, check the edge joints to make sure that the alignment is good and that the planking is going on in nice, fair curves with no humps or bumps developing. You will also want to check the edge of the last plank that you have installed to make sure that no bumps or unusual curves are developing along the edge that may cause difficulties when you try to fit the next plank. If a bump does develop, it is best to fair it out before installing the next plank.

Difficulty may develop toward the end of the planking job if the planks begin bending excessively in the *width* dimension, making it difficult to secure them in place. If this problem becomes severe enough, you can

rectify it easily by installing one or two maximum tapered planks to reduce the amount of curve in the width direction. Do this by marking the maximum amount of taper available in the width dimension, using a heavy lofting batten to mark a nice, even curve which extends from the middle of the plank out to a tapered point at each end.

Although the planking will simply run out at most areas of the hull and require no fitting, at some point along the keel the planking from one side of the hull will begin to butt into the planking from the other side. Carefully cut the planking of the side done first to a nice, straight edge that runs parallel to the centerline of the keel, so that an easily defined plane is available against which you can fit the planking that runs in from the other side of the hull.

Figure 7—Laminating second layer of veneer onto hull.

Veneer Laminations

After you have installed all the planking, begin preparing it just as you would a mold for further veneer lamination. First check to make sure that you have removed all temporary metal screws and properly recessed all permanent screws. Next, rough trim all of the planks which might run out at the sheer, the stem or the transom, so that you have a roughly defined surface on which to laminate veneers. Rather than trim the planking flush with these surfaces, allow them to extend an inch or two to provide a little extra area in which to extend laminating pressure. Later, after you have completed laminating, you can trim the planking flush with the desired surface.

Before you sand or fair, carefully check the entire strip plank surface for voids and crevices in the planking and in the joints between planks. Fill these voids, and holes in the planking at mold frame intersections where you have removed temporary screws, with a

Figure 6—Laminating first layer of veneer over faired strips. Note planking bench to right.

thick mixture of epoxy and low density filler. Rough fair the hull, and then begin laminating veneer.

You can laminate veneer to a strip plank hull exactly as described for the mold method in Chapter 19, except that with strip planking you can install the first and second layers of veneer with alloy staples which do not have to be removed. Leaving the staples in saves time and helps make the strip plank method a practical construction technique.

Figure 8—Forty-two foot hull with temporary molds removed. Hull is supported by permanent bulkheads installed during set-up. Note clean interior in which work can progress as exterior finishing is completed.

Begin the first layer of veneer about midpoint on the hull, using a thick low density adhesive mixture to bond it to the strip planking. Recess staples so that they will not be in the way of rough fairing in preparation for the second lamination. You can use the mechanical spiling system with this and succeeding layers, and greatly speed up the process. The strip plank hull is an ideal solid mold for laminating: you will find that you can laminate all layers of veneer quickly and efficiently, and probably in less time than it took to strip plank the hull. The quality mold surface also helps the hull surface remain very fair, with little work required between layers, up through four or five laminations of veneer.

You can remove the temporary frames from the interior of the hull at a point during construction when you have applied enough veneer so that the hull is rigidly self-supporting. It's possible to disassemble frames, but probably faster to saw them out, being careful not to damage the hull. You may have enough bulkheads and permanent frames in the set-up to support the hull, but it's more likely that you'll need to prop up the sheer, bow and transom with blocking to help distribute its weight. Do not, of course, cut the legs off permanent frames at this stage.

Figure 9—Launching 42 foot yacht. The natural finish highlights final layer of veneer laid fore and aft.

Final Finishing

With the temporary frames removed, you can work simultaneously on the interior and exterior surfaces. It's usually easiest to sand interior planking smooth while the hull is upside down, so that dust settles to the floor rather than to the bottom of the boat. Install good lighting in the interior, provide ventilation with fans, and wear a dust mask. If you have not done so already, cover all prefinished items with tape to protect them from damage from dripping resin and during sanding.

We use a polisher with 80 grit paper on a soft foam pad to rough sand and fair interior planking. When the surface is generally smooth and fair, we finish sand with orbital sanders and 100 grit paper until the surface is smooth enough to receive an initial coat of WEST SYSTEM resin.

Although it is not absolutely necessary, you may prefinish the entire interior while the hull is still upside down. It's our experience that all sanding and coating operations are much easier with the hull in this position than when it's upright. A good portion of the interior can be easily installed in an upside-down hull, as will be explained in more detail in Chapter 24. Just as with mold method hulls, it is more efficient to do a lot of exterior final finishing, including all fiberglassing, coating and sanding, before turning the boat over.

Build a cradle, as described in Chapter 19, in preparation for rolling. Unlike a molded hull, which you must lift up and off the mold and then turn over, a strip

Figure 10—Stripper canoes built by Herschel Payne. Western red cedar and WEST SYSTEM epoxy were used for both boats. The 15 foot model weighs 32 lbs. and the 18-footer weighs 48 lbs.

plank hull is simply pushed over, using mattresses and tires covered with carpet to absorb the load. Begin rolling by lifting one sheer continually upward, blocking the hull as you go. When you have raised the sheer to about a 60° angle, attach lines to it, some going in the direction in which the hull will be rolled and some leading in the opposite direction, so that people holding them on both sides of the hull can control it. Unless the boat is unusually large, a few people can pull it over, while others hanging onto the ropes on the opposite side snub their lines around a post or heavy machinery to slow the rate of fall until it sits gently on its bottom. Set the cradle under the hull and level it according to the waterlines so that you can complete the interior and install the deck.

Strip Composite Construction

The use of strip composite construction has been limited to stripper canoes, rowing shells, prams and dinghies. Although the strength and stiffness of stripper canoes have been proven through use for years, strip composites have never been subjected to controlled testing. There is no body of data from which to draw ideas for using stripper methods on other types of small craft.

We hope that this situation will change. Strip composite construction has some very attractive features. Veneer spiling and fitting are unnecessary and only mold frames are used, so the method is very quick. You can use lumber from your local dealer rather than veneers, which can be hard to find. The technique works well on compounded hulls and results in very strong and stiff small craft with little or no interior framework.

In an effort to expand its applications, we have examined several aspects of strip composite construction. Our approach has been to evaluate the relative effects of various weights and numbers of layers of glass cloth and to explore the relationships between these and wood core thickness in terms of stiffness, ultimate strength and weight. Our results provide preliminary suggestions on the best ways to build strength and stiffness into stripper hulls.

Glass fabric is used in strip composition construction to supply cross grain strength to wood planking. In more traditional methods, closely spaced ribs serve this function. While two layers of cloth and ¼ inch planking are sufficient to support a canoe, this schedule is inadequate for larger hulls. Two approaches to increasing strength and stiffness are adding extra layers of cloth and increasing planking thickness. Our testing indicates that, up to a certain point, adding more fiberglass to a hull justifies itself by increasing strength and stiffness disproportionately to the increase in weight.

Our data are intended to be used for the purpose of ranking materials and cannot be used to predict whether a material will prove satisfactory in service. Figure 11 shows the effects of increasing planking thickness while maintaining a typical stripper canoe fiberglass schedule. Data on ¼ inch okoume plywood with no cloth are provided as a control. Other testing has demonstrated that the impact resistance of a composite can be substantially increased by balancing panels with layers of fiberglass or aramid cloth on both interior and exterior surfaces.

Building a Stripper Canoe

Excellent detailed instructions for building stripper canoes with WEST SYSTEM epoxy have been published. If you have any problems finding a book on the subject, please call us for sources. The following brief outline presents but one of the many variations on the technique.

Setting up for a stripper canoe is not much different from setting up for a strip plank hull. You can use a standard four-sided strongback, but a three-sided, U-shaped foundation made of two 2 x 4's and one 2 x 6 is strong enough for a 17 foot canoe. Set up mold frames and stems to define the hull shape and bolt them to the strong back. Fair the set-up, and then tape the edges of the frames or cover them with plastic strips

so that they will not be bonded to the hull.

Many strippers are planked with western red cedar and sheathed, inside and out, with 4 oz. or 6 oz. fiberglass cloth. One of the most efficient ways to prepare stock for planking is to buy nominally ¾ inch thick flat grain boards, rip them to ¼ by ¾ inch edge grain strips, and then scarf them to length. Depending upon the design, only about 30% of the strips will need to be the full length of the craft.

Begin by planking the bottom of the canoe fore and aft, starting at the centerline and working out on each side. Edge glue the planks with a thickened low density epoxy mixture and use staples for temporary pressure until the epoxy cures. Wire brads or finish nails can be used at the stations. The flat bottom section of a canoe resembles a football.

When the bottom is planked, begin on the topsides. In most canoes, this and the bottom planking run at different angles so the strip which joins the two requires special fitting. Begin midway down the boat and work up and down from there. The strips should lie higher above the waterline at the bow than at the mid-section. Scribe and fit the final plank to the bottom.

Remove staples and nails when the epoxy has cured. Fair the canoe, first with a block plane and then with an 11 inch long sanding block. When you are satisfied, clean the surface and apply an initial coating of WEST SYSTEM resin. Allow this to cure, lightly sand and clean the surface again, and apply 4 oz. or 6 oz. woven fiberglass cloth.

Use the dry method for applying cloth described in Chapter 12 to apply the fabric. Fit and cut it and place

---

Figure 11—Preliminary results of testing of strip composite samples.

Twelve inch square samples of a variety of combinations of western red cedar and fiberglass cloth were weighed and subjected to increasing loads to failure. In all cases, 6 oz. glass cloth was applied to both sides of the samples. The goal of this experiment was to gauge the relative effects of wood core thickness and quantity of fiberglass cloth on strength, stiffness and weight in stripper construction. Samples became heavier with additional layers of fiberglass and epoxy, but up to a point strength and stiffness increased disproportionately to weight. In order to compare these results with conventional materials, we also tested a sample of ¼ inch okoume plywood which was not covered with fiberglass cloth. The plywood sample failed at 225 lbs., weighed 10.7 oz. and deflected .63 inch.

Cedar Planking Thickness	Average Pounds to Failure	Average Weight per Square Foot	Average Deflection at Failure
3/16 in.	214	8.0 oz.	.73 in.
1/4 in.	221	9.8 oz.	.49 in.
5/16 in.	300	11.6 oz.	.48 in.
3/8 in.	298	13.1 oz.	.32 in.

it over the entire hull exterior. Pour mixed resin onto the cloth and spread it out with a plastic spreader. The glass should be clear but slightly dull.

When the first layer of cloth has cured, apply a second layer to the bottom, allow it to cure, and lightly sand it, feathering the edges of the fiberglass. Coat the hull as many times as necessary to fill the cloth's weave entirely. After the resin has cured, sand again, first with 80 grit paper and then with 120 grit paper until the surface is smooth and dull.

At this point, build a cradle. Unbolt the mold frames and turn them sideways to free the canoe. Turn the boat over, and place it in its cradle. Sand the interior with a disc sander and soft foam pad as well as with a block where necessary. Apply fiberglass on the inside exactly as you did the outside, with one overall layer and a second layer in the flat bottom section.

Lay out the sheer clamp and trim it to shape. Laminate gunwales and breasthooks. Double check the width of the hull, and install thwarts. These are usually hung from screws which fasten up into the gunwales. Build or buy seats to your liking, install them, and finish the canoe as you would a strip plank hull.

Strip Composite Components

Strip composite construction methods can be used to build many boat parts. One of the more interesting applications is in building spars up to about 30 feet long. The same technique may be used to build cabin tops and other panels and components where design considerations favor low weight and minimal interior framing or where heavy compound curvature precludes the use of plywood.

In the past, solid masts were built by shaping a rectangular piece of wood into an airfoil and then, if weight was a problem, hollowing out the center. We suggest that instead of building spars this way, you begin with a male form which describes the shape of one half of the mast, strip plank it, sheath it with glass, make a second half, and then bond the two together. The resulting spar is lightweight and can be designed to receive specific loads.

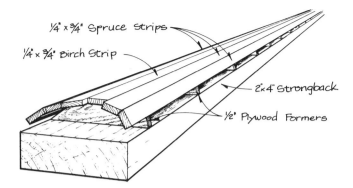

Figure 12—Building a strip composite spar.

Because this type of construction has not been widely used, we cannot recommend strip dimensions and fiberglass schedules. Smaller spars will probably require both high density wood strips and softwood. It is possible to taper the wall thickness and section of a freestanding mast, but as with all other aspects of strip composite spars, careful study must be made to correctly address anticipated loading.

A strip composite mast is built in two halves which are later joined. Set up a mold much as you would for a stripper canoe, except that it will only define half the spar. We suggest using ½ inch plywood for the formers, and that they be placed about a foot apart along a strongback as in Figure 12. Prepare desired stock for strip planking as described earlier in this chapter.

There are several ways to plank a strip spar. You can lay strips over your frames, spot bonding as you go, and then, when they are all in place, fill all the gaps with an epoxy/high density filler mixture in one operation. One builder reported that he was able to hold the strips in position with tape until he was ready to bond them. If you are reluctant to try one of these approaches, edge glue and staple the planking as you would on a stripper canoe.

When the resin between the strips has cured, remove the first mast half from the mold, and apply fiberglass to its inside. Make a second strip half, apply fiberglass inside, and then bond the two together. Fair the exterior surface and cover it with fiberglass cloth.

Chapter 21

The Stringer-Frame Method for Laminating Hulls

The advantages and disadvantages of the stringer-frame method for laminating hulls were discussed in Chapter 17. As we explained there, the stringer-frame system makes a framework which holds the skin in position and column to form a partial monocoque. It eliminates the need for a mold, permits installation of bulkheads and frames in the set-up, and produces hulls with excellent strength-and-stiffness-to-weight ratios. This method is particularly well suited to building long, narrow hulls with little compound curvature. The main drawback of the stringer-frame system is that you must begin laminating over a marginally adequate mold and take great care as you install the first two layers of veneer.

Frames for Stringer-Frame Construction

Many combinations of stringers and frames are possible, depending on the design, type and use of the boat. The most popular and perhaps easiest approach is to use web frames and bulkheads, both of which can be quickly and accurately sawn from commercial plywood, through the entire set-up. Later in this chapter we describe special I-beam framing which may be required in heavily loaded areas.

Frames serve two purposes: they form a mold until the hull is completed, and then they support the completed hull. Generally, in the stringer-frame method of laminating, frames are closer together than they are in the mold or strip plank methods. This is because the stringer-frame method uses relatively few longitudinal stringers to support the laminating process, while the other two methods use many stringers or planks. The long, narrow hulls typically designed for multihulls require numerous supporting web frames for rigidity and strength. In monohulls, with their fuller shapes, the need for supporting frames may not be as great, but a minimum number is necessary to support a set-up during building.

Web frames are cut from plywood, as opposed to laminated or sawn frames or plywood bulkheads. The thickness and width of web frames varies widely, according to the structural needs of the hull. Since the alternating grain of plywood veneers strengthens the frames in all directions, it's important to use balanced plywood with at least five alternating plies. A 3-ply

panel is usually much stronger in the direction of the two plies than in the direction of the middle layer. Even with balanced panels, it's important to lay out frames on the plywood so that its grain direction provides the greatest strength for a given frame shape.

With the stringer-frame method there is always a risk that a stringer may deform between frames during laminating. Deflection of even 1/16 inch presents significant fairing problems when the hull is finished, and ⅛ inch of dimensional change could be a disaster. Proper frame spacing and stringer size minimizes the possibilities of this sort of catastrophe.

The greatest distance between frames we've ever used was 24 inches, with 18 inch spacing being more common. If your permanent frames don't need to be this close together in the completed hull, use some temporary mold frames for molding support and remove them after the skin is laminated.

With the stringer-frame method, as with the strip-plank method, you can position prefinished bulkheads, frames, stem, keel and transom in the set-up with the temporary frames that are needed to support laminating. The only real difference is that instead of fastening stringers over the edges of the frames, as in the mold and strip plank methods, you notch them into all of the frames and bulkheads so that they are flush with the outer edges of these parts. Stringers are also let into the back of the stem, with their outer edges flush with the faired stem surface. Layers of hull skin are bonded to all of these parts and help to join them.

Stringers for Stringer-Frame Construction

Stringers, like frames, serve two functions. They, too form a reasonably substantial mold shape as the hull is built and support it when it is finished. It's difficult to temporarily reinforce stringers for laminating, so mold requirements supersede the requirements of the completed hull. Chances are that you will end up using more stringers than the structure actually needs in order to have a decent mold. Stringers may, however, be planed to smaller size after the hull skin has been laminated.

The main requirement of a stringer is that it not bend or deflect as veneer or plywood is bent around it during laminating. To minimize distortion, we always set

Figure 1—ROGUE WAVE's main hull set-up, stringers installed, and ready for planking.

stringers on edge, with the smaller dimension, or thickness, touching the skin, while the larger dimension, or depth, extends inward. A typical stringer for a 40 foot boat is 1½ inches deep and ¾ inch thick. We attach the ¾ inch side to the skin and run the 1½ inch side towards the interior. This makes a T-section which gives the completed hull great stiffness and strength. If the stringer was attached to the skin by its 1½ inch side, it would provide only about one third of the stiffness it offers in the ¾ inch dimension, and it would probably deform during laminating. This might lead to an unfair hull.

Since you will be stapling veneer and plywood to the edge of the stringer, it must be thick enough to permit stapling without a lot of *misses*. Although it's easy for a staple to miss even a thick stringer and missed staples can be removed before the next layer is applied, ¾ inch is a practical stringer thickness for stapling. We regularly, however, go down to ⅝ inch with little difficulty. Thinner stringers can be used, but may require very time-consuming and exact measuring to avoid misses.

Another consideration determining stringer size is the ability of the stringer to bend around the most severe curves in the hull shape. In certain situations, it may be necessary to laminate stringers out of two or three pieces to negotiate a curve. If so, use the set-up as a temporary form on which to clamp and form the laminate until the adhesive cures. Then remove the laminated stringer from the set-up and prefinish it prior to reinstalling it into the set-up. The laminated stringer has the big advantage in that it is sure to be very stiff and will resist deflection during the veneer laminating process.

Because of the variables involved, it is difficult to give advice as to stringer size adequate to resist deflec-

tion during laminating. Usually you can determine this for yourself by setting up a mock-up situation where you set a given size stringer between two points that would approximate the frame spacing. By bending some of the stock with which you plan to laminate over this stringer, you can get a general idea as to whether it will be adequate. As a general guideline, a 1½ inch by ¾ inch stringer is adequate for most laminating situations when used on frame spacings up to 24 inches.

The next decision is the spacing of the stringers along the frames. Initially it isn't a question of how many stringers are needed in the completed hull, but of the minimum number of stringers necessary for proper laminating to take place. Once again, the needs of the hull structure and those of the mold are different.

The main factor that determines stringer spacing is the shape of the hull itself. In areas with more curve, tighter spacing of stringers may be needed to define the hull shape properly, while flatter areas can rely on fewer stringers. When using *up to* 3/16 inch thick

Figure 2—Frames set up for proa SLINGSHOT. In this case, stringers for the bottom were marked off parallel from the chine and run out toward the keel. The single topside stringer was centered between sheer and chine.

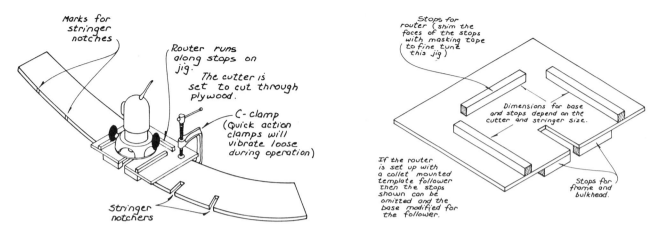

Marks for stringer notches

Router runs along stops on jig. The cutter is set to cut through plywood.

C-clamp (Quick action clamps will vibrate loose during operation)

Stringer notchers

Stops for router (shim the faces of the stops with masking tape to fine tune this jig)

Dimensions for base and stops depend on the cutter and stringer size.

If the router is set up with a collet mounted template follower then the stops shown can be omitted and the base modified for the follower.

Stops for frame and bulkhead.

Figure 3—Router jig for notching frames and deck beams prior to set-up.

laminating material, most stringers are spaced between 5 and 8 inches apart. If there are no sharp curves, it is possible to use even wider spacing than this, provided that thicker laminating material, such as ¼ inch ply, is used. For structural purposes, we have chosen our stringer spacings ranging between ten to twenty times hull skin thickness. For instance, stringers with 6 inch spacing with a ½ inch laminated skin would result in a spacing of twelve times skin thickness; a thinner ⅜ inch skin with the same stringer spacing would increase this ratio. Generally, it pays to be a bit conservative on stringer spacing, simply because stringers don't weigh very much and one or two more stringers per side add very little weight to the overall hull structure and can contribute measurably to a better molding surface.

On long, slim hulls without great amounts of compound curves, you can run stringers parallel to the sheer in succeeding rows. These will eventually run out at the keel in a curved arc. When the stringers are run parallel with the sheer, it is possible to prenotch all of the frames prior to setting them up. This can save a great deal of time in the long run because you can notch much faster at the bench than later, after the frames are set up. To do this, mark your standard spacing up from the sheer clamp on each frame, establishing the position of each stringer as it crosses the frame from the sheer all the way to the keel. Where it is feasible, we suggest using the router jig shown in Figure 3 to precut notches in frames.

More compounded hull shapes will not lend themselves to prenotching prior to set-up and the positioning of the stringers will have to be done more in accordance with the profile shape of the hull. Some hull shapes have curves around which the stringers can best negotiate at a given angle, and it is practicality that will determine stringer positioning. This same problem exists with the mold and strip plank methods, and has already been discussed. Here it is potentially more dif-

ficult because the stringers will tend to be larger, making them more difficult to bend than either the strips or planking used in the other methods. With heavily compounded shapes, it is also unlikely that the stringers will run parallel to one another. They will more likely taper toward each other as they go toward the bow or the transom from the middle spacing. This means that you may have to lay out each stringer individually to divide up the areas of the hull so that there is reasonably equidistant spacing between stringers. When spacing the stringers, pay special attention to any unusually hard curves in the hull. For example, the hard bulge created by the forward girth measurement point in a typical IOR rated ocean racer would be a problem area. In order to develop this very tight curve

Section through planking and stringers in "hard" bilge area.

Pressure from the planking forces the bilge stringer in and tends to force the stringers on either side out.

Solution is to increase the number of stringers in these high load areas

Figure 4.

according to the designer's lines, stringer placement is extremely crucial. Usually, you need up to three stringers to define such a tight curve properly, with the central stringer being in the exact apex of the curve and the other two being relatively close by to complete the definition of the arc over which the laminating material will follow. One of the problems caused by a hard bend is the extra loading that is applied to the stringers themselves. In this case, the central stringer takes all of the bending load and will tend to bend inward, while the stringers on either side that are holding the first lamination in the curved position will tend to deflect out when the lamination is attached to all three. If this is a problem, it is possible to support the stringers temporarily with supports from the floor or from the frames on either side. Another solution is to divide the bending load over two stringers rather than let one take the total load; thus you would have four stringers doing most of the work in defining a sharp bend, rather than just three.

Notching Frames for Stringers

When you have laid out all the stringer positions, check them with a batten for overall fairness. When you are satisfied with their placement, begin notching frames to receive stringers.

For this operation, we make up a marking gauge or fid, as shown in Figure 5. This is nothing more than a 3 or 4 inch long piece of the stringer stock we're using, with a slightly longer piece of plywood attached to the edge which ultimately faces the skin. The plywood pad extends a couple of inches beyond the stringer. In order to outline the stringer on a frame, we set the fid with the pad resting on the true edge of the set-up frame and the sample stringer flush against its side. It's important to make the gauge accurately, so that the stringer mark is perfectly square to the immediate perimeter of the frame on which it rests. We always mark stringer positions on all the frames with the stringer outline either above or below the mark on every frame. In other words, never draw the sur-marked position to the centerline of the stringer, but indicate that the mark is either the top or the bottom edge of the stringer.

When you have marked all of the stringer outline positions, you can begin notching. Many methods are used to notch frames to accept stringers. The simplest is to use a hand saw to saw along the sides of the marked notch down to and flush with the bottom of the notch. Make several more saw cuts in the center of the stock left in between the notch markings down to the bottom baseline. Then use a sharp chisel to cut

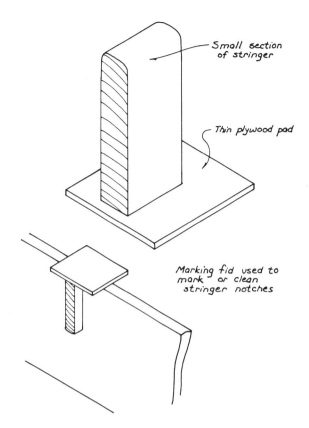

Figure 5—Marking gauge.

along the bottom of the mark in the slot on each side of the frame until you remove all material in the slot area. Until you get good with the saw, start by cutting the slots slightly undersize, and then file them out by hand to a snug fit with the stringer. Use a sample piece of stringer to check your notches. You can speed up the notching operation with the use of power tools, such as a reciprocating saber saw or a power circular saw with the blade set to the proper depth. We would advise caution in the use of either of these tools, however, because you need experience to perform accurate cuts.

Fitting and Fairing Stringers

An advantage of the stringer-frame method is that frames only need rough fairing as you set up. You can bevel and final fair the frames when you install the stringers. The stringers act as fairing battens: you can adjust them in and out of their notches to compensate for a frame which is too low or high at any point. If, as an example, a stringer makes a hard spot in one frame, correct it by filing its notch a little deeper until it lies fair. If, on the other hand, a stringer looks flat on a frame, shim it up in its notch with a small wedge.

During the process of fitting and fairing stringers in their notches, you will also fit the ends of the stringers to the stem and transom. You can cut triangular

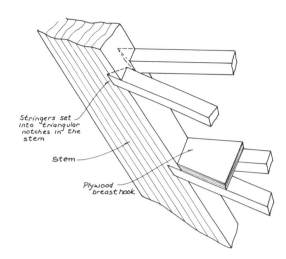

Figure 6—Fitting stringers to stem or stern post.

notches in the stem and fit stringers into them. We often notch stringers into the back of the stem lamination and then use triangular plywood breasthook-like gussets to make a triangular joint with the stringers on either side of the hull. With either method, fit the stringer at the stem and then set it into the notched frames working aft from the bow.

We usually notch stringers into a partial transom. Then, when the hull has been laminated, we add layers to the transom. We notch the partial transom and slip stringers into it in the same way we do with frames. However, if you have a full transom, you may want to cut triangular notches in it as you did the bow, so that the end grain of the stringers is not exposed.

When you have temporarily installed all of the stringers and they lie fair, mark them at various points so that you can remove them in preparation for final assembly. If you have not already done so, round off the exposed interior stringer edges between the frames, and sand and coat them. Prefinishing individual parts before they are installed is particularly important with this laminating method because a stringer-frame interior is difficult to coat and sand adequately later on.

Before reinserting stringers, apply a thick, high density epoxy mixture to the inside edges of all of the stringer slots in the frames. It is not necessary to apply resin to prefinished stringers before installing them, although in some situations coating both surfaces ensures better contact. If you have cut the notches carefully and the stringers fit snug, you will need very little outside help to keep the joints together until the adhesive cures. Usually, a few staples or a couple of clamps in the right places on each stringer will hold it in position. On permanent frames, remove all adhesive which squeezes out of the joints. We sometimes use this ex-

Figure 7—Fairing the molds on a stringer-frame set-up.

cess resin mixture to make small fillets between the stringers and frames to increase the bonding area.

In areas where the stringer is notched into a temporary frame, don't put adhesive in the notch because later you will want to remove the temporary frame

Figure 8—Stringers may be shifted slightly to facilitate bending, fitting or bonding.

without damaging the stringer. If the notch in the temporary frame fits tightly around the stringer, probably nothing else will be needed to hold the stringer in proper position; however, if it is a sloppy fit, further position the stringer with some fine cut wedges driven between the stringer and the gap that might exist on either side. In some cases, we have also used a small fillet, which we later chisel away, to hold a stringer rigidly to a temporary frame.

When all of the stringers are permanently installed, begin a final fairing of the entire hull surface. It is now very easy to bevel the frames, using the installed stringers as guides to achieve perfect bevels from frame to frame. If you have made any mistakes and have humps and hollows that need correction, these are still easy to take care of. Correct an offending high stringer or frame by planing it away until it fairs in with the rest of the hull. Correct stringers or frames that have low spots by laminating on a layer of ⅛ inch veneer or plywood and later fairing this addition in with the rest of the hull.

To the uninitiated, fairing intermittent stringers may seem difficult because most of the hull surface is still open space. With the strip plank or mold method, it is a little easier to sight along the hull because you are dealing with a solid surface that offers more telltale signs of humps and hollows that might be present. With the stringer-frame method, the planing that you do on one stringer or one frame affects a large surface

area in determining hull fairness. A good fairing batten and careful eyeballing will help you to achieve good overall fairness. Develop athwartship fairness by running the fairing battens at diagonal angles, as well as right angles, to the stringers. Check longitudinal fairness by sighting along your permanent stringers. In any areas of possible irregularity, clamp a large batten onto the offending stringer to see if it is, in fact, bending fair according to the batten. The favored tools for final fairing operations are a small hand held block plane, a smoothing plane (keep both fine set and very sharp), and an 11 inch, flat wood sanding block with 50 grit sandpaper.

I-Beam Frames

With the stringer frame system, it's possible to build a permanent, *I-beam-type frame*. The benefit of doing this is that it can greatly stiffen the hull locally while taking up little interior space. This type of framing is not usually required throughout a hull, but it can be very useful in an area of hard curves. We sometimes use it, too, for deck construction.

The I-beam frame has three parts: the load-bearing skin of the hull, a core composed of lightweight wood blocking and an interior load-bearing lamination. The blocking is inserted between stringers in the area of the frame. The lamination, which is formed in place over the stringers, is placed over stringers and bonded to the blocking. The sizes of blocking and lamination can be adjusted to handle anticipated loads. Because it is rarely subjected to high loading, we usually saw the blocking from low density wood stock, such as cedar, spruce or pine.

One way to build an I-beam frame is to insert the blocking between the stringers after final fairing of the stringers but before laminating the hull skin. We suggest fitting and bonding the blocking between stringers, flush on the interior and protruding enough past the hull profile for easy fairing for the planking. If you wait until after the hull is completed, and then try to fit the blocking from the interior, the job is much more difficult.

We usually do not install any blocking until the set-up has been finally faired. This way, we only have to fair it into the stringers to which it's attached. The blocking should also be faired smooth with the stringers on the inside surface to produce an even surface over which to laminate the third part of the I-beam. We make up and permanently install this piece before laminating the hull surface. (See Figure 9)

A second way to form an I-beam frame is shown in Figure 10. With this technique, saw a web frame flush

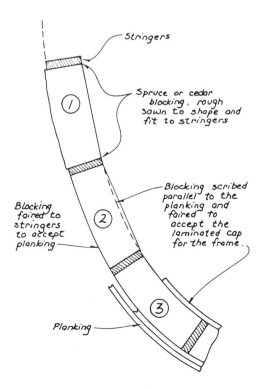

Figure 9—Blocking between stringers.

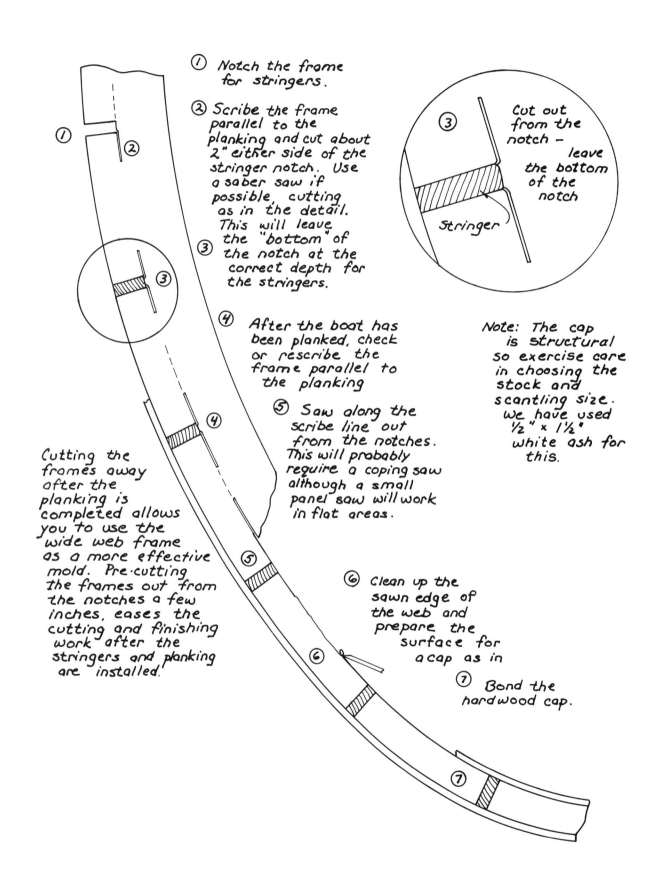

① Notch the frame for stringers.

② Scribe the frame parallel to the planking and cut about 2" either side of the stringer notch. Use a saber saw if possible, cutting as in the detail. This will leave the "bottom" of the notch at the correct depth for the stringers.

③ Cut out from the notch – leave the bottom of the notch

Stringer

④ After the boat has been planked, check or rescribe the frame parallel to the planking

⑤ Saw along the scribe line out from the notches. This will probably require a coping saw although a small panel saw will work in flat areas.

Note: The cap is structural so exercise care in choosing the stock and scantling size. We have used ½" x 1½" white ash for this.

Cutting the frames away after the planking is completed allows you to use the wide web frame as a more effective mold. Pre-cutting the frames out from the notches a few inches, eases the cutting and finishing work after the stringers and planking are installed.

⑥ Clean up the sawn edge of the web and prepare the surface for a cap as in

⑦ Bond the hardwood cap.

Figure 10—Making I-beam frame from web frame.

with the interior of the stringers, let the remaining plywood serve as blocking, and add a laminated frame to the interior. This will result in an I-beam which is probably stronger than the original web frame, but takes up less room.

To make a plywood web frame into an I-beam, fit and cut notches in the frame. Then saw starter cuts about 2 inches long on either side of each notch. Start each cut at the deepest part of the slot and run it parallel to the planking towards the next stringer. When you have finished laminating the hull, check the lines to be sure they are parallel to the planking, and then use a keyhole saw to connect them and cut away the excess frame. Use a spokeshave on the sawn plywood surface to fair it in with the interior stringer edges and bond the interior lamination in position.

Laminating on the Set-Up

The stringer-frame method offers a unique manufacturing opportunity: the stringers in the completed set-up can be used as a jig over which to laminate frames, interior sections of I-beam frames, keel floors, and any other parts which must be formed to the shape of the hull.

To laminate on the set-up, begin with rather thin, easily bended stock. Apply adhesive to all the strips needed for the lamination and wrap the pile in 4 or 6 mil polyethylene sheet, so that it can be handled without spreading epoxy on the set-up, framework, clamps or workers. Then clamp the stack to stringers in the area desired, adding several clamps between stringers for constant pressure to the laminate. We usually set up laminations as close as possible to frames so the stringers will be better supported and will not deflect under the pressure. If possible, choose a spot in the set-up with a little tighter curve than the piece you are laminating actually needs to have to compensate for springback.

As you laminate, take care to avoid damaging stringers and other parts of the set-up with clamps or resin. Cover vulnerable areas with masking tape and polyethylene sheet and use small plywood clamping pads to protect wooden parts. When the lamination has cured, remove it from the plastic and plane it to the shape and size desired. Final fit for positioning in the hull and prefinish the piece.

The First Lamination

Before laminating the hull skin over the completed stringer-frame assembly, carefully analyze the interior to identify operations which might be performed more efficiently now than when the hull is finished. The

Figure 11—Laminated floors over stringers. To ease the job of laminating and installing floor timbers, topside stringers have not yet been installed.

stringer-frame method requires that more attention be paid to this because the cluttered interior surface makes fitting interior items difficult. Laminated keel floors and frames, centerboard boxes, daggerboard trunks and interior furniture items are possibilities. Bunks, cabinets and other interior items are sometimes installed before the skin is laminated because they can be more quickly fit to and faired in with the overall set-up. The alternative is to fit these items later to a curved interior hull surface complicated with stringers and frames.

Figure 12—Positioning sheer clamp and topside stringers after installing laminated floors, blocking and first layer of plywood planking on bottom.

Several almost-complete interiors have been installed before any hull laminating, although in most cases this may not be possible. By comparison, the smooth interiors possible with the mold or strip plank methods are more easy to fit and join to than stringer-frame interiors.

The main purpose of the first lamination with the stringer-frame method is to provide an initial mold surface over which further laminations can take place. This first lamination can be either plywood or veneer. However, we much prefer plywood for this first layer for a number of reasons. Because the mold at this point must be considered inadequate, it is important to use the most stable laminating material available for the first layer to achieve the most solid and fair surface possible for further lamination. Plywood, because it is composed of at least three plies, is much more dimensionally stable in all directions than is veneer. Plywood also has the advantage that it already has sanded surfaces which are easily prefinished.

This is not to say that veneer cannot be successfully used; we have used it many times, as have many other builders. However, veneer does require a higher degree of skill. This is mainly due to the difficulty of controlling the unsupported edges of the veneer between the stringers. (They tend to curl one way or the other, requiring remedial action by the builder.) The stability of plywood makes prefinishing of the interior surface prior to installation practical, saving a good deal of interior finishing time later on. However, because of its unstable surface, we do not recommend that veneer be prefinished prior to application. The only advantages of veneer are that it may be a little bit lighter than plywood and is decidedly less expensive, but these advantages are greatly overshadowed by the extra work veneer requires on the first layer. With the second layer, veneers again become the preferred laminating material.

Since the object of the first layer is to make an adequate mold, you should apply the thickest layer of plywood you can for the stiffest possible mold surface. To help develop stiffness, run this first layer the shortest distance across the stringers, usually 90° to the stringer direction. The reasons for doing this are clear: if stringers are set at 6 inch spacing and the first layer of ply is installed at a 45° angle to them, 9 inches of wood grain will remain unsupported, while if the plywood grain runs at right angles to the stringers, there will only be 6 inches of unsupported wood fiber and the mold will be stiffer. The structural needs of the hull and the specifics of the building situation may make the ideal 90° angle impractical for your project, in which case you will have to make the best compromise you can.

Preparing Plywood Panels for the First Lamination

Using plywood for laminating poses an economic problem in the high waste caused by the limited 8 foot lengths in which plywood sheets are sold. We overcome this problem by sawing bevels on both ends of a

Figure 13—Coating 40 foot x 1 foot panels of planking stock. Scarfing together long lengths of planking stock like these cuts down on scrap rate.

4 foot x 8 foot sheet of plywood and then sawing the plywood into panels of the width desired for laminating. We next scarf together the individual panels, making plywood panels sometimes up to 40 feet in length from which we can cut proper laminating lengths. (See Chapter 10 for proper scarfing technique.) By taking measurements on the hull with a tape measure, we determine the panel length needed within a few inches and then rough cut this length from the long scarfed panel. The result is minimal (less than 5%) waste of plywood. With the high cost of plywood, the extra time required for scarfing usually pays big dividends.

After the scarf joints are completed, sand smooth the joining edges on both sides using either power or hand tools. Then precoat and sand all of the panels on one side prior to cutting to length and assembling them on the stringer-frame surface. While you can precoat the 4 foot x 8 foot sheet of plywood more quickly before you make the scarf joints and saw the panels into the desired width, this creates problems in that you must then make the scarf joints with great precision because the prefinished resin surface is more difficult to fair up to correct any minor misalignment.

The maximum plywood thickness which may be used in the first layer is determined by the hull curvature around which the panel will bend. Most hulls require plywood between ⅛ and ¼ inch thick, with 5/32 inch and 3/16 inch most commonly used.

The important thing to remember when choosing a thickness is that ¼ inch plywood is more than three times stiffer than ⅛ inch plywood and therefore much more difficult to bend over tight curves. Precoating with WEST SYSTEM* Brand epoxy will add to the stiffness and resistance to bending of a thin plywood panel. You might just make a radius with a given thickness of bare ply, but have the same piece break when you bend it around the same curve after it's been coated. With most of the hull area, this is not likely to be a problem, but there may be very tight spots where it's best to leave the wood uncoated to help in bending.

We have used one trick to bend a 3-ply panel around particularly sharp local curves without reducing its thickness. We scarf in a length of plywood with its grain running opposite the normal direction in the area of the curves and leave this section uncoated, so that it bends more easily. Later, coating both surfaces with resin will substantially improve the strength and stiffness of a "wrong way" piece.

Installing the First Layer

Assuming that you are applying the first layer at right angles to the stringers, start the master panel at a central location, as you would with the other hull laminating methods. Temporarily position it and mark its outline on the stringers and frames it covers. Apply a thick, high density epoxy mixture to all stringers, frames blocking, stem and keel surfaces which come into contact with this first panel. The adhesive should be so thick that it bridges any gaps, and, more importantly, does not run down any parts as it oozes from the joints.

Use either wide crown staples, which must be removed, or narrow crown alloy staples, which can remain in place, to hold the plywood in position until the adhesive cures. Narrow crown staples are faster because they don't have to be extracted, but they cost more and are more difficult to pull out when you miss a stringer. Insert the first staples at the edges of the panel where the stringers are easily visible. Then draw an accurate mark across the plywood panel to outline the exact locations of stringers for stapling within the panel.

With the stringer-frame method, proper spiling and fitting of the first layer are important for both aesthetic and structural reasons. The edges of the panels must be glued together to help form a rigid mold surface. They must fit well, and they should align themselves correctly between stringers where there is no support. The lay of the plywood strip is absolutely crucial to edge alignment. Pushing one edge of the ply in the wrong direction will result in pressures within the strip

* TRADEMARK OF GOUGEON BROTHERS, INC., U.S.A.

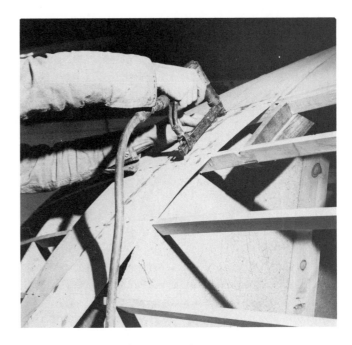

Figure 14—Stapling first layer of planking to topsides. Note laminated frame and blocking in upper right as well as limber holes cut in stringers next to blocking.

which will cause it to curl its edge away from its neighbor.

Spiling can be relatively easy with this method for laminating hulls. Overlap the plywood panels slightly as you hold them in temporary position, and then mark and scribe them from inside the hull, leaving small gaps in the marking where stringers are in the way. Use this line only for rough cutting because the overlap raises one panel edge higher than the other and the panels do not lie flush with the hull.

You can also use filler spiling systems with the stringer-frame method. Apply unspiled plywood panels at intervals down the hull as if you were using the mechanical spiling system described in Chapter 19. The gaps between panels should be just slightly smaller than the width of the panels that you are applying. Temporarily tack a standard width panel over a gap and mark both its edges for cutting and fitting from inside the hull. The advantage is that the filler panel overlaps the installed plywood panels on either side of it and lies reasonably true to the hull surface.

With the filler spiling system just discussed, you should begin final fairing in the middle of the panel. Plane the midsection edges of the filler panel so that it fits snugly in place and then work the ends of the panel in place, using a hand block plane lightly to remove material so that the panel will lie in best position and the edges will align properly. With the mold method, a "wild" edge can be tamed by applying enough staples to hold it in place until the adhesive cures. With the stringer method, you have nothing to staple to and can only rely on finessing the plywood panels into proper position so that the edges will line up by themselves.

The main disadvantage of the stringer-frame system is the extraordinary amount of time that you must spend in carefully fitting this very crucial first layer. We can't say forcefully enough, however, that taking the time to make sure that all of the edges between the plywood panels are not only well fit, but are properly lined and bonded with each other will save a great amount of time later on.

To edge glue the panels, use a well thickened high density resin mixture on both of the edges to be joined. A small brush or flat stick works well for applying the appropriate amount of epoxy, depending on the quality of the fit, directly to the edges. The difficult part here is matching the edges without getting epoxy all over the place. It's not so bad when you are applying resin to just one edge, but doing two edges at a time with the filler spiling system can be a bit messy.

After the plywood panels are stapled down, you will find that even with proper fitting and positioning there will be some misalignment of edges that will need to be corrected before the adhesive cures. Most edge misalignment is minor, requiring very little pressure to correct. There are two basic methods used to solve this

Figure 15—Transom of IOR ½ ton racer. Stapling pads align edges of plywood planks between stringers. Note staple lines along planking indicating stringer.

problem, both of which first require removing any excess adhesive from the edge joint areas on both the exterior and interior surfaces. The first method uses short staples and small scrap pieces of plywood that might measure 1 inch x 2 inches. Place the plywood pads directly in the area where misalignment is occurring. Position a staple through the plywood pad into the *low side* of the misaligned edges, drawing it up flush with the other edge. The staples should be short enough so that they will not protrude through the interior surface of this first lamination. (Use any number of these little plywood pads and staples wherever necessary.)

The second method is designed to solve more difficult alignment situations where maximum pressure is needed to bring the two ply edges into proper alignment. This method uses two opposing plywood pads approximately 1½ inches square. Drill a hole approximately the shank size of a number 8 screw on the pad to be used on the outside of the first lamination, and then drill a smaller pilot hole for a number 8 screw on the pad for the inside. Put a number 8 sheet metal screw with a washer through the outside pad through a hole drilled in the gap between the two misaligned edges of plywood to the inner pad, and screw both pads up tight until the edges are aligned.[1] This is a foolproof solution, but requires more time and energy than the staple method, and we only use it when absolutely necessary. With either method, use polyethylene sheet material or wax paper between the plywood tabs and the edges to prevent bonding between the two. However, even without protection, it is not a particularly difficult job to remove the plywood tabs with an offset chisel.

Another factor affecting edge alignment is the *width* of the plywood panel that is chosen. If a panel is too wide for the amount of compound curve present in the hull, the edges will tend to curl excessively between stringers. This not only contributes to edge alignment problems, but can cause extra work when fairing up prior to installing the second layer. The desire is always there to use as wide a width as you can get away with, so as to save some labor in fitting time by reducing the number of joints. However, with this method it is better to be a bit more conservative and use narrower panels than you might choose for the mold or the strip plank method; this might actually save time in the long run by reducing the labor needed to align the edges and fair the first lamination surface.

[1] There may or may not be a gap present between the plywood edges for misalignment to occur.

The first lamination of plywood is usually joined at the centerline along the keel, but this is not necessary if it would be advantageous — and the hull shape allows — it to join in another area, such as at a bilge stringer. As the panels run out at the transom, stem and sheer areas, allow a slight overlap of approximately 1 inch when trimming the ply so that you can laminate subsequent layers a slight bit beyond the actual hull. This will ensure good laminating pressure and a lack of voids in the completed hull when the edges are trimmed. Take extra care when bonding this first layer to the stem, keel and sheer. These are the critical joints in any boat; proper application of the first lamination to these members is always highly important.

Cleanup

If you want to achieve a nice looking, natural interior with the stringer-frame method of construction, proper cleanup is extremely important and, unfortunately, time-consuming. As plywood panels are installed over the stringer-frame support system, you must clean up the excess adhesive that exudes from the joints on the interior before it fully cures. Again, we must emphasize that the adhesive used should be thick enough so it will not run down the stringers or the plywood skin as it squeezes out from the joints because of the added cleanup difficulties this causes. It is not necessary that you remove the adhesive immediately; in fact, it is even a little easier to remove after it has started to stiffen or begun an initial cure. In this initial phase, the adhesive gets considerably thicker, losing some of its ability to adhere to other surfaces, and in this state it is easiest to remove. If you allow the cure to go beyond this state, removal of the adhesive becomes increasingly difficult and is all but impossible when the resin reaches a semi-rigid state. Depending on the temperature that you are working in and the cure rates you are getting with your resin mixture, you should plan your work so that you clean up at given intervals during the laminating process. If two or more people are applying the plywood strips on the exterior surface, interior cleanup can require the services of one person full time to keep up.

Cleanup is simpler and more efficiently done on prefinished interior surfaces. You can remove most of the excess adhesive that squeezes out of a joint using an inch-wide putty knife or a squared-off and sharpened piece of flat stick (such as a tongue depressor) that is approximately 1 inch wide. Deposit the excess adhesive, as it is removed from the joint, into a pot, scraping the blade edge reasonably clean on the lip of the pot. Occasionally, wipe the implement with a rag and solvent to remove excess adhesive that is starting to cure.

For the final cleaning operation, use a good solvent. Wash joint areas with a solvent-soaked lint-free rag to remove excess adhesive and to smooth out any leftover resin so you won't have to sand it later. Excess epoxy will mix with the solvent in the rag. This, combined with the wiping action, leaves the surface smoother than if it was sanded. Many solvents, including denatured alcohol, work well. Take appropriate precautions to prevent inhalation of solvent fumes.

During the cleanup operation, you will want to make sure that the gaps between the plywood panels are well-filled and relatively smooth. Sometimes the gaps may be so wide that the final wiping operation will remove too much resin from the gap area. When this happens, trowel some adhesive into the joint, allowing any excess to exude through onto the exterior surface, and then rely on hand sanding after the filler has cured to smooth up the interior surface area around the joint. It is important to check these edge joints between the panels carefully, because any gaps that are left unfilled can become potential points for resin to bleed through and run down into the interior when you apply the second layer.

When the first lamination is completed and the epoxy has cured, remove all alignment pads and temporary staples to prepare for rough fairing. Do this as you would on any other hull, but use sharp hand planes instead of sanding tools because the stringer-frame surface will be somewhat springier than the steadier surfaces produced by other methods. The first layer of a stringer-frame hull sometimes resists good fairing with a sanding block, but its springiness doesn't affect fairing with a sharp smoothing or block plane.

It's not unusual to find some low spots which need filling. Mix low density filler and epoxy to make a sandable fairing putty, and use this to fill these areas and any other voids. Take special care with voids which go all the way through to the first layer: fill them so that adhesive cannot seep through to the interior when you apply the second lamination.

Applying the Second Layer

When you have rough faired the first layer and are ready to apply the second, be sure that all stringer locations are marked on the outside of the first layer so you will know exactly where to staple. We generally mark stringers on each panel as we install it, and most of these marks survive rough fairing.

Before applying the second layer, give the first layer a coating of WEST SYSTEM resin to add stiffness and make it a more rigid surface for stapling. Allow this to cure, and lightly sand with a light duty polisher and foam disc pad. The coated surface also has better staple holding power, and this helps you develop more pressure as you install the second layer. A final benefit is that you will now have to apply epoxy only to the bonding surface of the second layer, rather than to both the first and second layers. This saves some time and a good deal of mess.

We generally apply a bit more adhesive to the second lamination than normal to try to make up for two possible deficiencies. The first layer will not have the high quality fairness achieved with the mold and strip plank methods, so we rely on thickened resin to fill some of the voids and hollows which may be present. The second and more difficult problem is that only limited pressure can be applied to some areas of hull as the second layer is installed. This means that the resin applied to the second layer should be free-flowing, not too thick but able to fill voids. We use low density filler mixed with resin to a thick consistency. In areas where we anticipate major voids, we apply large quantities of thickened resin to both the first and second layers to ensure that gaps will be filled.

You can do the second lamination with veneers instead of plywood with no difficulties. The general instability of the veneers is no longer a problem due to the fact that you now have a reasonable mold surface to staple to. Begin the second lamination in normal fashion by placing the master veneer in the central area of the hull at whatever diagonal angle you desire. Position succeeding layers of veneer on either side of this master, using either the hand or mechanical spiling system for fitting the edges. The only thing that is different from standard procedure is the stapling method used to bond this second lamination to the first lamination.

The areas where the stringers and frames are supporting the first lamination are the only really solid points on the mold surface and you need to utilize them well when bonding the second lamination to the first.

After you have positioned the veneer and attached it at the sheer clamp, keel, stem, transom and all other solid points, deal with areas between these members. To apply adequate pressure to these spots, use staples which are short enough so they don't penetrate the interior and leave holes which will need filling. If your first lamination was 5/32 inch plywood and your second layer is ⅛ inch veneer, you can successfully use ¼ inch long wide crown staples to achieve reasonable pressure without stapling into the interior.

Because the springiness of the mold will not permit

countersinking, all of these in-between staples will have to be removed. Use scrap veneer or plastic stapling strips to save time. If your staples are too long and break through the inner surface, adjust the depth of penetration by using thicker stapling strip material or by doubling standard plastic banding.

The best way to insert shorter staples in springy areas is to hold the staple gun firmly, with higher-than-normal pressure, on the veneer surface. The extra pressure helps the staple sink itself to the crown for maximum clamping between the two layers. Remember that you are applying the pressure and all the staple does is maintain it. If you hold the staple gun too lightly, the staples will not reach proper depth and will not have adequate holding power. If the stringers are relatively close and there is a fair amount of curve in the hull surface, you may need very few staples between them because the veneers themselves will develop sufficient bonding pressure.

You can generally tell whether a veneer is lying tight enough for good bonding by pressing it with your fingers in any suspect area during the laminating process. Any gaps between the veneers will move in and out with light finger pressure. Gaps are also likely to make a slight noise as the excess resin moves around. When in doubt, staple; no boat ever suffered from too many staples, but there have been a few which suffered from voids.

Depending upon the spacing of the stringers, we usually apply two to three short staples along all of the edges of the veneers where they meet between the stringers. These are usually the last staples applied in the lamination; this gives excess resin a chance to work its way out of the center areas of the veneer toward the edges before we apply pressure at this edge point. Sometimes there may be a wild edge or a warp in the veneer that fails to come down in position with the limited pressure that a short staple can apply. Solve this problem by having someone temporarily hold a small wood block on the interior side of the two laminations so that you can shoot a long staple through the first and second laminations and draw them together tight with the temporary block.

Checking the Second Layer for Voids

After the resin has cured and you have removed the wide crown staples, make a thorough check of the second lamination to detect any voids that may have developed between the two laminations. To do this, lightly move your hand over the hull surface and listen for a different sound than is usual for most of the surface. An area of veneer that is not well bonded to that beneath it will vibrate at a different frequency, producing a definite, higher pitched sound than that produced by veneers which are well bonded. Mark these suspect areas on the hull.

There are two ways to fill voids. The first, which is easier if you plan to laminate several more layers, is to cut out and remove the unbonded veneer. Fill the resulting gap with a thick mixture of epoxy and equal parts of high and low density filler. When this mixture cures, fair the surface smooth and apply more veneer over it. The second method to fill voids is to inject resin with a syringe into the immediate area of the void. If it is large enough, drill several holes at various points in the void to make sure that you are indeed filling it solidly with resin.

Once you have determined that the second layer is structurally sound, you will find that the hull surface is very rigid, creating a solid mold surface over which you can apply succeeding laminations easily in the normal manner as with the mold or strip plank methods. The only caution is that you should apply the third layer using staples that are short enough not to break through the prefinished interior surface. Refer to the earlier chapters on laminating procedure for a complete description of fairing and finishing techniques. The stringer-frame hull is rolled over in the same way as the strip plank hull.

Chapter 22

Hard Chine Plywood Construction

Hulls with round sections can be laminated with veneer or strips of plywood. Over the years, however, we have also used WEST SYSTEM* Brand epoxy with sheet plywood to produce hard chine hulls. Many hull shapes are well suited to sheet ply construction. Since plywood is already laminated, great savings in labor and possibly in materials result when it can be used in sheet form to build a hull.

The introduction of low-cost, plywood panels has been one of the most significant developments in wooden boat construction. Shortly after World War II, sheet plywood began to be widely used in all types and sizes of custom-built and mass-produced boats. It was immediately accepted because of its high strength-and-stiffness-to-weight ratios, its dimensional stability, its multidirectional strength and its convenient 4 foot x 8 foot size from which parts could be easily cut. The high pressure and good adhesives used in manufacturing plywood produce a high quality laminate.

Without question, the use of plywood has contributed to quality boat construction. The material is not, however, perfect. Plywood boats have had serious maintenance problems and, in many cases, short life spans. These deficiencies have been so severe that some boats specifically designed for plywood construction — the very popular *Sunfish*™ and *Sailfish*™ sailboats, are good examples — are now built with fiberglass, which is often heavier. Fiberglass was substituted for plywood not because it has superior physical properties, but because it is relatively easy to maintain. We solve many of these maintenance and longevity problems by using WEST SYSTEM epoxy in sheet ply construction.

Our hard chine construction methods differ from standard techniques most significantly in that we use resin to join all hull pieces and parts, while more traditional builders use screws, nails and mechanical fasteners. In the past, resorcinol or urea type adhesives were commonly used with fasteners, but no one expected the adhesive alone to provide necessary joint strength. Total bonding, in which 100% of each and every joint is made with a mixture of epoxy and filler, is now not only structurally possible, but often the easiest and least expensive way to join plywood panels.

Our methods also depart from typical plywood hard chine construction in their emphasis on coating and sealing. We coat all plywood with epoxy both during and after construction, encapsulating the wood to stabilize its moisture content and to protect it from the harmful effects of moisture. We can produce very light, stiff, strong and long-lived hulls by using the bonding and sealing qualities of WEST SYSTEM resin in combination with good plywood and lumber.

Best of all, sheet plywood is probably the easiest and fastest material to work with when building a hard chine hull. There are a number of reasons for this. For instance, the lofting of a hard chine boat is greatly simplified because most of its surface area is in a one-dimensional plane. When lofting a hull which has compound curvature, you must define all points on its surface, but with a hard chine hull, you only need to define the location of the chine, keel and sheer points on the lofting board. This simplifies and greatly speeds up the lofting process and enables you to develop a body plan in a fraction of the time normally required for a typical rounded hull shape. In addition, the time needed to mark, cut and assemble mold or permanent frames is greatly reduced because the process is much easier.

Frame Assembly

In other boatbuilding methods, mold frames are removed when the hull is finished. In hard chine construction, however, most frames stay permanently in the boat because the flat planes of plywood hulls usually require the support of substantial framework for adequate stiffness. Although frames can be made of plywood, the straight sections of hard chine hulls often make straight stock a better choice structurally and economically.

Usually, we decide early in the project on a standard size of frame material (1 inch x 3 inch stock is typical). Two main factors which determine the size of the frame material are the weight and size of the boat and the dimensions of the stringers and chines that will be notched into the frames. A notched frame must retain adequate load-bearing capacity. For example, if you are going to set 1½ inch x ¾ inch stringers on edge into 3 inch x ¾ inch frames, you can only count on 1½

* TRADEMARK OF GOUGEON BROTHERS, INC., U.S.A.

inches of the frame material to be load-bearing until the outer skin is applied. You will have to decide whether the 1½ inches of unnotched frame stock is adequate for your particular situation.

After you have decided on a standard dimension for the frame material, proceed to prepare enough of the desired stock to make all of the frames in the boat. In many cases, you can save time by rounding over (or "radiusing") what will be the interior edge, and then sanding and precoating all of the frame stock before it is sawn and assembled into frames. However, in some cases it may be easier to perform these finishing operations after you have assembled the frames.

All the frame joints which will meet either at a chine or keel must be at least as strong as the timber stock that is being joined. A joint system that we have used with great success consists simply of butt fitting the two pieces of timber together and then covering each side of the frame with a gusset of plywood. Orient the grain of the gusset so that each ply crosses the joint at a 45° angle, thus giving maximum strength. For accuracy, this assembly is best done in a two-step operation. First, cut the frame stock to proper size and take care to fit the individual pieces of the frame together, using nicely fitted butt joints as the only contact between the individual pieces. To ensure accuracy, temporarily position the pieces on a developed *full size* body plan from the lofting floor or a full size frame pattern that has been transferred to either paper or Mylar™, and use the full size lines as guides to lay out the frames. When you have fitted all of the individual joints to your satisfaction, insert wax paper or a thin polyethylene sheet under the edges to be joined to prevent any bonding with the surface on which the fitted frame stock is resting. Then coat the butting edges of the frame pieces with adhesive and reassemble them on the body plan surface. Hold the frame pieces in perfect position using small nails (around the perimeter) or weights until the adhesive cures.

Next, install plywood gussets at each joint on one surface only. The size and thickness of the gusset material are usually in proportion to the size and thickness of the timber stock used for the frames. Typically, we use ¼ inch to ⅜ inch thick plywood gussets on ¾ inch thick frame material. At the present time there are no scantling rules worked out on this relationship, but if you are in doubt, make a sample frame joint and try to break it. If a break occurs in the joint, make the gusset bigger.

Because we use gussets of a few standard radii, we can round and sand their edges and precoat them before installation on the frames. It's not necessary to make them as circles, but as much standardization of gusset size and shape as possible saves a great deal of time and labor. Study the lofting of your frames to determine the best gusset shape for your boat.

Use a high density adhesive mixture to bond the gussets and use either clamps or staples for temporary pressure. Clamps are simpler to use, so choose them wherever possible. If you are stapling, use either narrow crown alloy staples or wide crown staples. The former can be left in the hull, but the latter should be removed when the resin has cured. Be sure that any staples left in place are clear of areas which will be notched or beveled.

After applying the gussets to one side at each joint, install a spall, following instructions in Chapter 14, for additional support in the upper half of the frame. Use temporary diagonal bracing if you are working with a particularly large or unwieldy frame. This will help

Figure 1—Typical frame assembly showing gussets, filler blocking and position of structural members.

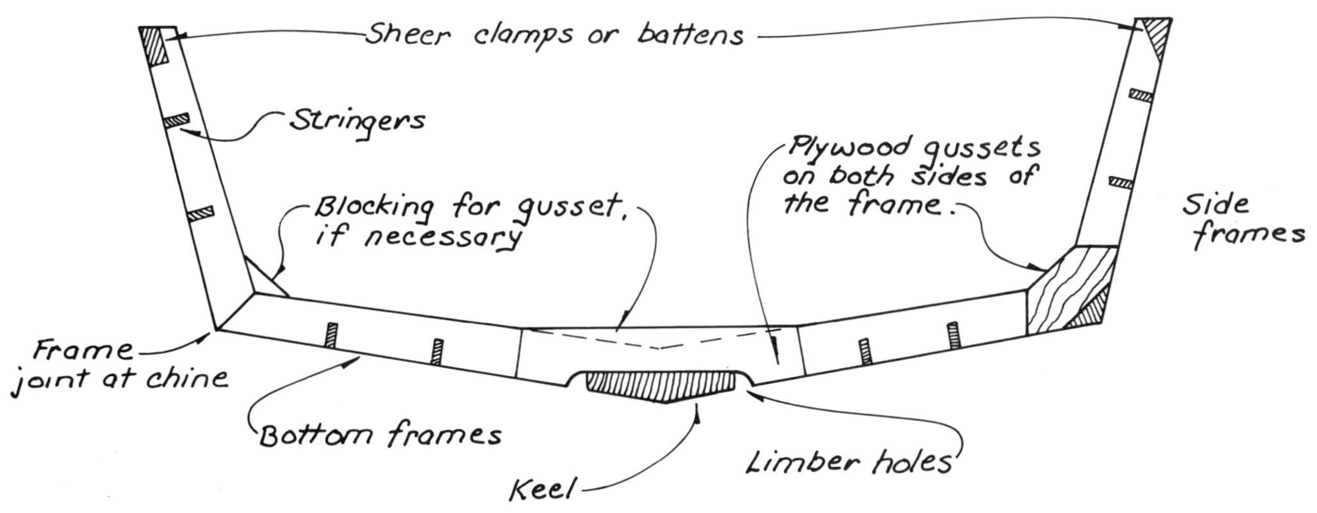

maintain accuracy when you turn the assembly over to attach gussets to the other side.

When you have installed gussets on both sides, reposition the frame on the body plan and check it for accuracy. Mark the centerline, appropriate waterlines and sheer measurements just as you would in the typical frame assembly procedure discussed in Chapter 14. It's convenient to lay out, cut and finish limber holes in the frames at this point.

Prefinish the frames as much as possible before installing them in the set-up. You may want to do this before marking the centerline, waterlines and sheer for the set-up. If you have already prefinished frame and gusset stock, touch it up to make sure that all surfaces are coated.

Setting Up

The process of setting up hard chine frames is identical to the standard procedure explained in Chapter 15. In practice, hard chine frames are easier to work with than regular frames because the chines serve as reference points for checking for minor errors in frame location. In some cases, the frames between the chine and keel will be straight, but in areas where the hull twists or flares out abruptly, such as the forward sections of a power boat, frames are designed to curve and accept the developed shape of the plywood.[1]

It's also considerably easier to fair hard chine frames than it is to fair frames for hulls with round bilges. In the initial stages of fairing, only the keel, chine and sheer areas are important. Lay a batten halfway between the

Figure 3—In this set-up for a hard chine trimaran hull, the builder has installed chines and is fairing frames.

chine and keel or the chine and sheer and make necessary corrections on the frames. Move the batten in either direction to check the bevel of the frames, and lay another batten on them from chine to keel and chine to sheer to check for irregular curves.

When the set-up is complete and the frames are finally faired, install the stem, keel and transom as described in Chapter 16. Sheet plywood construction is similar to the stringer-frame method in that it uses frames and stringers to support a thinner skin, but there are two major differences between the techniques. With sheet plywood, stringers are not always needed for support during building. Very little loading develops on any one stringer when plywood is applied over a hull surface, so generally there is little cause for concern about deforming stringers. Stringer size can therefore be based on the structural needs of the hull skin rather than on mold requirements.

The second difference is in the use of *chine logs*, longitudinal members which act as stringers for structural support at the chine joint and are critical for joining panels. In hard chine plywood construction, chine logs provide enough bonding area for holding the panels together and protect potentially vulnerable

Figure 2—Load-bearing bulkheads can be made from two pieces of thinner plywood with framework sandwiched in between. Bulkhead arrangement shown above handles main beam loads from trimaran outriggers.

[1] In cases like these, the hull is formed as a series of cones and/or cylinders. The plywood is still straight along certain elements, but these elements may no longer be parallel to the frames. The design of developed skin plywood hulls can be complex. For further information, we recommend *Modern Boatbuilding* by Edwin Monk. Charles Scribner's Sons, N.Y., 1973, or *Skene's Elements of Yacht Design* by Francis S. Kinney, Dodd, Mead & Company. N.Y., 1973.

areas of the hull. Chine logs should produce joints which are potentially stronger than the plywood.

As Figure 4 indicates, there are many successful ways to make chine joints. The sharp edges which usually result from these techniques do, however, obstruct hydrodynamic flow, and this is a major disadvantage of hard chine construction. Rounding sharp edges minimizes the problem, but requires innovative joining techniques which can provide large radii without compromising joint strength.

Some designs, such as the International Fireball dinghy, have two chines, each with flatter angles, on either side of the hull. These tend to expose a large amount of end grain on the overlapping plywood. The usual procedure was to avoid exposing end grain on the bottom of the boat, so the bottoms were put on last and the end grain exposed only on side surfaces. End grain well encapsulated in WEST SYSTEM epoxy has proven very tough and resistant to abrasion. Chines in this type of hull do, however, receive more abuse than any other parts of the hull and it may be worth adding glass cloth to more vulnerable joint areas to increase abrasion resistance if hard usage is expected. Glass tape, available in 3 inch and 6 inch widths, can be applied to chines and keels without a great deal of extra work.

To make a typical triangular chine log as shown in Figure 4, begin by rough-shaping the chine stock as close as possible to finished dimensions. Then scarf it to the proper length and attach it to the frames in the set-up. Notch each frame to allow the chine log to sit in position for final fairing. To speed up the notching process, make a small marking guide from a piece of sawn-off chine stock. As you lay out the notches, be careful to adjust for any twist in the chine as it extends from the bow to the mid-section and back to the transom. The angle of each frame at the chine will be different and you will have to shift the angle of the chine log to compensate. Divide the angle change at each frame so that you won't increase bonding area on one side at the expense of the other. You can get good indications of the angle change and notching depth from the body plan on the lofting board.

When you have completed the notching and fitting of the chine, bond it to the frames, using clamps for temporary pressure until the adhesive cures. Steel wood screws that are later removed are a good alternative if clamps are impractical. Staples are rarely used, because they will interfere with the heavy fairing that follows after the chine is permanently bonded in position. Because the chine in many boats is considered a major structural element, it is usually well fitted to the stem and transom. This is usually accomplished in the

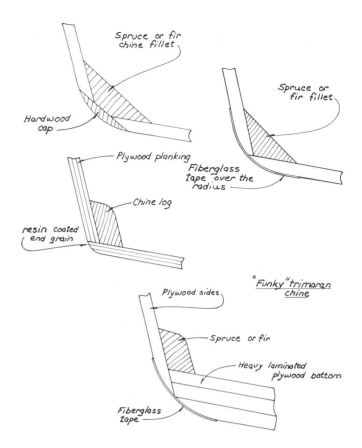

Figure 4—Typical chine joints.

stem by notching, but it can also be butted, provided that there is sufficient bonding area. Chines are always notched into the transom. Use either a triangular notch or a full notch, but the chine should not pass through the transom, exposing end grain. Bevel the chines using the same techniques used to bevel the keel as explained in Chapter 16. At each station where the chine intersects the frame, make saw cuts in the chine which represent extensions of the frame on either side of the chine. Then notch the chines down to their true shape at each frame station, as illustrated in Figure 5.

With most hulls it is then relatively easy to achieve a rough bevel on the chine using the notched-in bevel at each station frame as a guide. Assuming that the chine itself is bent around the frames in a fair curve, you can use the edge of the chine like a batten to determine whether your bevel is continuing fair from frame to frame. To assist your eye in determining this fairness between frames, you can lay a fairing batten directly on the chine and hold it temporarily with clamps to detect any high or low spots and mark them for further fairing. If there are unusually large spacings between frames it can be very helpful at this point to install any longitudinal stringers that are planned. Once the

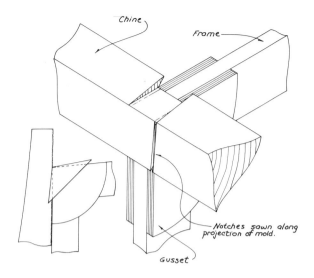

Figure 5—Notching the chine at the frames.

stringers are installed, you can use them as helpful guides to assist with the development of the chine bevel. Two or more stringers notched into the flat area of the frames between, say, the chine and the keel will act as excellent guides to help develop the true surface over which the exterior plywood panels will lie. You can use a straightedge to make a fair extension of the stringers down to the chine, indicating both the position and exact angle of the bevel on the chine at any point between frames. You can use the same technique, of course, to achieve proper bevels on both keel and sheer clamps.

Typically, the stringers are positioned across the frames parallel to the sheer at the desired intervals so that they run out at the chine, intersecting with the chine itself. This is not always necessary, and with certain types of chine systems, it is better to run the stringers parallel with the chines, allowing them to run out at the sheer and/or keel. As with rounded hulls, you can also position the stringers so that they taper toward each other as they enter the bow and transom area.

When the framework is finished, use a straightedge to final fair the flat surfaces between the chine and keel and the chine and sheer (and the chine and chine on a multiple chine hull). At no point should any of the athwartship frame edges be even slightly higher than any of the longitudinal members. This is especially important if you are using thinner plywood for the exterior skin because slightly high frames tend to produce a slight athwartship distortion which may be noticeable in the finished hull. Edges which are too low may also distort the hull shape.

Use a fairing batten and a piece of plywood measuring approximately 1 foot wide and 4 feet long to determine overall fairness in both directions. The plywood gives an indication as to how the panel will

actually lie when it is installed on the frame surface. Because you will be fairing flat surfaces, longer hand planes, such as jack planes, are very handy for final fairing.

Some boat plans may call for compounding or bending of the panels in two directions at the same time. You can accomplish this by curving the frames slightly between plywood joint positions, thus making the plywood bend in both directions. While this compounding does add to the stiffness of a plywood panel, difficulty can quickly arise if caution is not used on hard chine frame-supported plywood structures. Usually, the hard chine method of construction is chosen because of its ease and simplicity, and when you try to compound or bend plywood in two directions on a frame-supported surface, unwarranted complications can develop that can easily nullify any benefits gained. There are excellent and simple methods of compounding plywood which are explained in Chapter 23, but this compounding is done using a unique concept, where the compounded plywood surface does not have to be made to fit a preformed framework. (Also see discussion of compounding sheet plywood on decks and cabin tops in Chapter 25.)

Fitting Panels

You must first decide how large a plywood panel you can apply easily at one time. Generally, this depends on the size of the boat you are building. With smaller dinghies, it is common to apply a complete prescarfed panel over one section of the hull in one bonding operation. With larger boats, it will be easier to install smaller panels and perform the scarf joint assembly right in place on the boat hull, as discussed in Chapter 10.

Other benefits in using shorter panels include ease of handling and more efficient use of material because shorter panels create less scrap and are easier to mark and fit prior to final application. In any case, a 16 foot long panel is about the maximum length that you will want to install on any hull at one time. Our experience has been that it takes a very organized and coordinated effort by a number of people to apply large panels and to do a good job both in installation and cleanup. The main problem is time. You need time to apply adhesive to all of the stringers, frames, chines, keel, stem, etc. More time is required to position the panel and apply proper clamping pressure with staples. Even after the panel is in final position, a little more time will be needed to clean up the excess adhesive that squeezes out between the ply and the framework before it cures.

When scarfing in place on a hull, it's usually best to locate joints over bulkheads, frames and other solid components. If you are using plywood which is at least ⅜ inch thick, however, and have ample longitudinal stringers for support, it's possible to scarf anywhere without the totally-rigid support of a frame or bulkhead. With thinner plywood, you can scarf over temporary, plastic-wrapped butt blocks if a frame or bulkhead isn't handy.

There are a number of ways to mark panels for rough sawing and accurate scarf alignment. The easiest method is to clamp a sheet of plywood over the area it will cover and adjust it for minimal waste. Then draw pencil lines on the underside of the panel, using the chine and keel or sheer and chine as guides. Cut the sheet and check again for fit, and mark stringer and scarf locations. To speed things up later, tack the panel in place for this fitting and leave the nails in the plywood to help align it. Surmark the panel to facilitate installation. (See Figure 6.)

Scarfs should be evenly centered on frames. To pin down their locations, first determine the length of the scarf bevels. This should be eight times the plywood thickness, so if you were applying ¼ inch plywood the joint would be 2 inches long. To mark a 2 inch scarf on the panel, lay it out so that it centers on a ¾ inch thick frame and its edges extend ⅝ inch on either side. When the two panels are marked, saw the plywood along the scarf edges and machine the 8 to 1 bevel.

If fitting whole panels to your hull is impractical, use heavy brown paper to transfer the panel shape quickly from the framework to the sheet ply. Lightly staple the brown paper over the framework and trace the outline of the framework area that the panels are to cover. Remove the paper from the framework and cut out the marked perimeter. Then transfer the outline to the sheet ply. Because this method may be less accurate, leave a little larger safety margin beyond the marked edge as you are sawing out the panel. Position this rough cut panel on the hull and mark accurately for scarf joint location and any other marking that might be helpful (perhaps noting a gap area that may require more adhesive). Surmark the panels so that you can reposition them easily and accurately when you are bonding them in place.

It doesn't appear to be important whether you install the bottom panels or the side panels on a hull first. Ease in application and in cleaning up excess resin should be the determining factors. Normally, we prefer to apply the hull bottom (top when the hull is inverted) panels first, only because we can step in between the frames to get closer to the keel area.

When the panels are fitted and ready for installation,

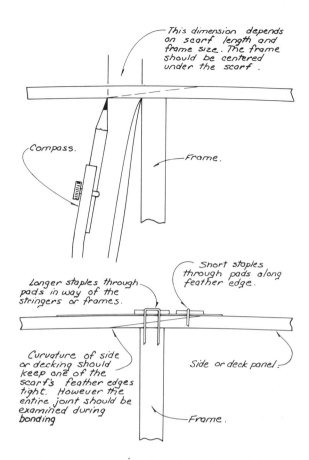

Figure 6—Marking and bonding plywood scarf joints on hull.

we always precoat and then sand the interior surface of each panel prior to installation. This saves on interior finishing time later on. An alternative to coating individual panels after they are cut out is to coat entire sheets of plywood prior to cutting out the individual panels. Although this method involves some waste, it can save time.

Marking Panels for Stapling

When bonding the panel to the general framework, you need to know where all of the stringers, frames and chine positions are so that you can accurately and quickly staple the panel to the framework in exactly the right places. To do this, mark the positions of all of the framework on the outside of the panel so that you can staple along these lines with accuracy. One of the advantages of running the stringers parallel with the chines or sheer is that you can make up a marking gauge to transfer the chine and stringer locations quickly to the sheet ply after it is applied in position. (See Figure 7.)

Another method is to draw the stringer locations on the interior of the ply, preferably after prefinishing it. Then transfer the marks to the outside by measuring from a point on the panel edge to a marked position or by drilling very small holes in the stringers and connecting them with lines on the panel exterior. Whatever marking technique you use, be accurate. Although missed staples can be removed and repaired, this takes time. Many missed staples can create substantially more work than the little effort needed to properly mark stringer and frame locations.

Applying Panels

Use a high density adhesive mixture slightly thicker than heavy syrup to bond the panels to the framework. If you have larger gaps to fill, you may need adhesive with a thicker, peanut butter consistency. Wash off precoated surfaces to remove dust and dirt and apply thickened epoxy to all joints. If the panels have not yet been coated, roll standard epoxy on any bare bonding surfaces before applying the thickened mixture. Use enough thickened adhesive so that some squeezes out of the joint. This indicates a 100% bond.

It usually takes at least two people to maneuver a panel. Try to avoid dragging it across the framework and smearing the epoxy all over. If you have tacked the panel for fitting and have left the nails in place, line them up with their holes and insert them. If you do not have the nails to guide you, line up surmarks and insert one or two locating staples at various central points on the panel to hold it in a general position while you check that everything fits as it should.

With sheet plywood we prefer to use narrow crown alloy staples which can be left in place. Narrow crown staples cause less damage to the plywood and, if they are slightly recessed, their holes are easier to fill and fair over for a smooth, easy-to-finish surface. Staples left in

chines may cause problems if you round over the joints, so use wide crown staples in this situation and remove them before you begin shaping. Difficulties may also develop at the keel and stem areas of certain types of boats.

Staples which are three times as long as the thickness of the plywood are usually adequate to hold the ply as it bends over moderate curves. In areas where the curve is so sharp that staples cannot hold the panel, use screws and large washers or other suitable types of pads for temporary clamping pressure and to distribute load until the adhesive cures. You can use nails with plywood pads, but we are not keen on the idea of using alloy boat nails and leaving them permanently in the hull. The main difficulty with boat nails is that their heads tend to show in the joint and greatly detract from a good surface finish.

After you have successfully bonded one panel to the framework, immediately clean up the excess adhesive that has squeezed out from between the joints. (See Chapter 21 for further discussion of cleanup procedure.) Installation of the second panel becomes more complicated because of the added difficulty of performing the bonding operation on at least one scarf joint at the same time that you are installing the panel. You should have already prefit and cut the scarf joint on this second panel. (Remember, with prefinished panels, you must cut the scarf joint on the opposite surface of the plywood on the second panel in order for the scarf bevels to mate.) With the second panel it is worthwhile to make a dry run to check the surmarks and make sure that alignment in the scarf joint is still accurate. Note any differences and change the surmarks to ensure an accurate final installation. Be very critical of your scarf joint alignment to prevent any misalignment of the beveled scarf cut on either panel which would cause unfairness in the skin. Because scarfing in place on the hull is a little more difficult than in a more controlled situation, we always provide a safety margin by applying an excess amount of adhesive to both beveled surfaces of the panels to be joined.

Pay special attention as you apply pressure to the scarf. Staple through a plastic-covered strip of plywood slightly wider than the joint for more uniform pressure over its surface. Use staples, nails or screws to apply maximum pressure through the joint to a solid member under it. To bring the exterior edges tightly together, use shorter staples which do not penetrate through the plywood. The interior edges of the scarf will probably need relatively little pressure because the curvature of the hull usually squeezes them together. If they do not fit tightly, remove excess adhesive and bring them to-

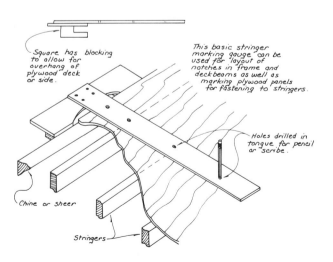

Figure 7—Gauge for marking stringer position on decks or side panels.

Figure 8—Applying adhesive mixture before bonding a panel to framework. Panel, lying against frames in foreground, will be scarfed in place.

gether with a plywood strip and shorter staples as you did on the exterior. (See Figure 6.)

If you are using ⅜ inch or thicker plywood, you can scarf in place on the hull without worrying about locating the joint over a solid member. In situations where you find that your sheet is only a few inches short of a frame and that you will have to cut off a substantial amount of material to retreat to the previous frame, the ability to scarf anywhere saves a great deal of plywood. Marking is simplified because the scarf doesn't have to be centered on a fixed point. Make sure, however, that

there is enough longitudinal support between the two panels to keep them reasonably aligned as you scarf.

Figure 9 illustrates two methods for scarfing between frames. The first, for thinner plywood, is to fit and bond blocking between stringers, with the centerline of the blocking lined up with the centerline of the joint. The second is to apply a temporary blocking. For this, use plywood thick enough to receive a staple. Cut it to the approximate width of the joint, and saw it to length to fit between the stringers. Someone on the underside of the boat should hold the blocking in position while another person staples through the scarf from the top.

The only difficulty with this method is that you need to support the interior blocking adequately so that it will receive staples, but not push so hard that you force the scarf joint up and out of fair during the assembly process. With thicker plywood this isn't too difficult, but it can be a problem with thinner material. You can minimize this problem by securing the scarf joint with staples at the stringers, keel, chine or any other solid area before applying pressure on the temporary blocking. One advantage of using the permanent rather than temporary blocking system is that this blocking can serve as a core over which you can manufacture a frame in the completed hull. In this case, frame material is laminated on the interior blocking surface, completing a rigid, I-beam type frame system, as discussed in Chapter 21.

When you have installed all of the panels in one section of the hull and the adhesive has cured, you can remove all temporary staples. We always remove the staples from the scarf joints and usually from the chine and keel because of the heavy fairing that may take place in these areas. The next step is to plane off the excess plywood smooth with the opposite chine surface so that you can fit and install the next panel on the other side of the chine to create a plywood overlap.

Composite Chine Construction

Many smaller boats and some larger ones have been built with no chine log at all. Instead, the plywood panels are joined with a composite chine made of fiberglass cloth or tape as shown in Figure 10. In most cases, especially with thinner plywood, it's easy to manufacture a fiberglass joint between two plywood panels which is as strong as plywood. This system can be useful in preventing the crack propagation at sharp corners which results from problems related to moisture and high stress concentrations. For instructions on the procedure, see the discussion of composite keels in Chapter 23.

The problem with this type of joint is holding the panels in position so that you can manufacture the

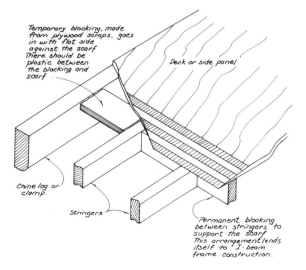

Temporary blocking, made from plywood scraps, goes in with flat side against the scarf. There should be plastic between the blocking and scarf.

Deck or side panel

Chine log or clamp.

Stringers

Permanent blocking between stringers to support the scarf. This arrangement lends itself to 'I-beam' frame construction.

Figure 9—Blocking for scarfing in place.

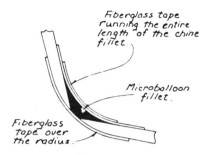

Figure 10—Chine joint using fiberglass tape over low density fillet.

joint. Molds are often unnecessary in sheet plywood construction because the boat's framework serves as a mold, but a jig or strongback is usually needed for composite chines. The jig may be male or female, and it may be similar to the one shown in Figure 11. Either way, it should allow you to temporarily assemble the panels with staples. After stapling the plywood, trim its edges so they fit well and join them with at least one layer of glass tape. When this cures, remove the hull from the form and apply glass tape to the opposite side to complete the joint.

The female jig or form has an advantage over the male type because the inside of the joint is taped first. When you remove the hull from the jig, you have the option of rounding over and fairing the exterior edge to the degree desired before you apply glass tape to complete the joint. You can also construct a composite chine over conventional framework. Sheet plywood can be used with a permanent stringer-frame support system to produce strong, seaworthy hulls, and the simplified chine system makes them easy to build.

There are endless variations for making up a properly strong composite joint. We normally make up some samples of the joint system that we plan to use and subject them to some simple destruction testing. Our standard measure of a successful joint is that all breakage occurs within the plywood rather than in the joint.

Final Fairing

Final fairing is the easiest part of hard chine plywood construction. If you had a fair framework to begin with, sheet ply should follow it precisely and make a smooth, even surface. Most fairing will be concentrated around chines, scarfs and the keel, where two panels of plywood have been joined. To fair a misaligned scarf, plane away as little wood as possible, and fill in low spots around the joint with a low density resin mixture. If the joint is critical, reinforce weakened areas from the inside. Before rounding over any joints at the chine or keel, true up the plywood edges. Use hand planes and

fairing blocks with 50 grit sandpaper to sharpen each edge, and then sight it for fairness. If an edge has flat spots or unnatural curves, do some corrective fairing. When you have developed a fair edge along the entire keel or chine, you can round it over with assurance that the overall chine or keel surface will continue to look fair after it is radiused.

The only limitations to the amount that you can round over either a keel or chine joint are the structural limitations of the joint itself. There have been cases where a well-designed joint has failed because more material was removed than was originally planned, leaving the joint in weakened condition. If you have any doubts about your particular joint, we suggest that you make up a sample joint of exactly the kind you intend to use and subject it to some simple destruction testing, making sure the joint will be stronger than either of the panels it is joining together. We generally make up a sample of our intended joint that is approximately 8 inches in length and subject it to whatever type of load we can dream up. If these loads cause our

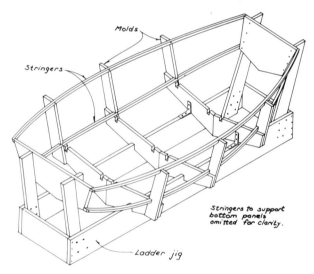

Figure 11—Female mold that could be used to efficiently produce a large number of composite plywood dinghies.

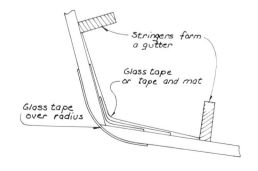

Figure 12—Taped seam on a Sea-Runner™.

Figure 13—Joints of Fireball dinghy temporarily held with wire. Fiberglass tape will be laid on the inside of these joints and the wires will be removed. Then fiberglass tape or cloth will be applied to the exterior of the joints. (Mark Lindsay)

steel screws that are removed after the bonding adhesive has cured so as not to interfere with planing or fairing operations.

Some problems can develop during fairing if you use Douglas fir plywood. As explained earlier, sanded fir plywood panels can be very uneven. Softer summer wood sands more easily than harder winter wood, so dishing results and becomes worse with more sanding. The only solutions are to keep sanding to a minimum and to use sharp hand planes for most of the fairing. We suggest that all exterior fir plywood surfaces be covered with fiberglass cloth and epoxy.

sample to break within the joint area, we build another sample, increasing the joint size or re-engineering it with a different concept until it is stronger than the panel itself and all future breaks occur within the plywood and not the joint.

Just as we use a stem cap piece in most boat hulls, with hard chine construction it is also possible to have chine caps and keel caps to help complete the rounding process with certain types of joint design. (See Figure 4.) The procedure is the same as with a stem cap. Plane a flat bevel on the chine or keel joint onto which you can laminate a single piece or multiple pieces of lumber stock. For temporary pressure we normally use

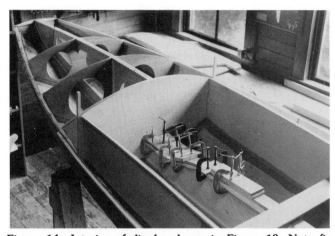

Figure 14—Interior of dinghy shown in Figure 13. Note fiberglass tape for joining chine, visible in forward sections. (Mark Lindsay)

Chapter 23

Building and Developing
Compounded Plywood Hulls

In our early years as boat builders, we became particularly fascinated with the concept of the Indian birch bark canoe. Here was a craft which was beautifully shaped, lightweight and strong. Best of all, it was of sheet material. The Indian birch bark canoe was built in a way just opposite to that in which boats are normally built: the skin was formed first and the supporting framework installed afterwards. First, the birch bark was removed carefully from a tree and roughly shaped into the form of a canoe. Then a supporting framework was installed to support the flimsy birch bark skin and better define the shape of the canoe. American Indians designed, engineered and constructed these birch bark canoes, which were the preferred method of transport by the early French explorers for a period of over 200 years.

In 1963, we used a similar developed skin method and plywood instead of birch bark to build a trimaran. Following traditional techniques, we "folded up" a hull and then installed interior framework to stiffen it, to better define its shape and to distribute high loading throughout its skin. We have been building boats this way for twenty years now, and have refined the technique to the point where compounded plywood construction is a practical method for a limited range of hull types and shapes.

With this boatbuilding technique it is possible to produce strong, lightweight hulls. We use it for catamarans and trimarans, but it is well suited to small day sailers such as the International Moth Class dinghy and may be among the best techniques for building racing canoes and rowing shells. Lofting, setting up and laminating are eliminated, so a boat can be manufactured in relatively few work hours. One disadvantage of compounded plywood construction is that its use is limited to shapes which can be developed easily by bending sheets of plywood in two directions. Another problem is that it's sometimes difficult to install framework in a preformed hull. In spite of these disadvantages, the method can be so successful that we think a discussion of its basic principles is worthwhile.

Boat plans and design information for compounded plywood construction can be hard to find. For this reason, this chapter includes an outline of the various design parameters we use in developing hull shapes and instructions on designing and building models. If you have purchased plans, begin with the specific techniques for building described in the first portion of the chapter. If you are developing your own compounded plywood hull, however, read over the sections on design before you start. In either case, the first step of any project should be to make up samples for testing. Experiment with keel joints and be sure that the plywood you have chosen will be able to bend around the hull's hardest curves.

Compounding Plywood

To *compound* a sheet of plywood, you bend it in two directions at the same time. All plywood can be compounded, but, as we will discuss later, the amount of compounding possible for a given sheet of plywood has not been firmly established, and, in general, the "compoundability" of a panel is determined by its thickness, by the number of plies used to make it and by the species of wood used. Plywood thickness is a limiting factor in the size of the hulls which can be built with compounded plywood construction. We have used up to ¼ inch 5-ply panels and usually choose the thickest plywood which can be bent to shape.

Different woods of the same thickness bend with varying difficulty. Although different species of woods may be used for compounded plywood construction, we almost always choose the very best okoume marine grade or birch aircraft plywood. Each species has its pluses and minuses; the important thing to consider with this boatbuilding method is that flaws and voids within a laminate may cause it to break when it is compounded. High quality panels should therefore be used.

Construction

To begin building a compounded hull, make two identical flat plywood panels. Each of these should be slightly larger than one half of the hull skin, so it's usually necessary to scarf two or more 4 foot x 8 foot sheets into a single piece. Sometimes we have been able to lay out both panels on a single sheet by alternating them end for end.

Precoating plywood with WEST SYSTEM* Brand epoxy increases its stiffness and affects compounding. We precoat only areas like the bow interior which will be difficult to reach in the folded hull, and these only if little compounding is required of them. Several of our STRESFORM* designs call for applying a layer of fiberglass cloth to the outside of panels before folding them into shape. As we discuss later in this chapter, fiberglass sheathing increases stiffness significantly. Should you decide to use this modification of the compounded plywood technique, make both a model and a test panel and check to be sure that it will be able to negotiate the hull's most severe curves.

The shape of a compounded hull is determined primarily by its *rocker profile,* its *keel angles* and its *sheer line,* all of which are explained in greater detail in the design section of this chapter. The amount of rocker cut along the bottom of the panels where they join to form the keel and the keel angles are the main factors in shaping the hull. The keel line cut establishes both the rocker profile and the potential for compounding while the keel angles describe hull fullness.

To understand the effects of these various lines, curves and angles, imagine what would happen if you joined two panels, both of which had perfectly straight edges, and bent them up. The result would be a cylindrical structure with no compound curvature. If, however, the edges of both panels are curved and held in a strong immobile joint at predetermined angles at the keel, they will be forced to compound as they bend towards each other.

Proper layout of the keel is crucial. The profile keel line must be absolutely fair, with no humps, hollows or flat spots which might be magnified in the hull after the fold-up process. The two panels must be exactly the same size. To be sure that they are, staple or nail them together and place them on a flat surface. Lay out a hull side on the top panel and then cut the two panels simultaneously. An alternative method is to lay out and cut one panel and use it as a pattern for the second.

Scribe a line on the inside of each panel approximately 2 inches up from the center keel joint. These

Figure 2—Plywood hull panels for a Tornado catamaran. These panels are cut from 5mm okoume plywood.

* TRADEMARK OF GOUGEON BROTHERS, INC., U.S.A.

lines will serve as guides later when the exact centerline of the keel is lost under the composite keel joint. The lines also help to make sure that the keel is applied evenly to both panels.

The next step on most hulls is to separate the panels and install a sheer clamp on each one. The sheer clamp, which is eventually an interior member of some hulls and an exterior member of others, provides rigidity to the upper part of the plywood panel. This is the only time during construction when it can be conveniently installed. Sheer clamp dimensions are usually a function of the thickness of the plywood: we generally use sheer clamps which are four to six times plywood thickness to gain sufficient surface area for bonding the deck to the hull. The sheer line edge determines the placement of the sheer clamps. We usually leave ours slightly high of the plywood edges so that there will be enough stock for any beveling which might be needed for deck crown.

Bond a sheer clamp on each panel and staple lightly to hold it temporarily in place. Too many staples will increase the stiffness of the piece, so use clamps if further pressure is necessary. While the epoxy is still wet, curve each panel in a longitudinal arc with the sheer clamp on the *inside* radius, even if it will eventually be on the outside of the hull. This forces a bit of a laminated curve into the two wood parts and helps to promote compounding in the plywood by compressing it along the sheer line. When the adhesive has cured, plane the sheer clamps so they will meet perfectly where the plywood panels touch at the bow. If the hull is double-ended also bevel them at the stern as shown in Figure 14.

Then round over and bevel the plywood panels along the keel line and stern edge. It's almost impossible for two sharp edges to mate accurately and they will not line up if they are left sharp. By rounding the edges you increase surface area and this makes it easier to adjust the panels for an accurate centerline. Before beginning, however, decide how you will temporarily hold the panels together until you can make a permanent keel joint. The technique you choose here will determine whether you shape the interior or the exterior panel edges.

We have used two reliable temporary holding systems, both of which act as hinges along the joint. With the first, we thread wire through holes along the keel line, and with the second we bond 2 inch wide nylon webbing to the outside of the panels along the joint. Whichever system you use, first clamp, staple or tape the panels together so that they will not shift as you align them. Double-sided carpet tape will effectively hold them, and will become an important part of the

Figure 3—Plywood panels and sheer clamps laminated to a large curve to help develop fullness in upper sheer area of completed hull.

nylon webbing system. If you use tape, however, apply it to a clean surface and be sure to remove any adhesive residue as soon as the webbing is firmly in place. Wash any surfaces to which tape has been attached with solvent and then sand them.

Nylon webbing, similar to seatbelt material, maintains better panel alignment than wire, especially around the stem area, and usually eliminates the task of straightening panel edges. To install it, round the inner edges of the plywood to a 1/16 inch radius and bevel a 45° angle from the curved area to the outer surface. Join the panels, interior surfaces facing, along the stem and keel lines with carpet tape, clamp tightly and check alignment. Then bond the webbing to the outside of the keel joint with a thickened mixture of Colloidal Silica and epoxy, holding it in place with

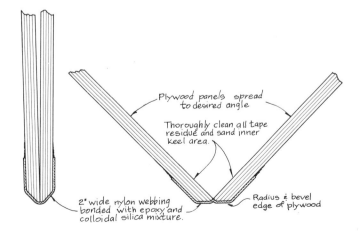

Figure 4—Joining plywood hull panels with nylon webbing.

spring clamps until the resin cures. Do not substitute fiberglass cloth tape for the webbing since it is too brittle when wet with resin to be used in this application. Webbing could be difficult to work with on asymmetrical hulls.

To use wires to hold the panels, lay out wiring holes along the keel line and bow (also the stern if the hull is a double-ender). These holes should usually be about ⅛ inch in diameter, ⅜ inch to ½ inch in from the edges of the plywood and about 4 inches apart. The holes on the two panels should be perfectly aligned, so double check them before drilling. Next, shape the inside facing edges. The easiest way to do this is to stack the pieces on top of one another, clamp them and round them both in one operation. Then place the panels on top of each with the interiors face-to-face. Cut No. 4 ground wire or other lightweight copper wire to about 5 inch lengths, thread a piece through each set of holes, bend it around and twist the ends loosely together as in Figure 5. Leave enough slack so that the wire will not dig into the wood when the panels are spread apart. We usually wire panels together along the keel to the top of the bow at the sheer line, but occasionally we leave the bow open at this stage to help develop more fullness along the keel line in that area. If you are building a double-ender, also wire or tape the stern.

When the panels are wired or held together with webbing, set them upright and begin opening them like a book. To distribute the weight of the panels evenly and better control the process, place sawhorses

Figure 6—Tornado catamaran hull panels held at correct angle with notched sticks and plywood form.

under the keel about one quarter of the hull length in from each end. Cut some sticks to length and insert them between the sheer clamps to hold the panels apart, and then measure the keel angle between the panels. As you spread the panels, clamp braces from the sawhorses to the sheer clamps on either side to make the unwieldy structure more manageable. There usually isn't much stability at this point — the panels are very wobbly.

We usually measure angles as three distinct parts of the keel line and let the rest of the hull fall fair between them. In the bow area, for example, we may work towards an 80° keel angle, while in the mid-section we might want an angle of 140°, and perhaps even 160° toward the transom. Three checking stations seem to be accurate for boats up to about 30 feet long.

One way to make sure that the two panels meet at the desired angle is build a simple jig or temporary frame support. This clamps to the exterior part of the hull and forces the two panels into the exact position you want. If you have three checking stations, make up three jigs, one for each position. Often, plywood doesn't lie flat as it is spread. Instead, it curls slightly inward and a straightedge shows a hollow on the outside of the panel. This means that if your jig is set for 120°, the plywood at the keel may only be spread to 110°. The solution is to spread the sheers further than 120° apart, until the panels are at the correct angle at

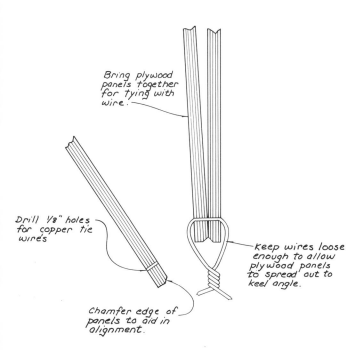

Bring plywood panels together for tying with wire.

Drill ⅛" holes for copper tie wires

Keep wires loose enough to allow plywood panels to spread out to keel angle.

Chamfer edge of panels to aid in alignment.

Figure 5—Wiring plywood hull panels.

the keel. Remember that the permanent joint will be made at the keel and it is only this angle which is crucial at this stage.

When the two panels are spread to desired angles, begin tightening the wires, if you are using them, until the edges are drawn tightly together and centered with a relatively straight keel line. If you have used webbing along the keel line, this step is eliminated. At this stage, wires may tend to pull way from each other at the keel line and leave gaps of up to ⅜ inch. Lightly tap each wire with a sharp tool and drive it into a V in the joint. As you do this, try to put your tool exactly in the middle of the wire between the two panels because an exact, accurate V promotes good alignment when you pull the pieces together. Twist each wire again until the edges are snug at the keel line.

During the tightening process, if one edge of a panel seems a little higher than the other, use finger or thumb pressure to hold the edges in alignment until they butt snugly. In some cases you can force wires to the left or right as you twist them to assist in raising or lowering one panel edge against the other. The goal of this final tightening is to snug the plywood panels against each other and to line them up so that there will be no humps and hollows along the keel line.

Occasionally, wire ties may be mutilated to the point where you lose control of the plywood edges around

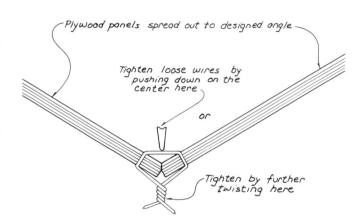

Figure 8—Tightening wires at keel joint.

them. The best solution to this problem is to snip these wires, remove them, start over with fresh ties and hope for better luck. Drill more holes and insert extra wires in areas which are particularly difficult. If you have further trouble, it's more than likely that you did not put enough radius on your edges and/or that a hump or hollow on a panel edge is throwing alignment out of kilter.

Constructing the Keel Joint

When the keel edges of the plywood panels are in position and any wires tightened, begin the process of building a keel joint. We recommend that you plan to manufacture the keel in a single day as this will eliminate sanding between layers.

The composite keel joint is one of the most critical parts of a compounded plywood hull. Although the size and composition of keel joints varies from hull to hull, basic installation procedure is very similar. Begin by filling the V formed by the two panels at the interior keel line with a fillet of thickened epoxy, lay in fiberglass cloth or tape, and apply more epoxy and fiberglass. The resin structurally joins the panels and, at the same time, serves as a core between the inner and outer layers of fiberglass.

There are no firm rules for the thickness and width of composite keels, but the fillet should at least cover protruding wires, if you are using them, so that you can evenly apply the glass over a smooth surface. The size of a keel joint, and especially its width, has a significant effect on the shape of the finished hull, and it is a rather rigid part of the structure which for the most part will not bend. If it is irregular, larger in some areas than in others, it may cause bumps and hollows. Variation of around 10% in the keel section is tolerable, but any more than this will lead to unfairness in the hull. (See Figure 9.)

Figure 7—Panels for trimaran outrigger hull showing temporary frame supports.

.

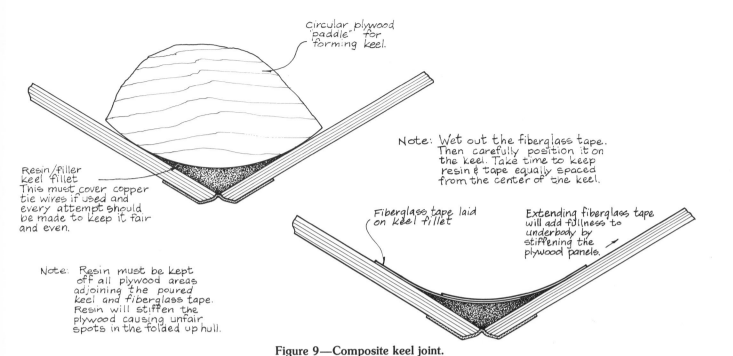

Figure 9—Composite keel joint.

To apply the initial keel joint fillet, add low density filler to epoxy to make a mixture which spreads easily but resists sagging. Apply it as smoothly and evenly as possible. The scribed lines on the interior of the panels aid in maintaining a balanced fillet as well as in laying the tape straight. Since leaning over the edges of the spread-out panels to reach the middle of the hull can be a bit difficult, we make several paddles, each resembling the keel shapes we want at a given part of the hull, and use them to remove any excess adhesive and to smooth the joint.

Figure 10—Applying glass tape over keel fillet on a 30 foot hull.

Apply fiberglass cloth tape over the fillet when the thickened resin mixture has partially cured. If you wait until the epoxy has fully cured, you will have to sand away rough edges. Catching the fillet while it is still pliable and malleable means that you can simply smooth potential rough edges with layers of glass cloth.

In manufactured keels, we usually use 10 oz. fiberglass cloth tape. This is available in various widths; we keep a supply of 2 inch, 3 inch, 4 inch and 5 inch rolls on hand for building various sizes of keels and typically install two layers of tape on both the inner and outer keel surfaces of hulls built with 5/32 inch to ¼ inch thick plywood. Like the width of the keel joint, the width of the glass tape influences the shape of the folded hull. Wider glass cloth adds stiffness to the plywood, and this keeps it from bending as much as it would if it were not covered with glass. As a result, the hull is fuller along the keel line and more compounding is demanded of the panels.

There are at least two ways to apply the fiberglass tape. You can install it dry, pressing it into the partially cured keel and then wetting it out with a stiff brush and non-fortified epoxy, but this can be a lengthy operation because of the awkward working posture. Since it's difficult to maneuver a squeegee from this angle, the dry method may also result in a little extra weight, and you might want to avoid this on a small boat. It's much more convenient to wet out a measured length of glass tape on a board which has been wrapped in plastic, remove excess resin with a plastic spreader, and then roll up the tape. Transfer it to the keel, unroll it in position, and smooth it out. Applying glass tape in the bow and other confined areas can be troublesome, so use the wet method in these spots.

To apply fiberglass cloth to the keel joint of a large boat, you may have to work out a slightly different procedure. A hull is very fragile until the keel has cured, so you can't get inside it to lay the tape. Instead, rig up a scaffold on which you can stand. Run a stick which is at least a foot longer than the widest point of the hull through the center of a roll of glass tape and rest its ends on the sheers. If the hole in the center of the tape is too small for the stick, bend a wire coat hanger into a U-shaped holder, bend the ends of the wire into hooks so it can hang from the stick, and use it to dispense the tape. Find a second stick — this one should reach the keel easily from the outside of the boat — and fasten a brush to it. We use the stiff, 2-inch wide brushes which are sold for cleaning automobile parts. Roll dry cloth tape onto the keel line and use the long brush to wet it out completely with epoxy.

No matter how you apply the fiberglass, closely watch the guidelines up from the keel as you work. Position the tape evenly on the panels because it will affect stiffness. If you are applying several layers of cloth, arrange them in an overlapping pattern so that their edges will be feathered. If you are using various tape widths, lay the widest first. Carefully control the epoxy since it too increases stiffness. Again use the marks as guides, and keep the resin lines equally spaced from the center of the keel.

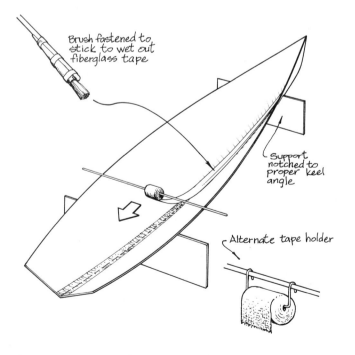

Figure 11—Applying fiberglass tape to composite keel of large hull.

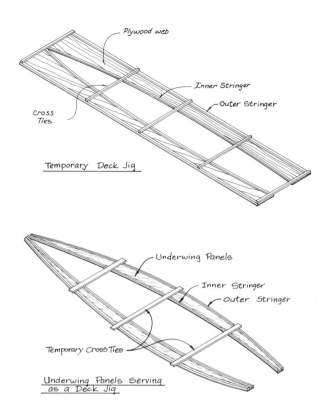

Figure 12—Typical deck jig and typical underwing panel.

Folding Up

When the keel and glass tape have fully cured, the plywood will be folded into the shape of the hull. A deck jig — usually nothing more than an outline of the deck perimeter from the top view — is necessary for this operation. Although deck jigs are usually temporary, in some designs they remain in the finished boat. In the main hulls of some trimarans, for example, a jig becomes an underwing panel, as shown in Figure 12. In these cases, the design and material used for deck jigs may be somewhat different, but their primary function is not.

Make the jig with a lip which slips over the edges of the sheer clamps when the hull is folded. This lip will hold the sheer clamps in their final positions. The jig is absolutely crucial to folding-up and must be accurately built. Fortunately, this doesn't require much time or material.

We usually design our deck jigs with a 1 foot wide plywood flange around the outer perimeter to serve as a sheer web separating two structural stringers. The inside stringer is more important because it is used to define the actual sheer profile, while the other stringer serves only as a structural member to help support the deck jig fixture. Manufacture one half of the deck jig first, and then duplicate it by making an identical half.

To determine jig measurements, loft the topside sheer profile on the floor, using perhaps four to eight

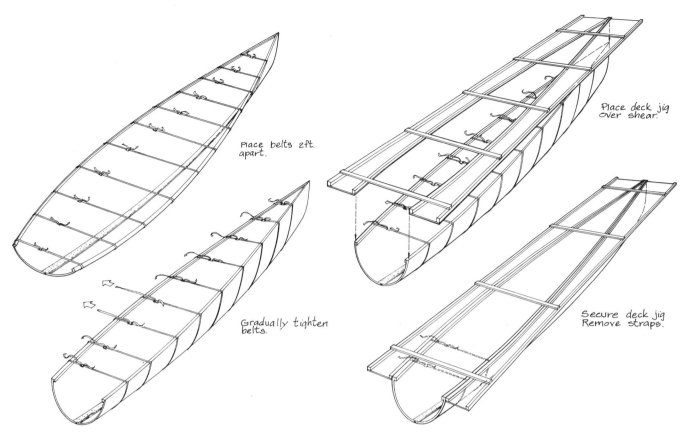

Place belts 2ft. apart.

Gradually tighten belts.

Place deck jig over shear.

Secure deck jig Remove straps.

Figure 13—Folding up with plastic strapping or belts.

measurement points from the centerline for guides. Find stock which will bend accurately to a fair and even curve and scarf it to form a stringer of appropriate size. This will be the permanent inner part of one half of the deck jig, so don't use a good lofting batten. Bond and staple foot-wide plywood panels to the top of the stringer, butting them as necessary. Leave some plywood overhanging.

Then bond and staple another stringer to the underside of the outer edge of the plywood. This piece should be about as thick as the inner stringer, but doesn't have to be made of quality stock. Lift the whole assembly from the floor, saw off the plywood overhang at the inner stringer and plane it flush. Make a copy of this half-jig, using it as a guide. For accuracy, we suggest that you tack the inner batten to the permanent sheer edge of the first assembly rather than to the lofting. Fasten plywood and an outer stringer as you did on the first.

Next, join the two halves of the jig with cross ties. These hold the pieces rigidly, help position them correctly and prevent any spreading in the middle of the jig. The cross ties rest on the sheers of the plywood panels and keep the jig from dropping down on the hull, but they tend to get in the way of interior work so

use as few as possible. In most cases, four is the least that you can get away with.

Getting this unwieldy hunk of joined plywood panels inserted into the deck jig is the most difficult part of compounded plywood construction and requires patience, skill and many workers. With smaller hulls, a few people can start working the two plywood panels into the deck jig by folding the two panels up toward each other. Then fold the bows together and insert the deck jig over the folded-up bow to hold that part of the hull in position. The fold-up team then works its way aft, slowly pushing the two side panels toward each other so that the lip of the jig is able to slip into position over the edge of the sheer, firmly locking the two panels. The problem with this fold-up method is that several other people must also help support the deck jig until it is positioned on the hull. The hull also needs a few more people to help support it, because as it is being folded up the bracing that was giving support is no longer effective because of the shape change. Once you have positioned the deck jig, the troubles are over because the once floppy hull becomes quite rigid and stable. Position temporary supports from the floor to the deck jig to hold the newly-shaped hull very firmly for further work.

Figure 14—Folding up a 30 foot trimaran hull with drawstrings. Note sheer clamps have been beveled at the stern so that they can be clamped together when hull is folded up.

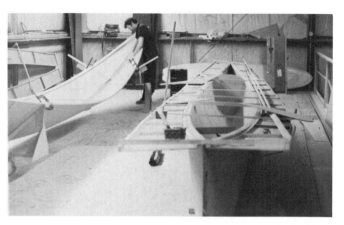

Figure 15—Folded hull with deck jig to right. Taping keel fillet in plywood hull panels to left.

Another way to fold panels is to use the plastic strapping and clips which have been developed to replace metal strapping in packing and shipping. Loop a series of these straps around the hull about 2 feet apart down its length, arranging them so that you have easy access to the clips. Force the sheer inward and take up on the strap. Work up and down the hull tightening each a little at a time, gradually increasing the tension. The boat will slowly and gently fold up, until eventually two people will be able to drop the deck jig in place. Things will look bad until the jig is installed, so don't be discouraged. With the jig in position, remove the straps and begin work on the interior.

Although strapping is better in most applications, especially with larger hulls and masts, you can also use light line to pull a hull into shape. Fasten screws into both sheers every 2 feet or so down the hull, setting the heads out far enough so you can wrap the line around them. Thread a drawstring around two screws, one on either sheer, and tie it with a rolling hitch. Tighten the strings up and down the hull by pulling on the knots with steady and progressive pressure.

Supporting the Compounded Plywood Skin

Every hull needs some form of minimal framework to distribute high load points over the hull skin, and the framework systems that we have used to accomplish load distribution have varied widely. Smaller boats,

such as the 18 foot Unicorn catamaran, rely on only three bulkheads and several stringers to distribute loads out over the 5/32 inch thick plywood skin, and this is sufficient reinforcement for a long-lasting hull. As boats get larger, however, they need more support for the skin because the loads are increasing dramatically while the plywood thickness may only increase a small amount, for example, from 3/16 inch to ¼ inch.

Another factor that affects the amount of framework needed for skin support is the stiffness of the skins themselves. If you improve the stiffness of the skin, less

Figure 16—Folded 30 foot hull with sub-level stringers laminated on inside.

framework is needed. Coating the ply panels inside and out with WEST SYSTEM resin will improve skin stiffness a great deal. A step beyond this is to laminate 4 oz. to 10 oz. glass cloth on both the inside and outside of the developed plywood hull. Although the addition of glass cloth will increase the weight of the hull significantly, chances are you will find that the hull skin is incredibly light, at this point probably not comprising any more than 50% of the completed weight of your hull. Thus, you may well be able to afford the extra weight. The main benefit of using glass cloth to stiffen the plywood hull panels is that it applies easily and quickly with effective results. Applying glass cloth on both the inner and outer hull surfaces is especially effective with 3-ply plywood, because it produces a 5-ply matrix after the plywood skins have been formed, which increases strength and stiffness significantly. When using glass, only apply it to the interior of the hull at this stage, leaving the outside to be glassed after the interior is completed and the hull can be removed from the deck jig and turned upside down. With the hull in that position, the outside layer of glass cloth is much easier to apply.

Another method to stiffen all or part of a plywood skin is to treat the developed hull as a mold and use it as a form over which to laminate veneers or more

Figure 18—Bonding experimental Verticel™ and fiberglass panels to inside of developed plywood hull. Sticks are providing pressure by forcing the Verticel against plywood hull. When this laminate cured, 10 oz. fiberglass cloth was bonded to interior side of Verticel core.

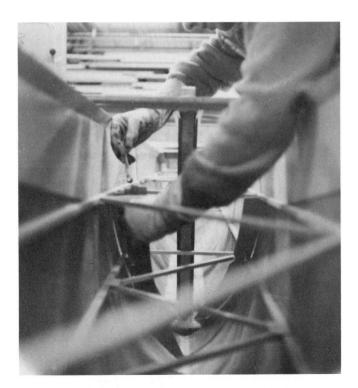

Figure 17—Struts and bracing for sub-level stringers in Tornado catamaran hull. Note small plywood gussets holding struts to stringers. Small plywood half-frames are being installed against hull skin. These frames will be filleted to skin. Centerboard case is vertical post in center of picture.

plywood. You can do this either on the inside or outside of the hull skin, but it is probably more easily and effectively done on the outside if the whole hull is to be covered.

Another interesting method that we have used, but which still must be considered in the experimental stage, is to laminate a honeycomb material on the inside of the compounded plywood hull, using a thickened resin mixture for bonding. We then cover the honeycomb with a layer of 10 oz. glass cloth to complete a sandwich panel that has a high degree of panel stiffness at a very light weight. The only difficulty with this approach is determining how best to distribute high load points over the interior of the hull skin with the honeycomb in place. In the case of the trimaran outer hulls shown in Figure 18 there were very few high load points involved, so they were a natural for this type of skin support. The beauty of the system in this instance is that the honeycomb and the 10 oz. glass cloth were easily installed on the interior with few labor hours and resulted in a skin that needed no further support.

Before installing any framework or doing any stiffening of the skin, make sure you are satisfied with the exact shape that the hull has taken. If not, you can easily make some modification of the shape at this point. For example, you can squeeze the hull in at various points or push it out at other points with temporary braces or supports. The interior structure that you then build in must be capable of holding these altered hull shape positions without losing any hull fairness after you remove the supports. At this point, you're down to "eyeball" boatbuilding because you have no body plan or given set of dimensions to go from. If you are building a hull you designed yourself, there are several parameters that you can establish early in the game as goals to shoot for in developing a given hull shape. These will be discussed later. If you are building from plans (for example, a Tornado catamaran), there is usually no guide to determine final hull shape other than the initial instructions for construction. Interestingly enough, however, the variation between hulls built by different builders (as shown by the class measuring templates) is surprisingly small in the Olympic class Tornado.

Bulkheads, Frames and Deck Beams

As in other methods of boat construction, bulkheads are used in compounded plywood construction as a major tool to distribute high loads over the skin area. With the fold-up method, we use bulkheads regularly to distribute high stresses caused by cross beams, masts, forestays, centerboards and staying points throughout the skin.

Because there are no lofted sections to go by, you need to determine the shape of the bulkheads by making up temporary patterns that can be fit to the hull and then used as templates to cut out the bulkheads. Make the patterns by fitting a piece of template material to each side of the hull. Join these two half pieces together with a brace at the top and an overlap or brace at the bottom to form a complete interior pattern of the hull at a given station. Then trace the pattern on a piece of plywood and cut out the plywood to form the bulkhead. You will probably need some final fitting of the bulkhead, but if you used the template system carefully, this should be minimal. (See Chapter 24 for more detail.)

Install the bulkheads by using a simple fillet on each side of the plywood to join it with the hull sides. Usually we add low density filler to the resin to make a lightweight fillet that provides a large bonding surface area between bulkhead and hull skin. You can further support the skin by laminating in place ribs manufactured of thin strips of wood which will bend easily around the hull. Stack laminate the wood strips on top of one another, using alloy staples that can be left in the laminate. Another method for skin support is to cut and fit

Figure 19—Structural members installed in 30 foot trimaran outrigger. Cross beam arm and centerboard case are braced and secured, with bulkheads and sub-level stringers in foreground.

Figure 20—Bulkheads reinforcing laminated stilts to which cross beams will be bonded.

deck beams. Generally, we use small leftover pieces of proper width plywood to construct them. The I-beam deck section (as shown in Figure 26) is very easy to install and provides the maximum amount of load-bearing support available per weight of deck beam. Usually deck beam failures are not so much material failures as they are failures of the joint where the deck beam meets the sheer clamp area. The I-beam deck beam system provides the maximum amount of bonding area at this joint and can eliminate this problem. Simple plywood deck beams are adequate in many situations, provided they have enough depth so that they won't break in tension, and that the point at which they join with the sheer clamp and hull skin area provides enough area that you can install a generous fillet to make a proper joint. Because the sheer clamps with

Figure 21—Laminated frames, box-type bulkhead, shelf and bunk bottoms all support developed plywood skin on this 35 foot racing trimaran.

plywood web frames and fillet them in place, using the same technique used to install bulkheads. (See Figure 17.) In some situations stringers might be needed to give further longitudinal support. We install stringers by holding them temporarily in place with staples and cross braces until the adhesive cures. When stapling through the skin from the outside to the stringer, we drill small holes to transfer the inside stringer location as a guide to stapling. It is also possible to install stringers on the undeveloped plywood panels before they are folded up, but we do not recommend that stringers over ½ inch wide be installed on the unfolded panels, because wider stringers will tend to cause hard spots and overly stress the plywood in that area during the bending process.

Depending upon the hull being built, you may have many other interior items to install. These might include centerboard or daggerboard cases, special compartments and, in larger hulls, interior accommodations. You can install some interior items after the hull has been removed from the deck jig; however, you must install large items now because the deck beams that are needed to hold the sheer in final position will be in the way later.

The deck beams are always the last items you install in the hull before you remove the deck jig. Deck beams serve an important function at this stage in supporting the upper hull area so that it will not change shape when you remove the deck jig. There are various combinations which we have used to make successful

Figure 22—Variety of framing, bulkheads and interior joinery employed in supporting plywood skin in this 35 foot trimaran.

Figure 23—Bunk bottom and laminated frames used to support hull skin.

this type of construction are fairly small, we have stayed away from any heavy triangular notching of the deck beams into the sheer clamps.

When the deck beams are installed and the interior support completed, you no longer need the deck jig. Remove it and turn the now-rigid hull upside down. Strip off keel webbing if you've used it. If you've used wires, you can snip them flush, but we find that extracting them makes fairing easier.

Fairing and Finishing

Then you can begin general fairing of the entire exterior surface of the hull. As a rule, there is little fairing to do, because plywood naturally compounds into an amazingly fair surface if you have done a good job of joining the panels. Usually the only real fairing is at the keel line itself, where it is common to have some small misalignment between the plywood edges that causes some minor humps and hollows. You can fair up the keel quickly with a combination approach of filling low spots and planing off some high spots. Try not to plane down into the composite keel; leave the point where the two pieces of plywood meet to act as a guide for fairing the keel straight. When you have trued up the keel line and stem, you can then round over the keel to whatever radius you want.

When the keel and stem are fair and radiused as desired, apply a minimum of two layers of 10 oz. glass cloth tape over the outside keel area. This glass cloth completes the structural composite keel and also pro-

Figure 25—Trimaran outrigger deck framing of plywood beams and spruce stringers.

Figure 26—Tension flanges for deck I-beams are bonded to underside of sheer clamp. Sheer webs for deck I-beams will be bonded to top of these flanges. They will look like the deck beams in Figure 24.

Figure 24—Deck beams being installed in Tornado hull. Note notches for stringer along centerline.

Figure 27—Construction on outriggers for 35 foot trimaran. These hulls will now be coated and fiberglassed. (See Chapters 11 and 12.)

vides abrasion resistance along the keel line when the boat is pulled up on the beach (a situation common with most lightweight multihulls). To apply glass cloth tape on the exterior keel line surface, just wet out the surface first with a light coating of resin. Apply the glass tape dry, firmly setting it in position in the resin. Then wet out the glass tape by adding more resin, either with a roller or by pouring it on the surface from a cup and smoothing it out with a plastic squeegee. We usually wait for the keel line taping to cure completely and then file or sand the glass tape edges as smooth as possible. Then we attempt to fair them in with putty, using low density filler. If the exterior surface is to be

covered with a layer of glass cloth, we wait to do this puttying operation until after we have applied the fiberglass cloth. Other areas of the hull may also need fairing. These could include the scarf joints and perhaps hollows that may have developed.

The final stage of hull completion is the fairing of the deck beams and installation of other deck structural items such as longitudinal stringers. (See Chapter 25.)

Design Guidelines for Model Building

At this time, the process of designing compounded plywood hulls is not very scientific. In fact, it's probably more a combination of art and common sense than anything else. Because the compounded plywood method promotes graceful shapes, we haven't seen any really bad hulls built using it, but that's about the only encouraging word we can offer.

The limitations of the compounded plywood system demand high length-to-beam ratios — 20 to 1 is not uncommon — and high prismatic coefficients with no sharp curves. These factors add up to hulls which drive easily through the water. The real design problems lie in achieving enough displacement for a given hull length, reducing the wetted surface to an acceptable minimum and arranging displacement throughout the hull for a sea-kindly and maneuverable boat which sits correctly on its lines when fully loaded. With compounded plywood construction, you can't always build what you draw, so including all of these design considerations in drawings is particularly complicated.

For centuries, model building has been an alternative to designing boats on paper. Nathaniel Herreshoff refined the technique, carefully shaping, testing and reshaping models until he was satisfied with a design, then taking the lines off the models for lofting. We use models for developing compounded plywood hulls because at this point in the development of the boatbuilding method it appears to be the only practical way to achieve accuracy.

By designing and building models on a scale of 1 inch to the foot, we have been able to project our results accurately from the model phase up to full size with very little error. We have built many models of a given design, slightly changing various parameters of each model hull until we finally achieved exactly what we wanted. Then we transferred the dimensions of the model to paper and expanded it up to where we could construct the full size version easily. Because of the limited hull shapes available with this system, the design work needed isn't really as complicated as you might think. Because the confines are narrow and there are only a few variations available, it usually

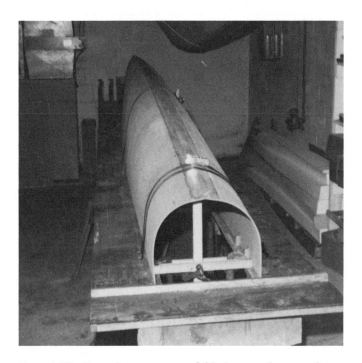

Figure 28—Tornado catamaran folded up and inserted into deck jig. Exterior keel has been faired and taped with fiberglass.

doesn't take very much model building to discover the scope of variables involved. It is helpful to understand the concept of developable surfaces, however. A high school textbook on sheet metal development is worth studying because the basic concepts discussed there are closely related to developing compounded plywood.

Your first step is to decide the basic parameters for the hull you are going to design and build. That decision involves the amount of displacement that is needed. For a given length of boat, there is a limit to the amount of displacement that you can achieve by compounding plywood. You may find out, for instance, that you need a displacement value of 700 pounds for the hull and you plan to build a boat 20 feet long. However, you may later find out that you are only able to get 500 pounds of displacement within that length and the extra 200 pounds may require that the boat be 22 or 23 feet in length. Another factor affecting this decision is the thickness of plywood to be used. Quarter-inch plywood cannot be bent as much as ⅛ inch or 5/32 inch plywood, and will reduce your displacement potential accordingly. A second decision concerns where the displacement is to be located along the hull. Do you want to have a lot of reserve displacement aft? Do you want fine bows or full bows, and how much reserve displacement will you need higher up in the bow area?

We continue to be amazed at the amount of compounding and the variety of shapes that we are able to extract from plywood panels. At this point, we can only give results of the amount of compounding that we were actually able to get on specific hulls that we have built in the past. To measure this compounding rate, we have determined the amount of compounding that takes place within a given 8 foot x 1 foot span at about midpoint along the hull. (Figure 29 gives these results.)

Once you have established the basic parameters for your hull, make a rough sketch of the shape and the profile of the hull you envision. This rough drawing is the catalyst to start the modeling process. The object is to begin the development of two model plywood panels that, when joined together in the proper method, fold up to form a close resemblance to the hull that you envision. An understanding of developable shapes will aid at this point in developing your first plywood panel cutout from your rough drawing.

The tricky part here is to establish lines on a flat panel which will, when the panel is compounded, produce the boat you want. As we mentioned earlier, the rocker profile, or side view of the boat, the keel angles and the sheer line ultimately define the hull shape.

Generally, on hulls with full afterbodies and transoms, the rocker profile in the flat panel is very similar to the keel profile when the hull is folded. For a given amount of rocker, a double-ended hull will have more

Figure 29—Compounding rates on Gougeon-constructed hulls

Boat name	Length of hull in feet	Plywood thickness	Athwartship bending (inches maximum over 1 foot)	Longitudinal bending (inches maximum over 8 feet)
VICTOR T (main hull)	25	3-ply (5 mm)	1½	¾
VICTOR T (outriggers)	17	3-ply (3 mm)	2	⅝
ADAGIO (main hull)	35	3-ply (6 mm)	⅞	1
ADAGIO (outriggers)	33	3-ply (6 mm)	1⅜	1⅛
FLICKA (outriggers)	30	5-ply (7 mm)	1 7/16	1
A CLASS CATAMARAN	18	3-ply (3 mm)	3	½
SPLINTER (main hull)	25	3-ply (6 mm)	1¼	1
OUTRIGGER CANOE	24	3-ply (4 mm)	1½	2
OLLIE[1] (main hull)	35	5-ply (7 mm)	1 7/16	1

[1]Outside of panels sheathed in 4 oz. fiberglass cloth before folding.

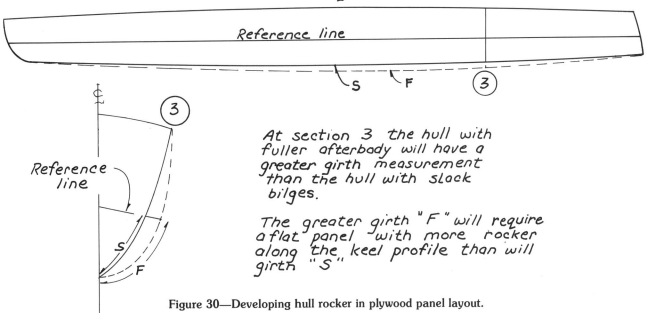

Flat panel for hull with transom and straight sheer

Reference line

S   F   ③

③

Reference line

At section 3 the hull with fuller afterbody will have a greater girth measurement than the hull with slack bilges.

The greater girth "F" will require a flat panel with more rocker along the keel profile than will girth "S"

S

F

Figure 30—Developing hull rocker in plywood panel layout.

keel rocker than a hull with a fuller afterbody, so on double-enders you can usually cut more keel rocker to achieve the desired amount of rocker in the completed hull. (See Figure 30.) Bow and transom profiles are pretty straightforward because the flat cut shape is very close to the compounded profile, except that the very tip of the bow will move aft slightly when the hull sheers are spread apart. You may have to work with the model a little and compensate for this to end up with the bow or transom you want.

The sheer line can be more difficult to determine than the keel line. The profile of a sheer line scribed on a flat sheet of plywood may be considerably different from the sheer line on a folded hull. The sheer on the completed hull is affected by many variables, including hull width, hull fullness and the amount of compounding within the structure, and it will usually require some adjustment to make up for curvature at the hull's midsection. Take all of these factors into account when determining the ultimate sheer line. Remember that the sheer line must curve evenly over its length, with no hollows or flat spots.

For basic clues on the sheer profile and height, look at the profile view and a reasonably drawn version of the body plan. The aft and mid sections of a hull usually demand more curve from the plywood, and the sheer is usually therefore higher at the bow, where the sections are much straighter. To develop a straight sheer line, add material in the midsection as shown in Figure 31 to make up for the curve there. Measure along the anticipated hull profile at each station to de-

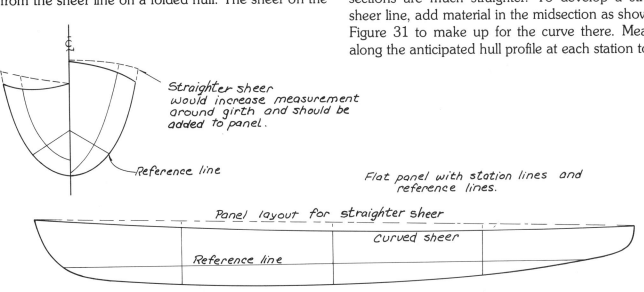

Straighter sheer would increase measurement around girth and should be added to panel.

Reference line

Flat panel with station lines and reference lines.

Panel layout for straighter sheer

Curved sheer

Reference line

Figure 31—Developing the sheer in plywood panel layout.

termine how much extra plywood is needed, and add this to the mid-sheer section of the layout. Then cut the panels for the first model.

Building the Model

The first model is usually only a rough attempt to achieve the hull you desire and will serve as a guideline for refinements that can be made with the next model. This first model will also give you a much better understanding of the compounded plywood hull development process. We have always built our models on a scale of 1 inch to the foot because we have learned by experience the thicknesses of plywood that we can use for the model which will scale up with reasonable accuracy to full size. We have used the following thicknesses of aircraft birch plywood purchased from aircraft supply houses. These thicknesses seem to be universally available.

Aircraft birch plywood	Scales to these full size panels (okoume plywood)
.8 mm	5/32 inch 3-ply
1 mm	3/16 inch 3-ply
1.2 mm	¼ inch 3-ply
1.5 mm	¼ inch 5-ply

While aircraft birch plywood is expensive, you can make a lot of models from one standard 4 foot x 4 foot sheet. Certainly the models are much cheaper than making full size mistakes that are costly not only in materials but also in time. Scaling between these two materials has been quite accurate. Several other factors must also be scaled properly, however, such as the manufactured keel and the sheer clamps. Remember that errors made in the models are projected to full scale by a factor of twelve, so everything you can do to maintain accuracy when building the models is essential.

Build the model as you would a full-size boat. First prepare two identical panels. Temporarily fasten them together and make and cut the keel, bow and sheer lines to the dimensions established in your drawings. True these up and make a *master template,* a third panel identical to the first two. This will serve as a record of the panels in this model and can be used as a pattern against which to make small changes in future models. Make a master template for *every* model so that you can clearly see the changes each new panel dimension brings.

The first step in assembling the panels is to install sheer clamps. These will, by necessity, be larger than

scale. A 1 inch square sheer clamp reduces to 1/12 inch square, which is too flimsy to adequately represent the real sheer clamp, so in this case we would increase the model sheer clamp to 3/16 inch square. Apply resin to the sheer clamps and hold them in place with spring clamps or clothes pins until it cures.

Bevel the exterior radius of the plywood, as you would on a full-size hull if you were using nylon webbing. Then join the two panels along the keel line and at the bow with duct tape or masking tape. Be careful to line the edges up perfectly. Surmarks help guarantee alignment fore and aft.

The next stage of the design is to decide how far apart and at what points to spread the panels to achieve the hull shape that you desire. If you have drawn a rough body plan view of the shape that you hope to get out of the compounded plywood, you can use this as a beginning point by simply measuring from the body plan the angles of the hull panels as they emerge from the keel line on both sides.

The panels join at specific keel angles. Divide the hull into four equal parts by drawing lines through it at the hull midpoint, a point between the bow and the midpoint, and a point between the midpoint and the stern. These three lines become measuring points for determining the keel angle. If the hull has a transom, include it as another measuring point. The size of the keel angle at the various lines will almost always fall within fairly narrow ranges. At the forward section line, it's usually between 80° and 90°, while the mid and aft section line angles are usually between 120° and 170°. Occasionally, if the transom is very round and flat, the stern line angle may be fuller than 140°, with the transom itself as much as 180° on some designs. Larger keel angles will provide more displacement and less wetted surface and are therefore desirable.

You are, however, limited by how much the plywood can be compounded, and by the amount of longitudinal rocker that is cut into the two plywood panels. Theoretically, if there were no rocker cut into the panels at all, you could join two panels at close to 180° included angle and then fold them up into a perfect half circle. As soon as the keel line of the panels is no longer straight and the panels have curved rocker cut into them, the 180° included angle is no longer possible and reduces accordingly in direct ratio to the amount of increase in rocker profile that you use in the plywood panel. Thus, a trade-off relationship exists between these two opposing demands on the plywood skin when developing compound curvature.

With the model you can go for broke and try for the largest amount of keel angle that you think you can get away with. If the stress is so much on the plywood panels that they break in the folding-up process, you can try less angle with the next model until you achieve a successful result. While this trial-and-error method may appear crude, we know of no more scientific method to use. No doubt it is only a matter of time until someone computerizes the compoundability of plywood panels with all of the different variations. This perhaps would reduce compounded plywood boat design down to a neat, tidy, mathematical program. But at the moment, experimentation seems the only way to proceed.

Carefully mark the bowline, centerline and stern line positions on the model panels, just as they are marked on the full sized panels, as measurement points for keeping track of the included angles that are used. For each measurement position, cut out a small plywood template with the exact included angle desired to form a V-shape into which you can spread apart the panels with accuracy. Staples or tape can hold the V-shaped plywood templates in place temporarily until the keel has cured.

As mentioned earlier, the width of the composite keel is also a factor in determining hull fullness. By preventing the plywood from starting its bend close to the keel line, a larger rigid keel effectively promotes the bend out further in the hull panel, developing more fullness (and displacement) in the hull. Thus, the larger keel also contributes to the compounding of the plywood structure, and must be understood as another warring faction that competes with the included angle and keel profile cut when developing compounding in the plywood panels.

With the small models, making the keel is the most sensitive and difficult part of producing a model hull that will scale up properly. To be more accurate, very carefully scribe two lines on each panel at the 2 inch and the 4 inch (scale inches) levels up from and parallel to the keel line all along its perimeter. Carefully install the poured keel, using a syringe to lay in a bead of thickened adhesive (using the 406 filler) that is made just thick enough so that it will not run, but not so thick that it is not easily applied by the syringe. (Load the syringes with this thickened material by pulling out the plunger.) Using the scribed lines as a guide for the manufactured keel width, carefully pour the keel down the center of the panels, trying to keep the bead as even and straight as possible. With just the syringe you can lay an accurate bead of resin in place, but if too much resin ends up in one area of the keel or not enough in another, you can use a small stick to scrape excesses carefully from one area and deposit them in another to even up the keel before the resin begins to cure. When performing this operation, it helps if the model is rigidly supported. You can usually accomplish this with the V-shaped plywood templates that are needed to hold the panels at their various angles anyway.

When the resin has cured, the keel by itself should be more than strong enough to support the two panels properly during the fold-up. There is no need to apply glass cloth tape along the keel line, as we would do with the full size hull.

The degree to which the panels are folded up toward each other is another factor affecting the amount of compounding that is induced into the plywood. U-shaped hulls with a lot of fullness down low and narrow decks will induce more compounding stresses within the plywood than a narrower hull with a wider deck. Deck width can be measured as a percentage of the height of the panel at its maximum point. A typical deck width-to-hull panel ratio is around 75%. For instance, if our panel height were 24 inches at its maximum size, a typical deck width would be approximately 18 inches. Any narrower ratio than this might exert extra bending and compounding forces upon the plywood for which you should make some allowance in the initial design by reducing some of the other compounding factors. The degree to which the plywood panels will be folded toward each other (or deck width) also affects the rocker profile. Narrow decks produce less rocker and wider decks promote more rocker. It is easy to witness this phenomenon by making several deck jigs for your model at varying widths and measuring the amount of rocker that is produced at the different widths. The compounded plywood concept of construction demands overall fair curves for all segments, including the deck profile. The profile of the deck should have gracefully flowing lines and not have any unusual fullness in the bow or straight lines that might contribute to distortions in the panels as they are being compounded. (See Figure 32.)

Make the deck jig for the model by carving one half of the deck line profile out of thin plywood (⅛ inch thickness works well), and then make a duplicate for the other side. Join these two pieces of plywood with cross braces at the bow and the transom and a third brace in the middle to complete the deck jig. Make sure that the plywood is thick enough and big enough so that no distortion of the deck jig will take place with only one brace in the middle. Then fold up the plywood model and insert it into the deck jig. The cross braces at the bow and the transom, together with the one in the middle, act as guides to hold the deck jig at the general sheer line position on top of the folded-up model. It is usually easy to fold up the model by hand

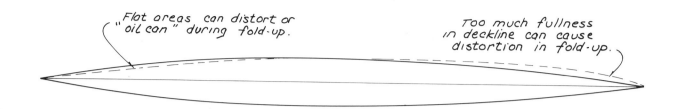

Figure 32—Considerations for deck plan on folded hulls.

and insert it into the deck jig, but occasionally another person is needed to help with this operation.

So that you can remove the deck jig and more closely evaluate the hull, complete the model by bonding on a precut deck to hold the hull in permanent position. For the deck use the same thin birch plywood that is used to fold up the hull. Cut out two deck panel pieces, one forward and one aft, that will fit between the three braces on the deck jig. Even though you can't cover all of the hull with the deck sections because some of the deck jig braces are in the way, this partial deck will give enough support to the sheers so that there should be no distortion once the deck jig is removed. Attach the deck by bonding it in place with thickened adhesive and holding it down with light weights until the adhesive cures. To keep the adhesive from bonding the deck to the deck jig and/or the deck jig to the hull, coat the deck jig carefully beforehand with a mold release (paraffin works well).

With the deck jig removed and the deck plywood faired smooth with the sheer, you will have a model hull that you can now study closely. Establishing waterlines on the model hull is necessary so that displacement values can be calculated. Choose the desired waterline position at both the bow and transom areas and set the model upside down on a flat plane. Prop the model up on blocks so that the marked fore and aft waterline positions are the same distance from the flat plane surface. Use a block and a pencil to draw a continuous waterline around the hull using the flat plane as a guide. Make sure that the model is also parallel in the athwartship direction during marking. (See Figure 33.)

With waterlines permanently inscribed on the model, you will now be able to take off measurements from the hull so that you can determine the center of buoyancy and the total displacement available at given waterline heights. You will also be able to figure your prismatic coefficient together with wetted surface area. For detailed instructions on how to figure all of these factors, consult Chapter 23 of Skene's *Elements of Yacht Design,* 8th edition, (Dodd, Mead & Co., New York, 1973). With this first model, you will undoubt-

edly find some parts of the hull shape that are not entirely to your liking. The object then is to determine what changes you can make in the next model to persuade it to look more like the hull you envision. Remember you might well have to compromise, because what you would like to get in a hull shape may be an impossibility with this method of construction.

If you decide to make a second model, you can measure the effect of the changes made in the second model against the first. From this data, you can assess a cause and effect relationship of any change. The more models you build with changes, the better your understanding of the compounded plywood process will be. We would advise anyone designing a hull for this process to spend at least a couple of days developing a number of models just to gain experience in the compounded plywood building method.

Going from the Model to Full Size

When you have developed a model hull that you are happy with, expand all the measurements of the model up to full size. The most important set of measurements will come from the master template, that is, the exact duplicate of the hull panels used in the successful model. Position the master template on ¼ inch square graph paper with the anticipated waterlines as

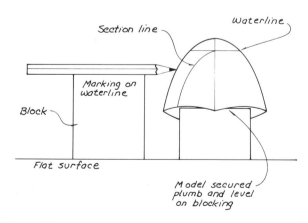

Figure 33—Marking waterlines and station lines on fold-up models.

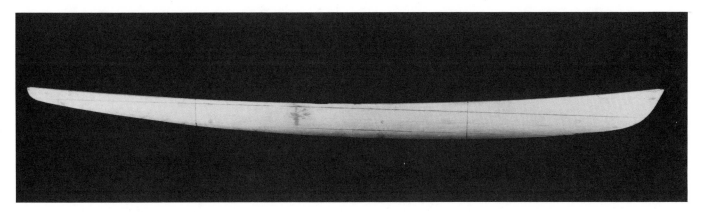

Figure 34—Model of outriggers shown in Figure 27. This model has been marked with waterlines and section lines.

parallel as possible to the horizontal lines of the paper. Then draw the perimeter of the template on the graph paper using fine lead with a sharp point for the best accuracy. Draw a longitudinal line through the approximate horizontal center of the panel. This becomes the reference line for all future measurements, and you can draw other longitudinal reference lines parallel to it if necessary. (See Figure 35.) Then make measurements of the keel line and sheer line using 1 foot to 2 foot intervals, depending on the size and amount of curvature involved. Closer measurement intervals, although they involve more work, produce more accuracy. In areas of rapid change such as might occur in the bow or transom, you may want to reduce measuring intervals down to as little as 4 inches to achieve enough accuracy. Then transfer these measurements to a full size plywood sheet that also uses a drawn center line as a main point of reference for all dimensions, with lines drawn at right angles to the center line at each predetermined measurement point. Lay down the center line using a tight cable, just as is done in lofting, for the best accuracy.

Carefully lift the measurements of the model panel from the graph paper, using a divider with fine points. Use great care and a sharp eye to interpret parts of inches from the scale ruler. List the measurements in a simple table under station positions for transfer to the full size plywood panel.

After you have transferred all measurements, use a lofting batten to connect all the measurement points. Because of the 1 to 12 scale-up, errors of plus or minus ⅛ inch are standard, with ¼ inch to ⅜ inch errors not uncommon. Using standard lofting techniques, try to pick the happy median between the measurement dots. Continue to adjust the lofting batten until it represents a fair curve with minimal variation from the measurement points.

A 90° angle is a 90° angle, no matter the length of its sides, so directly transfer the angles at which the panels are joined on the model to full size. The keel is, however, a different matter. It is the most difficult part of the model to scale up and accuracy here relies primarily on the craftsmanship of the builder. The difference between a 2 inch wide keel and a 4 inch wide keel is very small on a model, but quite significant on a finished hull.

The only other dimension to scale up is the deck perimeter, so that you can build a full size deck jig. This scale-up is not as critical as on the panel itself, and the main concern is with overall fair curves in the lofting batten rather than total accuracy on the deck width, where ¼ inch difference over, for example, 20 inches, would mean little difference in hull performance.

Using Fiberglass Cloth on Compounded Plywood Models

In the past few years we have begun significantly increasing the stiffness of some compounded hulls by applying a layer of 4 oz. or 6 oz. fiberglass cloth to the outside of panels before folding them. When 5-ply plywood is sheathed in glass cloth, the fiberglass basically turns it into the equivalent of a 6-ply panel.

Because these increases can be dramatic, this variation on compounding occasionally causes problems. We recommend that before attempting the procedure on an entire hull, you experiment with a model and then, if that bends successfully, that you test a 2 foot long section of the plywood and glass schedule which you plan to use, bending it to the hardest curves in the hull. In areas of tight curves, folding is sometimes easier if you moisten the inside of the plywood with warm water.

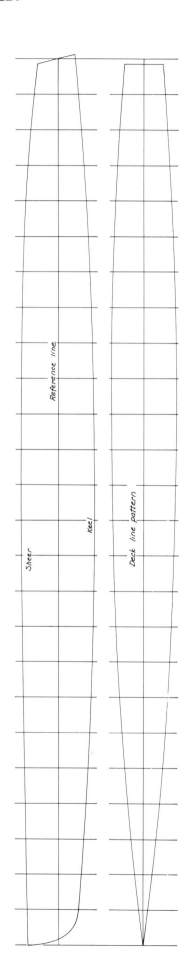

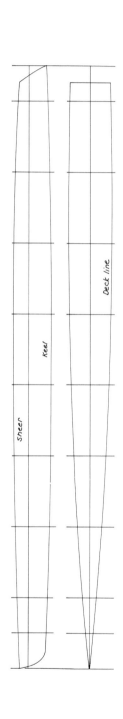

Stations	0	1	2	3	4	5	6	7	8	9	10	11	12	13	14	15	16	17	18	19	20	21	22	23	24	25	
Profile sheer above reference line	0-10-3	0-11-1	0-11-4	0-11-6	1-0-0	1-0-1	1-0-3	1-0-5	1-0-6	1-0-7	1-0-7	1-1-0	1-1-0	1-1-1	1-1	1-1	1-1-0	1-1-0	1-0-7	1-0-6	1-0-1	1-1-3	0-10-4	0-9-4	0-8-4	0-7-0	Sheer
Profile keel below reference line	0-7-0	0-8-1	0-9-0	0-9-7	0-10-7	0-11-0	0-11-4	1-0-0	1-0-2	1-0-4	1-0-5	1-0-6	1-0-7	1-1-0	1-0-5	1-0-4	1-0-0r	0-11-7	0-11-3	0-10-7	0-10-3	0-9-5	0-8-7	0-8-0	0-7-0	0-6-0	Keel
Half-breadth deck line from ℄	0-0-1-4	0-3-0	0-3-6	0-4-3	0-5-6	0-6-6	0-7-5	0-8-3r	0-9-2	0-9-6	0-10-2	0-10-4	0-10-7	0-11-0	0-11-1r	0-11-2	0-11-2r	0-11-2	0-11-2	0-11-0	0-10-2r	0-10-6	0-9-1	0-8-3	0-7-4		Deck
Profile sheer above reference line	0-3-0	0-3-6	0-4-5	0-5-0	0-5-2	0-5-3	0-5-2	0-4-5	0-3-5r																		Sheer
Profile keel below reference line	0-6-3	0-6-6	0-7-3	0-7-5	0-7-7	0-7-7	0-7-6	0-7-3	0-6-7	0-6-3																	Keel
Half-breadth deck line from ℄	0-0-1-3	0-2-4	0-4-2	0-5-5	0-6-6	0-7-3	0-7-5	0-7-5	0-7-2	0-7-0																	Deck

Figure 35—Hull and deck panels for VICTOR T. Offsets given in feet, inches and eighths of an inch.

Chapter 24

Interior Construction

Boat interiors can range from the very simple to the highly complex. Typically, large boats tend to have more complete interiors than small boats, and cruising boats have more highly developed interiors than racing boats. It has been said that a boat with a perfect interior has yet to be invented. The age-old problem of trying to put a lot of accommodations into a limited amount of space is a difficult design problem. We feel that boat designers really earn their money when it comes to interior planning and layout.

We are not interior design specialists, but we do have definite thoughts on interior construction. Our approach may be closer to the one used in aircraft design than traditional boat design in that we think that the interior should be an integral part of the structure, and it may offer designers more flexibility in the use of space and materials. We've had clear objectives as we have worked on interiors. Of these, keeping weight to a minimum, using the interior to improve the vessel structure, increasing interior utility and improving the appearance of the interior have been the most important.

Unfortunately, the joinery for most boat interiors will require a significant portion of the labor hours needed to build the boat. Professional builders are well aware of this problem, and many a builder has learned the hard way by underbidding this part of the boat. More than any other aspect of the boat, interiors require planning and strategy for the most efficient use of materials and labor hours. Over the years, we have developed a few simple techniques which have helped to reduce the labor hours needed for interior work and, at the same time, have made interiors more enjoyable on which to work. We present our suggestions here, but we must also emphasize that every boat interior will present its own unique construction problems. Careful thought, common sense and an open mind are all needed to choose the best construction strategy.

Keeping interior weight to a minimum

On racing boats, the weight of interior amenities has always been looked at with a very critical eye. The added weight of any interior, even on a heavy cruising boat, should be carefully considered. Interiors are usually nonstructural or secondary structural items, and need not be built with the safety margins required for the hull and deck structure. Construction with our methods can make interiors lighter. If you can save 200 or 500 pounds on a cruising boat's interior, you can lessen the vessel burden and increase its capacity to carry fuel, water or stores.

Using the interior to improve the vessel structure

With proper planning, it's possible to install many interior items so that they help to reinforce and support the hull skin. When bunks, shelves, cabinets and tables are correctly bonded to a hull, they can contribute to its strength and also add stiffness to the structure by holding the hull skin in position in their immediate areas. This is especially effective if the vessel is designed from the start so that interior items are laid out to provide the most support. The interior is no longer just dead weight for the hull to carry around. Instead, it contributes to the overall integrity of the vessel. By becoming structural, interior items at least partially pay for themselves on a weight-to-strength basis.

Increasing the utility of the interior

Unitized interior construction can minimize the up-keep and maintenance of the interior and allow it to be kept clean easily. Proper assembly and use of materials maximizes usable space. If, for example, you use fillets instead of large cleats to attach interior items to a hull, you can eliminate some room-consuming framework. When all surfaces are smooth and glossy, cleanup is easier. All of these increase the usefulness of the interior.

Improving interior appearance

When you use wood for boatbuilding, you can exploit the variety of wood grains and colors for simple but very attractive appointments. With wood, unlike other materials, no part of the boat must be concealed under headliners, ceilings or other facades, although these are sometimes desirable for covering frames, ribs and stringers. Effective use of various woods and combinations of woods can produce beautiful results with surprisingly little additional effort. We like naturally finished wood grain, but we do paint interior surfaces when necessary for better contrast, to lighten a dark interior or to aid in clean-up.

Figure 1—Six bunks, a galley and shelves bonded to the interior of this hull skin contributed to a noticeably stiffer structure.

Installing Interiors in Set-Ups

As we discussed in earlier chapters, portions of the interior, including bulkheads, frames, and other structural members, can be installed in set-ups for stringer-frame and strip plank construction. Other interior items, such as bunks, shelving and counters, can also be built into set-ups and these too can become structural. Major labor savings result from installing them at this stage rather than when the boat is completed. During set-up you can work in an unencumbered position from the floor with reasonably free access to all parts of the hull and fitting is often much easier.

Figure 2—Interior of boat shown in Figure 1. Note teak sole with white pigment/resin highlight.

One of the goals of this chapter is to identify the options and complications which affect the choice of methods used for interior construction. The amount of interior which can be installed during set-up depends on the complexity of the set-up itself. If you have many dummy frames and supports, you may have so many obstacles that it's difficult to judge if you will save time by installing the interior at this point or later. You will obviously need a great deal of planning and ingenuity from the beginning if you are going to install interior items in the set-up; we suggest that you begin planning during lofting, if not earlier.

To build interior items into a set-up, position them with excess wood extending to or beyond the true hull profile. Later, fair the excess in with the rest of the hull, using a batten and hand planes as you would to fair frames, stringers and bulkheads. (See Chapter 15).

Figure 3—IOR ½ ton racer. Bulkhead and partitions in set-up mixed with temporary chipboard molds.

Installing Interiors in Upside-Down Hulls

Work can begin on the interior and progress to a very advanced stage while the hull is still upside down. We admit that there are some problems with installing interiors in inverted hulls — such as learning to measure upside down — but there are also many benefits.

First, work can continue on the exterior of the hull as you build the interior. This is particularly efficient if you have a large crew and are trying to finish the boat as quickly as possible. When you work on the floor you have much more room than in an upright hull, so you can use more people and machinery. Some upright boats have only enough space for one or two people. With these, working from the floor can allow two or three people to move around and also make room for machinery. Another benefit is that you can set up small

Figure 4—Interior construction in upside-down hull of IOR ½ ton racer. Lighting and tools are set up. Note bandsaw in background at far right.

benches and machinery such as a band saw, disc sander and jointer inside the hull, and this saves labor.

When the hull is inverted you can save time by avoiding a lot of climbing. The average builder goes in and out of his hull several dozen times in the course of a day. With the hull upside down, you will have to duck under the sheer. (You can raise it 2 feet or more to make crawling in and out easier).

Another advantage of building the interior while the hull is upside down is that work in progress is always much cleaner. Shavings and sawdust drop to the floor rather than into the bilge, so constant cleaning isn't required. If you are building a boat with minimal shelter, an inverted hull can protect joinery, machinery and stock from the elements.

There are, however, some disadvantages to working in an upside-down boat. Since good lighting is essential to quality joinery, you will have to set up a lighting system, which may be inferior to general shop lighting, inside the hull. Overhead work tends to be tiresome and hard on the arms. Finally, you may need platforms or scaffolding to reach some portions of the interior.

Installing Interiors in Upright Hulls

As we have discussed, a major problem with the hull in the upright position is getting in and out of it. You should do anything you can to minimize this time-consuming problem. We always try to keep the hull as close to the floor as possible, installing all appendages such as keels and rudder late in the construction process. The difference of just 1 foot in height means that the worker has 1 foot less to climb up and 1 foot less to climb down each time he either enters or exits the hull. With hundreds of trips, this saves many extra hours.

Other steps can be taken to facilitate access to the hull. With some boats it's possible to leave the transom open so that workers will have easier access. Sometimes you can erect scaffolding to create a substantial amount of floor area at sheer height, and on this you can set up handy tools and a bench. In our shop we have a second-story loft 8 feet above the floor. We adjust the sheer height of hulls even with the loft and work out of it. If a hull is large enough, you can set up a workshop in the boat, and do a lot of machining right at the job site rather than outside it.

Proper planning of your work limits the number of trips you have to make in and out of the hull. By carefully organizing the job immediately ahead, you can gather the exact tools and the materials you will need. It's very aggravating to have to crawl up and out of the hull because you forgot your pencil or you don't

Figure 5—Interior of the IOR ½ ton racer after righting, before completion of interior details and installation of hardware and engine.

Figure 6—Transom left open for easy access to interior. Structural banks are also airtight buoyancy tanks for this lightweight laminated sloop.

have quite enough clamps to complete a bonding operation. Careful planning will help you avoid this. Pre-manufacture materials to the greatest extent possible before you carry them up inside the hull.

General Approach — Joinery

We rely on joints bonded with WEST SYSTEM* Brand epoxy for interior construction because they are often stronger and easier to make than fastened joints. All interior bonded joints must have adequate area for maximum strength, so we engineer them with this in mind. Although we often can use clamps and weights to hold parts in place as resin cures, we also use staple guns with fine wire brads or narrow crown staples. We set these fasteners in slightly and leave them in place; the small holes they make are hard to detect after filling.

We often use fillet joints in interiors, especially where curved surfaces meet. Fillets, described in detail in Chapter 9, save a great deal of time and are strong for their weight. Rounded fillets are also easy to keep clean. Plywood and wood parts can be bonded quickly to the curved inner hull surface by positioning them and applying a fillet of proper thickness on either side at the intersection of the mating materials. The alterna-

* TRADEMARK OF GOUGEON BROTHERS, INC., U.S.A.

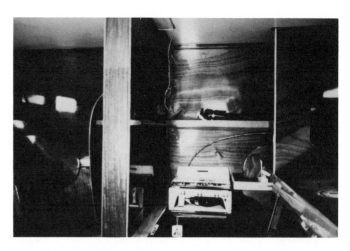

Figure 8—ROGUE WAVE's galley area after deck was installed. Sandwich construction of deck in this area required a headliner skin. This smooth plywood panel was painted white to lighten naturally finished interior.

tive to filleting is to laboriously attach shaped wooden cleats to the curved surface and to bond the parts to these cleats.

Materials

We often use plywood for interior construction because of its light weight and excellent strength and stiffness. It takes much less time to cut parts from large plywood panels than it does to piece them together from many small pieces of sawn stock. Most of our interiors have been built with ¼ inch (6mm) to ½ inch (12mm) thick ply. Except for bulkheads in larger boats, there is no reason to use thicker panels, and in many cases ¼ inch plywood will work if it has adequate supporting framework. We have also used much thinner plywood for making sandwich panels with a honeycomb core.

Nowhere is the use of prefinished plywood more important than in building interiors. The labor hour savings alone are well worthwhile and a much higher quality finish is usually the added bonus. We have found it beneficial to precoat whole sheets of plywood, usually on both sides, rather than to prefinish individual parts. (See Chapter 11 on coating.) You can coat large panels more efficiently and save lots of time in sanding. Smaller parts usually have to be hand sanded, so as not to sand through the coating around the edges, but you can machine sand large panels very quickly. The disadvantage of prefinishing whole panels is some waste of the prefinished panel. However, this must be weighed against the labor savings. In some situations, it may be best to cut out the parts first before prefinishing. In all cases, however, you should attempt

Figure 7—ROGUE WAVE's galley, pilot berth, navigation area and daggerboard case. All interior joinery was installed before deck was built. Circular pads on bulkhead are reinforcing gussets. Note lift-out access ports in cabin sole. Unfinished teak cockpit sole is in lower left of photo.

Figure 9—Design details for interior joinery. The basic designs are universal to boatbuilding, but modifications can be made to lighten the structures without sacrificing strength because they are bonded. We usually use fillets and triangular cleats instead of square stock for interior construction and get the same bonding area for less weight. It's easy to form corner pieces for settees, bulkheads and other molded items over common objects such as pipes and barrels.

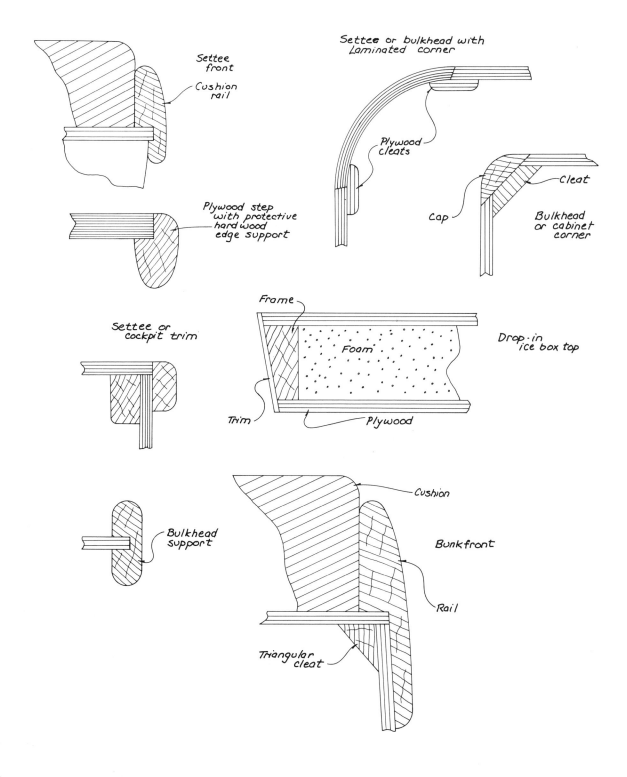

to prefinish the parts prior to installation rather than coat and sand the finished interior joinery after it has been installed.

When you are sawing parts out of plywood panels, sawing can chip out the upper face of the plywood edges, causing some unsightly scars which will show up in a natural finish. Using a band saw minimizes the chipping problem because it cuts downward and at a higher rate of speed. The more commonly-used saber saw presents a problem. You can tape over the line to be cut with clear cellophane tape or scribe a line with a sharp knife to minimize wood chipping. Using a sharp, hollow-ground saber saw blade with no set is also helpful. Generally, a precoated panel will not chip as badly as an uncoated panel.

Measuring

Before moving a completed hull from the set-up, we always mark a true waterline on its exterior and also at various places on the interior, if possible. (When using the mold method, you might have to use a marked sheer line as the reference line.) With a clearly marked exterior waterline, you can turn the hull over and then reposition it easily on its lines, so that the interior layout can begin.

Before you install any interior items, you must set the hull on its lines, both in the fore and aft and athwartship dimensions, so that proper measurements can be made. This is true whether the hull is in the upright or inverted position. With the hull plumb on its lines, you can use the level as the major tool to position interior layout dimensions accurately. With the waterline position known on the inside of the hull, you can measure all further interior dimensions either up or down from this reference line. The only other dimension to determine is the fore and aft reference from the station lines.

Making Templates

Fitting interior parts is one of the more difficult jobs of boatbuilding. Besides the normal curves that must be fitted *to*, a typical interior has numerous obstructions such as bulkheads, keel, frames and sheer clamps which a part must be fitted *around*. The normal complexity of this problem requires the use of templates to most efficiently define the final dimensions for a part. Trying to fit the part itself usually causes too much waste of material.

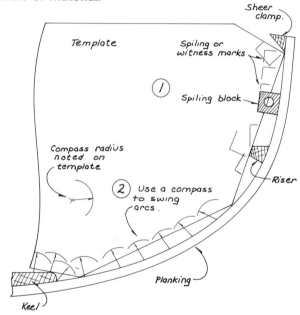

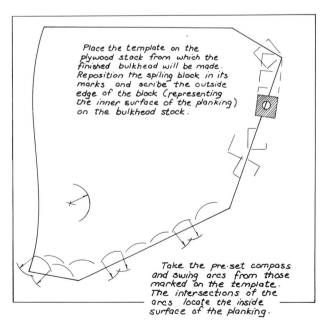

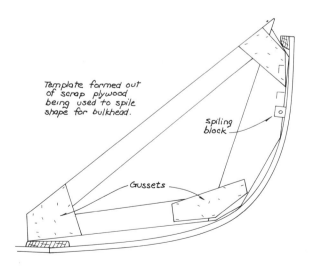

Figure 10—Template built up with scrap lumber and plywood gussets.

Figure 11—Two methods for spiling a bulkhead.

Any thin material that can be easily shaped is adequate for template material. We regularly use scrap pieces of plywood or veneer, which we temporarily fasten together with staples to quickly fashion a rough template that is as close to the desired final dimensions as possible. Initial mistakes in fitting are easily rectified by making additions to the template or dismantling and reassembling the template for another try.

Marking the template can be done with a compass or a spiling block, as described in Figures 10, 11, and 17. Sometimes two separate markings may be required to develop a close fit. After the first marking and sawing, the template will fit close enough so that the final marking and subsequent sawing will be much more accurate. A hand held block plane is the main hand tool used to machine the template to a final, and hopefully perfect, fit, but a spokeshave, offset chisel and file all end up being used at some point.

In some instances, a template may fit perfectly, with only a few gaps. Correct these by stapling on another piece of template stock to take up the gaps or measure and mark the gaps on the pattern so that the differences can be transferred to the actual part. When the template is finished, position it on the stock for marking. Then transfer the template measurements carefully, marking them with accurate lines.

It's easier to fit less complex parts right to the hull. Direct fitting can be particularly effective if you use the lofting as a guide for rough shaping parts before finally fitting them. Some builders rely heavily on lofting and cut interior parts so accurately that they need very little final finishing.

It's also possible to make many interior items outside the boat, where work is much more efficient, and to install them when they are finished. This can save a lot of time, but with more complicated parts the measuring problem can escalate, and when this happens time savings are reduced. As a general rule, it's best to build interior items which are easily fit to straight or gently-curved surfaces, or those which stand free, such as tables, outside the hull and then install them.

Bulkheads and Partitions

Bulkheads are considered structural parts of the hull, but in some boats, where they serve as partitions to separate accommodations, they are also functional parts of the interior. Because they usually contribute structurally, bulkheads are often of very sound construction. They are typically bonded to the hull in such a way as to be able to transfer considerable load to the skin.

Figure 12—Major structural bulkhead for GOLDEN DAZY is constructed with a framework sandwiched between two ½ inch thick panels of utile plywood.

To become interior partitions, bulkheads need little more than trim around exposed edges, as would appear in the walk-through. Installing trim on these edges improves their appearance and makes them safer than sharp plywood. Generally, all cutouts in bulkheads have rounded corners because sharp corners become points of stress concentration. All cutouts in a bulkhead theoretically have some weakening effect, so we often rely on the trim to strengthen and stiffen the weakened cutout area. Whenever we build what we consider structural trim, we laminate curves and corners instead

Figure 13—Bulkhead showing laminated hardwood trim on the walk-through.

of sawing them out of solid stock. We always scarf joints in structural trim although butt joints are more standard with most trim.

To insure privacy, the designer may specify a door in the bulkhead. With a small adjustment in the design of the trim, you can incorporate an adequate door frame system into the bulkhead opening. This only leaves the difficulty of building a door to fit this opening and frame system. The main problem with doors is that it is

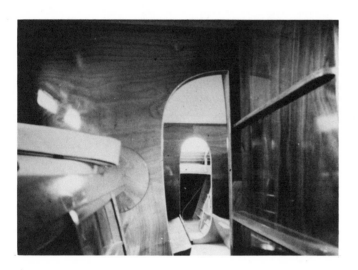

Figure 14—Opening in a structural bulkhead on ROGUE WAVE. Daggerboard trunk to right is bonded to this bulkhead.

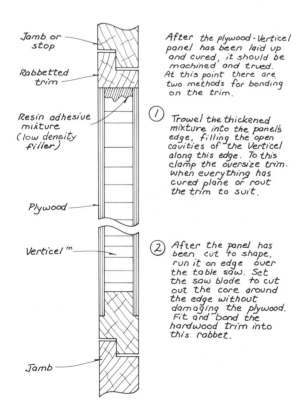

Jamb or stop

Rabbetted trim

Resin adhesive mixture (low density filler)

After the plywood-Verticel panel has been laid up and cured, it should be machined and trued. At this point there are two methods for bonding on the trim.

① Trowel the thickened mixture into the panel's edge, filling the open cavities of the Verticel along this edge. To this clamp the oversize trim. When everything has cured plane or rout the trim to suit.

Plywood

Verticel ™

② After the panel has been cut to shape, run it on edge over the table saw. Set the saw blade to cut out the core around the edge without damaging the plywood. Fit and bond the hardwood trim into this rabbet.

Jamb

Figure 15—Section through door showing core, skins and two methods of bonding trim.

difficult to get light ones which will stay perfectly flat. A ½ inch thick plywood door, if it is perfectly flat to begin with, will probably not stay that way forever. Like doors which are constructed for houses, the most successful doors for boats are laminated of two thinner sheets of plywood with a core material in between. These doors are light, strong and very stable, with an excellent chance of maintaining their original dimensions. (See Chapter 9 on laminating for details on cored laminating procedure.)

Partition walls, such as those which might be used to enclose a head, are generally nonstructural. They need only be strong enough to survive the rigors of hard sailing and in most situations ⅜ inch thick plywood is adequate. We have successfully used ¼ inch ply, sometimes including minor framing to improve overall panel stiffness. For large partitions, you may choose to use the core construction techniques outlined in Chapter 9. Core construction saves weight and results in stiff partitions with better sound-deadening quality than possible with a single panel.

Figure 16—Galley on 30 foot trimaran with bulkhead forward and hanging locker at lower right.

Cabin Sole (Floor)

The first part of the interior to be installed is the cabin sole, or floor, which will be walked on. Plywood from ⅜ inch to ½ inch thickness is generally used as the floor base, with proper support framing underneath. To achieve maximum headroom, most designers will strive to get the floor as low as possible in the bilge. This sometimes causes frustrating construction problems due to lack of room. We have found that bonding a portion of the floor permanently to the hull has helped locate the floor as low as possible within the

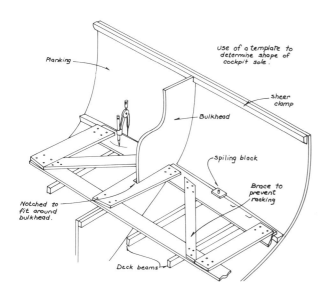

Figure 17—Spiling the shape of a cockpit sole.

only is refuse difficult to clean out of the bilge, but it can do a marvelous job of clogging bilge pumps. This is at best an aggravation, and at worst potentially dangerous. The lift-out portions of the floor should fit well with proper hold-down systems to keep them snugly in place — this will facilitate keeping the floor area clean. You should leave a minimum gap of 1/16 inch between all edges and for unusually large panels you should probably increase the gap.

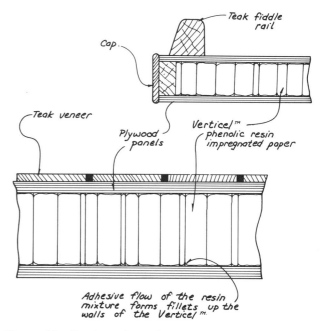

Figure 19—Sections through counter top and cockpit sole showing core construction.

hull cavity. The permanent floor also has great potential to contribute structurally to the overall strength and stiffness of the hull itself.

Obviously, portions of the floor must be removable to afford complete access to the bilge. This accessibility is important, both for cleaning and for repairing any damage which might occur. As a minimum guideline, you should be able to reach every part of the bilge with your hand when extending your arm through all available openings in the floor. With narrow, deep hulls, only a small percentage of the floor need be removable. (See Figure 20.) Wide, flat hulls, however, may require that a substantial portion of the floor be removable to permit suitable access to the bilge.

We feel that floors should be complete and integral enough to keep general debris out of the bilge. Not

Figure 18—Installing cabin sole framework in ROGUE WAVE. Structure supports the hull skin as well as the cabin sole.

Figure 20—Forepeak cabin sole with lift-out sections.

The bilge is the area of the boat most prone to dampness so give special attention to carefully coating all bilge surfaces to insure maximum protection. We further recommend that the bilge area always be clear finished — never painted — so that you can easily detect any moisture damage which might occur by noticing if the wood turns dark. A successfully designed and constructed boat should have dry bilges. The only way for moisture or water to get down below should be through open hatches or skylights, with wet sails or from people coming down from above. Like any other part of the interior, bilges should be ventilated, utilizing openings in areas which allow air passage but not allowing dirt and debris into the bilge.

Icebox Construction

We have constructed many successful iceboxes using ¼ inch plywood with light density closed cell urethane foam as the insulation medium. Usually, we design the inside of the icebox so that we will have the maximum amount of icebox room for a given amount of interior space, allowing for a minimum of 2 inches of insulation all around the exterior of the *inner icebox*. Two inches of foam are adequate for most situations, but we would advise against using any less. On occasion, we have used up to 4 inches of urethane foam insulation to get maximum cooling performance.

Begin by building the inner box. Since a major goal is to build a box which has a rounded, smooth interior with no difficult-to-clean sharp corners, we like to use large low density fillets on the inside corners to join side and bottom panels. It's most efficient to locate the opening on the top of the box and try to make it as small as practical for easy access. When the interior box is finished, but before assembling its top, apply a

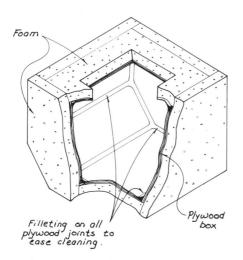

Foam

Filleting on all plywood joints to ease cleaning.

Plywood box

Figure 21—Cutaway of inner icebox construction.

minimum of four coats of WEST SYSTEM epoxy to its interior surfaces. We often add a layer of 6 oz. fiberglass cloth to the interior for abrasion resistance. Add white pigment to the final resin coatings to facilitate future cleaning: the white makes it easy to tell when you've got the icebox clean. Sand thoroughly by the third coat, so that the final coat will be smooth. When you have coated the box interior and the underside of the icebox top, attach the top.

Fit a neck around the perimeter of the top opening. This should be at least as high above the box ceiling as the thickness of the insulation you plan to use. To be sure that you will have adequate bonding area, make the neck from ½ inch or thicker stock or plywood. Give the exterior of the inner box a penetration coating of resin and allow it to become tacky before bonding precut pieces of foam in place. Then use a thick mixture of epoxy and low density filler to carefully bond the insulation to all exterior surfaces of the inner box, leaving only the top opening uncovered. An adhesive mixture which is sufficiently thick will act as contact cement, holding the foam in place without clamps. If difficulties arise, use tape or string to hold the foam in place.

When the interior box is finished, position it on a preconstructed base which will hold it at its proper height. Bond the foam on the bottom of the inner box to this base, using the same thick adhesive. Then install front and side panels around the foam perimeter. Although the panels don't have to touch the foam, it's ideal if it works out that they do.

If the icebox is located against the hull, leave a gap between the foam and the planking and don't try to fit it snug. Doing it this way requires less fitting and is therefore easier; having the foam tight against the hull serves little structural purpose. Make the lid for the icebox the same thickness of insulating foam as the base and bond to its inner and outer surfaces plywood as thick as that used on the inner and outer boxes. When the lid fits, install a lip around the perimeter of the box and add a handle to complete the job.

Tanks

Wooden holding tanks coated with WEST SYSTEM epoxy have been extremely successful, mainly because they are inexpensive and easy to build. You can build tanks to the exact size and shape you need and eliminate the time and expense of preparing drawings for a metal tank fabricator. While there are arguments in favor of building tanks permanently into the hull, we always make them as separate, usually removable, units so that if the hull is damaged, we can remove the tanks to repair it.

Figure 22—Forty gallon tank on ROGUE WAVE, constructed using fillets and fiberglass tape for all inside joints. The top of this tank forms part of cabin sole and tank is removable. Baffles are scalloped on upper edge so each compartment will vent. Three-eighths inch notches at the bottom of scallops are for longitudinal plywood frames to support the top.

The procedure for constructing the interior of a tank is similar to that used for the interior of an icebox, except that you can use cleats on the exterior corners to assemble the plywood panels if desired. Venting is needed to prevent build-up of gas pressure. Baffles should be installed to reduce the surge effect that can otherwise occur and to support the structure. If you use them, the number and size of baffles is proportionate to the size of the tank. A typical 40 gallon tank might have two or three baffles about three-fifths the size of the interior section area.

Build the tank in two halves, the main box, with or without baffles, and the top. To maximize space, you can mold curved side panels which conform to the contour of the hull out of sheets of plywood or veneer, and then assemble them with standard sheet ply to complete the tank. Depending on the size, shape and amount of support provided, ¼ inch plywood is probably strong enough for most tanks up to 40 gallons. Thickness of plywood for tanks is mainly determined by weight-per-square foot of unsupported area. Supports for a ¼ inch tank should be no more than 1 foot apart, assuming loading of 30 pounds per square foot.

Holding tanks do need occasional cleaning, so we always include a removable port in the middle to provide access to all parts of the tank. Coat the interior surface of the tank heavily with resin and apply a layer of 6 oz. fiberglass cloth to the interior. Try to make the interior surface as smooth as possible to facilitate cleaning.

We have made fuel tanks using the same basic tank construction techniques. Up to this point they have been very successful. However, we do not feel that we have enough experience with them yet to recommend them unconditionally. WEST SYSTEM resin is resistant to gasoline and fuel oil, so this does not seem to pose a problem. Our main concern is the safety of such tanks in the presence of fire. Wood tanks, unlike steel tanks, can burn, but steel tanks also appear to have their problems. Steel tanks can prevent open flames from getting to the raw fuel (or fumes), but they can't prevent the *heat* from getting to the fuel, and heat can be just as big a problem as open flames. Gasoline will spontaneously combust at about 900° F., but at much lower temperatures gas is rapidly expanded, creating tank-rupturing pressures. In the fight against heat (i.e., keeping the fuel as cool as possible), wood tanks have more potential than steel tanks because of wood's inherent insulating qualities. To minimize the fire problem, you could make wood tanks with thick walls that would take a long time to burn through, and provide extra protection with a coating of resin fortified with the 421 Fire Retardant additive. The thicker walls would also provide extra thermal insulation and the tanks would be very strong, with excellent puncture resistance.

We repeat that we have had limited experience with wood fuel tanks. No serious testing programs have been entered into, nor are there any existing safety standards. We do, however, feel that there is good potential for use of wood tanks.

Figure 23—Diesel fuel tank on ROGUE WAVE. The cockpit sole forms the top.

Windows and Ports

Windows provide light and, in many cases, much of the ventilation needed in the interior. Ports or windows which open yet can be made watertight are very difficult to make yourself, and the price of the manufactured ones is reasonable, so it is best to purchase these items. Traditionally, ports have been made of bronze or aluminum, but in recent years there have been a number of excellent plastic windows introduced on the market which we have found to be of high quality. Some of these plastic ports have unique design features, and we have installed them on the most expensive boats.

You can easily manufacture and install at low cost non-opening windows which only let in light. You can use standard Plexiglas™, but we highly recommend the use of Lexan™ because it is harder, has better scratch resistance, and is much stronger than Plexiglas. Choose a type and thickness of window comparable in strength to the cabin side or hull area which it is replacing.

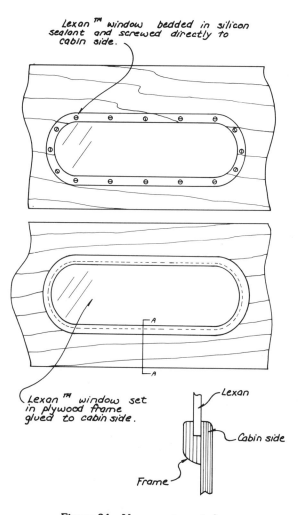

Lexan™ window bedded in silicon sealant and screwed directly to cabin side.

Lexan™ window set in plywood frame glued to cabin side.

Lexan

Cabin side

Frame

Figure 24—Non-opening windows.

To install windows as shown at the top of Figure 24, drill and countersink holes and screw or bolt the Lexan or Plexiglas to the cabin wall. You can install the window on either the exterior or the interior surface. We generally prefer the interior because the windows look better, but interior installation is potentially weaker and the cabin wall must be thick enough to provide holding power for fasteners. If it isn't thick enough, the area around the edge of the window will have to be built up with more wood in the immediate area of the fasteners.

Plastic glass comes with stick-on protective paper. Leave this paper in place to protect the plastic until the window is installed. Mark the window on the plastic — you want the window to overlap the cabin side by about an inch — and cut it with a band saw or saber saw, file edges smooth and radius the exterior corners. Drill fastener holes and fit the window in place. Just before you install it, peel off the paper from part of the plastic which overlaps the cabin. Rough up this area of the window with sandpaper and bed the window in position with silicone sealant, carefully removing any excess. Insert self-tapping screws or machine screws if through bolting is desired. Adjust the number of fasteners used to the anticipated severity of loadings. If you are going offshore, the joint between the window and the cabin wall should probably be as strong as the cabin wall. You can remove the paper on the window if you need light below, but it's sometimes better to peel it off after you have painted the interior.

Another way to install windows, also shown in Figure 24, is to bed them in silicone sealant as described above, but to finish them off in plywood frames which are bonded to the cabin sides. This is a little more difficult, but framed-in windows are more attractive than screwed-in windows, and this method is particularly effective for installing windows on thin cabin walls. Frames may be attached inside or outside, but we prefer to use them to enhance interior beauty. Wherever they are, the frames should have enough bonding area to ensure a strong window joint.

Another type of window is a "poor man's" lift-out window. This will keep out rain water, but may not keep out water if the window is hit with a solid sea. This type of window is particularly successful on lightweight boats which, because of their lightness, are not normally subjected to being boarded by large waves. Outline the cutout in the cabin wall on three sides with a trapezoidal framework which goes across the bottom and up two sides of the window, staying an inch to 2 inches away from any part of the opening. Deeply groove this framework so that any water entering will run down the groove to drains which are drilled through the cabin wall to the very base corners of the

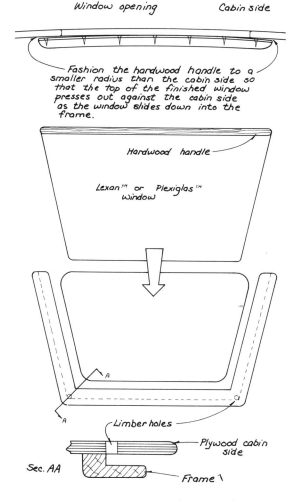

Window opening   Cabin side

Fashion the hardwood handle to a smaller radius than the cabin side so that the top of the finished window presses out against the cabin side as the window slides down into the frame.

Hardwood handle

Lexan™ or Plexiglas™ window

Limber holes

Plywood cabin side

Sec. AA

Frame

Figure 25—Low-cost lift-out window.

framework. Then cut out a glass window of the same trapezoidal shape as the framework, fit it into place and install a lifting handle on the uppermost part. To lift out the window, move it up approximately an inch or two and set it aside. You can then replace the window with a framed screen the same size to keep out bugs.

Electrical and Plumbing Systems

To do the best job on your boat's electrical system, it is wise to plan a wiring diagram before installing the interior. This is especially important if you plan on extensive use of modern electrical items. Plan the location of all lights, instruments, radio, pumps, refrigeration and engine. With these items located in the interior plan, lay out the best wiring routes. Then, as you construct the interior, make provisions for the wiring, such as predrilling holes in interior parts before they are assembled.

Most electrical wiring can be nicely concealed from view, but still be accessible for maintenance. You can hide wiring behind deck beams, in back of shelf fronts

and under bunks. Situate the master control panel in a central location which both minimizes the amount of wire needed and provides the best routes for hiding the wiring. Sometimes, it just isn't possible to hide all of the wiring, and you have to take other measures to cover it for a pleasing appearance. In these cases, make up U-sectioned coving from pieces of wood and with screws install it over the wires, so that you can remove the coving easily. You can use more exotic contrasting woods to make the coving, adding beauty to the interior with little extra weight.

In a wood boat, you can easily attach wiring to any part of the interior using various types of commercial staples or available wire mounts. Wood is also a natural insulator, and the wiring does not have to be shielded from the possibility of shorting out, as it does in steel and aluminum boats.

There are many pitfalls in a marine electrical system, and we suggest that you familiarize yourself with at least one good book on the subject, especially if your electrical system is to be extensive. One excellent text is *Your Boat's Electrical System* by Conrad Miller (The Hearst Corporation, New York, 1973).

In most boats, plumbing systems are rather basic and easy to install. We advise that you lay out your systems well beforehand to minimize the amount of piping needed. For example, install the water tank close to the sink and the holding tank next to the toilet. All through hull fittings are potential dangers to your boat, and we recommend that you buy only the best fittings (with shutoff valves) and install them properly. Design your interior items around your plumbing requirements. This is especially important with the engine if it is to be walled off or covered with an engine box. Allow room for the water intake, water exhaust, muffler system, fuel tanks and feeder lines.

Interior Final Finishing

We have always been enthusiastic about natural wood finishes. Some people criticize wood interiors for being too dark, and maintain that the only way they can be brightened up is with the use of light colored paint. For the most part, we feel that this objection can be overcome by using light colored woods. Spruce, ash, okoume and pine are all woods which finish light and are also beautiful in grain. It is our general observation that light woods occur in nature more commonly than do the darker woods. The widespread use of stains is also responsible for the reputation of wood as being dark in color.

This is not to say that we are against using solid colors on interiors. The tasteful use of colors in the right

Figure 26—Prefinished interior on IOR ½ ton racer.

places can accentuate natural wood grain finish and, at the same time, help to brighten an interior. Finishing countertops and tables with a light-colored Formica™ (easily bonded to wood with WEST SYSTEM resin) results in a durable, easily-maintained working surface. Painting the underdeck ceiling and bulkheads with light colors provides good light reflection. Choosing light-colored materials for cushions and curtains also brightens an interior.

Generally, it is thought that a varnished natural surface requires a lot of extra time, but many professional builders believe that the naturally finished interior is more attractive for the same amount of work than the painted interior. A solid color, especially with high gloss paint, will magnify imperfections in the surface. The same small imperfections in a varnished surface are camouflaged by the natural wood grain.

As we have already discussed, nowhere is prefinishing with our method of construction more important than on interior items. It's the same old story: coating and sanding of intricate parts is much more efficiently done outside the boat at a comfortable bench rather than inside, in cramped conditions. Not only are fewer labor hours needed, but a much better finishing job is possible.

To install the individual interior parts, carefully machine, assemble and hold them in position until all epoxy cures. Be careful to remove any excess resin from joints during assembly, while it is still liquid or semi-solid, to prevent a lot of difficult sanding and grinding later on. Fillets are normally installed during assembly. Try to make yours as neat and clean as possible, removing all excess material and smoothing fillets with a final pass of a filleting stick. If you haven't had a lot of experience with fillets, practice on some corner joints to improve your craftsmanship. To modify fillet color to match the interior of the hull, experiment with combinations of low density filler and 405 Filleting Blend. You can further adjust fillet color by adding pigment or tempera paint to the epoxy.

When the fillets are fully cured, lightly sand and recoat them with resin. At the same time, fill any staple holes or other depressions. A 406 resin mixture makes the best filler for small holes in a natural finish. The only caution is that this material is extremely hard when cured, so carefully clean away all excess.

When you have completed the interior and installed all trim, inspect all surfaces in preparation for varnishing or painting. Lightly sand the coated fillets as well as any areas which you have filled or coated, such as staple holes, dings or scratches. There may be areas in the interior where you would find it difficult to use precoated parts because of their unusual shapes. You will need to coat and sand these items when completed, using the standard coating sequence. The degree of fineness you choose in your interior sanding is a matter of taste. Professionally, for a varnish base, we go down to 220 grit paper when hand sanding (either

Figure 27—Clean, well finished interior built with WEST SYSTEM epoxy.

wet or dry). With machine sanding, we use 150 grit paper (and sometimes even 120 grit paper). For solid colors to look good, especially high gloss urethane, finer sanding may be needed.

When the interior preparation is completed, you will have the major job of cleaning up in preparation for the final finish coating. Begin this task by vacuuming all excess dust, dirt and debris out of the interior. We use a small portable shop vacuum with the standard attachments. Next, wipe down the entire interior, using soft, absorbent rags with a large pail of clean, warm water, rinsing the rag as you go. Make several trips around the interior surfaces, changing the water several times during the process. When the entire surface is as clean as possible, let it dry and then wipe it with solvent and cloth to remove any latent dust or contaminants which might remain on the surface. The final step is to wipe all surfaces with a tack rag.

Painting and Varnishing Interiors

The interiors of boats are much more difficult to varnish or paint than are the exteriors. The reason is very simple. There are many protruding items, such as bulkheads, beams and frames which you must paint around, as well as furniture which may need coating in difficult areas and on several surfaces. Complicating the process are items which should not be painted, such as windows, Masonite™ countertops and various hardware items. If you are an experienced and accurate painter, you can avoid these items. If not, we recommend that you cover and tape off these surfaces so that you do not inadvertently slop paint on them. (Note: From here on we use the words "painting" and "varnishing" interchangeably.)

Generally, we break up the painting job into two or more stages because the average interior requires more hours to paint than one or even two persons can expect to do at one time. For a boat 30 feet in length, it is not unreasonable to plan for 20 hours of interior painting — too much for even two people in one work session. Usually there are natural break points within the interior, at which you can start and finish a job without causing any unsightly overlaps. You can successfully paint the floor area, certain items of interior furniture and the ceiling apart from the rest of the interior. Mentally surveying the job beforehand and trying to identify the amount of work you can do at one time is important; if you get tired from painting too long, the quality of your work will go down, and all of the many hours of surface preparation will not pay off as they should. At all times during the painting, you will want to make yourself as comfortable as possible. This means proper ventilation, a reasonably cool temperature and good lighting.

We assume that you have designed a good lighting system to perform other interior work, but be aware that final painting requires "super" lighting to prevent missing areas and also to gauge the amount of coating you are applying in a given area. Too little coating material will cause dry spots, which will not have as much gloss as the rest of the coating. Too much coating will develop runs. You need to check your coating application continually, and this demands enough light. One answer to the lighting problem is the use of a portable lamp in conjunction with the general lighting system. You can carry the lamp with you to shine on the work immediately at hand.

We use high gloss varnishes and paints for interiors, mainly because they reflect light and make it easier to light these areas. As we mentioned earlier, glossy finish paints show more defects than semi-gloss or dull paints. Dull paints have their own disadvantages: they are usually porous and difficult to clean, and they always seem to be unsightly. Glossy paints, by contrast, are easy to clean and, if protected from sunlight, they will keep their gloss for many years and rarely need repainting. Because naturally finished interiors are generally protected from the sun, a high quality spar varnish with an ultraviolet filter is unnecessary. Instead, choose a varnish which is easy to apply and which dries to a high gloss.

As we discussed in Chapter 11, experience with a specific product is perhaps the largest single factor in a successful paint job. If you have used one system many times, you will be able to predict its reactions to temperature and humidity. Always test a new product in an inconspicuous spot to be sure that it is compatible with the cured WEST SYSTEM epoxy surface. To gain experience with any paint or varnish, begin by coating the forepeak, under bunks and other inconspicuous areas.

Sponge rollers deposit the right amount of coating faster and better than brushes, so use them for painting and varnishing whenever you can. Cut roller covers in half to reach nooks, crannies and broken surface area more easily. As you roll on a coat, go over the surface with a high quality brush to smooth it and remove any air bubbles. It's important to do this as soon as possible after rolling the paint on so that it will flow naturally and produce the smoothest surface. Use a brush to paint areas which you cannot reach with the roller.

Painting with a brush is a skill which must be learned. The object, of course, is to get the proper amount of coating onto the surface and smooth it out so that it will self-level and produce an even, fine textured coating over all surfaces. This is most easily done on a flat surface. The inside and outside corners of stringers, frames and other obstacles present coating problems which you must overcome. Corners become natural collection points for excess paint, and are a major source of paint runs.

A good brush is of primary importance. We advise investing in a good badger hair or fine bristle brush. There has been some success with the new foam brushes, and in some cases they appear superior in controlling coating thickness. However, they also seem to have a short life span, doing a good job at first, but getting progressively worse as the foam begins to break down.

It often seems impossible to control dust as you varnish, but you can take steps to minimize the problem. First, do everything you can to remove all dust and dirt from the interior before you begin varnishing. Do not let anyone else perform any operations which might create dust in the shop as you work. We go so far as to spray water on the floor around the boat. If the exterior of the boat is still dirty, cleaning the interior isn't going to help much — if you sit down on the dusty exterior,

the back of your pants will be contaminated and you'll carry dust down into the interior. This will also happen with shoes and anything else which becomes contaminated before going into the interior.

Just before coating an area, give it a final wipe with the tack rag. Keep the rag in your shirt pocket at all times. As you paint, you may discover contaminated spots. Stop and remove them before varnishing because contamination will both spoil the paint or varnish in its immediate area and affect the brush and coating material. Enough dust and dirt will give your finish a ''non-skid'' effect.

Time is important when you apply varnish. After rolling it on, you may have a very short period in which to play with a coating before it loses its solvents and starts to dry. Drying times vary, as do application conditions. In hot weather some paints will only give you a few minutes for corrections; others will provide 15 to 20 minutes of grace for touch-ups. Since they will give you more time in which to fill in places you've missed and to fix runs, we advise varnishing in cooler temperatures and the use of slower-drying coatings.

Chapter 25

Deck Construction

The earliest seagoing boats were built without decks, and as late as the thirteenth century the Vikings were plying the seas in their open longboats with crew and cargo exposed to the elements. During this period, however, the deck started to become a common addition to oceangoing vessels, and for very good reasons. The use of the deck improves the vessel in three areas:

(1) Decks keep water out of the hull, making it more seaworthy and protecting its contents and crew from the ravages of the weather. A canvas cover might serve to keep out rainwater, but it would never be adequate if the boat were boarded by huge seas. In certain types of boats, the deck must be as strong as the hull in order to withstand the surge of thousands of gallons of water pouring on it at one time.

(2) Decks provide a working platform for carrying out operations of the vessel. Deck design and layout can be crucial to crew safety and efficiency when handling the vessel, especially under adverse conditions.

(3) Decks improve the structural integrity of the boat. A hull with no deck is usually very wobbly because there is nothing to support the upper sheer areas. The same hull, with a deck installed, becomes an amazingly rigid structure with great resistance to twisting or torsion loads.

The deck can also serve other structural functions. Modern masthead rigs, with their large foresails, rely on a taut forestay to allow a good set on the foresails. To maintain a taut forestay, a great deal of pretensioning must be done on either the backstay or forestay. This generates forces which tend to bend the boat in an arc, causing the ends to raise up toward the mast. A properly engineered and constructed deck system can resist the high compression loads and thus prevent most of this hull deformation.

The deck must also be capable of withstanding high point loading wherever it occurs. Winches, cleats and other deck hardware can generate enormous strains which the deck must be capable of bearing.

Preparing the Hull for Deck Installation

Before work begins on the deck, make sure that all items which you can practically install in the interior are completed. This includes the engine, tanks, plumbing, some electrical fittings and any interior furniture items. Once you have installed the deck, interior work will be more difficult because of the restricted access and lack of good lighting.

Take measures to protect these installed interior items from general physical abuse that might occur during deck construction. Cover areas which could suffer from dripping adhesive with polyethylene film that is taped in place. Cover areas that could be walked or stepped on with cardboard cut to size. Tape it down to hold it in position.

The first stage of preparing the hull for the deck is to plane the sheer close to its final desired dimension. We assume that you have marked your sheer line carefully, but, in many cases, the sheer measurements may be replaced by the sheer clamp itself, the actual measurements having been obliterated in the process. If the sheer line you developed in the lofting and later in the set-up was fair, you probably will have little trouble final fairing the sheer to a high degree of exactness using the installed sheer clamp itself as the only guide.

Because the sheer line is such a prominent dimension defining the hull and deck intersection, it is more noticeable than any other dimension of the boat. If it is wavy or humpy, it can easily destroy the looks of an otherwise beautiful boat; therefore, make every effort to get this one critical part of the boat as fair as possible.

Fairing the Sheer

As you are planing the sheer line, you will want to begin developing the proper bevel on the sheer clamp for intersecting the deck. You can determine the angle at which the deck meets with the sheer clamp at each station from the lofting, but it is not really critical to achieve the exact bevel at this stage. Get the bevel reasonably close, leaving it a little on the high side. Later, when the deck profile is better defined, with some deck framework installed, you can easily final fair and bevel the sheer clamp angle. It is important at this early stage, however, that you accurately determine the final sheer line, because it is the main reference point for measuring. All future deck measurements used for installing the deck framing, cockpits and cabins are taken from the sheer line.

From the side view, sheers are usually relatively straight lines. Even a heavily curved sheer is not likely to curve more than a foot over the entire length of the boat. For this reason, a hand plane with an exceptionally long bed or sole makes the job of fairing the sheer line a lot easier. The long bed of the plane quickly detects humps and hollows over a reasonably long range. There is, however, a limit to what any plane can do. You must still determine the overall longitudinal fairness of the sheer by eye. Sheer line fairness is easiest to sight on narrow hulls, where there is minimum top view curve in the sheer profile. Wide hulls present the biggest problem, because there is no way to sight down the sheer and see all of it in the same sighting. The only way to view all of the sheer is to step back until you can see the whole hull from the side, but from this angle a slight variation is difficult to detect. Usually, the side view, together with careful observations of portions of the sheer from both directions (looking at the same section of the sheer from the bow view and then the transom view), will begin to give you indications of overall fairness. Visually compare a section of sheer on one side with that same section on the other side. If one side doesn't look quite as good as the other, try to find out why.

You can use other guides to help with your inspection of the sheer line. Position a fairly thick batten along the top of the sheer to see whether it lies fair with the sheer line. If the batten detects a hollow in the same area that your eye does, your visual opinion is reinforced, and you'll feel a lot better about planing the high spots on either side. Sometimes we cover the planed surface with blue carpenter's chalk to aid the sighting process. This marking helps the eye to define the actual sheer point, allowing you to measure it more accurately.

Planing down the sheers of most boats will probably be the largest single planing job in the whole project. A large boat may have a sheer clamp that is 2 inches thick bonded to a hull of perhaps 1 inch, for a total thickness of 3 inches. Planing 3 inches of stock around the entire outer perimeter of a hull can be a laborious undertaking. We have saved many hours of labor by using the Skil™ power plane to rough plane the sheer down to the point where you need hand planes only for final fairing. This power plane has a long bed which allows you to develop and maintain overall fairness as you are approaching the final sheer line measurement markings.

Once you have established the sheer line, you can further define the deck by shaping all of the bulkhead tops to the exact profile. You may have preshaped the bulkhead deck profiles from the lofting before you in-

stalled them in the set-up. In this case they only need to be final faired with the sheer and other bulkheads. With some boats especially those with plywood web frames, it is practical to make the deck beams a unitized part of the frame before installing the frame in the set-up. Then, after you turn the hull upright, you need only to final fair the precut deck beams before installing further framework such as longitudinal stringers. (See Figure 1.)

Figure 1—Web frames and deck beams in set-up.

Figure 2—Same deck beams with stringers in place, ready for decking.

Developing Deck Camber

All decks are curved, or have *camber,* so that rain or boarding seas will easily run off. Usually, this camber is given in the plans as so many inches of height for the widest deck beam. Using only these two dimensions, we usually make up a *deck tram* to lay out the deck curvature mechanically for the largest deck beam and then each succeeding smaller beam. Figure 4 shows this process in detail.

When you have to lay out only a few deck cambers, such as the bulkheads, you can lay out the camber geometrically for each deck curve method. This procedure is explained in Figure 3.

On narrow hulls, typical of multihull craft, you can shape all deck beams from a master pattern; all deck beams, no matter what their width, will simply be pieces of this one master arc. It is usual to use the geometric method to lay out the master pattern for the deck camber desired at the widest deck beam. Mark the master pattern with a centerline dividing the maximum deck width into two parts. Then match up this center with the intended centerline of any smaller beams which you can then lay out.

Some deck designs might have unusual shapes that will require full lofting to develop. This lofting usually

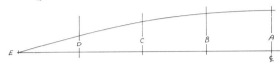

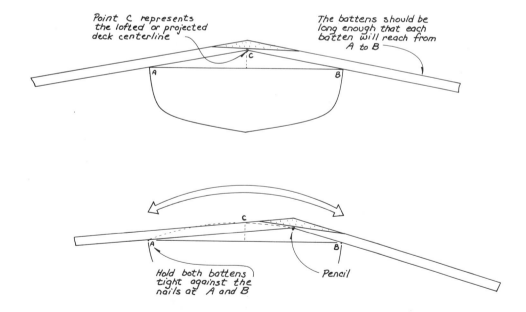

Figure 3—Geometric construction for deck camber.

Figure 4—Lay out the lengths of the largest deck beam on the lofting board or other suitable surface, such as a sheet of plywood. Using a base line for reference, measure up from the base at the center of the beam the maximum deck curvature height dimension (typically 3 inches to 6 inches in a 10 foot wide boat). Drive three nails into the layout surface, two at either end of the base line, which represent the beam ends (Points A and B), and a third (Point C) at the maximum beam height measurement, midpoint between the outer nail points. Position two straightedged battens, each at least a foot longer than the overall maximum beam, on the layout, with both battens meeting at the center nail and their middles resting on the nails at each end of the beam. Join the two battens at the center nail with a plywood cap, leaving a small gap in the apex of the battens in which to insert a pencil. You can then move this mechanical tram from one side of the beam to the other, using the two outer nails as a guide, to make a perfect arc over the entire width of the beam. As the beam width gets smaller, the tram will still continue to make a perfect arc in relation to the smaller dimension.

does not have to be as extensive as that done on a hull because the curves will not be as complex. Also, the dimensional accuracy will not be so critical. (This is not to imply that it will not end up being as fair as the hull.) Good examples of some modern designs that need lofting are those that incorporate a "blister" in the middle of the deck that acts as a cabin-type device to give headroom down below.

Deck Framework

The deck surface represents a substantial portion of the entire surface area of a hull. Because the deck is always the highest part of the hull, its weight is of major concern in trying to keep the center of gravity of the overall structure as low as possible to improve the seaworthiness and speed potential of the vessel. Usually, trimming weight in the deck pays better dividends than trying to trim it in the hull itself. You should do everything that you can to make an adequately strong deck at the least amount of weight within the proper safety margin.

Decks are relatively flat surfaces, especially when compared to the compound curved surfaces of a hull. With flat surfaces, the extensive use of a supporting framework is one of the best methods of giving strength and stiffness. For custom and even semi-custom boats, the framework-supported deck system is one of the most efficient and quickest methods of installing a deck system. This supportive framework can take many forms, depending on the type of boat and other variables, such as the cabin and cockpit layout. We use two basic framework concepts and modify each of these to fit the individual situation. The first method is rather traditional, using large athwartship deck beams to provide the main support, with smaller longitudinal stringers for further support. The stringers are sometimes minimized or left out if they don't serve a definite structural purpose. The second method uses a series of large, longitudinal beams, with smaller beams bent over the longitudinal beams in the athwartship direction. Generally, the second method is preferred on boats with wider decks, especially large keelboats. The first method is commonly used on boats with narrower decks, such as multihulls.

Longitudinal Deck Beam Concept

In the old carvel planked boats, the decks were planked just like hulls and athwartship deck beams made a lot of sense. When using plywood instead of planking as a decking material, however, the structural function of the deck beam changes. Deck beams used to be bolted carefully to a clamp and shelf arrangement

to hold the two sheers together. Now, plywood decking, bonded to the sheers, serves the same function and does a much better job in the process.

The major function of framework for decks is the same as for hulls: to best support the surface skin so that it will not buckle under high loads. The major loading on deck structures for many boats is longitudinal in nature, so it makes sense to orient a significant portion of the deck framework in a longitudinal fashion to help carry these loads.

The longitudinal beam concept has been used very successfully on many boats, and has some practical side benefits.

(1) Most interior traffic is fore and aft. Keeping athwartship deck beams to a minimum size increases the amount of headroom available for a given dimension of the vessel.

(2) The longitudinal beam concept can simplify deck framework construction.

(3) Properly positioned, the longitudinal beams can become strong points to which you can install major deck hardware for maximum loading potential.

Examples of longitudinal deck beam construction are shown in Figures 5 and 6.

The deck framing of the 42 foot sailboat shown in Figure 5 begins with the installation of four laminated longitudinal beams measuring about 1½ inches x 4 inches. We set them in proper position, using the existing bulkhead deck profiles and the sheer as the main

Figure 5—Longitudinal and smaller athwartship beams on GOLDEN DAZY.

saw. Remove the stock between the saw cuts with a chisel and true up the notch with a file.

You now only need to fit the frame or stringer to the existing notch. This involves transferring the bevel and the notch to the member to be fitted for a good mating. Cut the bevel on the ends to be fitted at the proper length, allowing the member to sit in proper final resting position in the notch. After the parts are properly fitted, bond them in place, using a thick adhesive mixture that will fill any gaps in the notch that may inadvertently exist between the members.

You can also use longitudinal beams to advantage as structural members to which to attach the cockpit or cabin sides. In Figure 9, the four longitudinal beams serve as supporting framework from which to hang a unique slingshot-shaped cockpit. We accomplished this by first installing the cockpit itself and then clamp-

Figure 6—Fore deck framing for ½ ton racer. Longitudinals will carry cabin sides and hanging cockpit.

measurement references. If necessary, we prop up the beams temporarily with posts from the floor of the hull, especially in places where they might sag a bit between bulkheads. We normally set the beams in place, keeping them fair to the eye as they are sighted longitudinally. We can check the positioning of the longitudinal beams at any station point that we desire with the template of the deck crown. When the longitudinals are in proper position, installing the rest of the deck framework is relatively easy.

We sawed the athwartship frames (shown in Figure 5) out of straight timber stock and they measured 1⅜ inches x ¾ inch. We then simply bent this stock around the four longitudinal beams to form a naturally curved deck crown that ended up being accurate enough so that little fairing was required.

We notched the athwartship beams as well as the longitudinal beams into the sheer clamp. The sheer notch, however, is of the triangular type where the athwartship beam is held captive and given complete support. (See Figure 7.) The triangular notch is a fast and efficient method of joining deck beams to the sheer clamp, and we have used this method for many years. We also use this method in a number of other areas where wood members need to be joined at approximate right angles.

To make a notch, first mark the dimension of the notch on the stock. The two critical dimensions of the notch are its length and depth. These dimensions will determine the bevel that the notch will take. The width of the notch will be determined by the width of the stock to be notched in. Then saw the two sides of the notch to the marked lines, using a fine-toothed hand-

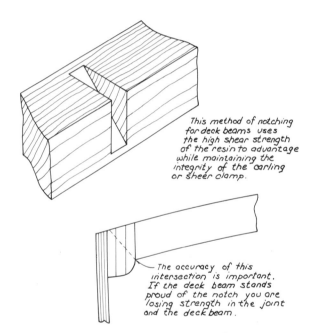

This method of notching for deck beams uses the high shear strength of the resin to advantage while maintaining the integrity of the carling or sheer clamp.

The accuracy of this intersection is important. If the deck beam stands proud of the notch you are losing strength in the joint and the deck beam.

Figure 7—Triangular notch.

Figure 8—Triangular notches were cut into a laminated beam before it was bonded to plywood frame. Longitudinal deck stringers were then easy to fit into position.

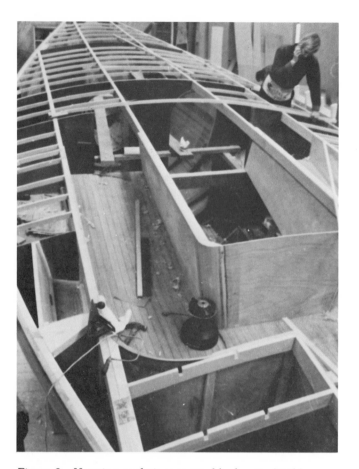

Figure 9—Hanging cockpit supported by longitudinal beams.

Laminated Deck Beams

More traditional laminated beams serve as the main support of the deck framework shown in Figure 11. The unusual shape of this deck made the longitudinal beam concept impractical. We lofted the heavily curved blister deck to determine the correct shape of each beam and then laminated the beams on the lofting floor using the block-on-floor method described in Chapter 9.

Because it's difficult to work on the under sides of decks, we prefinish all deck framing members. In this case, we shaped and coated the laminated beams and

Figure 11—Laminated frames and 1 inch x ¾ inch stringers used as framing for blister-type deck on ½ ton racer. Note plywood mast partner for keel-stepped spar.

ing the longitudinal beams to the various sides of the cockpit at the proper height. Also note the use of sawn-to-shape half beams in the athwartship direction in the cockpit area. These half beams span the short distance from the sheer to the longitudinal beams. They are fitted at each end, using the triangular notched method.

installed them with triangular notches at the sheers. To set each beam in proper position, we used the sheer dimensions on each side and the height at the centerline as reference points, measuring the height from a string which ran parallel to the waterline on the interior of the boat. Using standard hull fairing techniques, we faired the beams and notched smaller 1 inch x ¾ inch longitudinal stringers into each one. The deck had too much compound curvature to be covered with sheet ply, so we laminated two layers of 1 foot wide, 3/16 inch (6mm) plywood strips for a total deck thickness of ⅜ inch.

Cockpit Construction and Installation

Before installing any deck framework, we usually build the cockpit and set it in position. In most cases, it's easier to fit deck framing around the cockpit than to fit the cockpit around deck beams. Even if the two methods were equal, it's usually easier to fabricate the cockpit on the shop floor and install it as a unit than it is to build it from many pieces inside the cramped working quarters of the hull.

We always begin cockpit construction by building the cockpit floor. The cockpit floor, like the floor of a

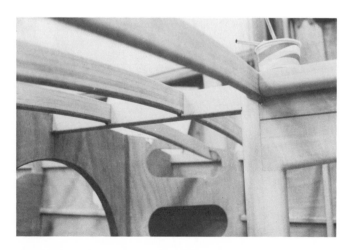

Figure 10—Laminated deck beams with centerline blocking and hardwood cap. At right are blocking and stanchion for deck-stepped spar.

house, serves as a foundation on which to erect the walls. We favor sandwich construction with a honeycomb core for cockpit floors, but a standard framework-supported floor similar to that used on the deck also works well. After we have constructed the floor, we saw cockpit sidewalls of appropriate plywood thickness and bond them to the completed floor to form a ready-to-install cockpit, as shown in Figure 12. The cockpit may be much more elaborate than this, with seats and lockers underneath. You can also add these before you install the whole unit in the hull.

Positioning the cockpit in the hull is not difficult. It must be centered and set at the right height in relation to the sheer dimension, or possibly to a waterline. Usually, there is at least one bulkhead in the vicinity of the cockpit, and you can cut this out to the exact dimension of the cockpit shape and use it as a positioning point for placement of the cockpit. With this initial support, you can true up the cockpit to the final dimension required. You may need temporary support to hold the cockpit in proper position until you can install enough deck framework to hold the cockpit installation rigidly in place.

Figure 13—Unusual slingshot cockpit is set in place on GOLDEN DAZY. It is trued up with temporary bracing and blocking, and then deck framework is installed around its perimeter.

Figure 14—GOLDEN DAZY's cockpit, viewed from the bow.

Figure 12—Cockpit assembly constructed outside the hull.

Decking Over

To final fair the deck framework, use essentially the same methods that are used to fair up a hull. Because the deck surface is almost flat in comparison to the curves on a hull, it is easy to see and correct imperfections, so fairing the deck framework is much less difficult than fairing a hull. Long bed hand planes are ideal for fairing up this large, flat surface area, and a large plywood batten measuring about 1 foot wide x 8 feet long also helps indicate how the plywood will lie on the various frame members.

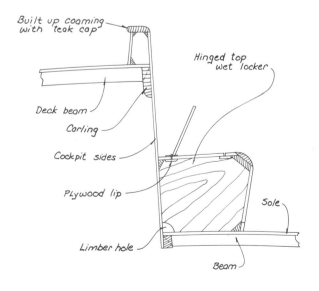

Figure 15—Cockpit seat detail.

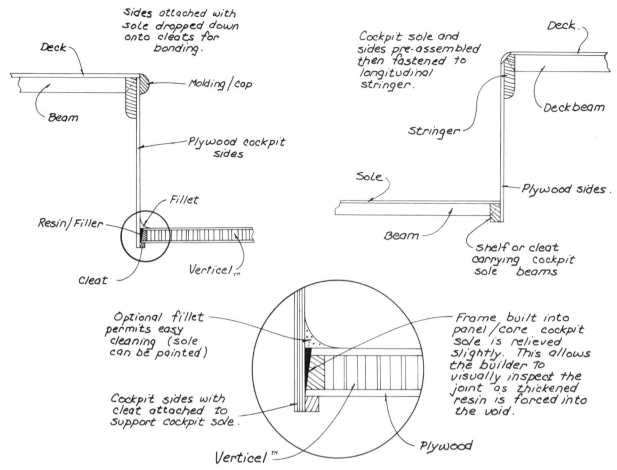

Figure 16—Cockpit construction details.

After the deck framework is faired, it is ready for the plywood decking. Decking thickness depends upon a number of factors, such as boat size and type, amount and spacing of supportive deck framework, and the type of service that the boat is likely to see. Generally, decks don't have to be as thick as hulls. A hull must be thick enough to withstand impact loads of hitting floating debris and the constant hydrodynamic loads of waves. The heaviest potential load on a deck is from a large boarding sea, and this enormous load, while awesome, is not particularly high on a pounds-per-square-foot basis when compared with the loads that a hull must withstand.

For most decks, the human body presents the greatest concentrated load the deck will ever have to withstand. Thus, our minimum criterion for a successful deck is that it be strong and stiff enough to prevent any substantial deflection when it is walked upon. A continually deflecting deck is likely to have a short life span, failing through fatigue at an inopportune moment.

In the end, there are no firm guidelines for deck thickness. If you use thin plywood, you will need more frames, and if you use thick plywood, you will need

fewer frames. A thin skin with a number of lightweight frames is lighter than a thicker plywood deck, but it also takes more time to build. We covered the deck framework for 42 foot long GOLDEN DAZY, shown in Figure 5, with two layers of ¼ inch plywood and laid ⅛ inch teak laminate over the ply. The resulting ⅝ inch deck was considerably thinner than DAZY's 1⅛ inch thick hull. The frame-supported deck on ROGUE WAVE, a 60 foot trimaran, on the other hand, was only ⅜ inch thick. Many small day racers have well-supported ⅛ inch to 3/16 inch plywood decking. OLLIE's deck is 5-ply ¼ inch plywood over light deck beams at 7 inch spacings.

Apply plywood decking in the same manner that you apply plywood panels to the hull framework in standard hard chine construction. (See Chapter 22.) As is the problem with hulls, decks normally present too large an area to cover easily with one prescarfed panel. Therefore, we apply the largest size panels that we can cut out of a 4 foot x 8 foot sheet of plywood and join them in place on the deck, using a deck beam or stringer as the point at which to make a scarf joint. Planning the scarf positioning may be a little bit more difficult on a deck than on a hull because of potential obstructions that must be fitted to, such as the cabin walls, hatches and cockpit. Because the underside of the deck will be seen by all, if natural finished, try to do the best job you can to hide the scarfs on top of a beam or bulkhead.

Figure 18 shows a method for applying a plywood panel to a compounded surface. We usually staple plywood, working along imaginary lines from the center out to the corners to minimize distortion. First we divide a panel into quarters and then into eighths and sixteenths until it is fastened around its perimeter.

Scarfing in place has advantages when applying plywood to decks. As we have pointed out previously, most decks have a small degree of compound curve which might cause some installation problems if you were to install a solid panel over the whole deck surface. This slight compound curvature is easily dissipated within the scarf joints when you apply many smaller panels over the same surface.

Sandwich Constructed Decks

With certain types of boats, a sandwich or core constructed deck system may be advantageous. This uses

Figure 17—Fore deck and beams fairings on ROGUE WAVE are plywood over stringers. Cabin area decks are sandwich construction using Verticel core.

the basic principle of separating two load-bearing skins with a core material. The main advantage of this type of deck is the smooth, unencumbered inner surface of the underside of the deck. The absence of any framework provides a surface which is easy to finish and, when complete, easier to keep clean. In addition, the sandwich deck provides a significant improvement in thermal and sound insulation properties over a

Figure 18 —Stapling plywood deck panels.

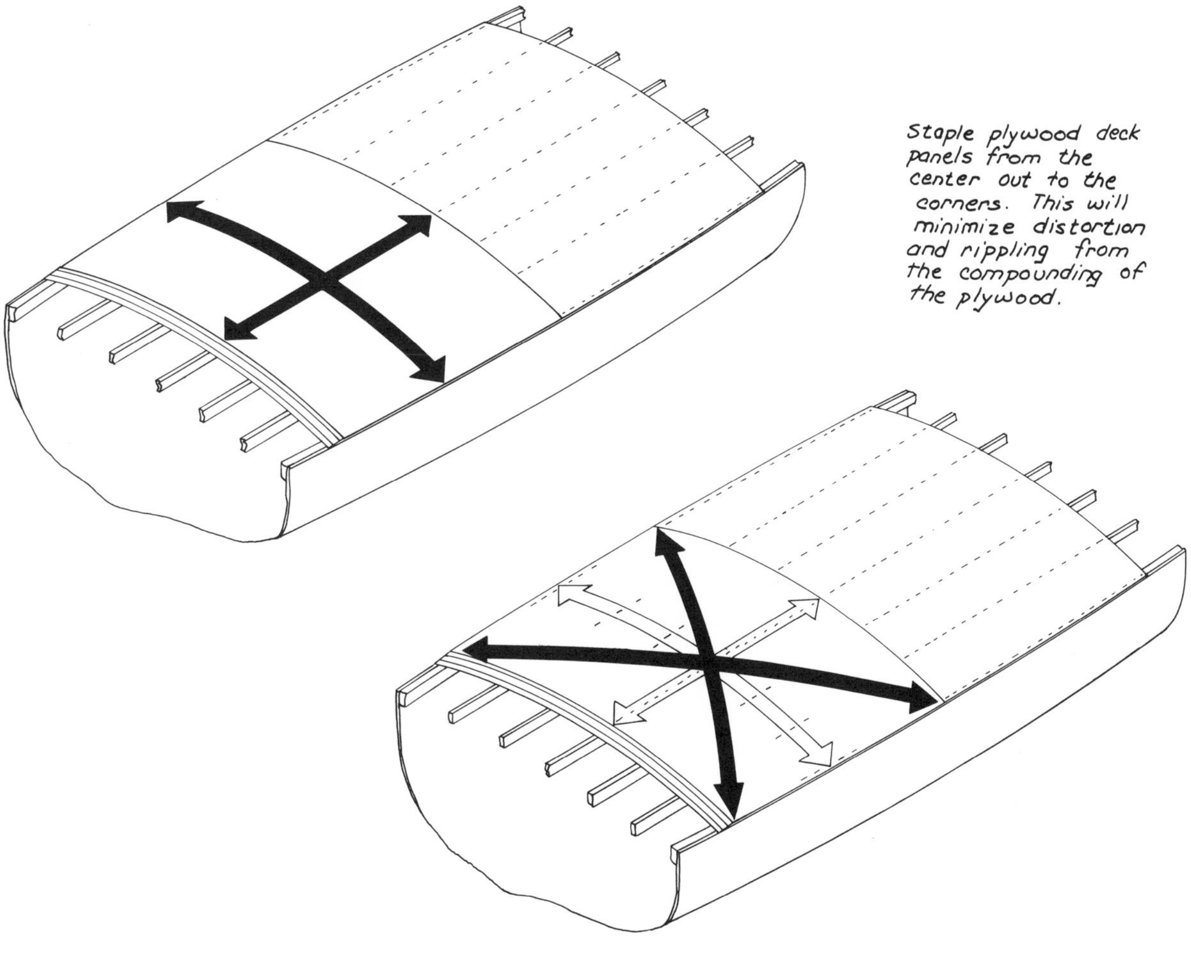

Staple plywood deck panels from the center out to the corners. This will minimize distortion and rippling from the compounding of the plywood.

Figure 19—Fitting and scarfing 3/16 inch plywood deck on main hull of proa SLINGSHOT. Note pads and blocking for hardware which are fit to stringers and frames.

standard frame-supported deck system. In hot climates, a deck that does not transmit heat from the sun can be a significant feature. It is also possible to build a lighter deck with the sandwich technique; however, this is dependent upon the application. It is our opinion that in most situations it is very difficult, on a weight-to-strength or weight-to-stiffness basis, to improve upon a well-designed frame-supported deck system.

Sandwich-constructed decks present added construction difficulties. For most boats, a sandwich-constructed deck takes longer to build than a frame-supported type and is also probably more difficult to execute by those with limited experience. A practical disadvantage of the sandwich deck is limited versatility when positioning deck hardware. Before you complete the sandwich deck, you must know the position of all deck hardware so that you can remove core material in the area of specific hardware items and replace it with appropriate solid blocking. Later, if you want to add some hardware items or move others to different locations, it will be difficult to do. With the open frame

deck, you can add more blocking easily to the underside of the deck wherever it is needed.

Figure 20 shows the core-constructed deck as used on the aft deck of a large multihull. This is a good application for the core deck because there is limited camber in the deck profile and very little hardware is to be installed. This boat will also spend a good portion of her time in the tropics, where the added insulation value is important. We began the deck construction outside the boat on a large prescarfed ⅛ inch thick piece of plywood that was prefitted to the deck perimeter and then set on a flat surface for further work. We positioned beams of ¾ inch thick stock, with a deck camber cut on the top, athwartship every 2 feet. We installed one longitudinal beam along the centerline by blocking in with 2 foot long pieces of the same ¾ inch stock. Then we positioned this partially-constructed assembly on the hull on top of false sheer clamps. Next we bonded Verticel™ honeycomb in place between the ¾ inch wood frames, using a thick, syrupy adhesive mixture to bond the Verticel only to the ⅛ inch plywood bottom. We faired the Verticel honeycomb down to the precut camber on the wood beams, using long fairing blocks with 50 grit sandpaper. Then we used long battens to fair up the entire deck surface, correcting any highs or lows in the wood beam members in the process. Finally, we bonded ¼ inch thick plywood over this faired surface, using standard size 4 foot x 8 foot panels to their best advantage with precut scarf joints and splicing the various panels together in place right on the deck surface.

Another core deck system is shown in Figure 21. This deck for a 26 foot monohull was on a flat floor. We laid out the accurate perimeter of the entire deck on the floor and then transferred it to a prescarfed ⅛

Figure 20—Aft deck on ROGUE WAVE with 3 inch thick Verticel™ core between plywood panels.

inch thick panel of plywood that had been prefinished on its underside. We then made cutouts in the plywood for the forward hatch, the cabin and the cockpit areas. We next fit the resulting plywood deck base with ¼ inch thick plywood beams, spaced on 3 inch centers. We cut these beams mostly from scrap plywood, using the mechanical tram method to develop a proper arc on each beam in a production-type set-up. Although this part looks laborious, one man cut the 104 beams needed in one day.

Installation of the beams on the plywood surface was easy, as we bonded each individual beam to a premarked position. We applied a bead of thickened adhesive to the bottom of each beam, then set the beam in position and held it there with temporary staples at each end until a cure was complete. We made a small fillet between the beam and the plywood by smoothing out the excess adhesive that had squeezed out from between the two members. We then placed this premanufactured deck base on top of the hull (Figure 21) and bonded it to the sheer clamps. The cabin sides, a preconstructed cockpit, hatch framework and all hardware blocking were installed in the deck base before we final faired the deck for decking over. For final fairing, we used a long sanding block with 50 grit paper and a hand plane to cut down a frame or added blocking to one that was abnormally high.

After we had completed the final fairing, we covered the deck over with 3/16 inch ply with stapling pressure applied out at the sheers, in perimeters around hatches, cabins, etc.. Because of the natural deck curve, we needed very little pressure to hold the plywood down flush against the ribs. In areas where contact seemed limited between deck and beam, we applied weights to the deck surface to hold it down until a cure was effected. We made scarf joints in place on the deck so that only standard size panels were applied at one time. We designed all scarf joints so that the center of the scarf joint occurred over one of the deck beams. Applying the adhesive to the small ¼ inch edge of each of the 104 small deck beams was tedious, and we used a common cake decorator-applicator. The cake decorator is capable of applying a very thick adhesive mixture in controlled amounts and in proper position to provide the best bond between deck beam and deck surface.

Blocking for Hardware

Hardware can develop extremely high stress concentrations on a deck which must be adequately distributed throughout the structure. Some hardware

Figure 21—Scrap strips of plywood used as core framing for sandwich deck.

items are more critical than others: the blocking for a major winch, for example, will have to be more substantial than the blocking for a simple cleat. It's difficult to decide how much blocking to use; to make a judgment, evaluate the loads on a given fitting and the direction — straight up or parallel to the deck, for instance — in which they are applied. Blocking is integral to the success of the hardware bonding techniques described in Chapter 26.

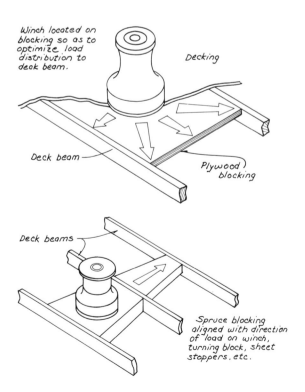
Figure 22—Blocking for hardware.

With frame-supported decks, blocking is usually installed by extending it to all surrounding framework and carefully bonding it to get the best load distribution. Thus, the framework pattern may affect your hardware location. The ideal location of the winch, as shown in Figure 22, is in the center of the framework in order to distribute its load over the greatest area. If the winch were located toward one side of the blocked-in box, it would reduce the load distribution potential of the deck-supporting framework, relying on the closest framework for a majority of support.

Because of its multidirectional laminations, plywood is an excellent blocking material to distribute loads over a wide area and is used in a majority of situations. Blocking is a good place to use all of your small scrap pieces of plywood. You can also use standard sawn wood stock for blocking, especially where you want to direct high loads over an immediate area such as would be done when blocking for sail track. In contrast to the old methods of blocking, we do not use high density hardwoods, but substitute lower density Sitka spruce or Douglas fir. These softwoods are adequate if you use the hardware bonding techniques detailed later in this book.

Most blocking is easiest to install before the plywood decking goes on. With core decks, the blocking must all be installed before the final layer of plywood is bonded on. It is much easier to fit, install and fair in the blocking to the bare deck framework than to install it laboriously from the underside of a capped-over deck. Sometimes, however, it's difficult to complete your deck hardware layout plan until the deck is fully completed and you can study it for a while. If this is the case, you're probably better off installing blocking for those items later on from underneath the completed deck, rather than installing it wrong in the first place and having to chisel out blocking that is not needed (if you're like us and can't stand to sail with unnecessary weight).

Cabin Construction

For construction purposes, the cabin is really an extension of the deck. It increases standing headroom and provides a place for windows or ports that will let in light and fresh air below. Cabins are always installed after the deck has been at least framed in, and usually after the deck has been completed. Design the deck framework with an opening for the cabin and sufficient framework around the opening perimeter for attaching the cabin walls. You will have to prebevel to the degree desired for the cabin walls.

Plywood is the most common material for making cabin sides. It should be thick enough to stand on its own with no further frame support for minimal deflec-

Figure 23—Sawn Sitka spruce blocking bonded to core deck at all structural frames and planed flush with deck profile. Note strip of blocking for adjustable sail leads to left.

Figure 24—All spaces between blocking in the deck shown in Figure 23 were filled with honeycomb core before the deck was laid.

Figure 25—Sandwich decks with framing and Verticel in place.

tion. You may laminate the walls out of several layers of plywood or veneers to get a desired precurved shape that might be difficult to form with a single piece of thicker ply. It is common to laminate the front wall of the cabin to provide attractive curves and improve windage. As we mentioned in Chapter 20, cabins can also be built with strip composite techniques.

Fitting cabin walls can be tricky. It is a good idea to make patterns of cheap paneling and then carefully cut the cabin walls to the exact pattern size before final fitting and installation. It is usual to install the walls of the cabin first, then join the corners with an appropriate wood gusset which has enough bonding area for a strong joint.

The most difficult part of building cabins is to establish a cabin top sheer line dimension. This may be a difficult dimension to take from the plans, and it is complicated by the fact that the type and shape of the cabin roof that is installed might dictate some of the final sheer line dimensions. For cabin tops with frame-supported roofs, build the frame using the same technique used for decking. Cover the framework over with sheet ply, or laminate it with strips of ply or veneer.

Because cabin tops are smaller and sometimes have more compound curves than decks, building a core-constructed cabin top or even a solid molded cabin top offers interesting alternatives to the frame system. Either one of these methods provides maximum head room with a clear underside surface and no beams on which to hit your head. The only problem with these two options is that you must first mold the cabin top and then fit it to the cabin walls. Therefore, for final fitting, we leave the cabin walls bare with no sheer clamps until the cabin roof has been fitted perfectly so that it meets the cabin walls on all four wall surfaces. At

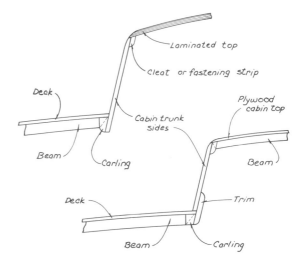

Figure 27—Construction details for cabin sides and tops.

this point, we install a cabin wall sheer clamp joining member around the newly-fitted upper perimeter of the cabin walls, so that we can then install the cabin roof permanently with proper bonding area.

A molded cabin top only ½ inch thick, especially one with compound curves, is rigid. You can easily mold this type of cabin roof out of multiple layers of veneer over a simple ribband mold made up beforehand to the desired shape. You can completely prefinish the interior surface of this cabin roof molding before installation.

When designing cabin structures, it is well to keep in mind the type and amount of the hardware that you may install on the cabin top surface. If major winches are to be located on the cabin corners, you should design the whole cabin structure to accommodate this extra load. Provide adequate blocking in proper places for hardware installation. Take care to make the blocking look nice because it is in a place where it will be continually viewed.

Deck Finishing

Prepare the deck for coating or covering with fabric in much the same manner as the hull, except that the overall fairness of the deck is usually not as crucial. The two most important criteria for the finished deck surface are attractiveness and safety. A non-skid deck surface contributes to safe and efficient movement and operations by crew members.

There are several ways to make non-skid deck surfaces. Probably the easiest is to purchase one of the commercial non-skid paint systems which can be applied over WEST SYSTEM* Brand epoxy and/or

Figure 26—Cabin roof built over cabin top and temporary forms inside the cabin. Small ½ inch wide x ¾ inch thick ribs spaced on 4 inch centers were laminated over the interior ply and faired smooth. Blocking for a headsail track was inserted at the edge of the cabin and a 3/16 inch ply roof was laminated over the assembly.

* TRADEMARK OF GOUGEON BROTHERS, INC., U.S.A.

fabric. The general procedure is to mix a non-skid compound with the base paint at a prescribed ratio and apply it over the sanded resin surface. Although the idea of mixing non-skid material directly into epoxy seems appealing, attempts at doing it are not usually successful. The 100% solid resin tends to cover the non-skid material, minimizing its effectiveness, and paint applied over the unsanded epoxy may not adhere well. Sanding the resin to improve paint adhesion further reduces the non-skid's potential.

Some of our customers have found that an alternative to mixing non-skid material with paint is to pour large quantities of sand ballast, available at hobby shops for use in miniature landscaping, over wet epoxy. To do this, mask off the perimeter of the non-skid area. Coat the enclosed surface with resin and then immediately cover the epoxy with a ¼ inch thick layer of sand ballast. When the epoxy has cured, brush and vacuum away excess sand and paint the surface, which should be rough everywhere. Use generous quantities of sand ballast to make sure that no glossy spots remain between particles since these may cause problems with paint adhesion.

You can also use 6 oz. or 10 oz. fiberglass cloth to make a somewhat less coarse deck. Mask off areas which you want to remain smooth and cover them with plastic. Bond the fabric to the surface, using techniques described in Chapter 12, but remove all excess resin with a plastic spreader. The weave of the cloth will provide the "non-skid" traction, so leave it exposed. When the resin has cured, scrub the area with water and a 3M Scotch Brite™ pad or steel wool until it is dull all over. Then paint the glass-covered area.

Another approach to a non-skid deck surface is to purchase the commercially available Treadmaster™ deck covering material. It is easy to bond this to the WEST SYSTEM resin surface using an adhesive mixture as the bonding agent. You can purchase this decking additive in a variety of colors and apply it in tasteful patterns wherever non-skid potential is needed. The disadvantages of this material are its added expense and the potential extra weight per square foot that may be objectionable on a smaller boat. Treadmaster is a flexible material adding no strength or stiffness to a deck surface.

Teak Veneer Deck System

You can achieve a very successful deck surface by laminating a layer of teak over a well-sealed plywood base. This veneer lamination of teak ends up being about ⅛ inch to 3/16 inch in thickness, which is thick enough to provide a durable, hard-wearing surface

capable of lasting for many years. The methods that we have used to apply this teak surface are described in the following paragraphs.

Prepare the deck plywood surface in normal fashion with a minimum of two coats of WEST SYSTEM resin prior to the application of the teak strips. This is done to provide a maximum moisture barrier directly underneath the teak surface which will protect the deck plywood surface and supporting framework from any moisture attack. Then sand the resin surface lightly in preparation for bonding the teak strips to the deck surface.

Before starting any bonding operations, determine a pattern for the layout of the teak strips. Traditionally, teak decks have always been laid parallel to the half-breadth deck line. However, we have also laid some decks with the planking parallel to the centerline that have been very attractive and also practical, more effectively contributing to compression load resistance. There seems to be no limit to the artistic possibilities in laying out a teak deck. (See Figure 28.)

Saw the teak stock slightly thicker than the desired finished dimension, leaving 1/32 inch to 1/16 inch extra to allow for the sanding process. Saw all of the strips to a given consistent width that most economically uses the stock you have on hand. Usually, we buy our teak in 2 inch thick rough sawn planks, and are able to get close to 1¾ inch finished dimension from this. We saw up the stock so that the 1¾ inch width of the teak strips will be edge grained. This minimizes expansion-contraction potential (very small with teak anyway) and makes for a more attractive and more evenly wearing surface than slabgrained strips would provide. You can do this by squaring your stock (sawing it into 2 inch

Figure 28—Intersection of teak deck, mahogany covering board and cedar topsides on GOLDEN DAZY. All three types of wood are no thicker than 5/32 inch and laminated in place with temporary staples. Note teak toerail with limber holes.

x 2 inch squares) and then turning it to the best position from which you can saw edge grained teak strips. It is crucial that the width dimension of all the sawn strips be exact, and that you cut the ends off of each strip exactly square. The thickness of the teak strips is not as critical and you can rough saw these, eliminating dressing with a thickness planer. You will take care of the teak thickness when sanding the deck later on. The strips should range from 6 to 12 feet in length. Strips any longer than this are difficult to handle when bonding them to the deck.

Next, make up an adhesive mixture using a combination of high density filler and 423 Graphite Powder. Add high density filler to the consistency of thick syrup and then mix in graphite at a rate of 5-10% by volume. This is enough to color the resin for the traditional black between the teak strips and, more importantly, to protect the epoxy from ultraviolet light. If you use too much 423 additive, however, you may have problems with excess graphite. Although we have never had any trouble with it, some varieties of teak are notoriously hard to bond. Try some sample joints with the teak you intend to use before applying it to the deck.

Install each teak strip by first coating it and the area on the deck where it will be applied with the adhesive mixture. Don't worry about applying too much resin: excess adhesive between the deck and the strips helps to guarantee that strips are bonded to the deck with no voids and very little will be wasted. Leave gaps of about 3/32 inch between strips for the traditional look and to ensure a positive seal between the edges of the individual planks. If little or no resin floods into a gap, you have an immediate indication of a potentially resin-starved area.

To maintain even gaps between strips, make a spacer which you can hold between them as you work. We usually make our "gap tools" from plastic, such as ABS℗, to which resin does not adhere well and from which it can be easily removed. Use butt joints where long strips are needed. Saw the ends of the planks square on a miter box or cutoff saw so that they will lie flat and coat them liberally with adhesive. Stagger joints for the most appealing effect.

There are many ways to hold planking down until the resin cures. The objectives are straightforward and any technique can be used if you keep them in mind. Strips should be in contact with the epoxy and, to avoid water damage in the future, there should be no holes in the deck. You can use ½ inch long wide crown bronze or steel staples, but aluminum staples are usually too soft to penetrate the teak. Try to use as few staples as possible — an average of one every 9 inches along the center of a strip and more in areas where the

teak curves severely will probably suffice. When the epoxy has cured, you can clip off the heads of bronze staples but you should pull out steel ones.

The legs of alloy staples may raise up from the surface at some point, and the holes left by steel staples can conceivably allow water to get in below the planking, so you may want to consider a slightly more time-consuming method for holding teak deck strips. We sometimes insert small sheet metal screws and washers, both of which have been coated with a mold release, into the gaps between planks. The washers hold the edges of the teak firmly until the epoxy cures and are easy to remove. Another technique which is particularly effective on cored decks is to insert self-tapping screws every 8 inches or so along the middle of a plank as it is laid. When the resin has cured, remove the screws, countersink each hole, and plug it.

When the strips are bonded in place, the deck is usually a mess, with black adhesive smeared on rough teak and, if you've used them, staples sticking up all over the place. At this point you should either remove the staples or clip their heads flush with the deck with sharp wire sidecutters. If you've chosen screws and washers or self-tapping screws, remove them. Then rough sand the entire deck with 50 grit paper and a hand-operated belt sander or a rotary sander with a good foam disc pad and thin plywood or plastic face. Rotary sanders are designed for this type of work and do an excellent job. Clipped alloy staples sand at about the same rate as teak and are about the same color, so they are almost invisible from a few feet when this operation is finished.

After rough sanding, the teak deck is relatively smooth but gaps and voids usually remain between some strips. Fill these flush with a resin putty mixture so that none are left anywhere on the surface. To make this putty, add Colloidal Silica to WEST SYSTEM epoxy until it is the consistency of a creamy peanut butter. Then add graphite powder as you did with the adhesive mixture. Trowel this evenly into the gaps, removing any excess on the deck to reduce the sanding required for a final finish.

After the puttied surface has cured, do a final sanding of the teak surface using 80 grit sandpaper. Usually, a rotary sander with a foam disc pad is adequate to achieve a nice, smooth surface. Another handy tool for final teak sanding, especially for getting in tight areas, is the modified air file sander (as described in Chapter 4). Inevitably, final sanding will involve some hand sanding with a block, especially when getting up around tight areas, such as cabins, hatches and cockpits.

After you have completed the final sanding, your

258

Figure 29—Deck of 26 foot LUDERS 16 framed-in and ready for plywood covering.

Figure 30—LUDERS 16 deck covered with ¼ inch 5-ply Gaboon plywood. The teak overlay contributes to deck strength and stiffness.

Figure 31—Installing teak planking parallel to sheer, beginning along outer sheer line and progressing toward the center of the boat. This is a sprung deck.

Figure 32—Deck planking and final sanding completed. Note herringbone pattern where planks meet along the centerline. Also note that teak begins several inches inboard from the sheer, with a painted cover board for an attractive effect.

deck surface is done. There is nothing more to do but install the hardware. If you spill any resin or paint on the deck surface, you need not worry. You can remove it easily with a little sanding.

Comments about the Teak Veneer System

We have had excellent results with teak decks which have ended up measuring about ⅛ inch to 3/16 inch thick. We feel that 3/16 inch thick is about maximum for this type of system, and we advise against using any thicker strips. The reason is that WEST SYSTEM adhesive bonding is able to overpower the expansion-contraction forces which occur in these thinner sections. Teak strips of much thicker dimension, such as ⅜ inch or ½ inch, might create forces so great as to overwhelm the adhesive, causing it to fail. We see no reason to go to any teak veneer thicker than 3/16 inch. We estimate that it will take at least 20 years of heavy foot traffic to wear through this thickness of teak, and should this unlikely event happen, you can easily replace individual planks of the teak.

The teak does not necessarily add any weight to a deck surface, and can be included as a part of the deck scantling system. A deck designed for ½ inch thickness of plywood might very well be made up of ⅜ inch plywood and ⅛ inch teak strips at much the same weight as if ½ inch plywood had been used. Although the teak can gain weight through moisture absorption, it is a high density wood, and does not gain weight appreciably as softwoods are prone to do.

Repair and Maintenance

Damage to teak deck surfaces, while not very common, is easy to repair. Set a router bit to cut the depth of the teak veneer and rout out the plank or planks to be removed. Replace with new strips of teak, bonding exactly as you did the original deck. Sand the new pieces flush with the rest of the deck surface and the job is done. It will look as good as new.

There are various treatments on the market for keeping teak bright. Some of these are excellent if you want to put the time into this type of upkeep, but they are

Figure 33—Teak planking on GOLDEN DAZY laid parallel to centerline. Installation was simplified because strips did not have to bend to the arc of the sheer line. This attractive pattern receives many favorable comments.

not necessary. A lustrous gray, sun-bleached deck can be very appealing.

Over a period of time, wet and dry cycles on the teak may have a tendency to raise some of the bronze staples up slightly from the flush surface. Sanding the staples flush with the teak deck surface, using 80 grit paper on a hand sanding block, easily solves this problem.

Chapter 26

Hardware Bonding

Hardware installation on wooden boats presents many problems. Even the smallest boats are usually equipped with cleats, winches and other fittings which must be screwed or bolted to wood surfaces. Unfortunately, hardware attached by normal methods reveals some of the weaknesses of wood. While wood's low density makes it an ideal hull construction material, this low density is a weakness where hardware is concerned. The extreme high point loadings which can be generated by hardware can easily overstress wood fiber.

High-load-bearing hardware is typically fastened to deck surfaces by through bolting. Nuts and washers are used on the underside of the deck to clamp the hardware firmly to the wood surface. Depending on the size of the washer, only a minimum clamping load can be applied on the nut before reaching the crush strength of the wood fiber. If the holes for the through bolts are the least bit sloppy, it's likely that the hardware on the deck will shift. To keep moisture from penetrating under the hardware and into the bolt holes and the vulnerable end grain exposed in the holes, various forms of bedding compound are used as sealants.

Over time, continual movement of the hardware tends to break down the elasticity of the sealant, and this eventually allows moisture to infiltrate the wood immediately surrounding the hardware installation. The invading moisture contributes to a general weakening of the wood fiber and sets up favorable conditions for dry rot. Dry rot should be detected early and the fitting should be removed and rebedded. If it isn't, serious structural damage can take place, possibly resulting in total failure of the fitting.

To overcome these problems, we have developed a different approach to attaching hardware: *hardware bonding.* We use WEST SYSTEM* Brand epoxy to bond fittings to wood fiber with the goal of distributing hardware loads over as large an area of wood fiber as possible. There are two distinct ways to achieve this load distribution. The first is to bond all screws, bolts and threaded rod directly to the surrounding wood fiber. The second is to bond the fitting itself to the wood fiber on which it rests. With the installation tech-

niques explained in this chapter and deck blocking installed as described in Chapter 25, hardware can withstand dramatically more load than hardware which is simply bedded in position.

WEST SYSTEM resin is an excellent adhesive for wood. It can also be used to bond metal to wood. In fact, it's this capacity to bond dissimilar materials which makes hardware bonding with WEST SYSTEM resin practical. Because there are some significant differences in the techniques used to bond fasteners up to ¼ inch in diameter and fasteners over ¼ inch in diameter, the following discussion focuses first on small fasteners and then on larger ones. Bonded fasteners and hardware can be removed following directions contained in this chapter.

Bonding Small Fasteners

There are several ways to bond fasteners with diameters of ¼ inch and less. All of these techniques will increase fastener load capacity. When a screw is inserted in wood, its threads break wood fiber. The screw keys into the wood — this mechanical keying makes the screw effective — but it does so imperfectly. Voids remain between the wood and the metal. When the pilot hole for the screw and the screw itself are wet out with epoxy, however, the epoxy molds to the shape of the screw threads and flows into all minute voids. Mechanical keying becomes far more efficient and the screw is therefore able to bear a greater load. The wood-resin matrix immediately surrounding the

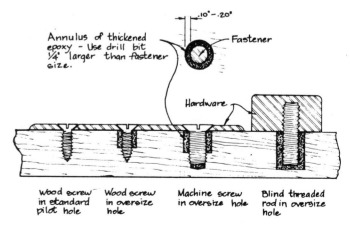

Figure 1—Bonded Fasteners

* TRADEMARK OF GOUGEON BROTHERS, INC., U.S.A.

fastener is stronger than wood alone and it distributes the fastener load more efficiently to the surrounding wood fiber.

The simplest and most common way to bond small fasteners is to wet out a standard size pilot hole, using a pipe cleaner or syringe to work epoxy completely into the hole and all of the wood fiber immediately surrounding it. Dab resin over the screw's shank and threads. Then insert the fastener and allow it to cure. The bonded screw will have much greater load capacity than an identical fastener inserted in an identical hole without epoxy.

To increase the amount of resin surrounding the fastener and, therefore, its holding power, a fastener may be inserted in an oversize hole. This creates an *annulus,* or ring, of epoxy between the metal and the wood. The diameter of the hole may be considerably larger than the diameter of the fastener. It can be up to twice the diameter of a small screw. We more typically recommend an annulus radius of between .1 and .2 inches, created by drilling a fastener hole with a bit about ¼ inch larger in diameter than the fastener. Drill the wood to the proper depth, fill the hole with epoxy, coat the shank and threads of the fastener with resin and set it in.

When very large holes are used for fasteners up to about ⅜ inch in diameter, the epoxy in them may "burn off" in an exothermic reaction and lose some of its physical properties, so relatively large annuli should be used only in situations where extremely high one-time pull-out loads are anticipated. It's a good idea to make and fill a sample hole in some scrap lumber to be sure that a fastener/oversize hole combination will not overheat.

In 1978 and 1979, we conducted tests to determine the relative effects of surface area on fasteners, comparing tension withdrawal of 1½ inch long flat head wood screws, ranging in size from No. 8 through No. 14, in dry pilot holes and oversize holes from 3/16 inch to ¾ inch in diameter. The screws were buried in ¼ inch plywood and Sitka spruce samples which had been constructed to simulate a deck and blocking.

The results of this experiment help to illustrate the effects of bonding fasteners. When a No. 12 screw was inserted in a standard size dry pilot hole, 901 pounds were required to withdraw it, but when an identical screw was bonded in a ¼ inch diameter oversize hole, 1,697 pounds were needed. It is significant that when the No. 12 fastener was bonded in a 7/16 inch diameter hole, with an annulus of only .15 inch, it failed in tension at 1,742 pounds. We therefore conclude that for tension withdrawal loading on No. 12, 1½ inch screws, there is no reason to use an oversize hole larger than

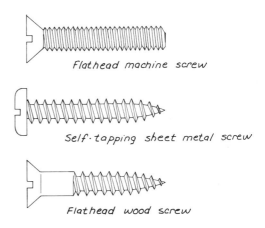

Figure 2—Screw types.

7/16 inch in diameter. At this point, enough surface area is available for load dissipation to overcome the breaking strength of the screw itself.

In the test, the No. 14 wood screw, with its larger shank, required a ¾ inch diameter oversize hole to reach its breaking strength of 2,746 pounds. A No. 14 screw bonded in a ⅜ inch diameter oversize hole was only capable of a load of 1,606 pounds, or slightly less than the No. 12 screw was capable of in the same size hole. All of the screws, from No. 8 through No. 14, had about the same load capacity when they were bonded in ¼ inch diameter holes.

In a second series of tests we compared wood screws to self-tapping screws in dry, predrilled pilot holes and in resin-soaked pilot holes. With both types of screws, the use of WEST SYSTEM resin increased fastener load capacity by up to 70%. We gain this phenomenal increase with little expense or additional effort, and use it in a majority of moderately-loaded hardware applications.

This test also showed the statistical superiority of self-tapping sheet metal screws to wood screws in both kinds of holes. The fully threaded shank of the tapping screw has more surface area and is therefore better able to key into the resin/wood matrix than the wood screw. Wood screws are inferior to tapping screws in tension withdrawal unless the smooth portions of their shanks are treated for bonding, a procedure which we think is neither time, nor cost, effective.

While our results show that bonding significantly increases the capacity of fasteners, they should not be interpreted to mean that small fasteners can be substituted for larger ones in any given application. Instead, the techniques described in this chapter can be used to increase safety margins and increase resistance to damage from dry rot.

Large Diameter Fasteners

Oversize holes and resin interfaces between metal fasteners and wood fibers become increasingly important with fasteners which are larger than ¼ inch in diameter. This is particularly true in situations where the potential of a bolt, machine screw or threaded rod must be maximized.

If you know the resistance load values of the different species of woods, you can determine the load capacity of a given large diameter fastener in pounds per square inch. Available square inches, of course, are figured on the diameter of the oversize hole, and not the diameter of the fastener itself. Average ultimate withdrawal resistance values for resin-bonded bolts, provided in Figure 3, are the pounds-per-square-inch load for bonded bolts in oversize round holes. Withdrawal resistance is affected by a number of variables, including fastener aspect ratio, length and shape, and these figures can therefore only serve as general guides.

The following average ultimate withdrawal resistance values for resin-bonded bolts from three species of wood were determined in tests conducted by Kurt Keidel at Ohio State University in June 1977.	
Honduras Mahogany	1,884 psi
White Ash	1,618 psi
Sitka Spruce	1,360 psi

Figure 3—Ultimate withdrawal resistance, selected boatbuilding woods.

To use these figures, calculate as follows. A ⅜ inch diameter bolt bonded in 3 inches of wood in a ½ inch diameter hole would have 4.5 inches of surface area. To find the load capacity of this bolt, you would also need to know the wood's ultimate withdrawal resistance value. Sitka spruce can withstand an average ultimate withdrawal load of 1,360 psi. Ultimate withdrawal resistance with a 4.5 square inch surface area for the bolt application would therefore be 6,120 pounds. If white ash were used instead of Sitka spruce, the average ultimate withdrawal load would increase to 1,610 psi. If Honduras mahogany were used, the average ultimate load would be 1,884 psi. Note that, depending on the number of load cycles, R ratio and other variables, safe allowable design loads should not exceed one half of the ultimate withdrawal resistance loads given above.

Shear Load and Fasteners

Hardware items are loaded in shear more often than they are loaded in direct tension, so we think an understanding of the shear capacity of fasteners is a very critical part of hardware bonding. We conducted numerous shear tests on various types and sizes of fasteners to determine their capability under various load conditions.

Most fasteners have less capacity in shear than in straight tension. In part, this is because fasteners tend to bend under shear load. This bending causes extreme high point loading, which begins at the upper wood surface immediately surrounding the fastener head and works down the shank as the fastener bends. To complicate the problem, the crush value for wood is way below what would be needed to withstand the high point loading generated by the bending fastener. Bonding a fastener in a resin/wood matrix will improve shear load capacity, but not as dramatically as it increases tension withdrawal. While an oversize hole with the resin matrix surrounding the fastener distributes load over more area, the extreme high point loading caused by the bending fastener can reach the compressive capability of the resin itself.

When fasteners are tested in tension, failure is easy to detect. When they are tested in shear, however, it is more difficult to determine when failure has occurred. We have a long-established rule that fittings should not move under normal maximum load, and for us fastener failure is detectable movement. Shear tests are difficult to design, however, and we could not use measurements of fastener movement as reliable indicators of failure. Instead, we used four measurement criteria, of which maximum load to detectable movement and maximum load with movement not to exceed a pencil line (.030 inch) were the most important.

In our tests, larger diameter fasteners proved

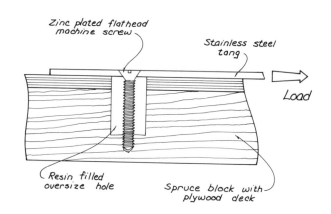

Figure 4—Sectional view of test sample for shear load on a bonded fastener.

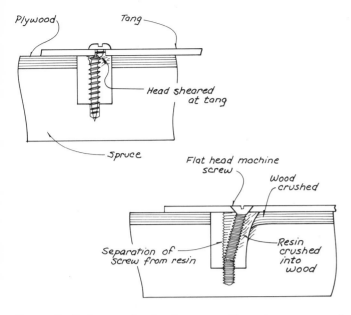

Figure 5—Failure modes for shear on self-tapping screws and flathead machine screws.

superior to smaller diameter fasteners in shear resistance, as might be expected. With wood screws, the value at detectable movement for a No. 8 screw was 435 lbs., while the value for a No. 14 screw increased only to 696 lbs. The increase between the two is not as large as the increase with standard size pilot holes in tension withdrawal testing. Fastener type made a difference in performance. Self-tapping and machine screws were generally superior to wood screws for shear load resistance, but tapping screws tended to have a lower ultimate breaking strength than wood screws.

High ultimate load capacity is good because of the generous safety margin it provides. Since we consider any movement to be initial failure, with a high probability that ultimate failure will follow in a period of time, our solution is to provide an appropriate safety margin. In selecting fasteners to secure a fitting, we therefore opt for either larger tapping screws or a greater number of tapping screws.

Machine screws have a distinct advantage as load-bearing fasteners because of their high initial resistance to movement and high ultimate failure capacity. This increased capacity is due to their larger core diameter and their fully threaded shank. Since machine screws also exhibited excellent tension withdrawal resistance, we think that for many applications they have the most potential and we use them just as we would wood screws or self-tapping screws. The only difference is that machine screws have blunt ends and therefore cannot cut their own holes, so we must drill pilot holes

with the right diameter drill bit and to the proper depth.

Self-tapping screws are our second choice of fasteners. They are usually superior to wood screws in tension withdrawal, especially to the pencil movement point. Wood screws, which were developed primarily for use in attaching two pieces of wood, seem to be only superior in ultimate failure in shear and this is of little consolation after large movement has occurred. They appear to have no significant advantage as fasteners for attaching hardware to wood. Wood screws are probably adequate for most hardware applications, but we see no reason to use them when tapping and machine screws are available at comparable prices.

As a rule, flathead screws are preferable to roundhead screws. This is especially significant when screws are loaded in shear, where tight mating with the hardware is critical to preventing hardware movement. A roundhead fastener inevitably has some slop between the fastener shank and the hardware hole through which it passes. While this gap can be partially filled with resin, this is not as strong as a tight metal-to-metal fit. If the holes in a fitting are not countersunk for a flathead fastener, you can usually taper them with a screw countersink or grind special bits to the proper countersink angle.

Shear load capacity of fasteners over ¼ inch in diameter depends primarily on the frontal surface area of the fastener available for load distribution. As a fastener gets larger, potential load carrying capacity increases at a much greater rate than surface area. Thus, the shear resistance of large fasteners does not improve geometrically.

Tests of 5/16 inch to ½ inch diameter, fully-threaded bolts show that, using pencil line movement as a criterion, shear capacity appears to grow linearly with the bolt diameter. While the strength of a ½ inch diameter bolt increased many times over the 5/16 inch diameter bolt, shear resistance increased only 45%, or about the same as the increase in frontal surface area.

In shear loading, fully threaded bolt shanks are superior to unthreaded shanks because of the greater surface area they present. The ability of the threads to key in the resin helps shear load capacity just as threads also help tension capacity. The shanks of some solid, rolled thread bolts narrow and widen in diameter. Beware of these — the thicker and thinner shank is a bad combination from several standpoints. For shear loads, the undersize shank presents a low frontal area and this results in low load potential. Secondly, with this type of bolt there is no guarantee that epoxy or epoxy mixtures will take up the gaps between the shank and the hole, so premature failure may result.

Procedures for Bonding Fasteners

Choose the specific technique you will use to bond any fastener after evaluating the loads to which it will be subjected. Heavily-loaded hardware, hardware which will be loaded in sheer and lightly-loaded hardware require slightly different procedures. Oversize holes are usually unnecessary for lightly-loaded hardware which can be attached with small screws, but up to a limit are advisable in other applications. Fasteners should be washed with soap and water or a degreaser but they need no other surface preparation. Always coat fasteners with resin before inserting them.

To drill a standard size hole for a machine screw, use a high speed metal drill with a diameter approximately one size under the size of the screw. To drill a pilot hole for a ¼ inch diameter machine screw, for example, choose a 7/32 inch diameter bit. The *interference fit* which results gives the screw threads plenty of bite into the wood fiber and ensures a good bond between the fastener and the wood when both are coated with epoxy. To bond a fastener in a standard hole, use a pipe cleaner or syringe to wet out the hole with WEST SYSTEM epoxy. Wet out the threads of the screw and install it immediately. When the resin has cured, the fastener will have about twice the safe working load in spruce or fir as the same screw installed without epoxy.

There are no firm rules about the diameters of oversize holes. We recommend that you aim for a cured epoxy annulus with a radius of .1 to .2 inches, so select a drill bit about ¼ inch larger than actual screw size. As we mentioned earlier, up to a point, larger oversize holes will provide higher one time capability, but for smaller fasteners this is balanced against the danger that resin pooled in a relatively large oversize hole may react intensely. Fasteners over about ⅜ inch in diameter are able to absorb the heat of this reaction and in this way "protect" the epoxy from its effects. For these reasons, we suggest the annuli for fasteners under ⅜ inch in diameter be kept at the lower end of the .1 to .2 inch range, and that you test holes and fasteners in scrap lumber before using them in a hull.

The immediate problem with installing fasteners in oversize holes is keeping them in position until the epoxy cures. The best technique is to drill the oversize hole approximately two-thirds to three-quarters of the length of the screw shank. This allows the bottom of the screw to bite into the wood. The fastener can then center itself in the middle of the hole and, at the same time, achieve enough holding power to hold the piece of hardware in place reasonably snug to the surface.

We usually use wood speed bores to drill oversize holes, grinding the tips to diameter and length as

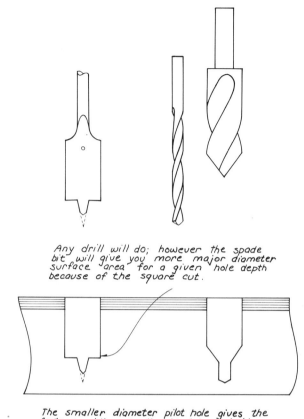

Any drill will do; however the spade bit will give you more major diameter surface area for a given hole depth because of the square cut.

The smaller diameter pilot hole gives the fastener bite into the blocking, holding the fastener and fitting until the resin cures. You can grind the long tip on the spade bit to avoid drilling through the blocking.

Figure 6—Drilling the pilot hole and oversize holes.

shown in Figure 6 for the screws we are installing. If, for example, we were drilling ⅜ inch diameter oversize holes into which we planned to insert 1½ inch No. 10 screws, we would buy a ⅜ inch diameter speed bore, leave its outer flanges intact, and grind its tip to the right diameter and length for a centering "bite" hole about ⅜ inch deep. Another way to drill oversize holes is to use two bits. Drill about three-quarters of the desired length with an oversize bit and then drill out the bottom with a bit which is smaller than the screw. In either case, keep drill tips sharp: in our testing, we noticed that wood fibers which are cut cleanly absorb epoxy better than fibers which have been burnished by dull drills. Burnished samples also failed more frequently than clean-cut ones.

Since you fill oversize holes with epoxy before inserting fasteners, it's easiest to work on near-horizontal surfaces, with gravity in your favor. After drilling a hole, remove all wood chips and fill it to the top with epoxy. Allow the resin to soak into the wood for 5 to 10 minutes. This waiting period is extremely important because a significant portion of the resin may be absorbed by the wood, especially in smaller holes. If you

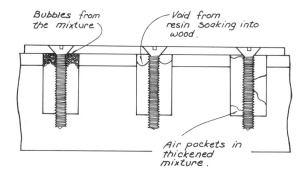

Figure 7—Problems in bonding fasteners.

insert the fastener too soon, the wood may continue to drain resin away from the screw. If, after waiting, you notice a significant reduction in the epoxy supply, add more before inserting the fastener.

In most situations, the fastener will take up a good deal of the volume of the hole and resin will be forced onto the surface as you insert it. To minimize this problem remove some epoxy from the hole with a syringe just before installing the fastener. You want some excess to flow out, since this will tell you that the hole is amply supplied with resin, so don't withdraw too much. A little experience will teach you how much you can remove without jeopardizing the wood/fastener bond.

Voids in oversize holes detract from the strength of the bonded fasteners and should therefore be avoided. Careful monitoring of resin absorption after the initial 5 to 10 minute waiting period will help prevent the voids which can result when the wood absorbs so much resin

Figure 8—Use a syringe to fill oversize hole.

that little is left for bonding the fastener. Other typical problems, shown in Figure 7, caused by air bubbles from the epoxy mixture and air pockets in the oversize hole, can be eliminated with efficient work habits. Stir the resin mixture carefully, getting as little air as possible into it, and always begin filling an oversize hole at its bottom and work up.

It's more difficult to install fasteners in oversize holes on perpendicular surfaces. Here, a two-step application procedure works well. First, use a pipe cleaner to wet out the hole with epoxy. Wait a few minutes, and then use a syringe to fill the hole with a thick mixture of epoxy and high density filler. The adhesive should be thick enough to stay in the hole without running, but not so thick that it cannot be administered with the syringe. To load it into the syringe, remove the plunger and force the resin mixture down into the barrel with a paddle. Begin injecting the resin into the bottom of the hole and work up. Try to avoid trapping air in the cavity as you proceed.

In situations where a screw hole — standard or oversize — is horizontal or extremely deep and the syringe is not long enough to reach to the bottom of the hole, slide a thin drinking straw over its tip. Insert the straw into the hole and, starting at the bottom and working up, inject non-fortified epoxy. Let this penetrate for a few minutes and then use the same tool and technique to inject a mixture of high density filler and resin.

Before inserting the fastener into the resin-filled hole, coat it liberally with the thickened resin mixture to mechanically fill all its threads. If an uncoated fastener is inserted in the hole, its threads may not completely fill with adhesive and the quality of the bond may be reduced. An advantage of the two-step process is that adhesive which oozes from the hole doesn't run and can be removed with a putty knife.

Removing Bonded Fasteners

The bond between a fastener and WEST SYSTEM epoxy is strong, but with the right procedures you can break it to remove the fastener from the wood. If you know you will want to extract a fastener at some point in the future, coat it with wax or a mold release before installing it. Although the wax will interfere with the metal/resin bond, it will not compromise the mechanical keying around the threads which provides the major load transfer capability.

Bonded fasteners can often be removed with reasonable force. If you have trouble loosening them, heat fasteners with a soldering gun or iron until the surrounding epoxy softens. Attach a cutting tip to a soldering gun and insert it in the slot at the top of smaller screws to free them. Larger fasteners with more root diameter can frequently be forced without breaking, but heating them to around 250°F softens the resin and makes the job much easier.

When you heat WEST SYSTEM resin to remove a fastener, you may destroy some of its physical properties. Drill out the hole completely and start afresh when you replace the fastener.

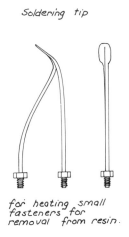

Soldering tip

for heating small fasteners for removal from resin.

Figure 9—Soldering tip.

Hardware Bonding

Bonding the contact surface of a fitting can contribute a great deal to load distribution over maximum wood surface. Proper bonding of a 2½ inch diameter paddeye, for example, can add up to 7,000 pounds of extra shear load resistance, assuming Sitka spruce with load parallel to grain.

We are usually primarily interested in improving the shear load capacity of hardware installations. It's difficult to make significant shear load improvements by bonding fasteners, but when a fitting is bonded to the wood on which it sits, it has far more capacity in shear than the fasteners used to attach the item have by themselves. In tension, the opposite is true: fasteners are always the predominant load distributors, so hardware bonding is of secondary importance. We therefore bond hardware mainly to improve shear strength, the main weakness of low density woods.

This improvement in shear capacity is especially significant with chain plate installations. Chain plates are usually very heavily loaded and their fasteners are always loaded in perfect shear. Chain plate movement has always been a common problem with wooden boats, but it is easily solved with hardware bonding. Design criteria for chain plates should include maximizing bonding surface area of the chain plate strap for maximum load distribution.

The bonding surfaces of many hardware items may already be grooved or rough and you can use this to advantage. The bottom of a typical winch base, for example, has deep machine marks as well as a hollow central core area. If resin is allowed to well up in this hollow area, it will form a fillet around the inner lip of the base and this will transfer load. Even if you do not make a good bond with the metal itself, the machine marks and core will provide excellent shear resistance through mechanical keying.

To increase the keying potential of any fitting, drill a series of small, shallow holes into which resin can flow. Ports, vents, hatches and other noncritical hardware items which will not be subjected to high loads probably do not need this special surface preparation, but they should be bedded in a thickened high density resin mixture to be sure that there will be no gaps between them and the hull surface to which they are fastened.

Preparing Metal Surfaces for Bonding

WEST SYSTEM epoxy can be used to make good bonds with most metals, an ability which makes the hardware bonding concept practical. There are problems with developing good bonds, however, and preparation of metal surfaces is necessary for good adhesion.

Metal surface preparation for adhesive bonding is a relatively new and complex field, and there are several schools of thought. For those interested in completely researching the subject, we recommend the *Handbook of Adhesive Bonding* by Charles V. Cagle (McGraw-Hill, Inc., New York, 1973). This is the best work on the subject that we know of to date. For the most part, super bonding with metals is not necessarily a requirement for metal/wood bonding. Invariably, wood grain strength itself is the limiting factor, and, in most cases, there is no need to achieve a resin-to-metal bond that is any stronger than the limiting factor of wood grain strength.

The following paragraphs describe preparation methods that we have used successfully on a variety of metals to achieve the wood grain strength criterion easily. Structural values which can be expected with various types of wood on a pounds per square inch basis are listed in the physical property tables in Appendix A. If you bond the hardware item *perpendicular* to the grain structure, you can assume only 60% of this figure. Shear strength properties of wood rarely exceed 2,000 psi, and usually are closer to 1,000 psi. You can make bonds with metals which are above 2,000 psi, but you need extremely good preparation of the metal surface.

Aluminum

Aluminum has always been difficult to bond, but simplified surface preparation systems have made the task somewhat easier. The first step of these preparations usually uses an acid wash solution to etch, clean and mill the surface. The second part, generally an alodine conversion coating, stabilizes the aluminum and minimizes the corrosion that may form upon contact with air before you apply epoxy the resin adhesive. The 860 WEST SYSTEM Aluminum Etch Kit contains all necessary ingredients and complete instructions. If you use another surface preparation system, carefully follow the manufacturer's instructions.

Steel (Including all 300 series stainless steels)

The preparation of a steel surface involves four steps. The first step is to get the metal surface as clean as possible. You can accomplish this with a solvent wash, using clean cloths to remove all grease and oils. You should wipe any unusually dirty surfaces several times, so that no possible contamination is left on the surface. The next step is to sand the surface with coarse sandpaper (60 grit or 180 grit wet or dry) to remove all mill scale and rust, exposing fresh, clean metal. Step three is to cover the sanded metal surface with a thin coating of standard resin. The fourth and final step is to immediately sand the metal surface (60 grit paper) again, while the resin is still in its uncured state. This procedure resembles wet sanding with water, but substitutes the standard resin for the water. The goal of this procedure is to expose fresh metal, allowing it to come in contact with resin immediately instead

Figure 11—Apply resin to bonding surface.

Figure 12—Wet sand resin into bonding surface.

of air, which can cause corrosion to begin quickly. (Besides contamination, corrosion is considered a major cause of poor bonding.) When you have completed the fourth step, you are ready to bond the hardware into position. Sometimes we allow this initial resin coating to cure for later bonding. Then all that we need to do to prepare the surface for bonding at a later time is to clean and lightly sand the cured resin surface for good adhesion.

Bronze Alloys

High copper content metals are particularly difficult to bond to, which is probably due to copper's fast oxidation rate. Most of the time, we prepare a bronze

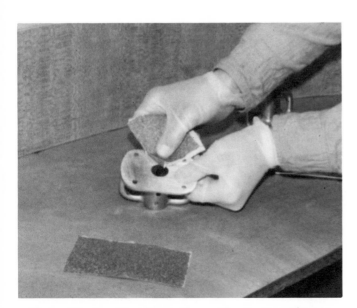

Figure 10—Sand bonding surface with coarse sandpaper.

bonding surface in the same manner as we do steel, but in addition, we try to abrade the surface physically as much as is practical to achieve mechanical keying between the resin and metal surface.

Procedures for Bonding Hardware

Hardware bonding has one disadvantage. In most cases, the procedure requires more time than normal hardware installation methods, because of the added steps required. After you have gained some experience with this new method, however, the extra time required will not be substantial, and we assure you that the results will be well worthwhile.

Bonding hardware in place is much easier if you do it before the boat receives its final paint job, but then the painting job is made more difficult because you must protect the installed items and paint around them. The only problem with installing hardware on a newly-painted surface is the possibility of contaminating the new finish. The hardware bonding process can be messy, and while keeping the newly-painted surface clean is possible, it involves a cost in time. In our own shop, we don't have a set policy, but look at the individual job and try to determine what installation procedure will save the most time. Often, we will install some hardware items before painting (especially difficult pieces, such as large winches and track), and then install the rest of the hardware items (those which are most difficult to paint around) after final painting.

Whether you are bonding hardware before or after painting, begin by positioning the fitting and carefully marking fastener hole centers. You can use any tool which makes a hole big enough to be useful as a center for drilling — we usually choose an awl for this job. Take particular care to center the starter holes in the fastener holes. When they are marked, check them. If one appears to be a little off, move it as needed for accuracy.

Next, remove the fitting and drill out the holes with an appropriate drill bit. The bit should be sharp and evenly-ground because dull bits tend to travel. To control the depth of the hole, stick a small piece of tape to the bit to mark the length of the fastener, remembering to subtract the thickness of the hardware. If you have a variable speed drill motor, start slowly and speed up after you have gone a quarter of the way. Sight your drill from the side and front to be certain that you are not angling it.

Hole sizes depend on the loads to which the hardware you are installing will be subjected. If you are working on a fitting which can be attached with small screws and will only be used in light load applications,

drill a standard pilot hole. If the item will be subjected to shear loads, as cleats are, drill a standard pilot hole and then switch to a drill bit which is about ¼ inch larger in diameter. Use this to drill out the upper half of the hole. If you are attaching a winch, mooring cleat, chain plate for standing rigging or other similar hardware, use coarse machine screws. Drill holes about ¼ inch bigger than the screws, ¾ of the depth of the hole. Then, use a bit 1/16 inch smaller than the screws to drill out the bottom of the holes until they are longer than the machine screws.

After all the holes are drilled, remove any wood chips from the individual holes and surrounding area. Then reposition the hardware to see if all drilled holes line up with those on the piece of hardware. (One of the advantages of using oversize holes for fastener bonding is that the fit is not so critical.) If everything lines up all right, leave the hardware temporarily in place with the fasteners set in their holes (using just a few turns so they don't fall out) and move on to the next hardware item and proceed to mark and drill for it. Preparing a number of hardware items simultaneously in this manner for the bonding procedure is more efficient than completely installing each hardware item individually from start to finish. The hardware placement, marking and drilling procedures are very different from those procedures needed for the bonding operation. Just gathering together the proper tools (or materials) for either operation requires considerable time, and you increase efficiency if you minimize this unavoidable start-up time.

If you are bonding hardware to a surface which has received its final paint finish, there is one more step that you must take before bonding begins. After you set the hardware in final position, draw a pencil line around its perimeter. Then remove the hardware and apply tape (usually 2 inches wide) around the perimeter of the pencil line, overlapping slightly so that the entire mark is covered. Reposition the hardware, using the drilled fastener holes as guides, and then carefully cut through the overlapping tape with a sharp blade, using the hardware perimeter as a guide. In this process, do not cut through the resin surface. Use only enough pressure on the blade to cut through the tape. Then remove the hardware and peel away the tape in the bonding area, leaving a taped outline which perfectly matches the hardware perimeter. The final step is to scrape away the paint in the bonding area down to the cured resin surface with a sharp edge tool, being careful not to disturb the taped outline border. You can then proceed with hardware bonding without getting resin on the painted surface immediately surrounding the hardware item.

You can prepare the bonding surface area on many hardware items well before installation. For example, you can surface treat aluminum items many hours ahead of actual bonding, if you take care that the bonding surface does not become contaminated. (Don't touch the bonding surface.) You can solvent clean and sand steel and bronze items ahead of time, and then at installation you need only coat them with resin and resand them before bonding. You should also clean the cured resin surface to which you will bond the hardware, using a solvent or water and ammonia. Lightly sand the surface, especially if it has not been sanded up to this point.

Next, apply epoxy to the hole. The techniques for doing this vary according to the anticipated loading on the fitting and the size of the hole. In all cases, however, a clock starts when you begin to work: the hardware must be in place before the resin in the fastener holes sets up. Oversize holes can contain resin concentrations high enough to speed up the exothermic reaction and shorten working time considerably. In hot weather, even with slow hardener, holes over ½ inch in diameter may start to gel in 20 to 30 minutes. Plan the installation procedure so that it can be completed as rapidly as possible.

If you have drilled standard pilot holes or oversize holes for small fittings which will be loaded in shear, follow the instructions under Procedures for Bonding Small Fasteners earlier in this chapter. If you are using coarse machines screws in oversize holes for heavy duty hardware such as a winch or mooring cleat, wet out the hole with WEST SYSTEM epoxy, and fill it with a thick mixture of epoxy and high density filler as described for perpendicular surfaces. Then coat and install the fastener.

When you have filled the fastener holes, coat both the hardware and the surface to which it will be bonded. If the surfaces mate perfectly, you can use epoxy with no additives, but if there are voids or gaps between them, mix high density filler with the epoxy to desired viscosity. Apply the mixture to both surfaces, using more where needed to fill gaps. (Try to visualize the high and low areas as the fitting is sitting on the bare surface.) With practice, you can apply the right amount of resin to the hardware, enough that there is reasonable excess to indicate 100% contact, but not so much that large globs squeeze out when you set the item in place.

After applying resin to the surfaces, put the fitting back in position and coat and install all the fasteners, tightening them until everything is snug. Clean away any epoxy which squeezes out as the item is bedded down. Use a putty knife to remove most of the excess, and paper towels or rags to clean up some of the thinner resin. We use solvent with rags on unpainted surfaces when this is necessary for a thorough job. If a lot of resin squeezes out, you have applied more than was needed, either to the hardware surface or to an oversize hole. Try reducing the quantity on the next item, until a small but healthy amount of epoxy squeezes out.

Casting Hardware in Place.

Sometimes, fittings must be set at specific angles to the hull surface to which they are attached. Winches, for example, are angled to maintain a proper lead. Lifeline bases, turning blocks and engine mounts often must be arranged in a manner which doesn't permit them to sit flat against a surface. Wedge-shaped wood bases and shims are usually used to support these items, but making them takes a great deal of time and skill. With the hardware casting process you can save a lot of time and end up with superior results.

To begin casting, clean the wood/epoxy surface and set the fitting in position, resting it on three points. One of these points is generally the lower end of the item itself and the other two are small, temporary wood props — wedges work well — cut to the right height. When you have the hardware exactly where you want it, load a syringe with a mixture of high density or 406 filler and epoxy. Inject the thickened resin within the perimeter of the fitting to build up several areas of contact between the two bonding surfaces, as in Figure 14. When this epoxy support or bridging has cured, carefully mark the position of the hardware and then

Figure 13—Bonded hardware on deck and cabin top of IOR ½ ton racer HOT FLASH. Several of the fittings have pads that were cast in place.

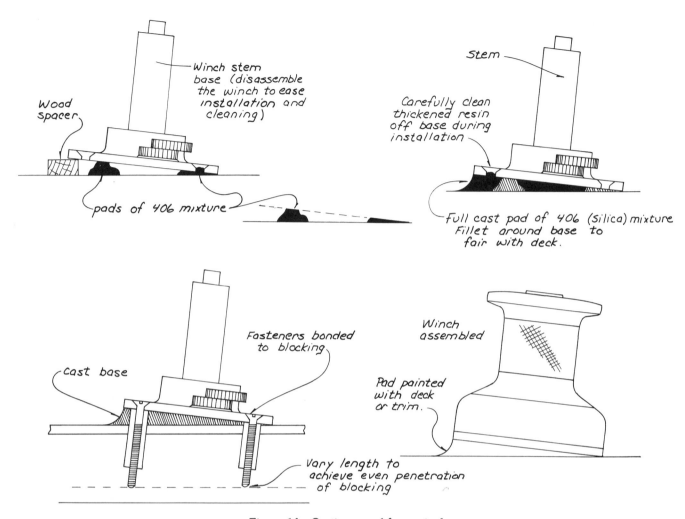

Figure 14—Casting a pad for a winch.

tap it with a mallet to break it loose. Up to this point you have drilled no holes and you haven't cleaned the hardware surface.

Remove the two temporary wood positioning points and fill the bonding area solid with sufficient amounts of a 406 resin mixture to fill all anticipated voids between bonding surfaces. If standard size holes for fasteners are to be used, you can prepare the hardware bonding surface for final bonding. If oversize holes are to be used, you'll need to remove the hardware once again after the casting resin has cured to drill the larger holes. At this point, if you have a piece of hardware with a lot of surface area, you may want to coat the hardware bonding surface with a release agent to facilitate removal. If a release agent is used, remember that after you remove the hardware you must clean both the resin and the metal surface carefully to remove the release agent material so that proper bonding can take place. Don't forget to mark the centers of the oversize holes to be drilled before removing the hardware. This may require chipping some excess cured resin out of the hardware fastener holes.

When you set the hardware in final position, excess resin mixture will flow out from the hardware perimeter and you will need to clean it away. This may require a bit of sculpting, especially if the cast portion is large. We usually make up a wood paddle to the shape desired, so that we can get the best effect when making a final pass across the uncured resin surface. If you don't get the results that you'd like, don't worry, because you can sand, file or refill the surface to develop the final result desired.

When the casting has cured, you can drill the holes for the fasteners and install the fasteners themselves in the appropriate manner. We caution you to remember to adjust the fastener lengths for the angle change of the hardware so that you get the same amount of fastener penetration into the wood fiber.

Removing Bonded Hardware

Use heat to remove hardware which has been bonded or cast in position. At temperatures above 250°F, cured resin begins to lose its physical properties. The resin softens and its bonding capability reduces considerably. Drill out all cured resin before reattaching the fitting to the deck surface.

Begin by removing any fasteners. Heat them, if necessary, with a soldering iron. When screws and bolts are loose, heat the fitting itself for a moment with a propane torch. A sharp rap with a mallet will usually dislodge the hardware at this point. If it doesn't break loose easily, don't force it. Heat it a second time with the torch and try again.

Bonding Ballast Keels to Wood Hulls

Heavy ballast keels, especially fin keels, can produce extreme high point loading. The problem is so difficult with some designs that even fiberglass boats using much higher density glass fiber have had difficulties at the keel/hull connection point. By applying our hardware bonding techniques to the process of keel installation, however, we have found a very successful solution to the problem of attaching keels.

The standard procedure for attaching a keel has been to use two rows of bolts, installed as close to the outer edges of the keel as possible. These run from the keel into the hull and usually through laminated floors which distribute load throughout the hull skin. The keel bolts are tightened with nuts inside the hull to snug the keel up against it. Large washers or plates distribute compression loads through the floors.

Unlike other pieces of boat hardware, keel bolts are subjected to alternating compression and tension loads; tension loads on keel bolts on a starboard tack change to compression loads on a port tack. When a boat with a standard, un-bonded keel installation heels, tension loads are transmitted through the bolts to the upper outboard edge and compression loads are transmitted directly from the keel to the wood it touches on the bottom of the boat. If the wood fiber in the immediate vicinity of the keel does not have sufficient crush resistance, the keel edge will begin to crush it. If the keel bolts are not continually tightened, the keel will loosen and this will cause movement which further damages the wood fiber.

When keel bolts are bonded in oversize holes in appropriate amounts and types of wood fiber, these problems are eliminated. A bonded bolt is far superior to the standard nut and washer in transmitting tension loads over a much greater surface area. More importantly, bonded keel bolts can withstand compression loads as well as tension loads, while up to this point keel bolts were never capable of distributing compression loads. Bonded bolts induce shear loading into the surrounding structure and it is irrelevant whether this

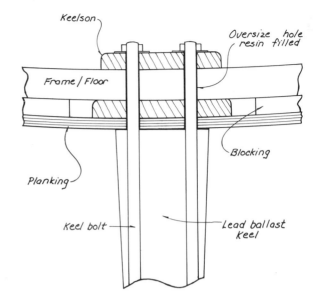

Figure 15—Sectional view of bonded keel bolts.

shear load is caused by tension or compression forces. The load change factor which causes such great problems in normal keel installations is of little concern when bonded bolts are used to distribute load.

In designing a bonded keel bolt installation, the goal is to achieve an arrangement which successfully distributes load over enough surface area that no part of the attached wood fiber is overloaded. Heavier keels will obviously cause more loading than lighter keels, but the bolt arrangement pattern may also be a big factor. In a thin-sectioned keel, bolts will be set closer together and this will cause higher input loadings to the bolts due to their decreased leverage. Other variables affecting load distribution are the number and size of the bolts and the thickness and density of the wood in which they are bonded.

We usually use higher density woods for laminated floors because of their substantially higher structural

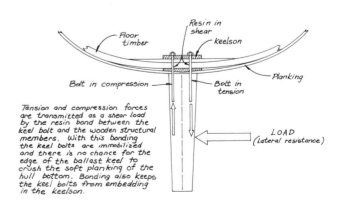

Figure 16—Design considerations in bonded keel bolts.

capacity, especially in sheer. Laminated floors are low in the hull cavity and centrally located, so the extra weight of denser wood is of little concern. We tend to choose Honduras mahogany and white ash because they are available in our area, but any of a number of wood species may be used as long as they bond well with WEST SYSTEM epoxy. Make a few sample laminations to be sure that the wood you select for laminated floors is compatible with WEST SYSTEM epoxy.

Installing Bonded Keels

Work out the details of the keel assembly early in your project. Its design will affect the interior structure of the hull and the number, size and locations of laminated frames. When you have decided how to achieve optimum load distribution, begin preparing for keel installation. Do this well in advance, so that when the time comes, the task of joining the keel and the hull can be accomplished with the least amount of grief.

Pour the keel as soon as possible so that you will have plenty of time to prepare it for final installation. Fair it and then rough up its surface with a wire brush to remove oxidation. Coat the keel with epoxy and, while the resin is still wet, scrub it again with the wire brush. WEST SYSTEM epoxy bonds well to clean lead surfaces. This coating will improve both paint adhesion

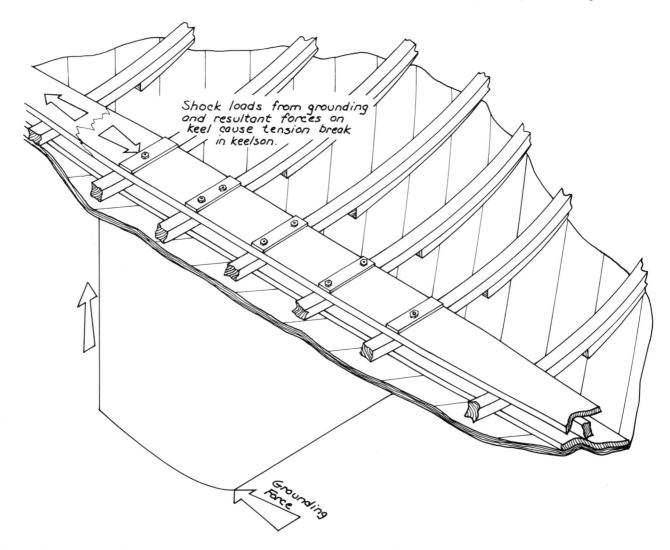

Shock loads from grounding and resultant forces on keel cause tension break in keelson.

Grounding Force

Figure 17—The I-beam/keelson combination provides the greatest strength and stiffness, both in athwartship and longitudinal directions. Besides great strength, the keelson concept provides a very necessary safety margin for grounding. When a boat of any substantial size with a modern, fin-type keel strikes an immovable object, such as a rock, considerable force is generated at the back of the keel, forcing this part of the hull inward, which, in many cases, can cause substantial permanent damage to the hull structure. In this situation, the keelson becomes a sacrificial part of the hull structure, and is capable of absorbing a great deal of energy before it breaks in tension (the strongest point of wood). A tension break on the keelson is easily repaired, requiring very little time and material. This is a great savings when compared to the possible damage that the hull itself could sustain without this arrangement. (In two instances, large IOR keel boats that we have built have had major groundings on rocks. In both cases, the keelson concept worked beautifully, absorbing most of the energy which was generated by the tremendous grounding forces.) See Chapter 16 for more details on keelson construction.

and the interface between the high density lead and lower density epoxy, and it will also reduce immediate oxidation. Fair the top of the keel where it will meet the hull. If it's very heavy, you may want to build a special fixture for the keel so that you can roll it around the shop. (See Figure 20.)

By far the easiest way to install bolts in a keel is to put them in a temporary fixture and pour the lead around them as the keel is made. When the bolts are in place, check them for dimensional accuracy. They must be perpendicular to the bonding surface of the keel and each must be parallel, both fore and aft and sideways, to the others.

The next step is make a pattern which sits on the top of the keel, as in Figure 18, to accurately record the locations of the individual bolts so that you can transfer them to the hull and drill holes to receive the bolts. For this you will need a sheet of plywood at least as long and as wide as the top of the keel. Mark the pattern with an accurate fore and aft position for the keel, so that when you line it up on the hull, the centerlines of the keel and hull line up. Then set it on top of the bolts. Line up the pattern and mark the location of each keel bolt. Rough cut bolt holes, allowing a wide margin around each one, so that the pattern drops easily onto the top of the keel. Push it down until it lies flush.

When this is done, make small square or round plywood pads for every bolt and drill the exact keel bolt hole diameter in the center of each piece. Slip a pad over each bolt, centering holes around the bolts,

and staple in place. Then ask several people to help you lift the pattern straight up and off the keel. If it catches on misaligned bolts, bend them as necessary. Correct any misalignment now: interference fits from out-of-parallel bolts can cause a great deal of trouble when the keel is installed.

If you haven't yet installed laminated floor timbers, use this keel pattern and the existing keel bolt arrangement as guides to do the job more accurately. If the floor timbers are already in place, adjust the pattern so that the bolts pass through all of them to best advantage. Position the plywood pattern carefully on the centerline and mark the bolt holes carefully on the floors or keelson.

Determine the diameter of the holes through the floors before you start drilling. The hole diameter should be at least ⅛ inch larger than the keel bolt. An important limitation on hole size is the size of each laminated floor timber. A larger oversize hole will distribute load over more surface area, but if you remove too much material, the floor timber may be weakened. Balance the surface area needed for load distribution against the dimensions of the floor timbers before making a final decision on hole size.

There are both advantages and disadvantages to increasing the diameter of an oversize hole. It's very difficult to maintain even 1/16 inch tolerances over a series of holes. If you increase hole diameter, you don't have to worry so much about close tolerances as you drill. Increasing the diameter by ¼ inch, for an annulus radius of .125 inch, makes the job of final fitting the hull and keel much easier.

To drill the marked keel bolt holes, either use a drilling jig or ask a few friends to help you do it by eye. In either case, you need a drill which has a big motor and in which you can chuck a large bit. The drill bit should have a long shank: in some situations 20 to 30 inches is an ideal length range. If you can't purchase drill bits which are long enough, have a machine shop weld a shank onto a standard bit.

The main goal of the drilling operation is to make all of the keel bolt holes exactly parallel, matching the bolt arrangement on the keel. Although it takes some time to fabricate, a drilling jig produces maximum accuracy. There are several ways to make jigs. One successful and simple method is to drill a hole in a large block of wood, using a drill press to make sure that it is absolutely square and perpendicular to the bottom of the block. Another method, shown in Figure 19, is to start with two pieces of stock, saw a line down the center of each, bond the pieces together, and use the kerfs as a guide for drilling. You can also rout half-holes in two pieces of wood and glue them together.

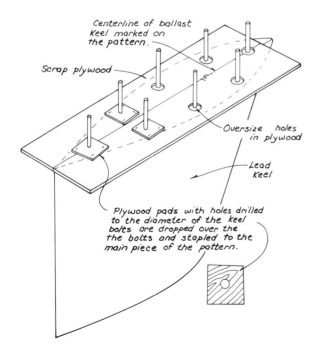

Centerline of ballast Keel marked on the pattern.

Scrap plywood

Oversize holes in plywood

Lead Keel

Plywood pads with holes drilled to the diameter of the keel bolts are dropped over the the bolts and stapled to the main piece of the pattern.

When you have made the jig, set it in the hull. Keep the bottom of the block in a perfectly flat plane to guide the drill bit as you move from hole to hole. To establish a common flat surface for all of the holes, clamp a thick sheet of plywood over the laminated floor on which you are working and check it with a level. Cut oversize holes in the plywood in the area of the drilling so that you can locate the marks you've made on the keelson or laminated floor. With the drill bit itself as a guide, drill starter holes at least ½ inch deep at all locations in order to line the jig up correctly. It's a good idea to use a clamp or cleat to hold the jig in place as you drill.

Although a jig is preferable, you can achieve reasonable accuracy using a simple sight method to drill the holes. This method relies on the coordinated efforts of three individuals: one to do the actual drilling, and two "directors" to sight the position of the drill bit with the use of levels. This method requires that the drill bit shaft be as long as possible, permitting maximum visual accuracy in lining up the drill. The two directors must be able to view the drill, one from the front and one from a side angle, using levels on end to sight and direct the proper positioning of the drill. The driller stands where he can see the two directors, who point out to him the direction that the drill motor should be moved to square the drill bit shaft with the level so that he can drill a perpendicular hole. With this method, the first 2 to 3 inches of drilling are the most crucial, because from there on it will be very difficult to change the direction of the drill. In order for this method to work, the hull must still be on its lines and the keel bolts must be oriented perpendicular to the waterline dimension as they sit in the ballast keel.

The lining up of the keel bolt pattern, marking of holes and the drilling operation can all take place either on the inside or on the outside (prior to turning the hull upright) of a hull. If you mark and drill from the outside, the only added difficulty is that you must mark the exact centerline of the hull and the fore and aft positions of the various laminated floor members. You should not remove the hull from its construction set-up before you transfer these dimensions and do the drilling. You can best transfer these dimensions with the use of a long level, both in the athwartship and longitudinal directions.

When you have drilled all of the holes, position the keel bolt pattern on both the inside and outside of the hull over the drilled holes to check them for accuracy. The holes will usually line up very accurately from the side that you started drilling from, but the opposite side of the hull may show some inaccuracy caused by improper lineup or wandering of the drill bit. Carefully mark these errors, and then use a round wood rasp to

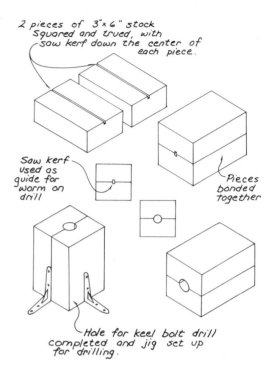

Figure 19—Jig for drilling keel bolt holes.

move the dimension of the hole toward the direction needed to straighten it out with the pattern. Usually, this situation causes no harm, only a slightly enlarged hole which has the positive effect of increasing surface area. The only disadvantage is the possible weakening of the laminated floor itself. However, this should be a minor problem in most situations. Make a final, careful check with the keel bolt pattern to assure yourself that the drilled holes in the hull will indeed receive the bolts protruding from the ballast keel with no interference from the wood itself. Then you can begin final preparations for a ballast keel/hull union.

Usually, this is the last major job on a boat, and you can do it just before launching. Up to the time you install the keel, you will probably want the hull close to the floor for easy access. In order to install the keel, however, you will have to jack it up high enough to have room to roll the keel and its bolts into position. When the keel is in rough position move it as necessary until you can lower the hull onto it.

When you have lined up the keel in position, you can set the hull down over the top of the bolts, leaving a gap of about 2 or 3 inches between hull and keel. At this point, you can take final measurements to note any possible discrepancies between the mating surfaces of the keel and hull. Check the keel bolts visually to make sure that there are no hangups which will prevent the hull from seating flush with the keel mating surface.

Coat areas of the mating surface on the bottom of the hull from the foremost keel bolt hole forward and from the aftermost keel bolt aft with a parting agent to prevent resin from bonding in these areas. The reason for this is that the ballast keel is a rigid, non-flexing mass, while the wood hull structure is not. Invariably, over a period of time, movement will take place between parts of the keel and hull. It will occur just beyond the outermost keel bolts, both fore and aft, creating small, hairline cracks. If you bond the keel with resin to the hull, these cracks will occur within the wood structure itself, providing points of moisture entry into the wood fiber. The parting agent causes the cracks to occur between resin surfaces, allowing water to seep harmlessly between resin-protected surfaces.

The lead surface itself should already be fairly clean, but a light sanding with some sandpaper will expose fresh metal for good bonding with the resin. The mating surfaces are now ready for a final fitting. The only thing left to do is to establish some reference measuring points to ensure that the keel itself is indeed in perfect position with the hull before any resin cures. Proper preparation should help ensure that the keel will settle in an accurate fore and aft position when the hull is set flush upon it, but sometimes a keel, rather than sitting perfectly true with a hull athwartship, will favor one side or the other. If you have accurate waterlines inscribed on the hull, you can take measurements from these points a set distance aft on either side down to the very bottom of the keel and adjust the hull so that this dimension is the same on either side.

The final setting of the keel requires the coordinated efforts of several people. Make up enough resin mixture at one time, using equal proportions of Colloidal Silica and high density filler, to cover the entire bonding surface of the keel. You need enough thickened epoxy to be sure that no gaps will remain anywhere between the hull and the keel, a quantity sometimes so

Figure 21—Rolling 10,000 lb. keel into position on specially-built handling fixture. Keel can be shifted slightly from side to side and fore and aft.

large that two or three people mix separate pots simultaneously. The mixture should be so thick that it will not run.

Liberally spread it over the entire keel mating surface. Lightly coat the bottom of the hull. Remember, however, that you begin to work with a time handicap the moment you apply the adhesive. The hull must be set down on the keel and trued up before the epoxy cures. In most situations this means that you have from 20 minutes to 1 hour for the operation. If you are well prepared this should present no problems.

When the hull is in final position, excess resin will squeeze out of the keel/hull joint. If the mixture is as thick as it should be, it will not run down the sides of the keel. Remove the excess and use it to make a fillet between the keel and the hull if desired. Use solvent and a rag to clean up any leftover adhesive on either the keel or the hull.

When the epoxy between the hull and the keel has cured, begin the second stage of bonding the keel. Use a syringe to fill each keel bolt hole to the top with regular epoxy. Feed each hole continually because large amounts will soak into the significant wood surface area in the hole. As you do this, it sometimes helps

Figure 20—Keel set up in handling fixture so that it can be final faired and moved.

to run a piece of wire up and down around the keel bolts. When this resin cures, install washers and nuts to complete the keel.

Removable Bonded Keels

The biggest problem with bonded keels is removing them. Bonded keel bolts can be extracted, but with difficulty. If for some reason you decide to remove a bonded keel, try using a cutter made from steel tubing which passes over the keel bolts.

If you plan to remove a keel on a regular basis for shipping or trailering, use the following alternate keel assembly technique. Instead of attaching bolts to wood fiber, thread or groove the exterior surfaces of sections of stainless steel pipe. Fasten the keel bolts through these sleeves, as shown in Figure 22. The bonded pipe transmits keel load through a large surface area. With a little modification, this basic idea can be used to attach other removable through hull fittings.

Choose stainless pipe or tubing of sufficient inner diameter to allow a keel bolt to pass through it. For each bolt hole, cut a sleeve which is long enough to touch the keel and protrude through the floors inside the boat. A lead keel is soft, so position nuts on the keel bolts before pouring it, just flush or slightly above the lead. These will separate the keel and the hull. Slide the pieces of threaded pipe over the keel bolts and firmly fasten them with nuts. You may have to fabricate temporary nuts which will pass through the holes in the boat and hold the pipe firmly to the keel. Seal the joint where the pipe meets the keel with thickened epoxy. Then install the keel as described for bonded keels. Lower the keel and saw off the excess pipe. Install the keel using a good gasket material around the keel bolt/pipe.

Bonding Through Hull Fittings in Tubes

Rudder and propeller shafts, cockpit drains and other fittings often pass through the hull in tubes to protect end grain wood. These tubes must be watertight, and they must bond well, but they are not always easy to obtain. We solve the problem by building piping for through hull fittings with WEST SYSTEM epoxy and fiberglass. There are several ways to do this.

One very popular method is to find plastic tube or metal rod of the right diameter and use it as a mold. Make sure that the mold is clean and that it has no nicks or scratches, and coat it with paste auto wax or another mold release.

Next, wet two layers of 4 oz. woven fiberglass cloth with epoxy and wrap them around the mold. Let the

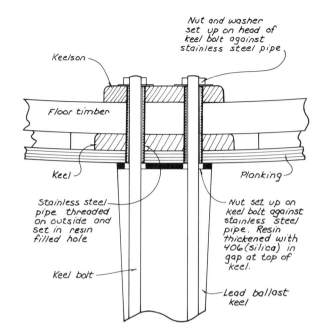

Figure 22—Removable bonded keel.

resin cure. Then, using a sharp knife, slice through the fiberglass along the length of the tube. Break the glass free of the mold, but for the moment leave it in place. The cut is necessary because the mold may not be perfectly round; without it, it might be very difficult to remove the finished tube. Wet out more glass cloth and wrap it around the tube until you reach the desired thickness. Some epoxy may seep into the cut, but this will not create any problems. Remove the fiberglass tubing from the mold when the epoxy has cured.

When a slightly modified technique, aluminum tubing may also be used as a mold. Coat the aluminum with a heat-resistant mold release — Teflon™ spray is a good choice — and wrap fiberglass cloth and epoxy around it as before. Then heat the tube to about 120°F with a hair dryer or heat gun. Keep it warm until the epoxy cures.

As the aluminum heats, both it and the wet-out fiberglass will expand. When it cools, it will shrink to original size, but the fiberglass/epoxy tube will remain slightly larger. This makes it possible to remove the new tube. If you have trouble sliding the glass from the mold, try pulling it off with pliers.

A variation on this second method can be used to make good fitting bearings. Mix WEST SYSTEM epoxy with Colloidal Silica or Graphite Powder and apply it to a Teflon-coated aluminum tube. Heat the tube until the thickened resin is fairly hard. Wet out fiberglass cloth with epoxy, wrap it around the tube and the adhesive mixture, and allow it to cure. Allow the part to cool and pull it off with pliers.

Appendix A

Wood Data

The following information is taken from various sources. In some cases, we have combined two or more sources in a single chart. You will note that listings of some species are inconsistent; this reflects available data. If you are interested in a serious study of wood, we recommend the Forest Products Laboratory's *Wood Handbook: Wood as an Engineering Material*, U.S. Department of Agriculture Handbook, No. 72, available from the Government Printing Office in Washington, D.C.

Terms Used in Charts[1]

Specific gravity (or density): The ratio of the weight per given volume of wood to that of an equal volume of water.

Modulus of rupture (static bending): The computed stress at the top and bottom fibers of a beam at the maximum load. It measures the ability of a beam to support gradually-applied loads for a short period of time.

Modulus of elasticity: The measure of a material's stiffness or rigidity. It is the ratio of stress per unit area to corresponding strain per unit length below the proportional limit. Deflection of a part under load is inversely proportional to the modulus of elasticity for the material of which the part consists. This modulus can be used in calculating the deflection of structural members under loads which do not exceed the proportional limit. It can also be used to calculate loads for long columns where stiffness is the controlling factor.

Work to maximum load: The capacity of the timber to absorb shocks which cause stress beyond the proportional limit and are great enough to cause some permanent deformation or injury to the timber. These are comparative values.

Compression parallel to grain — maximum crushing strength: The maximum ability of a short timber to sustain a gradually-applied end load over a short period. It is applicable to clear compression members for which the ratio of length to least dimension does not exceed 11.

Compression perpendicular to grain — fiber stress at proportional limit: The maximum across-the-grain stress of short duration that can be applied without permanent deformation to the timber.

Shear parallel to grain — maximum shearing strength: The ability of wood to resist shearing fibers or layers by one another along the grain.

Tension perpendicular to grain — maximum tensile strength: The average maximum stress sustained across the grain. This value is obtained by dividing maximum load by area in tension.

Side hardness — load perpendicular to grain: The values given are for the load, in pounds, required to embed a 0.444 inch diameter ball one half inch into the surface of a sample. Results are for comparison value only.

Impact bending — height of drop causing complete failure: A comparative value indicating a wood's ability to absorb shock.

Proportional limit: The limit of proportionality between stress and strain (deformation). Up to this limit, any increase in stress causes proportional increase in strain. Above this limit, strain increases at a greater rate for a given stress and usually results in permanent deformation. The proportional limit is used in deciding safety factors for wooden structural members.

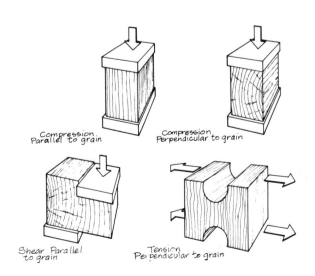

Compression Parallel to grain

Compression Perpendicular to grain

Shear Parallel to grain

Tension Perpendicular to grain

[1] Excerpted from National Lumber Manufacturers Association, *Wood Structural Design Data, Vol. 1.* (Washington, D.C., 1941), pp. 11-13.

A-1—Mechanical properties of woods commonly used with WEST SYSTEM* Brand Epoxy.[1]

For each species the first line is green material; the second line is adjusted to 12% moisture content.

Species	Specific gravity[3]	Static bending — Modulus of rupture (psi)	Static bending — Modulus of elasticity[2] (Million psi)	Static bending — Work to maximum load (Pounds per cubic inch)	Compression parallel to grain-maximum crushing strength (psi)	Compression perpendicular to grain-fiber stress at proportional limit (psi)	Shear parallel to grain-maximum shearing strength (psi)	Tension perpendicular to grain-maximum tensile strength (psi)	Side hardness load perpendicular to grain (Pounds)	Impact bending height of drop causing complete failure (Inches)
Ash, white	.55	9,600	1.44	16.6	3,990	670	1,380	590	960	38
	.60	15,400	1.74	17.6	7,410	1,160	1,950	940	1,320	43
Balsa, medium	.17	2,900	.58	—	1,805	100	300	118	100	
Birch, yellow	.55	8,300	1.50	16.1	3,380	430	1,110	430	780	48
	.62	16,600	2.01	20.8	8,170	970	1,880	920	1,260	55
Cedar, Alaskan	.42	6,400	1.14	9.2	3,050	350	840	330	440	27
	.44	11,100	1.42	10.4	6,310	620	1,130	360	580	29
Cedar, Northern white	.29	4,900	.64	5.7	1,990	230	620	240	230	15
	.31	6,500	.80	4.8	3,960	310	850	240	320	12
Cedar, Port Orford	.39	6,600	1.30	7.4	3,140	300	850	240	380	21
	.43	12,700	1.70	9.1	6,250	720	1,370	180	630	28
Cedar, western red	.31	5,200	.94	5.0	2,770	240	770	400	260	17
	.32	7,500	1.11	5.8	4,560	460	990	230	350	17
Douglas fir, coast	.45	7,700	1.56	7.6	3,780	380	900	220	500	26
	.48	12,400	1.95	9.9	7,240	800	1,130	300	710	31
Hickory	.64	11,000	1.57	23.7	4,580	840	1,520	340	NA	74
	.72	20,000	2.16	25.8	9,210	1,760	2,430	NA	NA	67
Lauan, light red	.41	7,500	1.44	NA	3,750	NA	840	NA	500	NA
	.44	11,300	1.67	NA	5,750	NA	1,090	NA	590	NA
Mahogany, Honduras	.45	9,300	1.28	9.6	4,510	NA	1,310	NA	700	NA
		11,600	1.51	7.9	6,630	NA	1,290	NA	810	NA
Meranti, dark red	.43	8,600	1.50	8.8	4,450	NA	NA	NA	560	NA
		12,100	1.63	11.7	6,970	NA	NA	NA	630	NA
Okoume/Gaboon	.37	7,300	1.14		3,900	NA	NA	NA	380	NA
Pine, loblolly	.47	7,300	1.40	8.2	3,510	390	860	260	450	30
	.51	12,800	1.79	10.4	7,130	790	1,390	470	690	30
Pine, longleaf	.54	8,500	1.59	8.9	4,320	480	1,040	330	590	35
	.59	14,500	1.98	11.8	8,470	960	1,510	470	870	34
Pine, white	.34	4,900	.99	5.2	2,440	220	680	250	290	17
	.35	8,600	1.24	6.8	4,800	440	900	310	380	18
Ramin	NA	9,800	1.57	9.0	5,395	NA	994		640	NA
	.59	18,400	2.17	17.0	10,080	NA	1,514		1,300	NA
Spruce, black	.38	5,400	1.06	7.4	2,570	140	660	100	370	24
	.40	10,300	1.53	10.5	5,320	530	1,030		520	23
Spruce, Sitka	.37	5,700	1.23	6.3	2,670	280	760	250	350	24
	.40	10,200	1.57	9.4	5,610	580	1,150		510	25
Teak	.57	11,000	1.51	10.8	5,470		1,290	370	1,070	
	.63	12,800	1.59	10.1	7,110		1,480		1,030	25

[1] Extracted from Forest Products Laboratory, *Wood Handbook*, U.S. Department of Agriculture Handbook No. 72. (Government Printing Office, Washington, D.C., 1974), pp. 4-7 — 4-17. Results of tests on small, clear, straight-grained specimens. Values in the first line for each species are from tests of green material; those in the second line are adjusted to 12% moisture content.

[2] Modulus of elasticity measured from a simply supported, center loaded beam, on a span depth ratio of 14 to 1. The modulus can be corrected for the effect of shear deflection by increasing it 10%.

[3] Specific gravity is based on weight when oven dry and volume when green, or at 12% moisture content.

A-2—Effect of Curvature on Bending Strength

Stress is induced when laminations are bent to curved forms. The following formula, drawn from the Forest Products Laboratory's *Wood Handbook*, p. 10-8, gives the ratio of allowable design stress in laminated curved members to that in straight members. You can use it as you plan and loft to determine the appropriate thickness of *each layer* of laminations for stems, frames, bulkheads, knees and other curved structural members.

$$1.00 - \frac{2000}{(R/t)^2}$$

where R is the radius and *t* is the thickness of the laminating stock. The values must be expressed in the same units.

Suppose, for example, that you wanted to laminate a frame for a mid-section of a Folkboat. On the lofting, the smallest radius of the bilge at this section is 24 inches. If you bonded a 1½ inch thick frame with ⅜ inch thick laminating stock, the strength of the curved laminate would be about 50% of the strength of a straight piece of similar cross-section, calculated as follows:

$$1.00 - \frac{2000}{(24/⅜)^2}$$

$$= 1.00 - \frac{2000}{4096} = 0.512$$

If you used ⅛ inch laminating stock, the curved laminated section would have about 95% of the strength of a similar straight piece.

In applying this formula, it's important to realize that more laminations require more work and result in greater waste of materials. Use common sense to balance the increase in strength gained by very thin laminating layers against their cost.

A-3—Bending to Small Radii

In tests conducted in our lab we attempted to determine the smallest radii to which selected *dry* boatbuilding woods and plywood would bend without breaking. Test samples were 24 inches by 6 inches. Average moisture content of the samples was 7%. The relation between the grain of the face veneer and the long axis of plywood samples is indicated below.

Veneers	Thickness (in inches)	Radius (in inches)
Dark red meranti	⅛	8
Douglas fir	⅛	12
Sitka spruce	1/12	11
Red cedar	⅛	10

Okoume plywood thickness (in inches)	Grain axis	
¼	5-ply Parallel	24
¼	5-ply Perpendicular	16
3/16	3-ply Parallel	16
5/32	3-ply Parallel	8
5/32	3-ply Perpendicular	6

A-4—Percentage increase in wood strength properties for 1% decrease in moisture content [1,2]

Species	Static bending				Compression parallel to grain — maximum crushing strength	Compression perpendicular to grain	Shearing strength parallel to grain	Sid hardn
	Fiber stress at proportional limit	Modulus of rupture	Modulus of elasticity	Work to maximum load [3]				
Ash, white	4.1	3.5	1.4	0.4	4.7	4.8	2.9	2.
Birch, yellow	6.0	4.8	2.0	1.7	6.1	5.6	3.6	3.
Cedar, northern white	5.4	3.6	1.8	- 1.5	5.9	2.3	2.8	3.0
Cedar, Port Orford	5.7	5.2	1.6	1.7	6.2	6.7	2.2	2.8
Cedar, western red	4.3	3.4	1.6	1.3	5.1	5.1	1.6	2.
Fir, Douglas	4.5	3.7	1.8	1.9	5.5	5.0	1.7	2.9
Hickory, true	4.9	4.8	2.8	- 0.7	5.9	6.6	- 3.9	—
Mahogany, Honduras	2.6	1.3	0.8	- 2.9	2.5	3.9	—	1.0
Pine, eastern white	5.6	4.8	2.0	2.1	5.7	5.6	2.2	2.
Spruce, Sitka	4.7	3.9	1.7	2.0	5.3	4.3	2.6	2.

[1] Extracted from Munitions Board Aircraft Committee. *Design of Wood Aircraft Structures, ANC-18, 1951* (National Technical Information Service/U.S. Department of Commerce Reprint AD-490 100, Springfield VA), p. 13.

[2] Corrections to the strength properties should be made successively for each 1% change in moisture content until the total change has been covered. For each 1% decrease in moisture content, the strength is multiplied by (1 + P), where P is the percentage correction factor shown in the table and expressed as a decimal. For each 1% increase in moisture content, the strength is divided by (1 + P).

[3] Negative values indicate a decrease in work to maximum load for a decrease in moisture content.

A-5—Tensile strength of plywood and veneer[1]

Species	% Moisture content at test	Specific gravity[2] of plywood	Tensile strength[3] of 3-ply wood[4] (pounds per square foot)	Tensile strength[5] single-ply veneer (1.5 pounds per square foot)
Ash, white	10.2	0.60	6,510	9,760
Birch, yellow	8.5	0.67	13,210	19,820
Fir, Douglas	8.6	0.48	6,180	9,270
Fir, white	8.5	0.40	5,670	8,510
Mahogany, African (Khaya)	12.7	0.52	5,370	8,060
Mahogany, Honduras	11.4	0.48	6,390	9,580
Pine, eastern white	5.4	0.42	5,720	8,580
Redwood	9.7	0.42	4,770	7,160
Spruce, Sitka	8.2	0.42	5,650	8,480
Tanguile (Lauan)	10.7	0.53	10,670	16,000

[1] Extracted from Michelon, Leno C. and Devereaux, Raymond J. *Composite Aircraft Manufacture and Inspection,* (Harper & Brothers, NY, 1944), p. 164.
[2] Based on oven dry weight and volume at test.
[3] Based on total cross-sectional area.
[4] Parallel to grain of faces.
[5] Based on assumption that center ply carries no load.
Data based on tests of 3-ply panels with all plies in any one panel the same thickness and species.

A-6—Oven dry weight of veneers of varying thicknesses by species[1]

| Species | Specific gravity[2] | % Air dry moisture content | Ounces per square foot veneer | | | |
| | | | Veneer thickness in inches | | | |
			1/16	1/8	3/16	1/4
Ash, white	0.58	8.9	3.02	6.04	9.05	12.06
Birch, yellow	0.63	9.6	3.28	6.56	9.84	13.12
Cedar, Spanish	0.37	7.3	1.92	3.85	5.77	7.70
Cedar, red	0.31		1.83	3.67	5.49	7.34
Fir, Douglas	0.51	6.2	2.65	5.30	7.96	10.6
Mahogany, African	0.46	8.0	2.39	4.78	7.17	9.57
Mahogany, Central American	0.49	7.9	2.55	5.10	7.66	10.20
Spruce, Sitka	0.38	8.9	1.98	3.96	5.94	7.94

[1] Extracted from Michelon and Devereaux, p. 163.

[2] Based on oven dry weight and air dry volume.

A-7—Approximate weights of finished Western red cedar laminates[1]

Number of ⅛ inch thick layers	Average pounds per square foot
4 (totaling ½ inch)	1.30
5 (totaling ⅝ inch)	1.65
6 (totaling ¾ inch)	2.00
7 (totaling ⅞ inch)	2.35
8 (totaling 1 inch)	2.70
9 (totaling 1⅛ inches)	3.00

[1] Includes weight of WEST SYSTEM resin used in bonding and coating all surfaces. All samples were weighed at the Gougeon Brothers, Inc. test facility.

Appendix B

Material Fatigue

Material fatigue is an extensive subject with many diverse elements and subtleties which make it difficult to understand. Throughout this book we discuss the fatigue resistance of wood, wood/epoxy composites and WEST SYSTEM* Brand epoxy and compare them with other materials.

In 1978, when we started an experimental wind turbine blade development program under contract to NASA, Gougeon Brothers, Inc. had been building boats for a number of years. Since then, we have been involved in an ongoing and extensive series of research and development programs. Most of our research has been basic material testing with an emphasis on long-term fatigue capability. Wind turbine blades, very dynamic structures, see high cycle loading in a difficult, fatigue-prone environment. In order to design long-lasting blades at the least weight, we must be able to predict blade life under these adverse conditions. To do this, it's necessary to know for how many millions of cycles a material can resist a given load.

This program has allowed us to produce well over 3,000 wind turbine blades, some of which have now seen five years of service with no failure within their designed load capability. We feel that much of the knowledge gained for wind blade development can also be used to support boat design and construction efforts. From our research we have learned ways to build strong, longer-lasting structures.

In Chapter 5, we discussed the comparative fatigue performance of common boatbuilding materials. We believe that it's more important to understand a material's capability after a million load cycles than its ultimate one-time load capacity. As we explained in that chapter, a hull will have experienced about a million fatigue cycles after about 833 operating hours. Since few boats are sailed constantly, it may take several years to reach this level. No one keeps track of sailing hours, but everyone knows how old a boat is, and this tends to foster an inappropriate level of confidence in the structure.

When evaluating materials for boatbuilding, most designers and engineers have focused on published one-time load to failure capability. The reason for this is simple economics. It's quite easy to apply an increasing one-time load on a test sample to the point of failure. The test takes only a few minutes, so many data points can be gathered in a day. In comparison, unloading and loading a single fatigue specimen 10 million cycles can require over a month of constant test machine cycling. A single data point may costs many thousands of dollars. Because of the high cost and time required, there is not a great deal of good fatigue data available for most materials, especially the composites which have recently become popular.

Another problem is that unidirectional materials are very difficult to test. Because of testing variables such as sample quality, results may have wide data scatter and this can confuse rather than clarify material capability. Most designers have therefore extrapolated their own endurance limits on chosen materials and taken arbitary guesses on some factor of safety. As many have found out, this can be a dangerous practice.

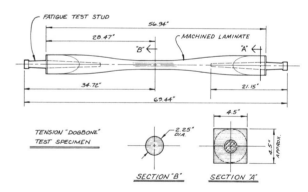

Figure 1—Dogbone test sample.

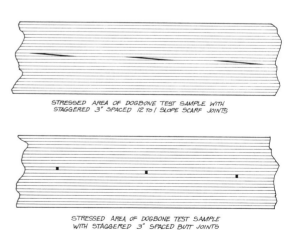

Figure 2—Butt and scarf joints in test samples.

* TRADEMARK OF GOUGEON BROTHERS, INC., U.S.A.

Fatigue Behavior of Wood

Wood is generally an excellent material to withstand cyclic fatigue loading for long periods of time. This, combined with its excellent natural resistance to stress concentrations, makes wood an ideal material for boat construction. Our comprehensive fatigue testing program has provided the first precise material capability data for wood.

To test wood laminate in tension fatigue as well as reverse axial tension-compression (cycling from complete tension load to complete compression load) fatigue, we designed the dog-bone sample shown in Figure 1. In all previous wood fatigue testing, a secured cantilever beam had been loaded repetitively until the beam failed. This work was done during World War II, on test machines which had limited capability, and this led to a great deal of flaw in early data. The early testing showed that wood was excellent in fatigue, but it failed to provide the quantitative results necessary to develop accurate design allowables.

Some results of our fatigue testing of ultrasonically graded Douglas fir/WEST SYSTEM epoxy composites are provided in Chapter 5. In spite of the induced defects of scarf and butt joints within samples, shown here in Figure 2, wood proved very resistant to fatigue. As we discussed in Chapter 5, we believe that longitudinal mechanical properties may be less important in the fatigue behavior of unidirectional materials than secondary or cross-grain capability. Materials failures in hulls are probably more the result of these secondary properties than of failure in tension or compression.

Fatigue Behavior of Glass Fiber

Figure 1 in Chapter 5 compares the performance of laminated wood, carbon fiber composite and fiberglass composite in fatigue. Wood may begin with less ultimate strength than either of these materials, but it maintains a higher percentage of its original strength through a million cycles than either of the other materials.

To test the fatigue behavior of glass fiber composites, samples were prepared using a transverse filament winding process, with approximately 80% of the fiber arranged longitudinally with the load path and the balance of fibers varied at 45° to 90° angles. All samples were tested in tension and compression, and some were tested in reverse axial tension-compression. Samples varied in their make-up. Two basic winding patterns were bonded with both polyester and epoxy resin.

Typical results of these tests are shown in Figures 3 and 4. Epoxy-bonded laminate with an average static

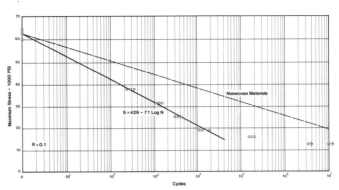

Figure 3—S-N curve for style 181 woven fabric reinforced polyester compared with nonwoven curve.

strength of 59,900 psi reduced to about 12,000 psi at 10 million fatigue cycles. Polyester-bonded laminate, by contrast, began with higher average static strength, 64,700 psi. When operating at 12,000 psi, however, 18 polyester test samples could only average 3.6 million cycles to failure, with data scatter ranging from 303,000 cycles to 10.1 million cycles.

These data suggest that resin plays a significant role in the long-term fatigue capability of glass composites. If only one-time, load-to-failure static tests are considered, the polyester samples are 8% stronger than epoxy. These capabilities are, however, more than reversed at higher cycles. At 3.5 million average cycles the polyester laminate retains less than 19% of its original strength.

Fatigue performance of woven fabrics is always inferior to unidirectional fiber performance because of stress at the points where fibers overlap. Polyester reinforced with woven glass retained about 20% of its original static strength after 10 million cycles. Little testing on glass reinforced laminate beyond 10 million cycles has been conducted, so it is difficult to really know at what point its endurance fatigue limit is reached. There is no clear evidence to support the theory that there may not be any endurance fatigue limit with glass laminates. Neither is there concensus on safe working limits for glass composites in applications which require

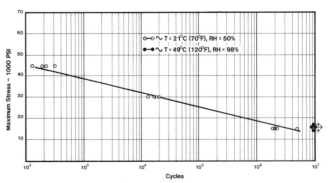

Figure 4—Baseline S-N fatigue life diagram for epoxy matrix composite with winding pattern Z, tested at R=O, 0=1 to 30 Hertz and various environments as noted.

very long fatigue cycle capability. Nonwoven, unidirectional glass laminates show a more linear fatigue slope, with less matrix debonding at lower cycles. Woven and non-woven laminates converge on the fatigue curve at high cycles where the fatigue capability of the glass fiber itself controls performance.

Fatigue Behavior of WEST SYSTEM Epoxy

Many fatigue test programs have focused on our WEST SYSTEM resins. Early on, we found that unreinforced resins are very difficult to test. This is primarily due to their low modulus: the samples are quite flexible and have to be tested at low cycle rates to avoid excess heat build-up within the sample.

Three test methods are used to generate our epoxy fatigue data: (1) compression fatigue where a cast cylinder of epoxy is compression load cycled between two platens, (2) bonded stud samples where a threaded steel rod is cast in epoxy and cycled in tension until epoxy failure occurs, and (3) torsion fatigue where a cast long square or rectangular prism sample is gripped at each end and twisted in opposite directions, which ultimately creates a torsional shear failure within the epoxy matrix.

The fatigue data and plotted trend lines in Figure 5

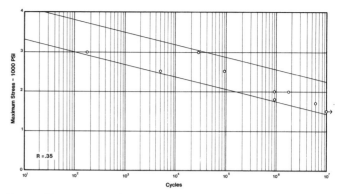

Figure 5—Torsional fatigue testing of WEST SYSTEM resin fortified with RG 144 asbestos fiber. Testing performed by the Advanced Energy Products Department, General Electric Corp., King of Prussia, PA, Fall 1982.

are the result of torsional fatigue testing. This type of test represents the type of shear loads which resin sees in a typical laminate. As can be seen, without continuous reinforcement, long-term fatigue cycle capability at 10 million cycles is about 40% of the material's one-time load capability, so reasonable design allowable values can confidently be used. The epoxy resin used in these tests was fortified with RG 144 asbestos fiber. We have since developed WEST SYSTEM 404 High Density High Strength Filler. The performance of the new filler exceeds that of asbestos.

Appendix C Scantlings for well-known

Boat Name	Total Weight (Pounds)	Ballast (Pounds)	Length (Feet)	Hull	Deck
GARGOYLE	2,400	850	22	⅜" total 3 layers ⅛" W. red cedar veneer	¼" okoume foredeck ⅜" okoume afterdeck 1 layer 1/10" teak 1" x 1½" spruce framing, 2" centers
ONYMITT	3,000	1,500	26	½" total 4 layers ⅛" W. red cedar veneer	Sandwich construction 3/16" plywood/ Verticel™ core spruce core framing
ACCOLADE	7,000	3,500	30	¾" total 6 layers ⅛" W. red cedar veneer	⅜" total 2 layers 3/16" okoume plywood over frames and stringers
BOOMERANG (formerly HOT FLASH)	7,500	4,000	32	⅝" total 1 layer ⅛" okoume plywood 4 layers ⅛" W. red cedar veneer	⅜" okoume plywood over stringers
ROGUES ROOST	7,500	2,800	35	½" total 4 layers ⅛" W. red cedar veneer	⅜" plywood
SWEET OKOLE	8,000	3,750	36	½" total 4 layers ⅛" W. red cedar veneer	⅜" plywood
SYLVAN	9,000	4,100	30	⅞" total 1 layer ½" W. red cedar strips, 3 layers ⅛" W. red cedar veneer, 1 layer polypropylene cloth	¾" total 1 layer ⅜" cedar 1 layer ⅛" cedar 1 layer ¼" teak
CHOCOLATE CHIPS	9,400	4,500	33	⅝" total 1 layer ⅛" okoume plywood 4 layers ⅛" W. red cedar veneer	½" total ⅜" okoume plywood ⅛" teak
WOODPECKER	10,630	6,250	37	11/16" total 1 layer 3/16" okoume plywood 4 layers ⅛" W. red cedar veneer	½" total 2 layers ¼" okoume plywood
MOODY BLUE	11,000	4,700	36	¾" total 1 layer ½" W. red cedar strips, 1 layer ⅛" W. red cedar veneer, 1 layer ⅛" African mahogany veneer	½" total 1 layer ⅜" W. red cedar 1 layer ⅛" okoume plywood
STAR	16,500	7,000	33	1" total 1 layer ⅝" W. red cedar 2 layers ⅛" W. red cedar veneer, 1 layer ⅛" African mahogany veneer	¾" total 2 layers ¼" cedar 1 layer ¼" cedar sprung and oiled
GOLDEN DAZY	18,500	10,000	42	1⅛" total 1 layer ⅝" W. red cedar strips, 4 layers ⅛" W. red cedar veneer	⅝" total 2 layers ¼" okoume plywod, 1 layer ⅛" teak
BAY BEA	20,000	9,000 in hull, 2,000 in dagger-board	45	1" total 1 layer ½" Port Orford cedar strips, 2 layers ⅛" W. red cedar, outside layer ¼" Port Orford cedar strips	¾" total ¼" okoume plywood 2 layers ¼" Port Orford cedar
WHITEHAWK	170,000	50,000	92	2½" total 1st and 3rd layers ⅝" white cedar, 2nd and 4th layers 5/16" white cedar, 5th layer ⅝" mahogany	1¾" total 3 layers cedar 1 layer teak

Information in this table has been drawn from designers, builders, owners and world literature. It represents a wide range of construction methods, sizes and weights for monohull sailboats.

boats built with WEST SYSTEM* Brand Epoxy

Interior Structure	Wood species used	Comments
¾" x ¾" spruce stringers (8 per side), ⅜" plywood bulkheads, 1" white cedar longitudinals	W. red cedar Mahogany Sitka spruce White cedar Teak	MORC racer designed by Lasher Performance Designs, Inc. Built by Bierig/Lasher
Sandwich bulkheads Structural accommodations No stringers	W. red cedar Mahogany, White ash, Sitka spruce	Sloop Designed by Gougeon Brothers, Inc. Built by Gougeon Brothers, Inc.
Laminated floors and frames Bulkheads No stringers	W. red cedar Mahogany, White ash, Sitka spruce	IOR-½ ton Designed by Bruce Kirby Built by Gougeon Brothers, Inc.
1½" x ⅝" Sitka spruce stringers, laminated floors Bulkheads	W. red cedar Mahogany White ash Sitka spruce	IOR-½ ton Designed by Gary Mull Built by Gougeon Brothers, Inc.
1½" x ¾" mahogany stringers (9 per side) Bulkheads	W. red cedar Mahogany, White ash, Sitka spruce	IOR-1 ton Designed by William Cook Built by Eric Goetz
1⅛" x 1½" Sitka spruce stringers (8 per side) Bulkheads, floors	W. red cedar Sitka spruce Mahogany	IOR-1 ton Designed by Bruce Farr Built by Louis Wake & Foo Lim
Laminated floors Some laminated frames Plywood bulkheads	W. red cedar Honduras mahogany Sitka spruce Teak	Double-ended cutter Designed by Henry Scheel Built by Van Dam Wood Craft
1¼" x ¾" Sitka spruce stringers (9 per side) Bulkheads	W. red cedar Mahogany, White Ash, Sitka Spruce	IOR-¾ ton Designed by Graham & Schlageter Built by Eric Goetz
1½" x ¾" Sitka spruce stringers, bulkheads Floors	W. red cedar Mahogany White ash Sitka spruce	IOR-1 ton Designed by Doug Peterson Built by Eric Goetz
Laminated floors and frames Bulkheads with structural trim Structural accommodations	W. red cedar Honduras mahogany White ash Sitka spruce African mahogany	IOR-1 ton Designed by Nelson/Merek Built by Van Dam Wood Craft
Laminated floors and frames Plywood bulkheads	W. red cedar African mahogany Sitka spruce Red oak plywood	Cruising cutter (all natural finish) Designed by Fred Ford Built by Van Dam Wood Craft
Sandwich bulkheads No stringers Laminated floors	W. red cedar Mahogany White Ash Sitka spruce	IOR-2 ton Canada's Cup, 1975 Designed by Ron Holland Built by Gougeon Brothers, Inc.
2½" x 1¼" Sitka spruce stringers (few), bulkheads Floors	W. red cedar Port Orford cedar Mahogany White Ash Sitka spruce	IOR-2 ton Designed by Britt Chance Built by Palmer Johnson
Bulkheads Structural accommodations Floors, frames	White cedar Pine, Oak, Ash Spruce, Mahogany Rare woods	Luxury racing ketch Designed by Bruce King Built by Lee's Boat Shop

Appendix D

Impact Testing on Reinforced Laminates

In 1985, we conducted two series of impact tests in our lab. In the first, we looked at the relative effectiveness of layers of fiberglass cloth in protecting a wood hull from rocks and floating debris. The results of this testing are useful for strip composite and stripper construction, so we have included them in Chapter 20. In the second set of experiments, we examined the effects of adding layers of fiberglass and Kevlar™ cloth to a laminated wood hull. Here, we were particularly interested in finding out how the location of the synthetic fibers in the laminate affected resistance to impact.

Before explaining our second test procedure, we should point out that some of the combinations of cloth used in this experiment are quite unusual and very expensive. We were attempting to determine the best schedule of Kevlar and fiberglass for a boat which will be sailed in a single-handed, round-the-world race and must therefore be exceptionally strong and damage tolerant. In most designs, and for most uses, the additional expense of this type of reinforcement is unwarranted. Our test used both woven and knit cloth, but the effects of fiber alignment and orientation were not apparent.

We tested the impact resistance of four samples. (See Figure 1.) The four panels, each about 12 inch x 15 inch x ¾ inch thick, were laminated with four layers of 3/16 inch cedar and WEST SYSTEM* epoxy. All samples had exterior sheathing of E glass cloth to simulate wooden hulls with exterior sheathing. In two panels, synthetic cloth was bonded between the innermost and the second layers of wood. Because of the practical problems with fairing Kevlar, exterior layers of this cloth were covered with fiberglass cloth in two specimens. Panel weight varied according to composition.

The samples were supported in the test machine around four edges and a 70 lb., 1½ inch, snub-nose steel projectile was dropped on each from 5 inches, 7.5 inches and 12.5 inches, resulting in energy levels of 350 in-lb, 525 in-lb and 875 in-lb respectively. All panels had shallow, 1 inch diameter dents on their top faces and minimal interior damage after the first drop.

As the projectile was dropped from greater heights, considerable differences in damage to the inner faces was evident. Samples which had reinforcing fibers between the inner layers of wood cracked much less than panels which had cloth on only their top surfaces. After the final drop, Panel 1, which had interior and exterior layers of aramid and an exterior layer of fiberglass cloth, had minor cracks on its interior surface. These were within a circular area about 2½ inches in diameter and would probably result in negligible loss of strength. Panel 2, which had E glass cloth on its exterior and inner layers and Kevlar sheathing, exhibited moderate cracks in an area about 5 inches in diameter. These might cause moderate loss of strength. Panels 3 and 4, which had no interior layers of synthetic fibers, showed extensive cracking on their inner faces. This could lead to substantial loss of strength.

The results of these tests can only be used to rank the various wood composites tested in order of their resistance to impact damage. They cannot be used to predict whether the materials will be satisfactory when used in a hull. It is, however, possible to draw some broad conclusions from them.

While adding fabric reinforcement to the outside of a hull can increase its strength, it may sometimes be desirable to laminate layer of cloth close to the interior of the structure. Panels which had synthetic fibers located near the panel back side were substantially better in resisting impact loads than panels which had only exterior sheathing. Additional layers of fabric will increase the weight and cost of a boat, but in certain situations, these extras are justified by the safety margin the cloth provides.

Since the completion of this test we have realized that we did not experiment with what might be the best combination of cloths. If Kevlar is bonded to an interior layer of a laminate, where it will be in tension, it can be used very efficiently. Fairing problems are largely eliminated when aramid is used, say, between the first two layers of a wood hull, but the fiber can continue to offer increased resistance to impact. The hull might then be sheathed with an exterior layer of fiberglass cloth for additional resistance to impact.

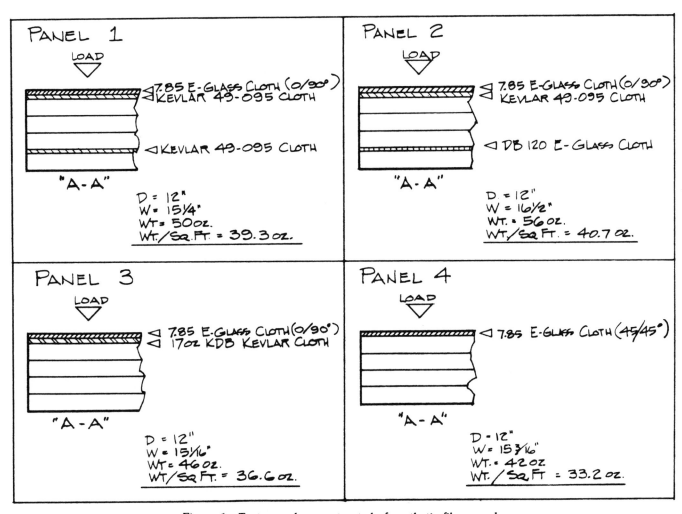

PANEL 1

LOAD ▽

◁ 7.85 E-GLASS CLOTH (O/90°)
◁ KEVLAR 49-095 CLOTH

◁ KEVLAR 49-095 CLOTH

"A-A"

D = 12"
W = 15¼"
WT = 50 OZ.
WT./SQ.FT. = 39.3 OZ.

PANEL 2

LOAD ▽

◁ 7.85 E-GLASS CLOTH (O/90°)
KEVLAR 49-095 CLOTH

◁ DB 120 E-GLASS CLOTH

"A-A"

D = 12"
W = 16½"
WT. = 56 OZ.
WT./SQ.FT. = 40.7 OZ.

PANEL 3

LOAD ▽

◁ 7.85 E-GLASS CLOTH (O/90°)
◁ 17 OZ KDB KEVLAR CLOTH

"A-A"

D = 12"
W = 15⁄16"
WT = 46 OZ.
WT./SQ.FT. = 36.6 OZ.

PANEL 4

LOAD ▽

◁ 7.85 E-GLASS CLOTH (45/45°)

"A-A"

D = 12"
W = 15³⁄16"
WT. = 42 OZ
WT./SQ.FT. = 33.2 OZ.

Figure 1—Test samples constructed of synthetic fibers, cedar and WEST SYSTEM epoxy. Arrow indicates direction of impact load.

Selected Bibliography

American Boat and Yacht Council, Inc. *Standards and Recommended Practices for Small Craft.* Amityville, NY: American Boat and Yacht Council, Inc.

Cagle, Charles V. *Handbook of Adhesive Bonding.* New York: McGraw-Hill, 1973.

Chapelle, Howard I. *Boatbuilding.* New York: W. W. Norton & Co., 1941.

Cook, Peter. *Boatbuilding Methods.* London: Adlard Coles Ltd., 1971.

Creagh-Osborne, Richard. *Dinghy Building.* Clinton Corners, NY: John de Graff, Inc., 1977.

Duffett, John. *Boatowner's Guide to Modern Maintenance.* New York: W. W. Norton & Co., 1985.

Forest Products Laboratory. *Wood Handbook: Wood as an Engineering Material.* U.S. Department of Agriculture Handbook No. 72. Washington, D.C.: Government Printing Office, 1974.

Gilpatrick, Gil. *Building a Strip Built Canoe.* Freeport, ME: DeLorme Publishing, 1985.

Gougeon Brothers, Inc. *Technical Bulletins Nos. 1-3.* Bay City, MI: Gougeon Brothers, Inc., April, 1985.

Guzzwell, John. *Modern Wooden Yacht Construction,* Camden, ME: International Marine, 1979.

Hazen, David. *The Stripper's Guide to Canoe Building.* Larkspur, CA: Tamal Vista, 1982.

Kahan, Del F. *Marine Electrical Practice. Pleasure Craft Direct Current Systems.* Newport Beach, CA: Marinetics Press, 1972.

Kinney, Francis S. *Skene's Elements of Yacht Design.* New York: Dodd, Mead & Co., 1973.

Marinetics Corporation. *Marine Electrical (catalog and handbook).* Newport Beach, CA: Marinetics Press.

Michelon, Leno C. and Devereaux, Raymond J. *Composite Aircraft Manufacture and Inspection.* New York: Harper & Brothers, 1944.

Miller, Conrad. *Your Boat's Electrical System.* New York: Hearst Corp., 1973.

Moores, Ted and Mohr, Merilyn. *Canoecraft.* Camden, East Ontario, Canada: Camden House, 1983.

Munitions Board Aircraft Committee. *Design of Wood Aircraft Structures ANC-18, 1951.* Springfield, VA: National Technical Information Service/U.S. Department of Commerce Reprint AD-490-100.

Wood Structural Design Data. Vol. 1. Washington, DC: National Lumber Manufacturers Association, 1941.

Offshore Racing Council. *Special Regulations Governing Minimum Equipment and Accommodation Standards,* January 1978. (Available from the U.S. Yacht Racing Union, Box 209, Goat Island, Newport, RI 02840.)

Pretzer, Roger. *Marine Metals Manual. A Handbook for Boatmen, Builders and Dealers.* Camden, ME: International Marine, 1976.

Spurr, Daniel. *Upgrading The Cruising Sailboat.* Newport, RI: Seven Seas, 1983.

Steward, Robert M. *Boatbuilding Manual, 2nd Edition.* Camden, ME: International Marine, 1980.

Tools and Their Uses. New York: Dover Publishing (U.S. Navy Bureau of Naval Personnel), 1973.

Vaitses, Allan H. *Lofting.* Camden, ME: International Marine, 1980.

Index